THE TR.
PHILOSOPHER

THE TRAGIC PHILOSOPHER
Friedrich Nietzsche

F. A. Lea

THE ATHLONE PRESS
London & Atlantic Highlands, NJ

This edition first published 1993 by
THE ATHLONE PRESS
1 Park Drive, London NW11 7SG
and 165 First Avenue, Atlantic Highlands, NJ 07716

© 1957, 1977, 1993 F. A. Lea

British Library Cataloguing in Publication Data

*A catalogue record for this book is available
from the British Library*

ISBN 0 485 12095 X

Library of Congress Cataloging-in-Publication Data
Lea, F. A. (Frank Alfred), 1915–1977.
The tragic philosopher: Friedrich Nietzsche/F. A. Lea.
p. cm.
Originally published: London: Methuen, 1957.
Includes bibliographical references and index.
ISBN 0-485-12095-X: £16.95 ($24.95 U.S.)
1. Nietzsche, Friedrich Wilhelm, 1844–1900. I. Title.
B3317.L37 1993
193–dc20 93-9875 CIP

Printed and bound in Great Britain by the
University Press, Cambridge

First published with the title
The Tragic Philosopher in 1957
by Methuen and Co.

CONTENTS

PREFACE TO
THE SECOND IMPRESSION

I am glad a second impression of this book has been called for, since it still seems to me sound as far as it goes; equally glad that the publishers will not let me undertake extensive revision, since it does not go nearly far enough, and if I once started trying to improve it, I would never know where to stop.

A lot of water has flowed under the bridges in the close on a quarter of a century since it was written. Then, in the years just after the War, Nietzsche was virtually unknown to the English-speaking world, except in caricature; his works were hard to come by, reliable translations non-existent. To-day, he is quite widely acknowledged, even by Freudians and Linguistic Analysts, to have "anticipated" their own leading ideas, and therefore to be "important". In other words, they have begun to catch up with him.

Credit for this change goes chiefly to Prof. Walter Kaufmann, whose *Nietzsche – Philosopher, Psychologist, Antichrist,* appearing in 1950, dissolved the incrustation of legend, and whose subsequent translations could hardly be bettered. I owe Prof. Kaufmann an apology for ignoring these in my original Foreword. Had the years during which fifty publishers were rejecting my manuscript allowed me to keep up with scholarship, I would certainly have profited both by his own work and by Richard Blunck's *Nietzsche: Kindheit und Jugend* (München, 1953) to correct mistakes in the earlier chapters. I would also have re-written Chapter X at least, in the light of Alwin Mittasch's *Nietzsche als Naturphilosoph* (Stuttgart, 1952), the first thorough study of a philosophy of nature apart from which the philosophy of mind is as easy to misinterpret as Aristotle's.

Yet the Nietzsche who matters to us is not the man who anticipated what others have made familiar: there is no point in going to a philosopher for what you already know, or think you do, and might have learned from him sooner. He is not even the man who pushed scepticism to its furthest limit and foresaw its practical implications, the "artist in

7

destruction and dissolution" whom Prof. Kaufmann concentrates on. The Nietzsche who matters is "that prophetic bird-spirit" who claimed, not without reason, to have "already lived through nihilism to the end, *to have it behind, beneath and outside himself*". It is he who has most to teach us. Or have we, perhaps stopped reacting against everything traditional from metaphysics to matrimony, and established a rational standard of human excellence by which to criticise institutions, evaluate trends and orientate our lives?

The Tragic Philosopher does not go nearly far enough, because it does less than justice to this Nietzsche. Part III, in particular, now strikes me as woefully deficient—though not surprisingly, since, when I wrote it, I was like an arrival in unknown territory, trying rather to take provisional bearings than to stake our definite claims. While I do not regret that, instead of presuming his case against Christianity sound, I examined it—a procedure so startling to critics as to win for this book the name of "a Christian interpretation", "the work of a believing Christian" —I do regret that, by so doing, I diverted attention to accidentals. The essential question is not whether Nietzsche's ideal has more in common than he thought with Jesus's, Paul's or Augustine's, but whether it is right. If it is, so much the better for theirs; if not, the only pertinent criticism is argument in favour of another.

I cannot repair these deficiencies now, though I have made some amends in my book, *The Ethics of Reason*. I hope that somebody else, equally struck by them and better qualified, will—not necessarily by adding to the number of books on Nietzsche, which can never be more than pointers or guides to his own, but by tackling as seriously as he did the fundamental problem of our time. To do this would be to do what every moral philosopher used to regard as his job; and never did it so badly need doing as now, when those with the requisite qualifications have mostly relinquished it to third-rate thinkers like me.

F. A. Lea, 1972.

FOREWORD

This book is not a biography: the external facts of Nietzsche's life have been recounted often enough. Nor is it a systematic exposition of his philosophy: George A. Morgan's *What Nietzsche Means* (Harvard, 1941) will hardly be bettered. Its principal aim is to trace the *development* of Nietzsche's thought, from 1865, the year of his 'conversion' by Schopenhauer, to 1888. Biographical matter has been introduced only so far as needful to elucidate his problems, and the solutions he propounded for them.

This being so, I have not felt called upon to join issue wherever I disagreed with him. The reader (even though he be reviewer) must realize that one can dissent without misrepresenting. On the other hand, neither have I refrained from criticism altogether. Nietzsche's views, when I first encountered them, antagonized at least as often as they attracted me. In the course of a six-years' struggle to make his 'perspective' my own, he compelled me, time and again, to 'take sides against myself'—with the result that much that used to appear false or extravagant now commands my sympathy or assent. But by no means all. To some of his conclusions I am more strongly opposed than before, and here and there I have stated reasons for opposing them.

Such a study as this cannot help being an 'interpretation'. From the broad web of Nietzsche's thought, the author picks out those strands that appeal to him, and, without even knowing it, weaves them into a new design. Must it, on that account, be pronounced 'false', a 'fiction' from start to finish? Nietzsche himself would have been inclined to say 'yes'. This is one matter on which I cannot agree with him—*could* not agree, in fact, without invalidating my agreement: since such a proposition would render, not merely all discussion, but all communication, impossible. The most I can acknowledge is that my interpretation is but 'relatively true', and that innumerable others are feasible, having equal or better claim to acceptance. This, however, I am both willing and eager to do.

Some further acknowledgements are called for. My thanks are due, in the first place, to Nietzsche's translators. This book being intended for English readers, I have referred, wherever possible, to the *Complete*

Works, in eighteen volumes, edited by Dr. Levy and published by T. N. Foulis. Though long out of print, and scandalously inaccurate, it is still the best edition available. Dr. Levy's *Selected Letters of Friedrich Nietzsche* (Heinemann, 1921) has likewise supplied some quotations. Only for material not yet translated—which unfortunately includes some of the most important—have references been given to German sources.

In the second place, I have to thank three friends, John Middleton Murry, Marcel Oppenheimer and Margaret Tims, for their kindness in reading the manuscript and giving me the benefit of their criticism. If *The Tragic Philosopher* is not as bad as it might have been, they must be partly responsible. If it succeeds in stimulating others to return to Nietzsche's own works, granting them the serious consideration they have so far been denied in this country, I myself shall feel richly rewarded.

April 1955   F. A. LEA

Abbreviations used in the Notes

THE following initial letters refer to Nietzsche's works in the English edition in eighteen volumes, edited by Dr. Oscar Levy and published by T. N. Foulis:

BT   *The Birth of Tragedy.*

GP   *Philosophy during the Tragic Age of the Greeks.*

FE   *The Future of our Educational Institutions.*

TS   *Thoughts out of Season:*
    I. 'David Strauss'
    II. 'The Use and Abuse of History'
    III. 'Schopenhauer as Educator'
    IV. 'Richard Wagner at Bayreuth'
    V. 'We Philologists'

H   *Human, All-too-Human.*
    I. Volume I.
    II. 'Miscellaneous Maxims and Opinions'
    III. 'The Wanderer and his Shadow'

D   *The Dawn of Day.*

JW   *The Joyful Wisdom.*

Z   *Thus Spake Zarathustra.*

BGE   *Beyond Good and Evil.*

GM   *The Genealogy of Morals.*

CW   *The Case of Wagner.*

TI   *The Twilight of the Idols.*

A   *The Antichrist.*

ER   *Notes on the Eternal Recurrence.*

NZ   *Notes for Thus Spake Zarathustra.*

EH   *Ecce Homo.*

WP   *The Will to Power.*

Except where otherwise stated, the numbers in the footnotes refer to the aphorisms, discourses or sections of a work, and not to the pages. This should facilitate the tracing of quotations in the German editions.

The initial N. stands for the 16-volume edition of Nietzsche's Works published by C. G. Naumann (later by A. Kröner), Leipzig. In this case, volume and page numbers are given in the footnotes.

First Movement

ROMANTICISM

'I never seek to provoke contradiction. *Help me* rather to formulate the problem! The moment your feeling turns against me, you no longer understand either my position or, therefore, my arguments. It is necessary that you should be a prey *to the same passion.*'

I

THE IDEALIST

Melancholy, irascible, very far from resigned, Arthur Schopenhauer departed this life on 21 September 1860. Less than half a century having elapsed since the publication of his greatest work, *The World as Will and Idea*, his philosophy was still virtually unknown to the universities, when, in the autumn of 1865, Nietzsche first alighted upon it. Chance, he was to say later, is the destiny that shapes our ends. A chance encounter in a second-hand bookshop inaugurated his own career.

Nietzsche was then a student at Leipzig, just turned twenty-one. Neither extravagant by taste nor lavishly supplied with pocket-money, he was not in the habit of buying whatever took his fancy. 'I know not what demon whispered to me: "take this book home".'[1] Take it home he nevertheless did, and the result was electric. He went on reading Schopenhauer far into that night, far into the following morning. By the time he laid the book down, he had undergone a religious conversion.

This conversion was his coming-of-age as a thinker. For this reason I am making it the starting-point of my study of his thought. Since, however, even the most powerful battery has to be charged before the starter will work, simply in order to understand this first climacteric in his development, it is necessary to know something of his antecedents. A brief survey will show that at least three factors had gone towards making it possible.

* * *

Friedrich Wilhelm Nietzsche, the eldest child of the pastor of Röcken in Saxony, was born on 15 October 1844. For most of what we know of his youth, we are indebted to his sister Elizabeth, two years younger than himself, who, according to her own account, was his confidante from childhood upwards, his unfailing helpmate and support. Nietzsche's recollection was different. 'For years', he wrote when he was forty, 'I have defended myself against Elizabeth like some desperate animal, but she will not stop tormenting and persecuting me.'[2] The last letter he addressed to her was a denunciation and adieu. Certain facts in her

[1] Works, Musarion Edn., XXI, 46.
[2] Quoted: Podach, *The Madness of Nietzsche*, Putnam, 1931.

narrative nevertheless emerge as indisputable: the first and most important being that the parsonage was a miserable home.

From the outset it must have been a disappointment to their mother.
Frau Nietzsche, herself the sixth of a neighbouring clergyman's eleven
boys and girls—and perhaps, for that reason, the more eager to assume
a position of domestic dignity and responsibility—had found herself,
as soon as she married, subordinated anew: in things spiritual to her
sister-in-law Rosalie, in things secular to her sister-in-law Augusta,
and in both to a mother-in-law who, though not always on the premises
like the others, was never far off them either.

Her husband, moreover, who might have been expected to uphold
her authority, turned out a broken reed. As often as disputes broke out,
he would close his eyes and retire to a world of his own—or, if that
failed to quell them, to his study—there to fast and pray until the spectacle of his anguish became insufferable, and pity enforced a reconciliation. Finally, in July 1849, when Friedrich was four years old, the pastor,
after months of painful illness and intermittent insanity due to softening
of the brain, died. Barely seven months later his youngest child, Joseph,
was laid beside him in the churchyard. Elizabeth can be believed
when she states that this double tragedy 'spread gloom over the whole of
our childhood'.

Nietzsche's first impressions were of discord, anxiety and bereavement. Nor was that all. The distracted widow (together with the inevitable Rosalie and Augusta) was transferred from Röcken to her mother-
in-law's house at Naumburg—where, there can be little doubt, she began
to cling ever more tenaciously to the only things that still 'belonged' to
her, her surviving children. At all events, she became what one would
expect, an anxious and possessive mother. The end of her trials was only
the beginning of theirs.

Friedrich and Elizabeth being now the object of her exclusive affection, she expected their exclusive affection in return: and this could only
be shown by their acting just as she wished. Her wishes being conditioned by her fears, high in the scale of values stood security, respectability and piety. Any failure to conform to these was not merely wicked
in itself, but a source of infinite suffering to her: and voices were not
lacking at Naumburg, Aunt Rosalie's as well as her own, to stress the
ingratitude of inflicting such suffering. Conformity was exacted by that
meanest of means, emotional blackmail.

Prematurely sensitized to the stresses and strains of this unnatural
feminine *ménage*, and driven for refuge into a private world, it is not
surprising that Nietzsche should have found it hard to adjust himself to

the very different surroundings of school. His queer preoccupations and pedantic manners, together with the family snobbery, made him an obvious butt. His misery at the Municipal Boys' School was such that he had to be sent to the Cathedral Grammar School instead. At the celebrated Schulpforta, which he entered at the age of fourteen, he was desperately homesick throughout his first term. He could make life tolerable to himself only by gathering a small circle of academically minded boys, among whom he was the acknowledged leader.

This habit persisted throughout his school career. Reading papers, exchanging views, with a couple of intimate friends, he was happy, and his intellect developed apace. Papers surviving from his eighteenth year bear witness to his astonishing precocity. Again and again we encounter whole passages that foreshadow his latest conclusions. 'Great is the domain of knowledge,' he exclaims at one moment, '*infinite* the search after truth'; and again, 'combat is the food which gives strength to the soul. The soul has skill to pluck out of battle sweet and glorious fruits. Impelled by the desire for fresh nutriment, it destroys; it struggles fiercely—but how gentle it can be when it allures the adversary, gathers it close against itself, and wholly assimilates it. . . .'[1]

At the same time, beset by the feeling of inferiority common among scholars at institutions where athletics are overrated, Nietzsche must often have longed to distinguish himself in more popular fields. Towards the end of his time at the Pforta, he began to shock his mother by getting into scrapes, and his teachers by neglecting his work. He was already pining for the relative freedom and independence of college life: and when, at last, in the autumn of 1864, he did arrive at the University of Bonn, almost his first act was to join the *Burschenschaft*.

The *Burschenschaften*, German student fraternities, were a survival of the Wars of Liberation. Revolutionary in their time, they were still proud of their superiority to everything merely academic. They were centres of social life, and sociability was what Nietzsche now wanted. He had made up his mind to be a boy among boys, or rather, a man among men. He flung himself accordingly into all the normal activities of the 'Franconia'. He marched through the streets in uniform, drank, sang, serenaded the girls in the streets—even fought a factitious duel. As far as appearances went, he achieved his object pretty successfully; as long as the novelty lasted, he may really have succeeded in outstripping the long, accusatory shadow of Naumburg church.

But it is one thing to change one's uniform; quite another to change one's self; and the truth must soon have come home to him, that loneli-

[1] Quoted: Halévy, *Life of Nietzsche*, Unwin, 1911.

ness and gregariousness, far from being mutually exclusive, may actually aggravate each other. A childhood conditioning as intense as his was not to be so easily escaped. The more normal his outward behaviour, the more abnormal he felt himself within. Try as he might, he could not really enjoy these activities; the very fact that he had to try told the tale: it was all play-acting. Nietzsche the *Burschenschaftler* was a mask. In a last desperate attempt to vindicate his manhood, it seems, he took to consorting with prostitutes—only, after two such experiments, to turn away in an access of self-disgust. And that was the end. Sick in body and mind, overpowered by the pangs of remorse consequent upon a puritanical upbringing, he broke with *Burschenschaft* and Bonn together. In the autumn of 1865, he was beginning his university career over again.

These were the circumstances, then, in which the memorable encounter with Schopenhauer took place, and these alone would have been sufficient to make it memorable:

'In young people if for the rest they have a tendency to δυσκολία ill-humours and annoyance of a personal kind are wont readily to take on a general character. At that time I was hanging in the air with a number of painful experiences and disappointments, without help, without fundamental principles, without hope, and without one friendly memory. To fashion for myself a suitable life of my own was my effort from morning till night. . . . Imagine now what effect the reading of Schopenhauer's main work must produce in such circumstances.'[1]

In Schopenhauer's bitter evaluation of life, as an everlasting oscillation between painful desire and still more painful satiety, Nietzsche 'saw a mirror in which I descried the world, life and my own soul in frightful grandeur'.[2] Of the World as Will, at least, he had more first-hand experience than is happily common at his age.

* * *

'I belong to those readers of Schopenhauer,' he wrote, 'who know perfectly well, after they have turned the first page, that they will read all the others. My trust in him sprang to life at once, and has been the same for nine years. I understood him as though he had written for me.'[3] Schopenhauer's resolute and scornful refusal to gloss over the harsh realities of existence was the first cause of the confidence he inspired in this melancholy, disappointed young man. The second was still more decisive.

By the time he was twenty-one, Nietzsche had outgrown the pietistic religion of his childhood. To a scholar of his precocity, submitted more-

---

[1] Works, Musarion Edn., XXI, 46. [2] *Ibid.* [3] TS, III, 2.

over to the strict philological discipline of Schulpforta, fundamentalism was an impossibility. 'We must expect a vast upheaval when the multitude discovers that all Christianity is founded on gratuitous affirmations', reads another of those prophetic sentences of 1862: 'I have attempted·to deny everything: ah, to destroy is easy, but to construct!'[1] Scepticism was in the air, and he had absorbed it naturally. In his autobiography he states that he never experienced anything in the nature of 'religious difficulties'.

In its time, however, this pietism had meant much to him. His further statement, ' "God", "the immortality of the soul", "salvation", a "beyond"— to all these notions, even as a child, I never paid any attention whatsoever',[2] is contradicted, not merely by Elizabeth's anecdotes, but also by his other reminiscences. Far from being indifferent to God as a child, he had been uncommonly preoccupied with Him. Perhaps God took in his mind the place of the father he had lost; assuredly the compensatory dream-world he created for himself at Naumburg revolved round the Christian sun. His ambition drew sustenance from the pulpit; at the ripe age of twelve he was already claiming to have seen God in all His glory! However soon it may evaporate, a faith as flattering as this must leave a perceptible void.

This void he had been dimly aware of throughout his year at Bonn—probably the discomfort it occasioned had encouraged his mild debauchery—and this void Schopenhauer filled. For was it not Schopenhauer's boast that he had retrieved the one truth at the heart of all high religions, and presented it at last in a form, not merely proof against rationalist criticism, but grounded in the *Critique of Pure Reason?*

According to Schopenhauer, the entire phenomenal world is the objectification of a single Will, the will to live. All the longing and satiety that make up the substance of our lives are caused by our failure to perceive this. We are enmeshed in the Veil of Maya. Where in truth there is unity, we assume multiplicity, ignorant that multiplicity, dependent on time and space, has no existence outside our own minds; where there is identity, we discover diversity. Thus the Will is at war with itself, and each, striving to live at all costs, lives at the cost of every other. Even reason, in man, is no more than the instrument whereby he at once pursues the same end more effectively and conceals from himself that it is the same.

Yet, says Schopenhauer, in man there does exist the potentiality of a different mode of experience, and occasionally—very occasionally—this potentiality is realised. He sees through the Veil of Maya. Suddenly

[1] Quoted: Halévy, *Life of Nietzsche.*   [2] EH, p. 28.

uplifted above the torment of willing, he is made aware of his true situation: he discovers himself in others, and so doing, loves others as himself. He is then confronted with a choice. Possessed with pity for all that lives, he may either devote his life to the alleviation of suffering, in which case he becomes an exponent of the only genuine ethics; or, seeing that no action of his can ever do more than alleviate it, he may adopt a more drastic remedy—the total suppression of the Will. He may, that is, by deliberate abstention from every physical pleasure, above all from procreation, so mortify the will in himself that he virtually ceases to live, even while his body still breathes. As ascetic saint, he therewith holds out to all the world the possibility of its final deliverance. And this, and nothing less, is what every high religion has taught. Hinduism, Buddhism, Christianity—they are so many antique mythologies transmitting this single truth, that life is a meaningless horror, and salvation the denial of life.

Schopenhauer, in short, belonged to that long line of thinkers, great and little, who, discovering from time to time a highest common factor in religions, forthwith conclude that anything higher than a common factor is inconceivable: that whatever they may contain over and above this 'perennial philosophy', therefore, may be dismissed as superstition, anthropomorphism and priestcraft. It is rather as though one should pronounce a sovereign equivalent to a penny, because they bear the same image and superscription. Only, in deducing his common factor, Schopenhauer showed an acumen rare among his successors, for he began by eliminating God.

God, he declared, was a thoroughly redundant hypothesis. Buddhism had long ago discarded it, and Christianity would have to do likewise, to merit the attention of philosophers. A Judaic inheritance, it actually militated against spirituality, if only because, as long as a creator was believed in, attempts would always be made to prove the creation good. See what insoluble problems this had posed even the great Augustine! The Founder of Christianity, on the other hand, and all his earliest disciples had known better: on their lips, the words 'world' and 'evil' were synonyms. Get rid of God, therefore, and the true religion of the Gospels will shine forth in all its purity. The world is evil—that is the premise of true religion; the world must be put out of its misery—that is the moral; and to put the world out of its misery means simply—to put it out.

Nietzsche was spellbound by this philosophy. No wonder! For years —ever since the decay of his faith—his seething ambition had lacked any definite objective. He had been the victim of what he afterwards called 'an extraordinarily dangerous dualism';[1] his nature had been divided against itself:

'The drama of his life opens with his attainment of moral and intellectual manhood. And how different everything looks now! His nature seems to be simplified fearfully, and torn asunder into two instincts or spheres. From its lowest depths a violent will gushes forth by every channel, cave and crevice to the light, in quest of power. Only a force completely free and pure could direct this will towards the good and beneficial. Had it been allied to a narrow intelligence, a will of such boundless and tyrannical desire might have become fatal; in any case a way into the open had speedily to be found for it—it could not remain long without pure air and sunshine.'[2]

Schopenhauer's philosophy provided that way. It reconciled Nietzsche's heart with his head. Without denying anything his instinct could affirm, or affirming anything his reason could deny, it re-established his earliest ideal.

God was an illusion indeed: but the man of God was a reality—and not only that, but by far the most important reality! In the light of this discovery, Nietzsche's very frustration and loneliness became insignia of election. He was one of those who, in Schopenhauer's words, 'on account of their higher intellectual power are made susceptible of far greater suffering than duller minds can ever feel, and are also placed in lonely isolation by a nature which is obviously different from that of others'. He acquired the courage of his singularity: and if it is hard to picture the philosopher we know fired by the ascetic ideal, let his own words tell the story:

'To this very day there remain as evidences for me of that sudden change the uneasy melancholic pages of my diary for that time, with their useless self-accusations and their desperate looking upward for the healing and reshaping of the whole kernel of man. Dragging all my qualities and aspirations in front of the Forum of gloomy self-contempt, I was bitter, unjust and unbridled in the hatred directed against myself. Even bodily penances were not lacking. ...'[3]

Nobody, it may be remarked, would have been more surprised by this reaction than Schopenhauer, who, odd, contradictory personality that he was, had never supposed that his philosophy could convert anyone (it had not even converted himself): the most that any world-view could do, in his opinion, being to provide a rational interpretation of

[1] TS, III, 3.　　[2] TS, IV, 2.　　[3] Works, Musarion Edn., XXI, 46.

aspirations proceeding from elsewhere. A rational interpretation, however, was precisely what Nietzsche needed—the aspiration to sanctity was already deep-rooted in his heart—and if *The World as Will and Idea* had given him no more than that, it would still have secured his allegiance.

As it was, it gave him still more. There was yet a third reason for the lasting impression it left, and this the most important of all. It was by virtue of this, indeed, that long after he had abandoned his penitential practices, he was still able to say of the book that it met 'the demand of every great philosophy to speak *sub specie aeternitatis*: "This is the picture of the whole of life: learn thence the meaning of thine own life".'[1]

* * *

Naumburg, with all its shortcomings, was not an uncultured home. Nietzsche's father had been a competent musician; he himself had inherited the gift, even as a child delighting local audiences with his improvisations on the piano. The father of one of his school-friends, Privy Councillor Krug, whose musical evenings were famous in the neighbourhood, had done much to encourage this interest. The father of another, Judge Pindar, had stimulated his taste for poetry by readings aloud from Goethe. In the repressive *milieu* of the Nietzsche household, music and poetry had gradually become the twin outlets for his emotional life. By his twenty-first year, his absorption in both was ecstatic. 'I was in love with art,' he recalled, 'passionately in love, and in the whole of existence saw nothing other than art—and this at an age when, reasonably enough, quite different passions usually possess the soul.'[2]

Two kinds of art in particular called forth his deepest devotion: the tragedies of Aeschylus and Sophocles, which he was lucky enough to be studying under the inspiring tuition of Ritschl; and the musical dramas of Wagner, just then beginning to be widely known in Germany. The one set before him an unsurpassed standard of formal perfection; the other so intoxicated him that, as he said, he tried in vain to preserve his critical faculties. Reciting Aeschylus, listening to Wagner, Nietzsche found himself transported into different and more glorious worlds: the frustrations of his everyday life were forgotten: the wheel of Ixion stood still.

Yet, the very intensity of his rapture at these moments had confronted him with a problem. What was it in these particular works that possessed such power over his soul? What was it in himself that responded so overwhelmingly? His restless intellect was demanding an answer to those

[1] TS, III, 3.   [2] CW, p. 86.

questions, and no answer had been forthcoming. So long as no answer was forthcoming, he was a troubled and divided man.

It was here that Schopenhauer came most decisively to the rescue. For Schopenhauer, loftily ignoring Hegel, claimed to be the first philosopher to give art an adequate place in his system. Not only was he, unlike other German thinkers, himself an artist in words, but in passage after eloquent passage he gave voice to an experience as intense as Nietzsche's own: and the whole third book of *The World as Will and Idea* was devoted to elucidating its significance.

This is not the place to attempt an exposition of Schopenhauer's aesthetics. It is enough to know that in all essentials they are identical with the later Shelley's. That is to say, the Genius, according to Schopenhauer, is a forerunner of the saint. He, the true, the intuitive artist, so far transcends his own individuality as to apprehend those Platonic Ideas which, through the medium of time and space (the *principium individuationis*), are refracted in the phenomenal world. These he depicts; and because he depicts these, and not merely their imperfect refractions, his works have the power of divesting the spectator, too, of his individuality, and so enabling him to participate in pure, timeless contemplation. Thus, the productions of Genius constitute a perpetual reminder that the Veil of Maya is not final, that the illusion is not indissoluble; they sound a summons to mankind to deliver the world from the world.

Two points in this theory, nonetheless, call for particular mention. In the first place, if what we call 'beautiful' is simply what we perceive in its Idea, then all things without exception must be considered potentially beautiful. The only difference between them is, that whereas some (Schopenhauer calls these 'the lovely') engage our emotions so little that detachment towards them is easy, others ('the sublime') demand an almost superhuman self-conquest to be regarded without disturbance of will. The greatness of an artist, therefore, is to be measured by his capacity for disclosing beauty in even the most terrible and questionable situations. It is on this account, Schopenhauer claims, that we attach such supreme significance to tragedy. Tragedy veritably is the summit of literary art.

In the second place, Schopenhauer assigns a quite peculiar status to music: since, he submits, while the architect and sculptor, the painter and poet, depict only the Platonic Ideas, the musician goes further still and depicts the Will itself, prior even to its 'adequate objectification'. He, in other words, transcends not merely time and space, but the very subject-object antithesis, and his art may be pronounced a direct representation of reality, 'the metaphysical to everything physical in the world, the thing-in-itself to every phenomenon'. A perfectly accurate, complete explanation of music, he affirms, would be 'the true philosophy'.[1]

One has only to glance at such a theory to realize how exactly it met Nietzsche's requirements. Here, once again, was the very thing he had been seeking—a rational interpretation of his own deepest intuitions. Here, at last, the meaning of art was related in the clearest possible way to the meaning of life itself. Neither poetry nor music need any longer be considered a graceful irrelevancy. By the same token, his individual talents were related to the sovereign ideal he had adopted. At one stroke Schopenhauer welded him into a unitary being.

As early as May 1863, when he still had a year of schooling before him, he had written home to his mother:

'Now I happen to be in the particularly unfortunate position of possessing a whole host of interests connected with the most different branches of learning, and, though the general gratification of these interests may make a learned man of me, they will scarcely convert me into a creature with a vocation. The fact, therefore, that I must destroy some of these interests is perfectly clear to me, as well as the fact that I must allow some new ones to find a home in my brain. But which of them will be so unfortunate as to be cast overboard? Perhaps just the children of my heart!'

At Bonn and Leipzig, this dilemma had persisted. If he was reading philology, and distinguishing himself by his studies of Theognis and Diogenes Laertius, that was only for want of any better or more obvious alternative. If he was gratified, as he certainly was, by the plaudits of 'father Ritschl', they were still insufficient to convince him that his vocation lay here and not elsewhere. He had no criterion by which to assess the importance of his interests, nor any definite goal to aim at.

Now all that was changed. Schopenhauer set before him an ideal which was not only congenial and exalted enough to enlist the full force of his ambition, but actually demanded the employment of every one of his manifold gifts. Schopenhauer fulfilled, as he put it later, the function of his ideal teacher: that of cultivating all his faculties, and at the same time bringing them into unison with each other, in the service of a single 'vital centre'.[2] It is hardly surprising that the ideal of the Genius soon moved to the forefront of his mind, practically eclipsing that of the Saint.

From the autumn of 1865 onwards, Nietzsche was able to face the world with a new confidence, in himself and his future. He had, in

---

[1] All quotations from *The World as Will and Idea* are taken from the translation by R. B. Haldane and J. Kemp (Routledge).   [2] TS, III, 2.

Schopenhauer's phrase, 'acquired character'. He would no longer, by striving after objectives alien to his nature, expose himself to mortification, 'perhaps the greatest of mental sufferings'; he would by concentrating on those pursuits for which he had a genuine aptitude, 'constantly and with full consciousness be completely himself'. He had a mission to discharge, and the power to discharge it. The philosophy of meaninglessness had given his life a meaning.

* * *

To those (the majority) for whom religion is opinion and poetry a pastime, all this must sound somewhat strange. They will prefer to derive Nietzsche's activities from motives more familiar to themselves. They will find it particularly hard to believe that the philosophy of a man of twenty-six (for Schopenhauer was no older when he composed *The World as Will and Idea*) could have effected so radical a transformation. Yet Nietzsche will always be unintelligible unless we appreciate the passionate nature of his intellectual pursuits. His entire emotional life was involved. It would be no exaggeration to describe his response to this book as love as first sight.

Moreover, he was not the first to fall for it. Tolstoy, sixteen years his senior, passed a whole summer 'in an endless ecstasy over Schopenhauer'. He was not even the first to discover in it a clue to the transcendent importance of Wagner's art. The selfsame discovery had been made, some seven years previously, by Wagner: and since this fact also was destined to influence him considerably, we may do well to dwell on it here.

Nietzsche, of course, could hardly have been aware of it at the time. 'In those days', he recalled long afterwards, 'it was the last of the Hegelians who rallied round Wagner. "Wagner and Hegel" was the battle-cry of the fifties';[1] and this battle-cry, shrill though it was, betrayed less confusion than most. In the massive polemics Wagner had fired off at his countrymen between 1848 and 1853, he had indeed shown himself, if not an orthodox Hegelian, at least a devotee of the theory I have called elsewhere 'the Romantic Myth'. That is to say, he had subscribed to the faith (of which Hegel's *Philosophy of History* presents the most elaborate formulation) that mankind, far from repeating the same monotonous round of errors, as Schopenhauer presumed, is progressing steadily through three distinguishable phases: one of spontaneity and unconscious union with nature; one of self-consciousness and alienation; and finally—in the imminent future—one of conscious reunion with nature and spontaneity regained. In *Art and Revolution* and *The Art-*

[1] L, 19.2.88.

Work of the Future, Wagner had actually evolved his own original variant of the Myth, widely extolled in its day, though generally forgotten in ours.

Once upon a time (so runs this variant), man's every action and word were the immediate expression of necessity, of his integral nature. No more in him than in any other animal was intellect at variance with instinct. His faculties, such as they were, were in unison one with another: in a word, he was whole. And since of the whole man—'the man of understanding united with the man of heart and the man of body'[1]—the natural speech is art, and of art the most natural form the drama, wherein all his faculties find harmonious utterance, this phase can be located in Greece. The Greeks, in their choral dances, celebrated an Apollo who truly reflected their own exuberant manhood: 'thus too, inspired by Dionysus, the tragic poet saw this glorious god, when, to all the rich elements of spontaneous art, he joined the bond of speech, and, concentrating them all into one focus, brought forth the highest conceivable form of art—the Drama'. Aeschylean tragedy, says Wagner, was the fine flower of the Greek religion, and that the religion of free men.

Subsequently, a time came when intellect broke away from its subservience to necessity. Suddenly made aware of his own individuality, man began, in fear and wonder, to speculate on the nature of existence: and thenceforth both inward and outward unison were at an end. No longer the spokesman of life, he became the bondslave of his own abstractions. Philosophy, science and the State subdued his instinctive nature, and would, if they could, have extinguished it altogether. In Greece, this Fall (it was nothing less) resulted from the institution of slavery. Even the Athenians, after all, were not universally free; the vast majority were slaves, to whom neither the religion nor the art of self-apotheosis could appeal. Slavery, accordingly, engendered a spirit of criticism, against which the votaries of Apollo were defenceless. Their religion fell a victim to the Sophists, their art to Euripides, who, in turning his back on the dance, turned his back on inspiration itself; and within the space of a few short years the glories of their culture were a dream. 'To Philosophy, and not to Art, belong the two thousand years which, since the decadence of Grecian tragedy, have passed until our own day.'

Under the rubric 'philosophy' Wagner includes Christianity: a faith, he declares, pre-eminently congenial to slaves, since, exalting self-contempt to the rank of a virtue and degrading the instincts and senses, it wages implacable war on all that is meant by the pride of life. His phase

[1] All quotations from Wagner's *Prose-Works* are taken from the translation by W. Ashton Ellis (Kegan Paul).

of self-consciousness and alienation, in fact, is virtually identical with the Christian era. Not until the Church lost its hold upon Europe, he says, were the arts able to spring up once more: and even the arts of the Renaissance had to blossom in lonely isolation.

However, the day is drawing near when this very usurpation of the intellect, which has been man's curse, will turn out to have been a blessing as well: for—the proof is before us—neither Christianity nor slavery can survive the culmination of science. Science itself must finally acknowledge the sovereignty of the unconscious, and therewith abrogate its own. In the conscious rediscovery of his unity with the rest of nature, man will again become whole, and in the knowledge of necessity, free. Further, thanks to the machine, this new freedom, unlike the old, will be shared by all humanity; while the arts, thanks to their intensive development in isolation, will be reintegrated into a drama outlustring even the Aeschylean. A new world-religion, a new world-culture, are at hand, to be at once the redemption and reward of a new, harmonious man!

For a moment, in 1848, Wagner seems to have believed that this consummation was at hand. The forces of instinct, embodied in the revolutionary masses, were on the brink of wresting the machine out of the grasp of their oppressors and making it the instrument of their emancipation. Bliss was it in that dawn to be alive! Later, disillusioned in the masses, he turned his hopes to a chosen few, the 'folk', whose response to his own music-drama—prophetic as that was of the art-work of the future—marked them out as the pioneers of a more gradual advance towards Utopia: but Utopia was still assured.

Thus, whatever else he may have been, the Wagner of those popular polemics was the very reverse of a pessimist. It was not for nothing that his name was coupled with Hegel's, and had Schopenhauer ever come across them, he would certainly have heaped the same scorn upon the one as the other. As if events transpiring in time could possess any ultimate significance! As if art could point the way to a happier life, its whole purpose being to deliver men from life! As if happiness were possible at all! *Art and Revolution* was like an anthology of all the tenets he loathed most.

'Wagner and Schopenhauer'—that war-cry, in the 1850's, would have sounded absurd indeed. And yet, within a few years of the publication of these works, and whilst he was still in exile for his part in the revolution, so successfully was Wagner seduced by *The World as Will and Idea* that not merely did he read it (by his own account) five times from beginning to end in a space of nine months, but he went on to read it back into everything he had hitherto written: declaring, in his subsequent Prefaces, that the right name for 'necessity' was the Will; that the 'love' which, so he had said, sprang from a reunion of instinct and intellect, marked really the suppression of instinct; that it could only be conceived as the symbol of a total renunciation; and that music was the speech of Nirvana. It was in the first flush of this new infatuation that he gave birth to *Tristan und Isolde*.

* * *

The Introduction to *Tristan und Isolde*, together with the Overture to *Die Meistersinger*, was performed at Leipzig on 27 October 1868—three years after Nietzsche's first encounter with Schopenhauer. Nietzsche attended the performance, of course; and in a letter the following day gave vent to his enthusiasm. 'I cannot bring myself to keep critically cool towards this music', he exclaimed: 'every fibre, every nerve thrills in me, and not for a long time have my feelings been so carried away as by the Overture just mentioned.' The ideal of the Genius still stood immovably before him: in Wagner's music he heard the very voice of that ideal.

For all that, Nietzsche was still a lonely and diffident figure. If he had discovered in Schopenhauer the philosophical teacher of his dreams, it was 'only as a book: and that was a great loss'. So much the more, he recalled, 'did I exert myself to see behind the book the living man whose testament it was, who promised his inheritance only to such as could, and would, be more than his readers—his pupils and his sons'.[1] If he had won over his few intimate friends, Rohde, von Gersdorff and Deussen, one by one to his point of view, it was only to realize that discipleship could never mean as much to them as to him. After all, they had fathers already; and no matter how great their fondness for music and poetry, it could not entirely eclipse those 'quite different passions' that usually possess the soul at twenty-four. Even stronger than his obsession with art, therefore, had become his craving to meet with a true, an intuitive artist, and the presentiment, still perhaps obscure, that only in the company of Genius would he really be 'among his own'.

Judge then his feelings when, within a fortnight of this concert, he was invited to meet Wagner in person! This was the day he had been dreaming of—the day, indeed, he had been working for, ever since he had discovered that Professor Brockhaus of Leipzig was the composer's brother-in-law, and begun to cultivate his acquaintance. In another long, detailed and excited letter to Rohde, he describes the great event: the comedy of errors preceding it, the introduction itself, and—highlight of the evening—his first conversation with Wagner:

[1] TS, III, 2.

'I managed to have quite a long talk with him about Schopenhauer. Oh, and you can imagine what a joy it was for me to hear him speak with such indescribable warmth of our master—what a lot we owed to him, how he was the only philosopher who had understood the essence of music! Then he enquired as to how the professors were disposed toward him; laughed a good deal about the Philosophers' Congress at Prague, and spoke of them as "philosophical footmen". Later on he read me a piece out of the autobiography he is now writing, a thoroughly amusing scene from his Leipzig student days which I still cannot recall without a laugh. He writes extraordinarily cleverly and intellectually. At the close of the evening, when we were both ready to go, he shook my hand very warmly and kindly and asked me to come and see him so that we might have some music and philosophy together. He also entrusted me with the task of making his music known to his sister and his relations, a duty which I undertook very solemnly to fulfil.'[1]

So Wagner himself was already a Schopenhauerian! It is not hard to imagine Nietzsche's joy. Everything fell into place: there was no longer the least room for doubt that his thought for the last several years had been tending in the right direction. The philosopher had ratified the music; now the musician ratified the philosophy—and not only in words. In Wagner the man Nietzsche saw the very incarnation of his ideal. 'The day I found Wagner', he wrote, 'I was happy beyond description. So long had I been seeking for the man who stood on a higher plane than I did, and who really comprised me.'[2] The Word of Schopenhauer was made flesh. No doubt he discharged his trust with the solemnity of a first communicant.

[1] L, 9.11.68.   [2] L, 3.2.82.

II

THE HELLENIST

'**N**ever yet have I known a young man reach *such* maturity *so* soon and *so* young as this Nietzsche... If it is given him to live long—which God grant—I predict that he will one day stand in the front rank of German philology. He is now twenty-four years olds, strong, active, healthy, physically and morally courageous, just made to impress kindred natures. . . . He is an idol and (without ever intending it) leader of the whole young philological world here in Leipzig.' On the strength of this testimonial from Ritschl, and his own contributions to the *Rheinisches Museum*, Nietzsche was appointed to the Chair of Classical Philology at Basle in 1869.

If he had reason for gratification, he also had reason for misgivings. Philology was not his vocation; he was tired of university life; at Basle he would be far from even his few intimate friends. He foresaw a monotonous round of academic commitments, only varied by those social functions at which he always cut the poorest figure. Nor were these misgivings unjustified. 'The most irksome feature of my life', we find him writing within a few months of taking up residence, 'is that I must be continually impersonating or representing somebody, either the teacher, the philologist or the man, and that I have always to begin by proving my metal to everybody I meet!'[1]

In society Nietzsche was out of place. Circumstances had conspired to make him take everything too seriously for small-talk. Even at Bonn he had been exasperated by 'the appalling arrogance with which in a twinkling men and opinions were disposed of *en masse*'[2] by his fellow-students. Either he had to hide his earnestness behind a mask of frivolity—and come away feeling that he had betrayed himself; or else he was mortified by what must appear the *gaucherie* of a very young man—and felt driven to assert his superiority. He might have become a hermit long before he did, but for a piece of news which practically coincided with his arrival at Basle: Wagner had come to live in the neighbourhood.

This, of course, changed the whole outlook. He lost no time in following it up. Diffidently indeed—for he was fearful of intruding on the Master—but fortified by the invitation of six months before, Nietzsche

[1] L, 15.2.70.　　　　　　[2] L, 25.5.65.

presented himself at Tribschen that May; and the acquaintance thus renewed, swiftly ripening into intimacy, did more than anything else to shape his course over the next seven years.

As it happened, his visit could hardly have been better timed. For once in his stormy career, Wagner was enjoying comparative peace and security. Relieved of his financial embarrassments by the patronage of the young King of Bavaria, and happily united with Cosima von Bülow, he had just resumed work on *The Ring*. At the same time, he was but too well aware that the staging of *The Ring* would depend on the completion of the Bayreuth *Festspielhaus*, and that on the raising of funds beyond even King Ludwig's means. To overcome the indifference or hostility of the German public, propaganda and propagandists were required. In Nietzsche he saw the man he was looking for.

That is not to say that Wagner exploited Nietzsche. On the contrary, the man he was looking for was one who so thoroughly understood his mission, and shared his own sense of its importance, that he would need no urging to devote himself to it whole-heartedly. For many years past, he had given up hope of meeting such a man. Embittered by repeated reverses, he had grown suspicious, jealous, overbearing, and certainly quite capable of fleecing his admirers unscrupulously. But Nietzsche was different. From the first Wagner warmed to him genuinely, throwing off his customary reserve, and entrusting him with responsible commissions. In Nietzsche he saw, perhaps, even more than an ally—a portent: the first of a new generation, who would respond to his art as their elders had never done.

What Nietzsche saw in Wagner we know; and if, as he later confessed, he had 'depicted an *ideal monster*'[1] the reality was at least sufficiently like it to make such discrepancies as there were of small account. His letters of this time are ecstatic. To von Gersdorff, for instance, he writes on the 4th of August:

'I have found a man who reveals to me, as no other does, the image of what Schopenhauer called the "genius" and who is penetrated through and through by that wonderfully deep philosophy. This is no other than Richard Wagner, concerning whom you must not accept any judgement to be found in the press, in the writings of musical experts, etc. No-one knows him and can judge him, for the whole world stands on a different basis and is not at home in his atmosphere. In him there rules such an unconditioned ideality, such a noble seriousness of life, that near him I feel as if I were near the divine.'

[1] CW, p. 86.

On Nietzsche's lips, this is no mere hyperbole. Being near Wagner, he repeats, is like taking 'a practical course in Schopenhauerian philosophy'.[1] Strange though such phrases may sound to us (remembering those 'twenty-four silk dressing-gowns of different colours'), they only show how completely the image of the Genius had replaced that of the Saint in his mind. Writing to his mother a few weeks later, he is no less enthusiastic:

'Never have I been happier than during the last few days. The warm, hearty and increasing intimacy with Wagner and Frau von Bülow, the complete agreement between us on all the questions that chiefly interest us, Wagner absolutely in the prime of his genius and marvellous creations only just coming into being, glorious Tribschen arranged on such a regal and ingenious scale—many things conspire to exhilarate me and strengthen me in my calling.'[2]

Truly, Nietzsche was now 'among his own'. At Tribschen, history was being made, and he was to bear a part in it. Not merely a minor part either: he was veritably the right hand of the Master. To him Wagner entrusted manuscripts—the *Autobiography* and *State and Religion*—as yet destined only for the few; to him he assigned the final correction of his proofs. And when the day's work on 'Siegfried' was done, discussions on art and philosophy would ensue, in the course of which he paid Nietzsche the honour of listening attentively to his theories—even incorporating them in his own works. Cosima too, it should be remembered, took part in these discussions, and little by little began to figure in Nietzsche's mind as the ideal consort for a man of genius. He and his friends, who were soon introduced to the household, would speak of Wagner as Dionysus, von Bülow as Theseus, and Cosima as Ariadne.

From his mother, of course, he was careful to conceal the true relationship between Dionysus and Ariadne. That would have started a wave of disapproval. Even as it was, her jealousy was aroused. When Friedrich spent Christmas with the Wagners, and was presented with a couple of rooms to occupy as often and for as long as he liked, she suspected that Tribschen was becoming more than his spiritual home—and justly. Tribschen was, in fact, far more his home than Naumburg had ever been. Here all the irritating conventions and constraints were forgotten; he was welcomed as one of the family, not only by Wagner and Cosima, but equally by their children and servants. He would even undertake domestic commissions—taking infinite pains, for example, over the choice of the children's Christmas presents.

[1] L, 16.6.69.   [2] L, 30.8.69.

There were times, admittedly, when his very eagerness to please carried Nietzsche away. He would, as Elizabeth observed, echo opinions of Wagner's which he did not genuinely share. There were others when the Master's demands on his limited leisure became excessive, and he realized the danger he ran of becoming a mere sounding-board. Then he would absent himself abruptly for weeks. Taking all into account, however, it cannot be denied—nor did he himself ever deny—that he gained as much as he gave in the course of their long association. It was during the first year of his residence at Basle that he read, marked, learned and inwardly digested those polemics of 1848–53, which Wagner was reissuing in his *Works*.

*   *   *

The 'Tribschen Idyll' was the background of Nietzsche's development at Basle. In the foreground stood his university work. But the two were intimately connected. Schopenhauer had shown him the significance, not only of Wagner's music, but also of Aeschylus' poetry. 'Thanks to our philosopher,'[1] he believed, he held in his hand a key to the Hellenic genius, such as had been lacking even to Winckelmann, Lessing and Goethe. In classical research he was using this key, and his lectures reflected the trend of his research. The subjects he chose at the beginning of 1870 were 'The Ancient Musical Drama' and 'Socrates and Tragedy'.

'Every day', he wrote to Rohde that February, 'I get to like the Hellenic world more and more.'[2] 'To like', was an understatement. His mystical conception of Genius had led to a profound and passionate absorption in the Hellenic world: such that he could say—again without hyperbole—'Greece has the same value for us as the saints have for Catholics.'[3] Whatever it may have been later, his philology at this time was no merely academic routine. He was already projecting a major work, to be entitled 'Greek Cheerfulness', in which he would make use of his principles to illuminate every aspect of Greek life; and though this project was never carried out (it is a fact we shall have occasion to revert to, that none of Nietzsche's great projects ever was carried out) those essays and fragments that remain, above all *The Birth of Tragedy out of the Spirit of Music*, bear witness to the originality of his thought.

The Birth of Tragedy was actually published at Wagner's instigation. Wagner stood in need of support; and Nietzsche, rather than be classed with those false friends of genius who keep their opinions to themselves until they become public opinion, risked his professional career by

[1] L, 7.11.70.   [2] L, 15.2.70.   [3] N, IX, 68.

reassembling the material of his lectures and giving it a polemical twist in the interests of Bayreuth. To an outstanding degree, therefore, it reveals the inter-relation of all that most deeply concerned him.

He had some reason to regret this demonstration of loyalty in after years. Not merely is the book 'badly written, heavy, painful, image-angling and image-entangling, sugared at times even to feminism, uneven in tempo, void of the will to logical cleanliness', and much more to the same effect (it was the only one of his productions whose demerits he lived long enough to see), but it is 'full of precocious, unripened self-experiences':[1] that is to say, of ideas which had not had time to grow inter-connected and inter-related. He was changing even while he wrote it. The experience of 'intellectual pregnancy' was still new to him; he had not yet learned to let his thoughts mature in their season, to resist whatever calls on his magnanimity might precipitate a premature birth. *The Birth of Tragedy* is a seven-months' child.

To the student of his mind, however, its very contradictions have an interest of their own—and these ought not to be exaggerated. While Schopenhauer and Wagner have both contributed largely to his thesis, it is by no means a mere *pastiche*. He treats his authorities freely, not to say high-handedly. 'I was the first,' he claimed, 'to distil out of them both a kind of unity':[2] and the unity is natural, organic. Every page bears the stamp of his own unique personality.

* * *

Nietzsche's debt to Schopenhauer is obvious from the start. He rejects out of hand the Romantic theory of the Greeks as a race of 'naive' children, propagating art out of sheer delight in their unbroken unity with nature. The Greeks, he asserts, had a quite unusual capacity for suffering, and this had been stretched to the utmost by the bloody wars and fratricidal cruelties preceding the foundation of their State. Far from being optimists, they were natural pessimists, who had proved by bitter experience the truth of Silenus' words: 'What is best of all is for ever beyond your reach: not to be born, not to be, to be nothing. The second best, however, is soon to die.'

Their devotion to the plastic or 'Apollonian' arts—under which heading he includes, not only painting, sculpture and architecture, but also the Homeric epic—can be traced directly to this. The Greeks had need of these arts in order to make existence endurable. The Olympian world, as portrayed by their poets and sculptors, bore the same relation to their knowledge 'as the rapturous vision of the tortured martyr to his sufferings':

[1] BT, p. 5.   [2] L, 19.2.88.

'How else could this so sensitive people, so vehement in its desires, so singularly qualified for *suffering*, have endured existence, if it had not been exhibited to them in their gods, surrounded with a higher glory? The same impulse which calls art into being, as the complement and consummation of existence, seducing to a continuation of life, caused also the Olympian world to arise, in which the Hellenic "will" held up before itself a transfiguring mirror.'[1]

The Greeks had to idealize life, before they could reconcile themselves to it—let alone regard it as the highest good; the Homeric dream-world was the medium of this idealization.

To Schopenhauer also Nietzsche owes the concept of a metaphysical unity, preceding and transcending multiplicity. If, he suggests, the suffering of man has given birth to an illusory world, in the contemplation whereof he finds peace, may we not infer that the suffering of a God has given birth to that other illusory world, of which we ourselves form a part? And for the same reason—in order that in the contemplation thereof He may find peace? May we not be justified in imagining a Being simultaneously condemned, through his dismemberment into individuals, to reproduce the world as we know it, and redeemed by the contemplation of this world, in an eternity beyond our understanding?— 'For this one thing must above all be clear to us, to our humiliation *and* exaltation. . . that we have our highest dignity in our significance as works of art—for only as an *aesthetic phenomenon* is existence and the world eternally *justified*:—while of course our consciousness of this our significance hardly differs from the kind of consciousness which the soldiers painted on canvas have of the battle represented thereon.'[2]

The operative words in this passage are those that Nietzsche himself underlines. It belongs to the essence of this conception that, seen with the eyes of God, the world would appear neither moral in the Christian sense, nor rational in the Hegelian—but it would appear beautiful.

Finally, Nietzsche imports from Schopenhauer the idea of music as an art *sui generis*: for, to the question, whether it is possible for a man to see the world with the eyes of God, he, like a true mystic, replies with a forthright Yes: 'We are figures in the dream of a God, who divine how he dreams.'[3] This capacity is precisely what distinguishes the musical genius: 'the Genius, in the act of artistic production, coalesces with the primordial artist of the world',[1] so expressing at once the primordial pain and the primordial redemption in appearance. It is for this

---

[1] BT, 3.   [2] BT, 5.   [3] N, IX, 191.

reason that music must be set apart from the plastic or Apollonian arts. It may be termed Dionysian.

Having paid tribute to Schopenhauer for this distinction, however, Nietzsche goes on to point out that even he, the only philosopher to have understood the essence of music, did not follow up his insight to the end. He forgot, or failed to realize, not only that the lyric originated in music, but (this was Wagner's belief) that the drama is an extension of the lyric. Both lyrical and dramatic poetry, therefore, ought also to be classed as Dionysian.

Schopenhauer's own treatment of the lyric is notoriously inadequate. Puzzled as he was by its apparent subjectivity (his theory demanding absolute objectivity as the *sine qua non* of art), he was reduced to ascribing to the poet a rapid oscillation between willing and not-willing, between 'the aesthetic and the unaesthetic condition'—and so to classifying such poetry as 'an imperfectly attained art'.[1] If however, as its name implies, and none other than Schiller has declared—the lyric springs from 'a musical mood', then no such anomaly exists. The poet before ever he begins to rhapsodize, has been released from his individuality, 'become one with the Primordial Unity'.[2] He is therefore no longer to be conceived as identified with the passions he depicts, even though these passions be his own. 'In truth, Archilochus, the passionately inflamed, loving and hating man, is but a vision of the genius, who by this time is no longer Archilochus, but a genius of the world, who expresses the primordial pain symbolically in the form of the man Archilochus'.[3] The lyric is, so to speak, 'emotion recollected in tranquillity', or at any rate, in detachment. It presents a god's-eye view of the man.

And what applies to the lyric applies to the drama as well: since 'it is by no means necessary that the lyrist should see nothing but the phenomenon of the man Archilochus before him as a reflection of eternal being; and tragedy shows how far the visionary world of the lyrist may depart from this phenomenon, to which, in fact, it is most intimately related.'[4] Once he has coalesced with the primordial artist, in other words, the poet is free to select a more cogent symbol for the primordial pain than is provided by his own discontents: and this is exactly what he does, when, emerging as tragedian, he sets the most terrible realities before us, and at the same time endows them with beauty.

It had long been known that among the Greeks of the sixth century B.C. 'tragedy sprang from the tragic chorus';[5] and that the chorus, in at least two of its earliest forms, consisted of leaf-crowned revellers,

---

[1] BT, 5.   [2] *Ibid.*   [3] *Ibid.*   [4] *Ibid.*   [5] BT, 7.

dancing and singing in honour of Dionysus. Seizing on this fact, Nietzsche submitted his own metaphysical interpretation of the rapturous mood into which these revellers were thrown by the strains of the Phrygian flute:

'Under the charm of the Dionysian, not only is the covenant between man and man again established, but also estranged, hostile or subjugated nature again celebrates her reconciliation with her lost son, man. . . . Now is the slave a free man, now all the stubborn, hostile barriers, which necessity, caprice, or "shameless fashion" has set up between man and man, are broken down. Now, at the evangel of the cosmic harmony, each one feels himself not only united, reconciled, blended with his neighbour, but as one with him, as if the veil of Maya had been torn and were now merely fluttering in tatters before the mysterious Primordial Unity.'[1]

In this state of intoxication, the reveller believed himself identified with his god—and he was not deluded! The *principium individuationis* being ruptured, he truly was united with the primordial artist of the world, whose suffering and redemption alike sounded forth in the notes of the music. Collectively, the votaries of Dionysus were plunged into a musical mood: and the deeds enacted on the stage bore the same relation to the chorus as his visionary world to the lyrist.

Hence it is that in the drama, as in the lyric, we encounter so strange an incommensurability between the sentiments actually articulated, and the mood which the poetry conveys. In every line of an Aeschylean tragedy, may be observed 'a certain deceptive distincness and at the same time an enigmatic profundity, yea an infinitude of background'.[2] The former appertains to the visionary world; the latter proceeds from the genius—and would be intensified to a still higher degree by the original musical accompaniment. Only, of course, the tragic hero is an incomparably more impressive symbol than the subjectively willing and desiring man Archilochus. In fact, his prototype, in every case, is none other than Dionysus himself: the myth of whose dismemberment, distribution and ultimate reconstitution, exactly expresses 'the consideration of individuation as the source and primal cause of evil, and art as the joyous hope that the spell of individuation may be broken, and the augury of a restored oneness'.[3] The later heroes, Prometheus, Oedipus and the rest, are one and all 'but masks of this original hero, Dionysus'.[4]

* * *

It was in this phenomenon of the 'Dionysian' that Nietzsche believed

[1] BT, 1. [2] BT, 11. [3] BT, 10. [4] *Ibid.*

himself to have discovered the 'profoundest principle of the hitherto unintelligible Hellenic genius':[1] and whatever we may think of his metaphysics, there can be little doubt that he was right. Burckhardt acclaimed
it instantly a discovery of the first importance; subsequent research has
tended to corroborate his opinion.

Referring to primitive communities, at the 'pre-animistic' level of
development, Lévy-Bruhl has written: 'At the time when souls and
spirits are not yet individualized, the individual consciousness of every
member of the group is and remains strictly attuned to the collective
consciousness. It does not distinctly break away from it: it does not even
contradict itself in uniting with it; that which dominates it is the uninterrupted feeling of participation'. According to this and other authorities, the ritual dances of tribes which have arrived at the 'animistic' level
(and so assign a soul of its own to the totem-animal in particular) are
designed to restore this feeling of participation. The state of mind that
Nietzsche attributed to the Dionysian reveller, therefore, was virtually
that of those Hopi dancers whose ceremonies so fascinated D. H. Lawrence; and one can but admire the insight that enabled him, ignorant as
he was of all that anthropology has since recorded, to divine it with such
precision. Together with his colleague Bachofen, he thereby opened the
way to a more realistic view of the Greeks than anyone had yet attained:
for even the Greeks of the fifth century B.C. had, as he was quick to
point out, more in common with their primitive ancestors than they had
with present-day Hellenists.

The Hellenists of the centuries following the Renaissance mostly
made the natural mistake of re-creating the Greeks in their own image;
they conceived them practically as contemporaries, whose very myths
were no more than attempts—somewhat fantastic attempts—to account
rationally for natural phenomena. They would have been equally per-
plexed and distressed by the notion of Aeschylus or Sophocles as the
spokesman of a 'Dionysian' mentality. Nietzsche, on the other hand,
maintained that their submission to 'pre-conscious' states was precisely
what made Aeschylus and Sophocles what they were: that is, not merely
the two greatest poets, but the two greatest spiritual forces, of their time.
The myths had originated in these states; as often as they were in danger
of degenerating into playful superstitions, the tragedians charged them
anew with an ever deeper significance. He believed, in common with
Wagner, that the constant re-enactment of the tragedies did more than
the temple ceremonial, perfunctory as that often was, to preserve and
replenish the religion of the Greeks—and so, indirectly, to inspire what-

[1] BT, 20.

ever was memorable in their culture. We do not have to endorse his own Schopenhauerian interpretation of the 'Dionysian' in order to agree with him about this.

Indeed, although he claimed to be indebted to Schopenhauer for his discovery, it will be noticed that Nietzsche arrives in the end at a standpoint very like Wagner's. Not merely does he hold that the Greeks, at least in their moments of creativity, were freed from the 'spell of individuation', but, he goes on, this source of their strength was at the same time a source of weakness. They never became fully conscious of what their achievement implied. Their very trust in instinctive wisdom prevented them from elaborating a philosophy adequate to their experience: and it was due to this that their culture succumbed so quickly to rationalism.

Thus Euripides, keenly alive though he was to the effect produced by his predecessors—to that strange incommensurability between the sentiments expressed by their heroes and the mood conveyed by the poetry —because he was unable to explain it, could only account it a defect. Possessed by the dogma, 'to be beautiful, everything must be intelligible', he endeavoured to rectify the drama, and succeeded in ruining it. 'To separate this primitive, all-powerful Dionysian element from tragedy, and to build up a new and purified form of tragedy on the basis of a non-Dionysian art, morality and conception of things—such is the tendency of Euripides which now reveals itself to us in a clear light.'[1]

From this point forward, as a whole, the argument of *The Birth of Tragedy* follows closely the lines laid down in *The Art-Work of the Future*. It is (and the fact deserves stressing, because it has been generally overlooked) little more than a re-presentation of Wagner's Romantic Myth. Nietzsche even attributes the critical spirit to a growing preponderance of the slaves, 'at least in sentiment'.[2] He departs from Wagner only in his characterization of Socrates: 'the specific *non-mystic*, in whom the logical nature is developed, through a superfoetation, to the same excess as instinctive wisdom is developed in the mystic.'[3]

This is as original as it is bold. Socrates, we are told, represents 'a turning-point and vortex of so-called European history'[4]—his prodigious confidence in the power of the human understanding having determined, both for better and for worse, the whole future development of Europe: for better, inasmuch as it made possible the advancement of science; but for worse, inasmuch as it was, and is, linked with a profound illusion—namely, 'that by means of the clue of causality, thinking reaches to the depths of being, and that thinking is able not only to per-

[1] BT, 12.   [2] BT, 11.   [3] BT, 13.   [4] BT, 15.

ceive being but even to *correct* it'.[1] This illusion, spreading over Europe like a fog, made impossible as long as it lasted a tragic perception of reality. Upon Socrates first and foremost, therefore, Nietzsche fastens responsibility for the dissolution of Hellenism.

However, the rays of the sun have already pierced, and are even now on the point of dispelling, this fog. 'The extraordinary wisdom of *Kant* and *Schopenhauer* has succeeded in gaining the most difficult victory, the victory over the optimism hidden in the heart of logic, which optimism is in turn the basis of our culture.' Reason has defined its own limitations; science itself must shortly resign its claim to see into the heart of things: so the way is open once more to a '*tragic perception*, which, in order even to be endured, requires art as a safeguard and remedy'.[2] All this is thoroughly Wagnerian; and it is here, of course, that Nietzsche presents Wagner in person, the Aeschylus of the new dispensation; the type of the '*music-practising Socrates*',[3] as he calls him, in whom scientific and philosophical understanding are united with Dionysian wisdom.

The conclusion of *The Birth of Tragedy* is tremulous with hopes and half-hopes. What does the twofold apparition of German music and German philosophy portend, if not the emergence in Germany itself of a new culture—a culture inspired, like the Hellenic, by a living, native mythology; and yet, unlike the Hellenic, insured from the first against the destructive critique of rationalism?—

'My friends, ye who believe in Dionysian music, ye know also what tragedy means to us. Here we have tragic myth, born once again from music—and in this myth ye can hope for everything and forget what is most afflicting. What is most afflicting to all of us, however, is—the prolonged degradation in which the German genius has lived estranged from house and home in the service of malignant dwarfs. Ye understand my allusion—as ye will also, in conclusion, understand my hopes.'[4]

Thus Nietzsche's polemical purpose is accomplished. Not only are Schopenhauer and Wagner used to illuminate the Greeks, but the Greeks to illuminate Schopenhauer and Wagner—and perhaps someone else as well.

* * *

Nietzsche called Schopenhauer his 'first and only teacher'. The first he may have been, but hardly the only: he owed as much, if not more, to Wagner. *The Birth of Tragedy* is a synthesis. It is a synthesis, however, and no mere *pastiche* because, in the last analysis, he owed most of all to himself.

[1] BT, 15.   [2] BT, 18.   [3] BT, 17.   [4] BT, 24.

Despite his own claim, it is questionable whether he was really indebted to Schopenhauer even for his discovery of the Dionysian. It might be truer to say that he was indebted to the Dionysian for his discovery of Schopenhauer. He hints as much when he writes, 'the dithyrambic votary of Dionysus, therefore, is understood only by those like himself'.[1] Like Lawrence, Nietzsche had more than the average modern man's experience of 'preconscious' states. The mood he attributed to the intoxicated reveller was substantially his own, in the composition, or even appreciation, of music—when every nerve, every fibre, thrilled in him, and he felt the urge to dance and caper, as he ultimately was to do on the hills overlooking Nice.

He had sought in Schopenhauer an explanation for his individual ecstasy. It is no accident that he should have found an even better explanation for the collective ecstasy of the Greeks. *The World as Will and Idea*, after all, is little more than a modernised transcription of the age-old philosophy of the Vedanta; and that philosophy may well represent the first great attempt, on the part of an Aryan-speaking people, to elucidate a 'feeling of participation' which had grown precious in proportion to its rarity. It fitted Nietzsche because it was cut to fit.

What is more, even what he borrowed from Schopenhauer he modified drastically. A quite brief acquaintance with *The Birth of Tragedy* is enough to show that, apart from the concept of a Primordial Unity, and that of music as an art *sui generis*, next to nothing of the original system survives.

In particular, although Nietzsche upholds the Apollonian artist as a saviour, communicating that timeless contemplation which is the highest attainable on earth, he will have nothing of the doctrine of Ideas. So far from the artist revealing eternal archetypes beyond appearance, he merely creates 'pleasurable illusions', doubly removed from the truth—illusions, moreover, 'seducing to a continuation of life'.[2]

Even the visionary world of the tragedian belongs to no different order: it serves as much to conceal as reveal the awful Dionysian reality. Just as long as the spectator of a tragedy keeps his eyes on the symbolic figure before him, he cannot help being deluded into the belief that the doom he is witnessing is that of one individual alone, Prometheus or Oedipus, and not that of all humanity, himself included. At the very moment when music is exciting him to an ecstatic recognition of the nature of life itself, he is persuaded that its only effect is to heighten the appeal of particular scenes:

[1] BT, 2.   [2] BT, 3.

'Thus does the Apollonian wrest us from Dionysian universality and fill us with rapture for individuals; to these it rivets our sympathetic emotion, through these it satisfies the sense of beauty which longs for great and sublime forms: it brings before us biographical portraits, and incites us to a thoughtful apprehension of the essence of life contained therein. With the immense potency of the image, the concept, the ethical teaching and the sympathetic emotion—the Apollonian influence uplifts man from his orgiastic self-annihilation, and beguiles him concerning the universality of the Dionysian process into the belief that he is seeing a detached picture of the world, for instance, Tristan and Isolde, and that, *through music*, he will be enabled to *see* it still more clearly and intrinsically.'[1]

It was owing to this illusion, Nietzsche says, that the Greek, no matter how completely he might abandon himself to Dionysian raptures, was spared the sense of futility which would otherwise have assailed him in the intervals: for it is with the god-intoxicated ecstatic as with the ordinary drunken reveller—he has to pay for his excess on the morning after. Having glimpsed the transitory, phenomenal nature of all that makes up human existence, how can he escape a 'longing for nothingness',[2] such as Indian Buddhism, for this reason, posits as the *summum bonum*? If the Greeks did not go the way of the Indians, it was because they had learned to veil the reality from themselves, or surmount it anew, as often as it threatened to engulf them.

As a logical pessimist, therefore, Nietzsche ought to have condemned the Apollonian. He ought, like Plato, to have banished the artist altogether, who created a mere illusion of illusion. It was only by adapting the doctrine of Ideas that Schopenhauer had secured his reprieve.

Nietzsche, however, does nothing of the sort. His passion for art is such that he no longer values 'self-annihilation' as an end, but only as a means—to the creation of works of art. He actually speaks of the 'longing for a Buddhistic negation of the will' as a 'danger';[3] and, far from condemning the Greeks for their concealment, he commends them for it. It was only by virtue of this that the artist could preserve himself in existence: 'art saves him, and through art life saves him—for herself'.[4] If the naked truth involves a denial of life, and art can subsist only upon illusion—so much the worse for truth, and not for art! Such is really Nietzsche's moral.

His instinctive exaltation of the Genius over the Saint has, in fine, led him to uphold what is virtually an assertion of the will-to-live. All his lip-service to Schopenhauer, therefore, cannot dissemble the fact that

[1] BT, 21.   [2] *Ibid.*   [3] BT, 7.   [4] *Ibid.*

lip-service to Schopenhauer, therefore, cannot dissemble the fact that it is not really Schopenhauer at all whom he is extolling as Wagner's philosophical counterpart. A system of unqualified pessimism would not safeguard the new Hellenism but sap it. That philosopher of the future who has gained the most difficult victory, whose system 'we may unhesitatingly designate as *Dionysian wisdom* comprised in concepts',[1] is none other than Nietzsche himself: *The Birth of Tragedy* is his philosophy.   * * *

This claim is not advanced openly: it is implicit, rather than explicit. It is nonetheless clearly present, and in later years Nietzsche confessed to it. What, then, are we to say of this philosophy? Happily, there is no need to say much. The self-contradictions and confusions of *The Birth of Tragedy* speak for themselves. Even its fundamental postulate, the Primordial Unity, cannot be adequately defined.

As we have seen, Nietzsche begins by postulating a God eternally impelled by His suffering to create the phenomenal world, in order that in the contemplation thereof He may be eternally redeemed. This is his justification for the continuance of life, and therefore of art. It follows that union with God is by no means the peaceful affair that most other mystics have depicted. It is accompanied by shrieks of anguish: 'from the highest joy sounds the cry of horror or the yearning wail over an irretrievable loss'.[2] Nietzsche makes no secret of the fact that there is a sexual, indeed sadistic, element in this consummation. He suggests that the Dionysian rites of the Greeks were derived from the Babylonian Sacaea—festivals whose centre 'lay in extraordinary sexual licentiousness, the waves of which overwhelmed all family life and its venerable traditions; the very wildest beasts of nature were let loose here, including that detestable mixture of lust and cruelty which has always seemed to me the veritable "witches' draught".'[3]

As time goes on, however, Nietzsche's god is gradually transformed. We hear less of the suffering, and consequently less of the 'redemption in appearance'. Dionysus cheers up, and before the end becomes almost entirely joy—joy, moreover, not in the contemplation, but in the sheer creation, of the world. Union with Him, accordingly, now becomes nothing more nor less than a rapturous submission to the procreative force of nature, expressing itself in an 'unchecked effusion of the unconscious will'.[4] It is the inmost workings of this will that find symbolic reflection in tragedy and the tragic myth.

Nietzsche, as we have seen, was changing even while he wrote *The Birth of Tragedy*. It is this that makes it so difficult a book to understand

[1] BT, 19.   [2] BT, 2   [3] *Ibid.*   [4] BT, 21.

—if truth be told, the most difficult of all his books. His thought had not crystallized even by the end: and to attempt a criticism at this point would be premature and unprofitable. We shall do better to follow it to a provisional conclusion in his closely related lectures on *Philosophy during the Tragic Age of the Greeks.*

* * *

These lectures were not written out until 1873, after they had been delivered more than once; and of course they were left unfinished. This time there was no Wagner to insist on publication: indeed, it was partly Wagner's pointed indifference to an enterprise promising no benefit to Bayreuth that resulted in their abandonment. Yet they are important, and mark, in many respects, an advance on *The Birth of Tragedy.* The style is succinct and clear; the matter arranged with full respect for 'logical cleanliness'; and though the pen-portraits of particular philosophers may be fanciful, occasionally inaccurate, one cannot but envy the students who had their classics presented in such a form.

Nietzsche's curiosity concerning the pre-Socratic philosophers was natural enough. He believed that there were two fundamentally different kinds of philosophy: on the one hand, the Socratic, which was hostile to art, and to which the two thousand years since the decadence of Grecian tragedy belonged; on the other hand, his own, which was not only friendly, but complementary, to art. He saw his own kind emerging in Germany *pari passu* with the emergence of tragedy: nothwithstanding his reservations with regard to the 'unconsciousness' of the Greeks, he could not help suspecting that a similar phenomenon might have been witnessed during their tragic age—and his suspicion was quickly confirmed. Hence the curious claim, reiterated in the course of these lectures, that 'the Greeks, as *the* healthy nation, have *justified* philosophy once and for all by having philosophized, and that indeed more than all other nations'.[1]

The characteristic of this second kind of philosophy, which, unlike the Socratic, is a manifestation of health—and must, for that reason, appear quite unphilosophical to those who stand within the Socratic tradition—Nietzsche describes at the outset. It is a philosophy that proceeds as much by intuition as by reason: whose first proposition, indeed, 'had its origin in a mystic intuition . . . the proposition: *Everything is one*'.[2] It takes for granted, in other words, a harmony between the external world and the internal, and will hold as true of the former only what corresponds to the latter, and is known to correspond by the immediate satisfaction it brings. It proceeds by divining the similarity in

[1] GP, 1.　　　　　　　　　　　[2] GP, 3.

dissimilars, the instrument of this divination being Fancy: 'Lifted by the latter, philosophical thinking leaps from possibility to possibility, and these for the time being are taken as certainties'.[1]

Such a mode of thinking, obviously, is more characteristic of poets than philosophers. Nietzsche's basic proposition may remind us of Baudelaire's '*La première condition nécessaire pour faire un art sain est la croyance à l'unité intégrale*'. But this of course he gladly admits. It is exactly what we should expect. The only distinction between the poet and the philosopher is that the latter has to formulate his vision conceptually:

'The philosopher tries to make the total-chord of the universe re-echo within himself and then to project it into ideas outside himself. . . . What the verse is to the poet, dialectic thinking is to the philosopher: he snatches at it in order to hold fast his enchantment, to petrify it. And just as words and verse to the dramatist are only stammerings in a foreign language, to tell in it what he lived, what he saw, and what he can directly promulgate by gesture and music alone, so the expression of every deep philosophical intuition by means of dialectics and scientific reflection is, it is true, on the one hand the only means to communicate what he has seen, but on the other hand a paltry means, at bottom a metaphorical, quite unfaithful transposition into a different sphere and language. Thus Thales saw the Unity of the "Existent", and when he wanted to communicate this idea he talked of water.'[2]

That is not to say that the function of the intellect is merely to 'rationalise'. On the contrary, the philosopher fails in his task if he does not submit his hypotheses to the strictest possible criticism, and present them in the most cogent possible form. Thales' proposition, 'All is water', was not merely a rationalisation of the mystic intuition, 'Everything is one'; it was a highly plausible scientific theory—the most plausible up to its time. But, whereas the scientist, as such, accepts this irrational assumption only in the form that reality is rational, and forgets that he has accepted it at all, the philosopher, like the poet, accepts it in the form that reality is harmonious, and bears it in mind to the end.

The early Greek philosophers, Nietzsche contends, were all distinguished to a greater or less degree by this mode of thinking. They constitute what Schopenhauer, 'in opposition to the Republic of Scholars, has called a Republic of Geniuses'.[3] They were no mere logicians; they must have played a part second only to that of the tragedians in deepening and purifying the Hellenic mind. Indeed, there

[1] GP, 3.   [2] *Ibid.*   [3] GP, 1.

was one whose thought was so essentially Dionysian that he all but merits the title, 'tragic philosopher'.

This was Heraclitus of Ephesus, who 'has as his royal property the highest power of intuitive conception'.[1] Heraclitus resembles Schopenhauer in maintaining that things have no existence apart from their interaction, and that this interaction takes the form of a continuous conflict: 'Out of the war of opposites all Becoming originates; the definite and to us seemingly persistent qualities express only the momentary predominance of the one fighter, but with that the war is not at an end; the wrestling continues to all eternity'.[2] At the same time, he differs from Schopenhauer in refusing either to regard this flux as evidence of a Fall or to postulate an unchanging Being. He actually denies Being. He has so far overcome the sentimental or moral repugnance which the conflict commonly excites, that he is able to envisage it, not merely with calm, but with positive delight. This, Nietzsche states, is no small achievement, since 'the eternal and exclusive Becoming, the total instability of all reality, which continually works and becomes and never *is*, as Heraclitus teaches, is an awful and appalling conception, and in its effects most nearly related to that sensation by which during an earthquake one loses confidence in the firmly-grounded earth. It requires astonishing strength to translate this effect into its opposite, into the sublime, into happy astonishment.'[3]

Heraclitus, in short, all but arrived at the point of envisaging existence as an aesthetic phenomenon; it was by virtue of this that he was able to conceive the author of existence as an artist, or rather as a child, building up and demolishing sand-castles—at all events as innocent of anything like moral bias. And since to survey the flux of Becoming with the happy astonishment of a child is veritably to survey it with the eyes of God, Heraclitus, may be said to have enunciated a wisdom, 'sufficient for the latest mankind'.[4] This is all we know on earth, and all we need to know: 'the world needs truth eternally, and therefore she needs Heraclitus eternally'.[5]

Thus, in *Philosophy During the Tragic Age of the Greeks*, Nietzsche's metaphysics undergoes yet a further metamorphosis. From being a sufferer seeking redemption in appearance, and an almighty procreative force rejoicing in its power, the Primordial Unity has finally resolved itself into the world-child Zeus! And here we can no longer forebear to ask what validity, if any, attaches to an 'intuition' that returns such contradictory verdicts. Did Nietzsche himself not begin to suspect that behind that peephole in the *principium individuationis* so beloved of

[1] GP, 5.   [2] *Ibid.*   [3] *Ibid.*   [4] GP, 8.   [5] *Ibid.*

Idealists (that peephole through which Kant had espied a categorical *imperator*, Hegel a universal logician, Schopenhauer an arch-misanthrope), there might stand, no god at all, but—a mirror?

As a matter of fact, he did. As early as September 1866, in a letter prompted by Lange's *History of Materialism*, he had submitted to von Gersdorff that 'the thing-in-itself is not only unknown to us, but even the conception of it is neither more nor less than the offspring of an opposition conditioned by our organization, concerning which we do not know whether it has any meaning at all outside our experience': in other words, that Schopenhauer's initial asumption was really no more than an assumption, and that his system could be justified, if at all, only as a work of art.

If we look closely enough, we shall find traces of the same suspicion in *The Birth of Tragedy* itself. For example, hardly has the author accustomed us to the idea, fundamental to his whole conception, that the 'metaphysical comfort' imparted by tragedy represents an assurance, outlasting our momentary coalescence with the Primordial Unity, that 'eternal life flows on indestructibly beneath the whirl of phenomena',[1] than, abruptly, he designates this too an 'illusion'—a mere mirage projected by 'the avid will' to 'detain its creatures in life!'[2]

Moreover, in a succession of cryptic notes, dating from the very years of *Philosophy During the Tragic Age of the Greeks*, Nietzsche seems virtually to adopt the argument against himself. It is not, he declares here, the 'instinct of knowledge' that is satisfied by Heraclitus' philosophy; it is simply the 'aesthetic instinct',[3] and the same applies to all philosophies: 'the beauty and grandeur of a construction of the universe (*alias* a philosophy) is what determines its value at present—that is to say, one judges it as a work of art'.[4] Again, if it is true that 'Heraclitus will never age',[5] it is true, not because his system embodies some 'eternal verity', but simply because, like 'immortal poetry', it responds to an unchanging need of human nature: 'philosophy is poetry beyond the confines of experience, an extension of the mythical instinct'.[6] Finally, and most conclusively of all, the metaphysician 'discovers the truth by inventing it, and invents it by discovering it':[7] whether there is a future for metaphysics, therefore, depends on whether or not he can continue to do in full consciousness what he has always done hitherto unconsciously:

'The creation of a religion would consist in this, that one awakened *faith* in the mythical construction he had erected in the void: i.e. that

---

[1] BT, 17. [2] *Ibid.* [3] N, X, 133. [4] N, X, 126.
[5] N, X, 128. [6] *Ibid.* [7] *Ibid.*

it corresponded to an extraordinary need. It is *unlikely* that this will ever happen again, after the *Critique of Pure Reason*. On the other hand, I can imagine an altogether new kind of *artist-philosophers*.'[1]

In these notes, and not for the last time, Nietzsche himself supplies the most instructive criticism of his own 'construction of the universe'.

It was, on the face of it, unlikely that the 'philosophy of the future'— a philosophy by definition uniting Dionysian wisdom with scientific understanding—should turn out to be no more than a variant, however eccentric, of the first great attempt ever made by an Aryan-speaking people to solve the mystery of existence. Nietzsche's claim, in *The Birth of Tragedy*, to have already sketched such a philosophy, was premature to say the least—and at the back of his mind he knew it. While, therefore, he may have succeeded in suppressing his doubts for the present, it could only be a question of time before they returned to afflict him. The paragraph just quoted stands like a summary or prospectus of his views in years to come.

[1] N, X, 122.

III

THE EDUCATIONIST

Nietzsche had barely completed his first year at Basle when, in July 1870, the Franco-German War broke out. His immediate reaction was characteristic. 'Here is a frightful thunderbolt', he cries in a letter to Rohde, 'Our whole threadbare culture is sliding into the arms of the most horrible of devils. . . . We may already be at the beginning of the end. What a wilderness! We shall again need cloisters. And we will become the first *fratres*!'[1] His fear was for what remained of European culture; his care, to keep it alive.

During the ensuing weeks, his sentiments underwent some change. After all it was to Germany—the country of Kant and Schopenhauer, Luther and Wagner—that he looked first and foremost for the rebirth of Hellenism. He was persuaded that the Germans had only to emancipate themselves from their long intellectual subservience to France to discover a genius of their own, capable of kindling a new Renaissance. While far removed from a thoughtless patriotism, therefore, he watched the unfolding of events with growing sympathy for the Imperial cause; and, as German casualties began to mount, bewailed the Swiss nationality he had taken, which prevented him enlisting himself. At last, in August, he did win permission to serve with the ambulance corps.

His first-hand experience of military service, however, was brief and disillusioning. Though he shared the typical scholar's hankering for the life of a man of action, Nietzsche was eminently unsuited to the part. For one thing, he was far too sensitive. The strain of attending the sick and dying told on him body and mind. Within a few weeks he had succumbed to dysentery and diphtheria himself, and even at Naumburg, where he was sent to recuperate, the scenes he had witnessed continued to haunt him for weeks. 'I am not right yet,' we find him writing on October 20, 'Besides, the atmosphere of my experiences had spread like a gloomy mist all about me, and for a time I never ceased to hear the plaintive cries of the wounded. It was therefore quite impossible to pursue my plan of returning to the seat of war, and now I must content be with watching and *pitying* from a distance.'

Not only was Nietzsche too sensitive, he was too intellectually

[1] L, 20, 7, 70.

detached. He could not escape his vocation simply by stepping into uniform. Even under the walls of Metz, he was to be found pondering *The
Birth of Tragedy*; and no sooner was he out of earshot of the guns, than
all his earlier misgivings revived. If he had hoped that the sufferings of
his countrymen would serve at least to dispel 'the optimism hidden in
the essence of logic', he could have made no greater mistake. The resounding military victory over France had precisely the opposite effect:
and the truth was not long in coming home to him. 'If only we are not
forced to pay too dearly for this huge national success in a quarter where
I at least refuse to suffer any loss', he writes in November. 'Between
ourselves, I regard the Prussia of today as a power full of the greatest
danger to culture';[1] and in another month's time, 'I am gradually losing
all sympathy with Germany's present war of conquest. The future of
German culture seems to me now more in danger than ever it was. . . .'[2]

His forebodings were too surely confirmed. The immediate effect of
the war was to consolidate the hold on Germany, not merely of Prussia
but of the Prussian philosophy. To all but a few, it seemed as if nothing
more was needed to vindicate Hegel's contention that history was on the
side of the Germans, their State 'God walking on earth'—a contention
which, from his own viewpoint, was little less than Satanic.

For Nietzsche held with Schopenhauer that the State, far from being
an end in itself, was merely a means to an end, and a more or less
deplorable means at that. The true end of man on earth was the self-
abnegation of the Will. If the State, by preserving order, enabled the
Saint or Genius to realize this the more effectively, its existence was
justified, and so was the devotion it inspired in the breast of the ordinary
citizen. The moment it overstepped that limit, it became a threat to be
countered at any cost. In an essay, *The Greek State*, written early in
1871, he expressed this viewpoint forcibly, invoking Plato's *Republic* in
support: 'The proper aim of the State, the Olympian existence and ever-
renewed procreation and preparation of the genius—compared with
which all other things are only tools, expedients and factors towards
realization—is here discovered with a poetic intuition and painted with
firmness'. Small wonder he returned to Basle more anxious than ever
concerning the future of Germany!

Schopenhauer once remarked that what distinguishes the false philosopher from the true is this: that the 'perplexity' of the one arises from
a comparison of books, that of the other from a contemplation of life.
By this criterion, Nietzsche was a true philosopher. It cannot be em-

[1] L, 7, 11, 70.   [2] L, 12, 12, 70.

phasised too strongly that his thinking was experiential through and through: determined from first to last by the urge to make sense of experience. 'I have always put my whole body and life into my writings', he was to say towards the end. 'I know nothing of purely intellectual problems.'[1] It was out of his reflection on this very peculiarity that his 'political philosophy' took shape.

This experiential approach, of course, was what isolated him in university circles. At Leipzig, he had turned to the teachers for help, and turned in vain. Not merely had they no solution to his problems, but— he had quickly discovered—they were incapable of apprehending them as problems. To them, philosophy was simply a subject, like any other taught at the universities. They knew all about the systems of the past— at any rate up till the time when they themselves had been students; they could compare and contrast Plato and Aristotle, Spinoza and Kant; they might even, on occasion, profess adherence to this or that school: but of philosophy as a personal need, of philosophy as a way of life therefore, they had no inkling whatsoever. The very possibility of such a thing had never entered their heads. It was at Leipzig, as he confessed, that Nietzsche acquired that contempt for the 'philosophical footmen' which he afterwards expressed so pungently:

'The only way to criticize a philosophy that is possible and proves anything at all—namely, to find out whether one can live by it—has never been taught at universities: only a criticism of words about words. Imagine a young head, without much experience of life, being stuffed with fifty systems, in the form of words, and fifty criticisms of them, all jumbled up together—what an overgrown wilderness it will come to be! What a mockery of a philosophical education! It is, in fact, avowedly an education, not for philosophy at all, but for a philosophical examination; the usual result being, as we know, the pious ejaculation of the much-tried examinee, "Thank God I am no philosopher, but a Christian and citizen of my State!"'[2]

To the professor, philosophy is a profession: at best a profession of faith entirely divorced from practice; more commonly a respectable *métier*. To the amateur, it may be a passion: Nietzsche among the professors had felt like a lover among philanderers.

He had been forced to work out his salvation for himself, with only Schopenhauer to lean on. What would have become of him without Schopenhauer? That question must often have crossed his mind; and one of his aspirations, on his appointment to Basle, had been to save his

[1] N, XI, 382.　　　　　　[2] TS, III, 8.

own students from having to tread the same uncertain path. At all events, he had sworn to Rohde, he himself would never degenerate into a 'Philistine':

'Philosophical seriousness is already too deeply rooted in me; the true and essential problems of life and thought have been too clearly revealed to me by that great mystagogue, Schopenhauer, to allow of my ever being obliged to dread such a disgraceful defection from the "Idea". To infuse this new blood into my science, to communicate to my pupils that Schopenhauerian earnestness, which is stamped on the brow of the sublime man—such is my desire, such is my undaunted hope. I should like to be something more than a mere trainer of efficient philologists. The present generation of teachers, the care of the coming generation—all this is in my mind.'[1]

Philology, of course, not philosophy, was Nietzsche's 'subject' at Basle; but how intimately the two could be associated is shown by *The Birth of Tragedy*. His hope had been, first to arouse in his pupils a response to Greek literature akin to his own, and then to interpret that response—thereby bringing all their faculties into unison with each other, in the service of a single vital centre. It was the ideal he had proclaimed in his Inaugural Lecture on *Homer and Classical Philology*.

As we have seen, however, Nietzsche found himself scarcely less isolated at Basle than he had been at Leipzig. The Swiss dons, with rare exceptions, proved no more capable than the German of sharing his aspirations. Hence his deep-seated *malaise*, his hankering after a more congenial situation. When he exclaimed, 'we will be the first *fratres*', he was far from merely building castles—or monasteries—in the air. He meant it seriously. How seriously was shown when, soon after the war, Rohde happened to echo this exclamation. Crediting his friend with an earnestness equal to his own, Nietzsche replied by return of post, proposing that they should save up to establish 'a new Greek Academy', and so 'effect a breach with philology as it has been practised hitherto and its aspect of culture'.[2] The project, as he had already conceived it, was to be parallel and complementary to 'Wagner's Bayreuth plan':

'Even supposing we get but few adherents, I believe, nevertheless, that we shall be able to extricate ourselves pretty well—not without some injuries, it is true—from this current, and that we shall reach some islet upon which we shall no longer be required to stop up our ears with wax. We shall then be our own mutual teachers and our books will be

[1] L, 13, 4, 69.   [2] L, 15, 12, 70.

only so much bait wherewith to allure others to our monastic and artistic association. Our lives, our work, our enjoyment will then be for one another; possibly this is the only way in which we can *work* for the world as a whole.'[1]

Nothing came of this, naturally. Nietzsche's friends were never as single-minded as he; and Rohde himself, though he did not know it, was already well on the way to becoming a normal 'Philistine'. Nietzsche had to content himself for the present with sharing a house at Basle with two other congenial spirits, Overbeck and Romundt. But the project, in one form or another, continued to attract him at intervals for many years afterwards.

Meanwhile, that very urge to make sense of his experience, which had drawn him to Schopenhauer and Wagner (alone of his contemporaries), had driven him to philosophize himself, creatively adapting their ideas; and the more he philosophized, the better he came to understand what had animated these men—and not only them, but also those early Greeks whose systems bore the stamp of their personalities. It was an urge of precisely the same kind. And so, at long last, there dawned on Nietzsche the realization that this, and nothing else, was what really distinguished the Genius. All that he had hitherto emphasized—mystical self-abnegation, pure, timeless contemplation—all that was at most the ultimate outcome and fruition. Whether in philosophy or art, the experiential approach itself was the *sine qua non*.

The experiential thinker and the Genius were one and the same. This discovery marked an epoch in Nietzsche's thought. No sooner had he made it than many other things became clear to him. In particular, he saw for the first time exactly where the present educational system was at fault. As a system that ignored this approach, not merely was it irrelevant, it was actually hostile, to Genius. In other words, it actively frustrated the realization of man's true end.

At the same time he saw, or thought he saw, why this system had become what it was: why, that is to say, institutions founded by humanists as devoted as himself had been so far perverted from their aim, that the art of passing a philosophical examination had usurped the place of philosophy on the curriculum, the ideal of the 'useful official'[2] that of the 'complete man'.[3] It was because these institutions had for generations been subordinated, slowly but steadily, to the State—a State that demanded of its citizens, not culture, but 'unconditional obedience'.[4] Assuredly it was no accident that Prussia, even now, was appointing

[1] L, 15, 12, 70.   [2] FE, p. 31.   [3] N, IX, 424.   [4] FE, p. 31.

wherever it could professors of the Hegelian persuasion: 'It would perhaps be no exaggeration to say that, in the subordination of all strivings
after education to ends of State, Prussia has appropriated, with success,
the useful heirloom of the Hegelian philosophy, whose apotheosis of
the State in *this* subordination certainly reaches its height.'[1]

Thus, when Nietzsche spoke of the danger to culture involved in the
Prussian ascendancy, he was not speaking of something abstract and
remote, but of a danger he himself had encountered, and was countering
still. His 'political philosophy', rudimentary though it was, sprang like
all his philosophy directly from his own experience. Moreover, since
he was incapable of divorcing theory from practice—their divorce was
precisely what he deplored—it reacted directly upon it. From this time
forward, his mind was seldom free from projects of educational reform.
And as luck would have it, early in 1872, came an opportunity to voice
them.

* * *

His dissatisfaction with Basle was by no means reciprocated. By
every criterion but his own, Nietzsche seems to have been an admirable
teacher. He had that first qualification for education ('the most delicate
technique that has ever existed in art'),[2] a living interest in his subjects.
Combining duty with pleasure, instruction with research, he would communicate the keenness of discovery, and his lectures were said to be as
enthralling as a French novel. Indeed, when it became known that he had
refused an appointment elsewhere, his students wished to hold a torch-
light procession in his honour, whilst the authorities, no less impressed,
substantially increased his stipend. Even before this he had been invited
to deliver a series of public addresses, *On the Future of Our Educational
Institutions.*

In the circumstances, this invitation may have been slightly embarrass-
ing. The youngest member of the staff, a comparative newcomer at that,
Nietzsche could hardly fail to see the risk he ran of offending the very
people who had favoured him, if he gave direct expression to his views.
It was for this reason, no doubt, that he couched the addresses in the
form of a dialogue, circumventing, not for the last time, 'the use of the
little word "I"'.[3] If the device was transparent, it served all the better
as a polite *apologia.* At the same time it gave him a chance to point his
moral symbolically.

Having disposed of his difficulty in this way, however, he took full
advantage of the occasion, both to set his own thoughts in order and to

---

[1] FE, p. 87.   [2] FE, p. 45.   [3] EH, p. 90.

lay them before an intelligent, influential audience: with the result that the five addresses, in the form in which they were ultimately published (it need hardly be said that he had intended to expand them), constitute a document of considerable intrinsic as well as biographical interest. They merit, in fact, more attention than they usually receive from his readers—who, all too often, approach these earlier works seeking (and therefore finding) nothing but 'anticipations' of his later.

The characters of the dialogue are four: two raw young students, on the one hand; an elderly philosopher and his companion, on the other. The philosopher (who may fairly be identified with Schopenhauer) is represented as awaiting a friend, and discoursing to his companion merely to fill in the time. The students (Nietzsche and Rohde), though longing for enlightenment, receive it quite unexpectedly in the shape of the words they overhear. The personal reminiscence here is unmistakable; and so it is again at the end, when, the philosopher's friend having failed to appear, his signal-call is nevertheless heard, hailing from the least expected quarter—out of the mouths of other students.

Through the lips of this imaginary philosopher, Nietzsche describes the education he desired. By this standard he passes judgment on the education he knew, beginning with the public schools and going on to the universities. It is worth noting, therefore, that there is nothing 'reactive' about his criticism, harsh though it often is. He stands at the opposite pole from those reformers, commonly labelled 'progressive', who start out with a fixed resentment against the existing order, and arrive at their views of what should be by the simple expedient of ideal-izing whatever is contrary to it. His creative deed is his 'yes'.

Thus, the aim of the public schools, as he sees it, being single and irreplaceable—to awaken a genuine response to Greek art and literature —Nietzsche has nothing but praise for the thoroughness of the ground-ing they already give in Latin and Greek: 'the most wholesome feature of our modern institutions'.[1] He himself owed much to the discipline of Schulpforta (Latin and Greek had not come to him easily), and always gladly acknowledged it. Where he finds fault is in their neglect of German: since, he insists repeatedly, 'the beginning of all real culture'[2] is the correct usage of the mother-tongue. If their Hellenism really meant anything to the teachers, they would at least so far model themselves upon the Greeks as to treat their own language with meticulous respect. Instead, they allow German to be grossly abused: either studying it solely from an etymological standpoint, or else regarding it as a medium for compositions to be judged, not by their manner, but their matter—

[1] FE, p. 63.   [2] FE, p. 58.

compositions, moreover, in which boys are encouraged to pass judgment on poetical works, and even ethical issues, which they are totally incapable of appraising.

The correct usage of the mother-tongue, however, can be acquired only by incessant practice. The teacher therefore should make his pupils express the same thought time and again, ever more happily. Not until they have learned in this way to appreciate all the subtleties of the language, will they be capable of a genuine feeling for the works of the great German poets—and then they will approach these works with a becoming humility and reverence. 'Everybody should, himself, be aware of the difficulties of the language: he should have learned them from experience: he must reach after long seeking and struggling the path our great poets trod in order to be able to realize how lightly and beautifully they trod it.'[1]

This is very characteristic. Nietzsche goes on to compare the difficulty of learning to write with that of learning to march—a comparison which recurs frequently in his books. Unlike some of the minor Romantics, he himself would never allow that 'inspiration' could be a substitute for technical proficiency. *Laissez-faire, laissez-aller* was as abhorrent in art as in economics. Inspiration was a prerequisite of greatness, to be sure: but before it could achieve its results, mastery of the most exacting forms must have been brought to a second nature.

Only when boys have begun to master the German language, he concludes, can they be expected to appreciate the German classics; and only when they have begun to appreciate these, can they be expected to acquire a real enthusiasm for the Greeks. 'Once more, therefore, we need the same leaders and tutors, our German classical writers, that we may be borne up, too, by the wing-strokes of their past endeavours—to the land of yearning, to Greece.'[2]

His constructive approach is the same when he comes to deal with the universities, whose first objective, as he sees it, is to initiate students into philosophy. Only, of course, his indictment of their shortcomings—their veritable betrayal of their mission—is a great deal more severe. The better he knew what had animated the philosophers of the past, the more preposterous it seemed to him that people who had no inkling of this should presume to interpret their works—the more pernicious, indeed, since it was the very student who knew best the meaning of 'perplexity' who suffered the worst frustration. He asked for bread and was given a stone; he was lucky if the stone was not dropped on his head. In the concluding address, Nietzsche draws on all his remembrances of

[1] FE, p. 58.   [2] FE, p. 61.

Bonn and Leipzig to depict the plight of the adolescent, who, on leaving school, finds himself 'in the highest degree in need of a guiding hand, because he has suddenly and almost instinctively convinced himself of the ambiguity of existence, and has lost the firm ground of traditional views'.[1]

At this age, he declares, 'the natural and the most immediate need of youth is, so to speak, a self-surrendering to great leaders and an enthusiastic following in the footsteps of the masters'.[2] Yet what does it meet with instead?—Professors! Professors who (it is their only excuse), owing to a similar dereliction in their own youth, have long since abandoned any attempt to solve the riddle of existence, and now seek what comfort they can get from an arid, sterile, exclusively oral and theoretical exposition of past philosophies: 'Their comfort, however, certainly does not counter-balance the sufferings of one single young man with a thirst for culture who feels the need of a guiding hand, and who at last, in a moment of discontent, throws down the reins and begins to despise himself. This is the guiltless innocent: for who has saddled him with the unbearable burden of standing alone?'[3]

To many, and especially the kind of educational reformers mentioned above, Nietzsche's indictment of a system which aims at 'implanting independence in the place of the dependence, discipline, subordination, and obedience implanted by former generations that thought it their duty to drive away all the bumptiousness of independence',[4] equally with his endorsement of surrender to great leaders and masters, cannot fail to sound obscurantist. All the more essential is it to realize how closely he is adhering to his own experience.

The kind of surrender he is speaking of is either made spontaneously or not made at all. If we grant his initial assumption, that the young man arrives at the university imbued with a deep sense of the significance of art, it is unthinkable that he should devote himself to anyone other than a philosopher—a philosopher, moreover, capable of providing him with a rational interpretation of this significance, and so with an ideal to live by. What Nietzsche requires of the educationist is what Schopenhauer bequeathed to himself—nothing more and nothing less. One may recall the letter he wrote from Leipzig to a friend who had suggested his writing a critique of Schopenhauer: 'One does not write a critique of an outlook on the world; one just either accepts it or does not accept it; to me a third standpoint is unintelligible.'[5] What he requires of the student is that he should embrace a philosophy 'with that simple manly faith which compelled an Ancient, wherever he was, whatever he did, to

[1] FE, p. 128.   [2] FE, p. 134.   [3] *Ibid.*   [4] FE, p. 127.   [5] L, 20, 10, 68.

deport himself as a Stoic, when once he had pledged his life to the Stoa'.[1]
Let a man but try to live by his philosophy, he intimates, and criticism
will follow soon enough—the only kind of criticism that is possible and
proves anything at all.

That, however, is not all that will follow. By the time he came to
compose these addresses, Nietzsche had advanced some distance beyond
the position of the Inaugural Lecture. He no longer regarded even initi-
ation into philosophy as the final objective of the universities. A further
ideal had dawned upon him, which, emerging also from his own experience, finds its first formulation at this stage.

* * *

He himself, we have to remember, had surrendered, not to one great
master, but to two. In doing so, he had discovered, what perhaps he
had long suspected, that 'a reciprocal predisposition prevails in the hierarchy of spirits'.[2] In other words, that if the young man with a thirst for
culture stands in need of a philosophical teacher, the teacher stands in no
less need of sincere and devoted disciples. Without them, he is in desperate danger of succumbing to the hardships and temptations of isolation. 'When, however, in spite of all this, leader and followers, fighting
and wounded, have found each other, there is an impassioned feeling of
rapture, like the echo of an ever-sounding lyre, a feeling which I can let
you divine only by means of a simile.'[3]

The simile concerns a great conductor with his orchestra, and there
can be no doubt that Nietzsche's thoughts, when he wrote these words,
had wandered back to those early days at Tribschen. What had he and
Wagner alike not suffered from the incomprehension of their fellows?
Not until their first encounter had either felt truly 'among his own'—
for Wagner had confessed to him lately that, but for his encouragement,
he might never have completed *The Ring*.

Now, looking back on the history of German literature, Nietzsche
had grown aware that the same smug indifference and hostility, against
which Wagner was forced to contend, had been the common lot of
almost every one of its foremost representatives. Winckelmann, Lessing,
Goethe, Schiller—they had all been at war, more or less, with the spirit
of their times; half the energy which might have gone towards their
creations had run to waste in exasperated self-vindication:

'So you are proud of your poets and artists, my good Teutons? You
point to them and brag about them to foreign countries, do you . . .?
For each of them, however, up to this very moment, you have always

---

[1] GP, 2.   [2] FE, p. 140.   [3] FE, p. 141.

been the "resistance of the stupid world" that Goethe speaks of in his "Epilogue to the Bell"; towards each of them you acted the part of apathetic dullards or jealous narrow-hearts or malignant egotists. In spite of you they created their immortal works, against you they directed their attacks, and thanks to you they died so prematurely, their tasks unfinished, stunned and shattered in the battle.'[1]

The conclusion was unavoidable. Simply in order that the genius should rise to his full stature, it was imperative that he should be surrounded by men of his own kind—cultured men, complete men, men of the only kind who could justly appraise his achievement.

Such had been his position in Greece: and that was why Greek artists and philosophers had achieved such unrivalled perfection. They had not been isolated; they had not been continually driven onto the defensive. On the contrary, they had been completely at one with their society, and their greatest productions stood out as the fine flower of an entire civilization. In Greece, complete men were not the exception, but the rule: 'If we could rightly interpret the total life of the Greek nation, we should ever find reflected there only that picture which in her highest geniuses shines in more resplendent colours.'[2]

Nature requires the genius: the genius requires a culture. Just when Nietzsche reached this conclusion is impossible to say: but with it his hellenic studies must have taken on still deeper significance. It was no longer Greek literature or philosophy *per se* that focussed his attention, but rather the total life of the Greek nation. And, inevitably, his educational ideal underwent a corresponding change. It was no longer enough for him that students should acquire a taste for the classics, or even a philosophy of life; the aim of the university could be nothing less than to impart a conception of hellenic culture as a whole, considered as the prototype and supreme exemplar of what every true culture should be. Only then, when they were so possessed with this ideal that they would never rest content until the German spirit had found analogous embodiment, could the future of Germany be safely entrusted to their charge: since 'once that feeling for Hellenism is aroused, it immediately becomes aggressive and must express itself by indulging in an incessant war with the so-called culture of the present'.[3]

* * *

In these addresses Nietzsche describes the education appropriate to a genius. He makes no secret of this. If the genius is the aim of the universe, it follows that his well-being should be the aim of the university.

---

[1] FE, p. 106.   [2] GP, 1.   [3] FE, p. 62.

'These individuals must complete their work: that is the *raison d'être* of their common institution.'[1]

At the same time, he denies, very rightly, that it is an education appropriate *only* to genius. When the philosopher's companion raises the obvious objection—'If it be only in connection with these rarest natures that true culture may be spoken of, how are institutions to be founded on the uncertain existence of such natures, how can we devise educational establishments which shall be of benefit only to these select few?'[2] —the philosopher retorts emphatically, 'not a few, even of those whose talents are of the second or third order are suited to such co-operation, and only in the service of such a true cultural institution do they feel that they are discharging their duty'.[3] In point of fact, by re-defining the genius as the experiential thinker, Nietzsche has given the term a wider connotation than it had for Schopenhauer. He might have been well advised to discard it altogether in favour of the 'complete man'.

For all that, it scarcely needs pointing out that such a system of education would be appropriate only to a minority, and a small minority at that. He himself stresses this too. It is essentially a classical education; and if his teaching in the High School at Basle had taught him anything, it was that even the first condition of a genuine taste for the classics—the ability to master the mother-tongue—was lacking to all but a few: 'among many thousands, perhaps hardly *one* can legitimately claim a hearing as a writer'.[4] So far from expecting that everybody would benefit by it, Nietzsche was convinced that the attempt to give everybody a classical education was, not merely foolish, but positively harmful. In the first place, a teacher faced with 'unselected youths, huddled together in a confused heap',[5] was prevented from giving his best even to those with the requisite qualifications. In the second place, he was condemned to manufacture out of the others yet a further generation of 'Philistines' —of men with no real understanding of either art or philosophy, but just enough superficial acquaintance with both to feel entitled to criticize and pontificate. He was condemned, in other words, to expose the genius of the future to the very fate it had endured in the past, defeating his own aim.

For these reasons, Nietzsche regarded the 'tendency to spread learning among the greatest possible number of people' as an evil second only to the 'tendency to minimize and weaken it'[6] in the interests of the State. Between them, he pointed out, these two evils had already gone far towards discrediting a classical education altogether. So obviously

---

[1] FE, p. 112.   [2] FE, p. 104.   [3] FE, p. 113.
[4] FE, p. 54.   [5] FE, p. 73.   [6] FE, Preface.

worthless was it to the many, that its value to any was being called in question; and before long it might well be cast overboard in favour of some other discipline, more relevant to the bureaucratic ideal. He intended his educational establishments for the few, and only the few.

At this point, therefore, a further question arises: what is to be done for the many? The obvious answer would seem to be that they should be endowed with a course of instruction equally appropriate to their own particular abilities. There appears, after all, no reason why that 'certain moral sublimity', which, as he says, far more than the 'degree of talent',[1] qualifies a man for association with genius, should be confined to those of literary leanings; it might just as well find expression in the work of the craftsman, the doctor, the scientist, or even the statesman. As Goethe reminded Eckermann (in a conversation which Nietzsche was later to quote approvingly), 'genius does not depend upon the business, the art, or the trade a man follows, but may be alike in all'—and if genius does not, still less does the appreciation of genius. Were it otherwise, indeed, it is hard to see how a culture, in Nietzsche's sense, could ever come into being. The fine arts would always and everywhere stand out in reproachful contrast to every other product of society.

Strangely enough, however, he himself contradicts this answer flatly. He maintains, in effect, that the capacity for moral sublimity veritably is confined to those with literary leanings: and shows himself utterly indifferent to what becomes of the others. Anything, we are given to understand, is good enough for them—or too good. 'I for my own part know of only two exact contraries: *Institutions for culture and institutions for livelihood*. All our institutions belong to the second class; but I am speaking only of the first.'[2] To the second class he abandons willingly all who 'promise to turn out civil servants, or merchants, or officers, or wholesale dealers, or farmers, or physicians, or technicians'.[3] For him, a true education and a classical are synonymous.

* * *

Why was this? The explanation is not far to seek. It was to Schopenhauer originally that Nietzsche owed his conception of the genius; and Schopenhauer was, to put it mildly, an intellectual snob. Although he did allow on one occasion that the genius excelled the ordinary man only by possessing to a higher degree the capacity for self-transcendance, as a general rule he maintained, with savage iteration, that the vast majority of human beings was congenitally incapable of any aesthetic contemplation at all, let alone creation. And it is highly probable that

[1] FE, p. 114.   [2] FE, p. 98.   [3] FE, p. 95.

Nietzsche, when he first encountered *The World as Will and Idea*, was particularly attracted by this notion. He was, at that moment, emerging from his humiliating attempts to act the man among men: how gratifying then to learn that what he had taken for an inferiority of degree was in truth a superiority of kind!

I do not mean to overrate the 'compensatory' factor in Nietzsche's make-up. It is very far from being, what the tyros of Adlerian psychology eagerly represent it to be, a simple and sufficient explanation for whichever of his opinions they happen to find repugnant; and even if it were, it would be no argument against these opinions—since, as he himself pointed out, and they have still to learn, our knowledge of the origin of a thing tells us nothing as to its value. Nevertheless, the factor was there, and it may well have been partially responsible for his long adherence, and occasional reversion, to Schopenhauer's misanthropic view: for—and this is what really matters—that view is unwarranted by the evidence. He himself supplies the *reductio ad absurdum*.

He has extended the term 'genius' to include anyone—be his talents only of the second or third order—who shows a genuine aptitude for the fine arts. Beyond that he refuses to extend it: with the result that, in his essay on *The Greek State*, even the manufacturers of those vases and utensils, justly rated among the most precious relics of antiquity, are summarily denied any credit for aesthetic creation. The Greeks, he asserts here (in contradiction to Winckelmann), regarded the occupation of a craftsman as shameful—and they were right, since art can never proceed from the will to live, or even to earn a living. *Ergo*, it can only be the prerogative of a leisured few, exempt from the need of supporting themselves. *Pulchrum est paucorum hominum.*

That this is absurd, the history of the fine arts themselves is enough to prove. Neither Michelangelo nor Shakespeare nor Mozart was exempt from the need of supporting himself. Moreover, if it is true that 'it is impossible for a man, fighting for the continuance of a bare existence, to become an *artist*', it is no less true that as soon as he has secured a bare existence he begins to fashion works that are not merely useful but beautiful. Wagner pointed this out, citing it as a good reason why nobody should have to fight for the continuance of a bare existence. The ornaments on a Grecian vase, he contended, were different only in degree, not in kind, from the friezes of the Parthenon.

To Nietzsche, however, Coomoraswamy's celebrated dictum, 'the artist is not a special kind of man, every man is a special kind of artist', would have sounded, at this stage, perverse; and with his characteristic intellectual ruthlessness (that *terribile demonstrazione*, which Vasari ascribed to Leonardo) he pursued the deductions from his own premise to their logical conclusion.

'In order that there may be a broad, deep and fruitful soil for the development of art, the enormous majority must, in the service of a minority, be slavishly subjected to life's struggle, to a *greater* degree than their own wants necessitate. At their cost, through the surplus of their labour, that privileged class is to be relieved from the struggle for existence, in order to create and to satisfy a new world of want. Accordingly we must accept this cruel-sounding truth, that *slavery is of the essence of Culture.*'

He does not even stop there. Slavery can only be enforced by the power of the State; the only kind of State that will enforce it—in the interests of the cultured few, and not those of the money-grubbing many—is a military State, wherein the hierarchical principle is accepted implicitly: 'Be it then pronounced that war is just as much a necessity for the State as the slave is for society, and who can avoid this conclusion if he honestly asks himself about the causes of the unequalled perfection of Greek art?'

Who can avoid this conclusion?—Anybody sufficiently versed in history. Nietzsche himself had avoided it very successfully, when he diagnosed contemporary Prussia as a power full of the greatest danger to culture. The scorpion stings its own head.

In his public lectures, it need hardly be said, he was less outspoken than this. It is possible, indeed, that he had already altered his verdict. But his bias still lay in the same direction, and was reinforced by his loathing for the 'Philistines of Culture'. His very insight into the problem (and it is a real problem, more acute than ever today) constituted by those who had received, and been corrupted by, an education for which they were unfitted, blinded him to the parallel problem (no less outstanding) of those who had not received an education for which they were eminently fitted. 'The greatest danger,' he writes, 'is that the ignorant classes should be contaminated by the dregs of existing culture.'[1] Hence it was that he wished to deny the majority, not merely a classical education, but any education whatever. In this matter, he cannot be wholly absolved from the charge of 'reactiveness'.

* * *

Nothwithstanding these aberrations, the addresses *On the Future of our Educational Institutions* were a resounding success—if success is to be measured by applause. Fashionable Basle thronged to hear them, and

[1] N, X, 290.

Jakob Burckhardt, who shared Nietzsche's worship of the fine arts and had wept with him over the vandalism of the Commune, was warm in his approbation. In the spring of 1872, the young professor's future seemed assured. He had justified the expectations of the authorities. Had he been nothing more than a professor, he might have looked forward confidently to a long and prosperous university career.

Unfortunately, or fortunately, Nietzsche was so much more than a professor that his success had the very opposite effect. He knew too well what it was worth. He knew that it bespoke no intention of putting his proposals into practice, or even of debating them seriously: and since it did not, what object was there in his remaining at Basle?

Up till now he had been able, more or less, to reconcile his professional duties with his personal predilections. The subjects he had treated in his lectures were subjects that naturally engrossed him. He would, in all probability, have written books on the birth of tragedy and the pre-Socratic philosophers even if he had never occupied a Chair of Classical Philology. Now this was no longer possible. With his discovery of the significance of Hellenic culture as a whole, his own classical education had reached its goal—philology had no more to teach him. His own Hellenism had become aggressive, and was clamouring for incessant war with the so-called culture of the present. *On the Future of our Educational Institutions* was really his declaration of war; and that declaration had to be followed up—if not at Basle, then elsewhere.

If he had been ill at ease in the academic world before, therefore, he was more than ever so now. His letters betray a continual undertone of impatience, with his colleagues, his duties, the whole career to which he was committed, and to which every new obligation appeared to bind him more tightly. What is more, in the summer of 1872, two further factors served not only to aggravate his impatience but to turn his eyes back towards Germany.

The first of these was Wilamowitz-Möllendorff's attack on *The Birth of Tragedy*, a pamphlet satirically entitled *The Philology of the Future*, which so far discredited Nietzsche's academic standing as to reduce his students the following autumn to two. Wilamowitz, by concentrating on points of historical detail, succeeded in making him appear as unreliable in his facts as he was biased in the interpretation he set on them (and his criticism was in some respects just). At the same time, he showed such characteristic incomprehension of the central argument of the book —above all of the conviction distinguishing it that philology should be related to life, classical research to the problems of the day—that nothing could have been more effectively calculated to remind Nietzsche, supposing he needed reminding, of how widely his outlook diverged from that of the professional philologist. His reaction may be summarized in the sentences he wrote not long afterwards:

'The condition of philologists may be seen by their indifference at the appearance of Wagner. They should have learned even more through him than through Goethe, and they did not even glance in his direction. That shows that they are not actuated by any strong need, or else they would have an instinct to tell them where their food was to be found.'[1]

The second factor that aggravated his impatience was Wagner's own departure from Tribschen: the Bayreuth plan being by this time so far advanced as to demand his presence on the spot. For Nietzsche this was like a bereavement. The tale is told how, while the Wagners were packing, he himself sat down at the piano, giving vent to his regret in a succession of mournful improvisations. Once more he was fated to be alone—and not merely alone, but 'out of it'. All the summer he must have been conscious of great things afoot at Bayreuth, in which he no longer bore a part. Small wonder he was torn by the ambition to strike a blow for German culture on his own account!

For Nietzsche, like Wagner, still believed in the 'German genius'. Towards the end of his public addresses, he had recalled how students returning from the Wars of Liberation, eager to build a new Germany, had been betrayed by the old authorities in State and University. The courage and loyalty of the simple German soldier in the recent war had convinced him that such eagerness still prevailed, and that it was still only those old authorities who stood in the way of a cultural renascence. The smug bourgeois might extol Bismarck's *Reich*, if not Bismarck himself, as God walking on earth, the Philistine be well content with the universities as temples of Dagon, but behind the façade of unity there were thousands who already knew better:

'The first who will dare to be quite straightforward in this respect will hear his honesty re-echoed back to him by thousands of courageous souls. For, at bottom, there is a tacit understanding between the more nobly gifted and more warmly disposed men of the present day. Every one of them knows what he has had to suffer from the condition of culture in schools; every one of them would fain protect his offspring from the need of enduring a like oppression, at whatever cost to himself.'[2]

[1] TS, V, 80.   [2] FE, p. 44.

Such was also Wagner's persuasion. Consequently, when, a year later, Nietzsche drew up his *Appeal to the German Nation* on behalf of the Bayreuth plan, he expressed himself still more forcibly: 'The Germans will only appear worthy of respect and be able to exercise a salutary influence upon other nations, when they have shown how formidable they can be, and yet will succeed in making the world forget how formidable they have been by the intensive manifestation of the highest and noblest artistic and cultural forms.' Like so many other idealists, before and since—and not only youthful ones—he imagined that a willingness to die for one's country betokened a willingness to live for it; and this time, he was resolved, leadership should not be wanting.

But what could he do in his own particular sphere? There seemed very little he could do. His new Greek Academy obstinately refused to materialise. The only possibility, it seemed, was to throw out still more 'bait'. In the spring of 1873, accordingly, he settled down to the composition of a series of ringing polemics, the *Thoughts out of Season*.

IV

THE HUMANIST

(1)

Nietzsche intended to write thirteen *Thoughts out of Season*. The number proved unlucky and he completed only four: 'David Strauss, the Confessor and the Writer' (1873), 'The Use and Abuse of History' (1873), 'Schopenhauer as Educator' (1874), and 'Richard Wagner at Bayreuth' (1875–6). The first two complement one another; so do the second. The four together mark the culmination of the first phase of his philosophy.

The polemical form suited both his spirit and his intention. Bruno Bauer called 'David Strauss' the finest polemic in German, and although, as Strauss's foremost rival in the field of New Testament criticism, Bauer may have been biased, there can be no disputing either the brilliance or the force of its style. These 'unseasonable (or over-seasoned) thoughts',[1] as Nietzsche called them, having ripened in his mind for years, were ready to burst on the world. He saw himself, moreover, in the guise of a 'soldier of culture', destined to 'turn German bravery into a new direction',[2] so that they present a masterly example of that 'spiritual warfare' which he was later to extol as the sublimation of war itself.

They also present an object-lesson in true patriotism, since Nietzsche never had any patience with the collective self-adoration that usually goes by the name. He was just as vehement in his denunciation of the evil traditions of his countrymen as he was passionate in his devotion to the good. His sentiments, indeed, recall Wordsworth's, and it is no surprise to learn that he was dubbed a francophile and enemy of the German Empire. If he attacked the Empire, however, it was because he believed it to be betraying the German genius: to that he remained loyal from first to last. He could hardly do otherwise, seeing that he embodied it.

His long apprenticeship to the Greeks had given him a unique insight into the minds of his great predecessors—Lessing, Goethe, Schiller, above all perhaps, Hölderlin, with whom he acknowledged a peculiar affinity. From his own experience he had learned what imperious instinct it was that had driven these men one after another, with an ardour and tragic

[1] L, 31, 12, 73.   [2] TS, I, 1.

intensity unparalleled outside Germany, 'to the land of yearning, to Greece'. They were figures, he declared, 'whose every movement, the expression of whose every feature, whose questioning voice and burning eye, proclaimed the one fact *that they were seekers*';[1] and what they had been seeking was the secret of a genuine, native culture, of the only kind in which they themselves could have lived and worked unendangered.

This being so, there was only one way of honouring them, and that was 'to continue seeking with the same spirit and with the same courage, and not to weary of the search'.[2] Anything less betrayed a shameful indifference to all that they had stood for. Their labours would not be rewarded, nor would their spirits be at peace, until Athens had been built in Germany's green and pleasant land.

Yet how many of those who professed to honour them felt any such obligation? Statues might be erected to their memory, new editions of their Complete Works be issued: on every side one assumption remained unchallenged—that the works of genius were so many 'works of art', whose sole and sufficient purpose was discharged in the provision of spare-time entertainment for the many and topics of conversation for the few. That the artist had any function beyond this, that art itself bore any relation to 'life'—this was a thought as remote from the patron of the gallery as the thought of philosophy as a way of life was from the university professor. Everywhere the values of the Philistine were accorded absolute validity; art and philosophy tolerated just so far as they accommodated themselves to these:

'The Philistine really does not at all mind giving himself up, from time to time, to the delightful and daring transgressions of art or of sceptical historical studies, and he does not underestimate the charm of such recreations and entertainments: but he strictly separates the "earnestness of life", by which he understands his profession, his business, his wife and child, from such trivialities, and among the latter he includes almost everything to do with culture. Therefore, woe to the art that begins to take itself seriously, that makes demands which affect his income, his business and his habits—his Philistine's earnestness, in short. From such an art he averts his eyes as though it were something indecent; and, affecting the attitude of a guardian of modesty, he cautions every unprotected virtue on no account to look.'[3]

It was his indignation with this complacency—which the establishment of the Empire had only augmented—that burst forth like a torrent in Nietzsche's first polemic.

[1] TS, I, 2.   [2] *Ibid.*   [3] *Ibid.*

He had no personal acquaintance with David Strauss, still less any personal animus against him. For the author of *The Life of Jesus*, he had even a qualified respect—it had helped to liberate him, as it had many others, from the trammels of Christian fundamentalism; he was genuinely distressed when he learned that his polemic had reached the old scholar on his death-bed. Strauss's latest work, on the other hand, *The Old Faith and the New*, was perfectly representative of the attitude he despised—how representative was shown, not only by the phenomenal success it enjoyed, but also by the bewilderment with which Nietzsche's attack was received. Neither Strauss nor his admirers could conceive of a man taking art so seriously. It was much the same fifteen years later, when *The Case of Wagner* appeared: everywhere some personal motive was looked for. It might be envy, it might be vanity, it might even be incipient lunacy: that a man should 'suffer from the fate of music as from an open wound'[1]—that was incomprehensible.

It was as a type that Nietzsche picked on Strauss—the type of the 'Culture-Philistine'. As he explained afterwards, 'I avail myself of a person only as a powerful magnifying-glass, with which to render a general but insidious and elusive threat visible.'[2] That, of course, is why his satire provoked such widespread resentment: had Strauss's tastes been at all eccentric, it would have been welcome. That too, is why it is still so readable: for—need it be said?—the type was by no means confined to Germany, nor to the nineteenth century. We have only to substitute Wordsworth for Winckelmann, Coleridge for Lessing, Blake for Goethe, Keats for Schiller, Shelley for Hölderlin, in order to find in these pages a perfect portrayal of the cultured Englishman's attitude towards his 'classics':

'What does our Culture-Philistinism say of these seekers? It regards them simply as discoverers, and seems to forget that they themselves only claimed to be seekers. We have our culture, say her sons; for have we not our "classics"? Not only is the foundation there, but the building already stands upon it—we ourselves constitute that building. And, so saying, the Philistine raises his hand to his brow.'[3]

The term 'Culture-Philistine' (*Bildungsphilister*), as Nietzsche coined it, denotes not merely the smug bourgeois, whom so much effort has been made to *épater*, but also the *épateur*, the smug intellectual. 'Supposing', he exclaims on another occasion, 'a man is working at Democritus. The question is always on my tongue, why precisely Democritus? Why not Heraclitus, or Philo, or Bacon, or Descartes? And then,

[1] CW, p. 121.   [2] EH, p. 24.   [3] TS, I, 2.

why a philosopher? Why not a poet or an orator?'[1] Why indeed? We
ourselves may well ask the same question, confronted as we are with an
interminable succession of 're-valuations' and 'new judgements' and
up-to-date estimates of this, that or the other writer—assuredly inspired
by no vital concern. To 'live by' art or philosophy in England today
means exactly what it meant in Bismarck's Germany—to make a living
by writing about artists and philosophers. Whence it has come to pass
that the most astonishing work 'never produces an effect, but only a
criticism: and the criticism itself produces no effect, but only breeds
another criticism'.[1]

Instead of spurring men on to accomplish what their creators began,
Nietzsche saw the works of genius being exploited by the Philistine for
the very opposite end: to justify his acquiescence, and reinforce his
pride, in the existing state of affairs. The spectacle exasperated him, as
well it might: and all the more because he knew what it signified for the
genius himself. Let a man but continue seeking now in the same spirit
as those whom the Philistines had come to regard as immortal (and
innocuous), and what sort of reception did he get? As long as possible
he was ignored; when that became impossible, he was attacked; finally,
he was disposed of, most satisfactorily of all, as 'abnormal'—which was
exactly what he was. For the Philistine, however, with his rock-like
certitude that normality is synonymous with health, abnormality could
mean one thing only—disease. Thus the sayings and strivings of genius
were classed with those of the insane. 'Are you aware,' Nietzsche remarks in a letter of this time, 'that a certain alienist has proved in the
most "dignified language" that Wagner is demented? And you are
probably aware that the same thing has been done for Schopenhauer by
another alienist:

'You see to what measures these "healthy people" resort. True, they
do not decree the scaffold for the discomforting *ingenia*, but this sort of
sneaking and malevolent creation of suspicion answers their purpose
much better than the sudden removal of their enemies; they undermine
the confidence of the rising generation. Schopenhauer forgot this
dodge! It is singularly worthy of the vulgarity of the vulgarest age . . .'[2]

Not, perhaps, so apt as George II's 'I wish he'd bite my other generals':
but certainly no less to the point.

It is always the same. An original thinker bursts on the world: for a
moment men are shaken, abashed, outraged even. It is only for a
moment. Before he has damaged a single conceit, the blessed truth dawns

on them, 'He is a genius!'—and relief shines on every countenance.
'He is a genius! There is no need to take him seriously. All we have to
do is sit back and enjoy the performance—paradoxes brilliant as fireworks—applauding from time to time!' and how ungrateful it is of the
performer not to acknowledge our applause! But when, worn out with
trying to make himself heard, the genius is at last driven beside himself,
why, relief turns to positive exultation: 'There, he's mad! You see how
right we were not to pay any attention . . ?'

It is truly an ironical spectacle, that of the normal man (the man who
has just spent sixty years on a sustained attempt to wipe out the culture
and ruin the populace of Europe) setting himself up as a paragon of
health! Yet the 'dodge' to which Nietzsche refers has only been perfected with time. Nowadays the whole paraphernalia of psycho-analysis
is enlisted in its support. Although the assumption—or presumption—
that we have nothing to learn from genius, genius everything to learn
from us, is not always so overweeningly obvious as it is in the very title
of one recent production, *Mr. Carlyle, My Patient*, it is to be traced, to
a greater or less degree, in more than half the biography and criticism
published in this country today. At all costs, the rare, the exceptional,
the abnormal, must be discredited!—That is the *leitmotif* still of the
British intelligentsia.

More clearly than any man of his time, Nietzsche was alive to the
danger (as well as the impertinence) of this assumption. For dangerous
it is. If the normal is the criterion of the right, then the actual is the
criterion of the ideal: and once that dogma has gained credence, it will
not be long in reaching its term, in the 'worship of Reality as the
Reasonable—that is to say, in the canonization of success'.[1]

On the road that leads to that worship, the Germany of the 1870's was
already far advanced. The arrogance natural to a rising class, and a
nation newly united and conscious of its power, had received a tremendous impetus from the Hegelian ideology: so that, to Strauss and his
fellow-bourgeois, Hegelians almost to a man, the military victory over
France seemed like a vindication, not merely of the material, but equally
of the spiritual, superiority of the *Reich*.

Nietzsche poured vitriol on this superstition. The victory, he pointed
out, had been due to 'severe military discipline, natural bravery and
sustaining power, the superior generalship, unity and obedience of the
rank and file—in short, factors which have nothing to do with culture'.[2]
It bore no relation whatsoever to the spiritual merits of the combatants.

[1] TS, I, 7.   [2] TS, I, 1.

German culture, far from having proved its superiority to the French, did not so much as exist. 'Culture is, before all things, the unity of artistic style in every expression of a people's life.'[1] Judged by this standard, France might truly be called cultured; Germany was barbarous. What passed for a German style was just 'a riotous jumble of all styles';[2] and so it would inevitably remain, as long as the Philistine remained.

The Germans, he declared in *The Use and Abuse of History*, have certainly accumulated a prodigious amount of knowledge, especially historical knowledge, which is duly reflected in every department of their civilization, from language to architecture. They are indisputably the most learned people the world has ever seen. But, because they have accumulated this knowledge in response to no experiential need, they have never converted it into an expression of their life. It remains, from first to last, superficial, abstract, aggregate:

'Knowledge, taken in excess without hunger, even contrary to desire, has no more the effect of transforming the external life; and remains hidden in a chaotic inner world that the modern man has a curious pride in calling his "real personality". He has the substance, he says, and only wants the form; but this is quite an unreal opposition in a living thing. Our modern culture is for that reason not a living one, because it cannot be understood without that opposition. In other words, it is not a real culture but a kind of knowledge about culture, a complex of various thoughts and feelings about it, from which no decision as to its direction can come.'[3]

Between what the Philistine knew and what he was, there was a gulf—if, indeed, he *was* still anything at all. Nietzsche had his doubts about that too. Underneath this vast panoply of learning, might not the celebrated inward life, 'too weak and ill-organized to provide a form and external expression for itself',[4] have already withered away, without anybody being the wiser? In a few incisive sentences, he disposed of the prevalent cult of 'objectivity', invoked to dignify this state of affairs: ' "pure knowledge without reference to consequences", knowledge, in plain terms, that comes to nothing'.[5] The academicians, he records derisively, 'go so far as to suppose a man who is *not affected at all* by some particular moment in the past the right man to present it. This is the usual relation of the Greeks and the philologists. They have nothing to do with each other—and this is called "objectivity"!'[6] Such objectivity has as much in common with that perfect detachment which is 'actually

[1] TS, I, 1.   [2] *Ibid.*   [3] TS, II, 4.   [4] *Ibid.*   [5] TS, II, 6.   [6] *Ibid.*

the powerful and spontaneous moment of creation in the artist'[1] as a concept has in common with an Idea.

Not merely have the Germans no culture at present, but they are doing everything possible to ensure that they shall have none in the future. Their whole educational system is designed expressly to forestall and atrophy the experiential approach. In a memorable paragraph, Nietzsche resumes the argument of his public addresses:

'The monotonous canon runs thus: the young man has to begin with a knowledge of culture, not even with a knowledge of life, still less with life and living itself. This knowledge of culture is mixed and instilled into the youth as historical knowledge: that is to say, his head is stuffed with a vast mass of ideas drawn from second-hand acquaintance with past times and peoples, not from immediate contact with life. He desires to experience something for himself, and to feel a close-knit, living system of personal experiences growing within him: but his desire is dazed by the intoxicating illusion that it is possible, in a few years, to amass within himself the highest and notablest experiences of ancient times, and of the greatest times too. It is the same insane method that carries our young sculptors off to art-shops and galleries, instead of to the studio of a master, above all the one studio of the only master, Nature. As if one could pick up on a brief tour through history the technicalities and artistries of past times, the very fruits of their lives! Ay, as if life itself were not a handicraft, demanding thorough and diligent learning and unsparing application, if we are not to have mere botchers and babblers as the issue of it all!'[2]

What wonder if men submitted to an education like this turned out 'incarnate compendia, abstractions made concrete!'[3] The typical end-product of such a system was the specialist—a creature reduced to an appendage of his one, lop-sided faculty of research. And if, as was widely assumed, the be-all and end-all of life was the smooth running and continual aggrandisement of the State, then indeed nothing could be more satisfactory. But suppose that was not the be-all and end-all?

In his public addresses Nietzsche had treated Hegelian *étatism* as the cause of this perversion of education; in *The Use and Abuse of History* he treats it as a result. It is, he infers, the very emptiness of the modern man that compels him to fall down and worship the State—he has nothing to pit against it. Equally, it is his very incapacity to dominate history that compels him to venerate it. He is the victim of his upbringing. Thus the exaltation of Germany by the Philistines becomes, in his

[1] TS, II, 6.   [2] TS, II, 10.   [3] TS, II, 5.

view, a symptom of their degradation. Not only is their culture a negation of culture, but their philosophy is a negation of philosophy.
Hegelism is simply the apotheosis of modern vacuity.

'I believe,' he writes, 'there has been no dangerous turning-point in
the progress of German culture in this century that has not been made
more dangerous by the enormous and still living influence of this
Hegelian philosophy';[1] and, in words that deserve to be engraved, he
designates some of its effects. It has 'accustomed the Germans to talk
of a "world-process", and justify their own time as its necessary result';[2]
it has 'put history in the place of the other spiritual powers, art and
religion, as the one sovereign, inasmuch as it is the "Idea realizing itself"
the "Dialectic of the spirit of the nations", and the "tribunal of the
world":

'History understood in this Hegelian way has been contemptuously
called God's sojourn upon earth,—though the God was first created by
the history. He, at any rate, became transparent and intelligible inside
Hegelian skulls, and has risen through all the dialectically possible steps
of his becoming up to that self-manifestation: so that for Hegel the
highest and final stage of the world-process came together in his own
Berlin existence. He ought to have said that everything after him was
merely to be regarded as the musical coda of the world-historical rondo,
—or rather, as simply superfluous. He has not said it; and thus he has
implanted in a generation leavened throughout by him the worship of
the "power of history", that practically turns every moment into a sheer
gaping at success, into an idolatry of the actual: for which we are now
wont to adopt the very mythological, and at the same time very German,
phrase "to adapt ourselves to circumstances". But the man who has
once learned to crook the knee and bow the head before the power of
history, nods "yes" at last, like a Chinese doll, to every power, whether
it be a government, or a public opinion or a numerical majority; and
his limbs move correctly as the power pulls the string. If each success
manifest a "rational necessity", and every event shows the victory of
logic or the "Idea", then—down on your knees quickly, and let every
step in the ladder of "success" have its reverence! There are no more
living mythologies, you say? What, religions are dying out? Just look
at the religion of the power of history, mark the priests of the mythology
of Ideas with their scarred knees!'[3]

It is forceful, and fearfully true. Perhaps, now that another seventy
years have elapsed, we are better prepared to appreciate its truth.

[1] TS, II, 8.　　　[2] *Ibid.*　　　[3] *Ibid.*

Nietzsche's insight, however, did not stop short even here. There was, he persisted, no such thing as the Idea; the world did not move forward of its own momentum towards some divine consummation; if the workings of any sovereign power could be traced at all in the great historical process, it was the power, not of God, but of human self-interest—'so far as there are laws in history, the laws are of no value, and the history of no value either'.[1] Yet, such was the fatal optimism, or optimistic fatalism, implanted by this ideology that it was not beyond the range of modern man to dispense with the Idea in theory and continue to cling to it in practice—in other words, to ascribe the same purpose, and pay the same honours, to his own self-interest as he had hitherto done to God!

'In Christian terms, the Devil is the Prince of this World, and the lord of progress and success: he is the real Power behind all "historical powers", and so it will essentially remain, however painful that may sound to the ears of a time accustomed to deifying success and historical power—a time well-versed in giving new names to things, even to baptising the Devil. It is truly an hour of great danger. Men seem close to the discovery that the egoism of individuals, groups or masses has been at all times the lever of historical movements: and yet they are in no way disturbed by the discovery, but proclaim that egoism shall be our God. With this new faith, they begin quite deliberately to build future history on egoism: though it must be a clever egoism, one that imposes certain restraints upon itself that it may endure, one that studies history precisely in order to recognize the foolish kind of egoism. Their study has taught them that a very special role is allotted to the State in the future world-system of egoisms: it is to be the patron of all the clever egoisms, to protect them with the power of its military and police against the frightful outbreaks of the foolish egoism . . .'[2]

Nietzsche was at fault in one particular only: the discovery had already been made. A quarter of a century had gone by since the publication of *The Communist Manifesto*.

In all other respects he was right. We might even say that history had vindicated his insight, had his purpose not been to contravene history. At all events, he followed the Philistine cult of normality to its ultimate consequences; and it was partly because he saw these so clearly that he pitted against it so vigorously his own religion of genius. It was not, he affirmed, for the genius to adjust himself to society, but for society to adjust itself to the genius—and quickly too, if it was to be saved from

[1] TS, II, 9.　　　　[2] *Ibid.*

utter degradation. To the idealization of the real, he opposed the realization of an ideal; and to all the cowardly or unscrupulous opportunism
dignified by the name of 'submission to historical necessity', a
summons to swim against the current—for 'you will find that the virtuous man will always rise against the blind force of facts, the tyranny
of the actual, and submit himself to laws that are not the laws of fickle
history'.[1]

* * *

'Must life dominate knowledge, or knowledge life? Which of the two
is the higher, and decisive power?'[2] That was the question with which,
in one form after another, Nietzsche strove to confront his contemporaries. His own answer, of course, was clear and emphatic. A genuine
culture could only be the expression of 'complete, mature, harmonious
personalities'.[3]

If, however, such personalities were to be given a chance to emerge,
the existing system of education would have to be abolished root and
branch. There must be no more forcible feeding. A new system would
have to be installed, the distinctive feature of which would be a curriculum adjusted to the real needs of youth: for 'the whole feature of
study lies in this: that we should study only what we feel we should like
to imitate; what we gladly take up and have the desire to multiply. What
is really wanted is a progressive canon of the *ideal* model, suited to boys,
youths and men'.[4] It was to the establishment of such a system that he
summoned his readers in *The Use and Abuse of History*.

He did not deny that a generation educated in accordance with this
principle would be ignorant by contemporary standards. He insisted
upon it. 'They will have unlearned much and have lost any desire even
to glance at what those educated men especially wish to know: in fact,
their chief mark from the educated point of view will be just their want
of education; their indifference and inaccessibility to many famous, and
even to many good things'.[5] But, he insists, what knowledge they do
possess will be related directly to their experience; it will be a means, and
only a means, to a fuller and richer life—and that is what counts: 'at the
end of the cure they are men again and have ceased to be mere shadows
of humanity'.[6]

Reading these words, we are reminded again of D. H. Lawrence,
whose lifelong protest it was that the modern European was becoming
so enslaved to general concepts, to abstract ideas and ideals, that his
instincts could no longer make themselves felt. We even fall in love,

[1] TS, II, 8.   [2] TS, II, 10.   [3] TS, II, 7.
[4] TS, V, 178.   [5] TS, II, 10.   [6] *Ibid.*

Lawrence averred, in conformity with some theory of love, derived
from the philosophers or the films: and the function of the novel, as he
saw it, was not very different from that which Nietzsche attributed to
music: namely, to quicken men's dulled sensibilities, by conducting
their affections into channels where they must feel afresh, and feel for
themselves.

Nevertheless, one difference between the two men is all-important.
Nietzsche was, and remained to the last, completely free from that
obstinate anti-intellectualism which pervades most of Lawrence's writings, and may be associated with their general formlessness. However
vehemently he might insist on 'correct feeling' as the pre-condition of
'correct thinking',[1] it never became a substitute. With respect to music
itself, he would not allow that the purpose of art had been attained until
correct feeling and correct thinking had been united one with the other,
and, by virtue of that unity, been transformed into something greater
than either. Music, he wrote, 'signifies a return to nature, and at the same
time a purification and remodelling of it; for the need of such a return
took shape in the souls of the most loving of men, and, *through their art,
nature transformed into love makes its voice heard*'.[2] That intellect, as well
as emotion, should be enlisted in the service of life, is the whole burden
of *Thoughts out of Season*. Nietzsche might have understood, but he
certainly would not have approved, the truly fantastic cosmology with
which Lawrence ended his *Fantasia of the Unconscious*.

While, therefore, he deliberately stressed the 'ignorance' of his new
generation, by contemporary standards, he was very far from thinking
of it as ignorant in itself, let alone glorifying ignorance. On the contrary,
he was convinced that it was only when learning ceased to be cultivated
for its own sake, that it would really begin to flourish as it ought: first,
because those who had no inclination for it were a stumbling-block to
those who had, and secondly, because those who had, and those alone,
were capable of carrying it to new heights. He knew that there would
always be some with a need for science and history; their need, before
anything else, was what he wished to see met.

It was not science, but the abuse of science, that Nietzsche attacked—
its advancement at the expense of man. In this respect he was a typical
Romantic; and once again, perhaps now that another seventy years have
elapsed, we are in a position to appreciate his maxim,' It is necessary,
not to destroy, but to subordinate science.'[3] Goethe, he observes, was
alive to this abuse, demanding that 'science should only influence the

---

[1] TS, IV, 5.   [2] *Ibid.*   [3] N, X, 114.

world by way of a *nobler ideal of action*'[1]—and behind Nietzsche's ideal of the complete, mature, harmonious personality, it is constantly Goethe whom we glimpse. Not only is he quoted in the opening sentence of *The Use and Abuse of History*, but other sayings of his crop up throughout *Thoughts Out of Season*: sayings, one and all, which reflect the man at his best, the mature, self-aware thinker of the *Conversations with Eckermann*. It is no surprise to learn that Nietzsche was deep in Eckermann at the time. Reading these conversations, he remarked, 'one may well ask oneself whether any man in Germany ever attained to a comparably noble form'.[2]

In the same way, it was not history, but the abuse of history, that called forth his violent protests. Taken in excess, without hunger, it could have a paralysing effect on the will; it could weaken the '"plastic power" of a man or a community or a culture: I mean the power of specifically growing out of one's self'.[3] But no-one knew better than he what enrichment it could bring to the man who turned to it naturally— or could receive from him in return. After all, only those to whom history had a vital meaning could really begin to understand it: 'the language of the past is always oracular: you will understand it only as builders of the future who know the present'.[4] What could the savant cultivating his 'objectivity' in a senior common room, make of a Renaissance or Reformation?

'The deeper the roots of a man's inner nature', Nietzsche claims, 'the more of the past will it appropriate or dominate, and the mightiest and most formidable nature would be known by an historical sense which, though unbounded, would be in no danger of being overrun. It would assimilate and digest the past, however foreign, turning it, so to speak, into blood.'[5] This was his fundamental claim: and he had the best possible warrant for it. We have only to study *The Use and Abuse of History* closely, to realize that what he is saying is nothing other than what he is doing. The explicit is implicit as well. Thus, citing what he calls a life-serving, as distinct from life-stultifying, approach to the past, 'suppose', he exclaims, 'one believe that no more than a hundred men, brought up in the new spirit, efficient and productive, were needed to give the death-blow to the present fashion of education in Germany: he will gather strength from the remembrance that the culture of the Renaissance was raised on the shoulders of such another band of a hundred men'.[6] The polemic itself is his summons to that anonymous hundred.

[1] TS, II, 7.   [2] N, X, 279.   [3] TS, II, 1.
[4] TS, II, 6.   [5] TS, II, 1.   [6] TS, II, 2.

A year earlier, Nietzsche had surmised that thousands of courageous souls would spring to arms at such a summons: men like himself, who, though they had suffered the effects of a perverse education, had yet retained sufficient vitality to recognize its perversity and dedicate themselves to its overthrow. Bearing on them 'the marks of that sorrow which an excess of history brings in its train',[1] they would not, indeed, for their own part win more than 'a foregleam of the happiness and beauty of times to come';[2] from their Pisgah they would only be able to direct others towards it. But their very historical knowledge would prove the appointed means of telling where it was necessary to be unhistorical: 'for the origin of historical culture, and of its absolutely radical antagonism to the spirit of a new time and a "modern consciousness", must itself be known by a historical process. History must solve the problem of history, science must turn the sting against itself'.[3]

In *The Use and Abuse of History*, he is a little less sanguine. He looks for only a hundred men. Still, a hundred will suffice; for the youth of Germany, sound as this still is, will readily respond to their call: 'Set this free, and you will set life free as well.'[4] And he is confident that the hundred will be forthcoming. After all, the truth is so obvious that 'man must learn to live, above all, and use history only *in the service of the life that he has learned to live!*'[5] Moreover, he avers (perhaps with Burckhardt in mind), already 'one finds that the greater and more developed "historical men" are conscious of all the superstition and absurdity in the belief that a people's education need be so extremely historical as it is: the mightiest nations, mightiest in action and achievement, have lived otherwise, and their youth has been reared otherwise'.[6] The appeal, once more, is to Greece:

'In certain centuries the Greeks ran the same risk as we do, of being overwhelmed by what was past and foreign, and perishing on the rock of "history". They never lived proud and aloof. Rather was their "culture" for a long time a chaos of foreign forms and ideas—Semitic, Babylonian, Indian, Egyptian—their religion a veritable battle of all the gods of the East: much as German culture and religion today are an internecine chaos of all foreign nations and bygone times. And yet, Hellenic culture became no mere agglomeration, thanks to that Apollonian dictum ["Know Thyself"]. The Greeks learned gradually to *organize the chaos*, by thinking back to themselves, to their own true necessities, according to the Delphic teaching, and letting all sham necessities go. They thus came into possession of themselves, and did not long

---

[1] TS, II, 10.   [2] *Ibid.*   [3] TS, II, 8.
[4] TS, II, 10.   [5] *Ibid.*   [6] TS, II, 8.

remain the epigoni of the whole East, overburdened with its inheritance. After a hard struggle with themselves, they most felicitously increased and enriched the treasure they had inherited, by their practical interpretation of that dictum, and became the ancestors and models for all the cultured nations of the future.

'This is a parable for each one of us: he must organize the chaos in himself by thinking back to his true needs. He will want all his honesty, all the sturdiness and sincerity in his character, to help him revolt against second-hand thought, second-hand learning, second-hand action. He will begin then to understand that culture can be something more than a *decoration of life*—in other words, a concealment and disfigurement of it, for all adornment hides what is adorned. And thus the Greek idea, as against the Roman, will be discovered to him, the idea of culture as a new and finer nature, without distinction of inner and outer, without convention or disguise, as a unison of living, thinking, appearing and willing. He will learn from his own experience that it was a higher force of *moral* nature that gave the Greeks victory over all other cultures; and that greater veracity must needs be a first step towards the promotion of *true* culture, even though such veracity may at times damage seriously the current standards of education, may even help to bring down the entire edifice of merely decorative culture.'[1]

That is the grand conclusion of *The Use and Abuse of History*—the best of the *Thoughts out of Season*, and one of the best of all Nietzsche's works. Whoever has no sympathy with this, may as well disregard the others—Nietzsche is not for him. Whoever, on the other hand, has once entered into its spirit will, I think, sooner or later find himself scaling the tortuous track that leads out onto *Thus Spake Zarathustra*.

I myself know of few books, and none of comparable brevity (it comprises a mere hundred pages) that contain so many fine things finely said. One is tempted to go on quoting interminably. And yet—it is a melancholy reflection—this book is as new and true today as when it was written. In other words, it has had 'no effect'. Far from a hundred men responding to Nietzsche's summons, not a single one responded. His voice died away into silence: and it was then, I believe, as he waited for the response which never came, that he realized at last just how out of season he was. Only once, or at most twice, again in his life, was he to experience quite the same confidence in himself, his mission and his readers.

[1] TS, II, 10.

(2)

It is a striking fact that, notwithstanding his reverence for Schopenhauer and avowed antipathy to Hegel, Nietzsche was at least as remote from the one as the other in his attitude towards history. Indeed, it would not be going too far to say, even at this stage, that he had slightly more in common with Hegel. For Schopenhauer, not content with repudiating the worship of reality as the reasonable, denied that history could afford any inspiration to action at all. The most it could do was to enhance a man's sense of the incorrigible wickedness, irrationality and futility of all human endeavour, and thereby hasten his adoption of that attitude of total indifference which was the one thing to be desired.

In *The Use and Abuse of History*, Nietzsche dubs this attitude the 'super-historical', and invokes it, along with the 'unhistorical', as an antidote to the overpowering of life by history. There is, however, an unmistakable sneer behind even the lip-service he pays it. He expounds it tersely at the beginning of the book, only to add, 'but we will leave the super-historical men to their loathings and their wisdom: we wish rather today to be joyful in our unwisdom and have a pleasant life as active men who go forward, and respect the course of the world'.[1]

He does not, be it noted, deny the truth of Schopenhauer's verdict. On the contrary, he underlines it, repeatedly referring to all historical ideals, his own included, as 'illusions'. But the interpretation of history, whether in word or act (and of course the word is an act), was in his view a creative art; and as in *The Birth of Tragedy*, so here, he sets a higher value upon art than he does upon truth itself.

Throughout *Thoughts out of Season*, indeed, his line of thought runs much closer to the early Wagner's than it does to Schopenhauer's. If we overlook the theoretical pessimism (as it is very easy to do), we shall find that they are practically identical. Not merely do Nietzsche's views on the dominance and eventual self-negation of science, on the nature and mission of art, and on the vocation of the German people, coincide exactly with those of *The Art-Work of the Future*, but even his vision of the culture to come is scarcely distinguishable from Wagner's.

This is surprising, but hardly contestable. Although certain passages are lifted bodily from *The Future of our Educational Institutions*, there is nowhere, in *Thoughts out of Season*, any suggestion that this culture is to be the close preserve of a few; nowhere the least trace of that contempt for the common mortal which he had inherited from Schopen-

[1] TS, II, 1.

hauer. Taste is no longer confined to the fine arts, or artists: furniture and buildings, utensils and clothing, are expressly cited as fit subjects for aesthetic creation and contemplation. When Nietzsche spoke of the unity of style in *every expression* of a people's life, he meant precisely that. At one point, indeed, he breaks out into an apostrophe that might have featured in *Art and Revolution* itself: 'Rise to the conception of a "people"; you can never have one noble or high enough!'[1]

In his earlier works, Wagner had opined that a rational society would do away with labour as the factory-operative knows it, tolerating only such occupations as give scope for aesthetic fulfilment. He had been a socialist of the William Morris persuasion: and there is more than a hint of William Morris in Nietzsche's presentation of his views. Listen, for example, to his indictment of a class which 'had but one idea, to use its power as hard-heartedly and craftily as possible in order to render the impotent—the people—ever more serviceable, base and un-popular, and to rear the modern "worker" out of them'; a class which 'robbed them of their greatest and purest things, born of their deepest needs, in which their soul, the true and only artist, humbly expressed itself: their myths, songs, dances, and their inventiveness in speech, in order to distil therefrom a voluptuous antidote against the fatigue and boredom of its existence—the modern arts'.[2]

Here, it may be granted, Nietzsche is merely reporting Wagner; he cannot be assumed to have subscribed to these views himself—although his exposition is singularly perceptive and sympathetic. But the following in his *ipse dixit*, and it sounds like a recantation:

'That an art could arise which would be so clear and warm as to flood the base and the poor in spirit with its light, as well as to melt the haughtiness of the learned—such a phenomenon had to be experienced though it could not be guessed. But even in the mind of him who experiences it today it must upset all previous notions concerning education and culture; to such an one the veil will seem to have been rent in twain that conceals a future in which no highest good or highest joys exist that are not the common property of all. The odium attaching to the word "common" will then be abolished.'[3]

It is a far cry from *The Greek State* to this; and it may, of course, be argued that even here Nietzsche is speaking with his tongue in his cheek. Not all the declamations of *Richard Wagner at Bayreuth* can be taken at their face value. But I do not believe that he is: the conclusion accords too well with the whole spirit and tenor of *Thoughts out of Season*. Once

[1] TS, II, 7.   [2] TS, IV, 8.   [3] TS, IV, 10.

the plastic power of life, rather than the intellect as Schopenhauer understood it, is held responsible for artistic creation, the further step of acknowledging every man to be potentially a special kind of artist is virtually inevitable. Agreeing with Keats that 'Memory should not be called Knowledge', Nietzsche might, after all, have borrowed Keats' words to describe his ideal, 'a grand *democracy* of Forest Trees'.

The gradual departure from Schopenhauer, which this betokens, and which we have traced in other connections, culminates in the third of the *Thoughts out of Season*, 'Schopenhauer as Educator': since, as every reader must have remarked, the name 'Schopenhauer' here stands for little else than 'the philosophical genius'[1]—and what Nietzsche knew about the philosophical genius, he knew at first-hand. In one of his letters, he actually repeats certain passages from this essay, adding in a marginal note, 'you can read all this in print in my Schopenhauer; but they are at the same time my own experiences and feelings'.[2] It would be nearly, if not quite, true to say that the correct title would be 'The Educator as Schopenhauer'.

The philosophical genius, as defined here, is simply the completely sincere and honest man, who thinks back to himself, to his own true necessities, letting all sham necessities go; and the process by which he achieves this end is the same that Nietzsche has already tried to define in *Philosophy during the Tragic Age of the Greeks*:

'But how can we "find ourselves" again, and how can man "know himself?" . . . This is the most effective way: to let the youthful soul look back on life with the question, "what hast thou up to now truly loved, what has drawn thy soul upward, mastered it and blessed it too?" Set up these things that thou has honoured before thee, and maybe they will show thee, in their being and their order, a law which is the fundamental law of thine own self. Compare these objects, consider how one completes and broadens and transcends and explains another, how they form a ladder on which thou hast all the time been climbing to thy self: for thy true being lies not deeply hidden in thee, but an infinite height above thee, or at least above that which thou dost commonly take to be thyself.'[3]

Intuition, in other words, is still the first requisite: a reliance on what Keats would have called 'the holiness of the heart's affections', and what Nietzsche himself, following in Wagner's footsteps, now identifies with love. Only what compels the response of love is 'true'; only what

[1] TS, III, 7.   [2] L, 22, 1, 75.   [3] TS, III, 1.

responds with love, the 'true self'. And the second requisite, as we should expect, is reason: since, if the deliverances of intuition are not to be falsified, if they are to find an adequate formulation, there must be no compromise with any creed, however plausible or consoling, that cannot stand up to the most ruthless intellectual crossfire: 'Everything that can be denied deserves to be denied; and real sincerity means the belief in an existence which could not possibly be denied.'[1]

Thus, the procedure Nietzsche attributes to 'Schopenhauer's man' (as he calls the philosophical genius) is simply his own procedure; and equally his own is the suffering he describes as its outcome—such a swallower of formulas being compelled, not only to part with his own cherished convictions, but to endure the incomprehension and hostility of others who feel theirs to be threatened. Nietzsche departs from his own experience only in a single respect, namely, when he declares that 'the man who looks for a lie in everything, and becomes a willing friend to unhappiness, may have a marvellous disillusioning';[2] that is to say, that this very suffering 'serves to quench his individual will and make ready that total revolution and reversal which it is the very meaning of life to realize'.[3] This, at the time he was writing, could only have been a surmise.

*　*　*

In making use of Schopenhauer's name in this way, Nietzsche was not, of course, acting entirely arbitrarily. Schopenhauer, for all that he displayed to the full the very German propensity for spinning intellectual cobwebs, for all that he loved to seize on some tenuous analogy, refine on it page after page, and let it go only reluctantly after it had yielded the last thread of corroboration (what appears to the average English reader just too good to be true, appearing to him too good to be false), knew well the meaning of 'perplexity' and his system was born of it. He too was an experiential thinker. That is why, even to those who reject this system as a whole, it can still make a strong appeal. Being what he was, moreover, he could not help reflecting on what he was: so that at intervals all through his work we encounter psychological observations which carry their authenticity on their face. Nietzsche could legitimately have appealed to some of these—as he certainly did draw upon them—in support of his characterization.

The dissertation on 'acquired character' in Book IV of *The World as Will and Idea*, for example, was one of those passages whose truth was only confirmed by his subsequent experience: so much so, that when he came to write his autobiography, he took a phrase from it for the sub-

---

[1] TS, III, 4.　　　　[2] *Ibid.*　　　　[3] *Ibid.*

title. The penultimate Supplement, again, 'On the Denial of the Will to Live' furnished him with more than merely that quotation from Eckhardt ('the quickest beast that will carry you to perfection is suffering') which he happened to use himself. 'For true integrity, inviolable justice', Schopenhauer affirms here, 'this first and most important of cardinal virtues, is so hard a task that whoever professes it unconditionally and from the bottom of his heart has to make sacrifices that soon deprive life of the sweetness which is demanded to make it enjoyable, and thereby turn away the will from it, thus lead to resignation.' Here, if anywhere, was the warrant for Nietzsche's surmise.

Nevertheless, these are the very sections of Schopenhauer's work that bear least relation to its thesis. The one is introduced parenthetically—it 'is not of so much importance for ethics proper as for life in the world'; the other amounts to a qualification of the supreme value set originally on deliberate asceticism. If Nietzsche was indebted to these, therefore, his indebtedness only confirms his independence. Moreover, as we have seen, even ideas he was justified in attributing to Schopenhauer, he treats from an angle that would have surprised that philosopher. If his interpretation of 'true integrity' is entirely his own, so is the significance he attaches to the denial of the will— for, it need hardly be said, he is far from regarding this denial as an end in itself.

True, in *Thoughts out of Season*, he still pays lip-service to the saint. 'The sincere men who have cast out the beast' are, we are told, 'the philosophers, artists and saints.'[1] Nature requires all three 'for a metaphysical end';[2] and man should so organize his life as to facilitate their emergence—co-operating consciously with nature's unconscious purpose, helping her to realize that redemption after which the whole creation groaneth and travaileth in pain together until now. He even goes so far as to call Christianity 'one of the purest manifestations of the impulse towards culture and the production of the saint'.[3] But actions speak louder than words, even when the words are Nietzsche's: and, whereas he portrayed the philosopher in *Schopenhauer as Educator* and the artist in *Richard Wagner at Bayreuth*, there is no evidence that he even considered portraying the Christian or Buddhist.

Finally, in the notes for *We Philologists*, he gives unequivocal expression to his belief that 'this conception'—the conception of the denial of the will—'has now become deeper: it is above all a discerning denial, a denial based on the will to be just; not an indiscriminate and wholesale denial';[4] and a little later suggests that 'the man who today

[1] TS, III, 5.   [2] *Ibid.*   [3] TS, III, 6.   [4] TS, V, 189.

wishes to be good and saintly has a more difficult task than formerly: in order to be "good", he must not be so unjust to knowledge as earlier saints were. He would have to be a knowledge-saint, a man who would link love with knowledge.'[1] It is not easy to see how the knowledge-saint would differ from the philosopher himself.

Nietzsche really values self-annihilation only as a means, to creative achievement in the world. The mission of the philosophical genius, therefore, would be consummated, not in the immediate realization that 'everything is one', but in the formulation of a new world-view to embody and safeguard this truth: a world-view which, having room in it for all that intuition could affirm, and yet affirming nothing that reason could deny, would have the effect of reintegrating the man who embraced it—of presenting him with a picture of the whole of life, whence he could learn the meaning of his own life, and so of uniting him with others in a common purpose and ideal.

* * *

Such a world-view as this Nietzsche had indeed at one time discerned —or thought he discerned—in *The World as Will and Idea*. As in *The Birth of Tragedy*, therefore, so in *Thoughts out of Season*, Schopenhauer is acclaimed as the philosopher of the future. His work, we are told, is redolent of victory—victory over all the temptations that beset modern man when he strives for sincerity: loneliness, self-contempt, above all that 'shattering despair of truth itself'[2] which drove Heinrich von Kleist to suicide. 'We cannot decide whether what we call truth is really truth, or whether it only seems so to us', Kleist had cried after reading Kant, 'my one highest aim has vanished, and I have no more.' Schopenhauer had surmounted this despair: 'the pioneer to bring us from the heights of sceptical despondency or "critical" renunciation to the height of tragic contemplation'.[3]

Even in *The Birth of Tragedy*, however, we saw reason to question the genuineness of these acclamations. Although Schopenhauer's system had, in its time, released Nietzsche's creative energy, that energy had manifested itself at once in such modifications of the system that it could hardly be called Schopenhauer's any more. Only the concept of a metaphysical unity survived, and that on sufferance. By the time he composed *Schopenhauer as Educator*, this concept had gone the way of the rest. Not merely does Nietzsche never expound the system he extols so loudly, but—the omission is striking—he never so much as alludes to his own. In none of its protean forms does the Primordial Unity reappear. By this time, in fact, the scepticism which had hovered in the wings of *The Birth*

---

[1] TS, V, 191.   [2] TS, III, 3.   [3] *Ibid.*

of Tragedy, was moving to the front of the stage. He no longer really believed in any metaphysical reality whatever.

'Schopenhauer's man' had ousted Schopenhauer, the philosophical genius outgrown the philosophy. It had proved impossible after all to go on consciously championing an illusion, no matter how edifying it might be. The very sincerity which (as he liked to think) Nietzsche had inherited from Schopenhauer, forbade it. If everything that could be denied deserved to be denied, if real sincerity meant the belief in an existence that could not be denied, then—the inference was inescapable —that dubious 'thing-in-itself' had to be called in question. He had called it in question—with what result, let his own words of twelve years later recall:

'When, in the third *Thought out of Season*, I gave expression to my reverence for my first and only teacher, the *great* Arthur Schopenhauer, I was for my part already in the throes of moral scepticism and dissolution, that is, as much concerned with the criticism as with the deepening of all pessimism down to the present. I already did not believe in "a blessed thing", as the people say, not even in Schopenhauer. It was at this period that an unpublished essay of mine, "On Truth and Falsity in an Extra-Moral Sense" came into being.'[1]

The essay (long since published) fully bears out this confession. By the time he wrote *Schopenhauer as Educator*, Nietzsche himself was in the position of von Kleist. He himself had succumbed to the 'shattering despair of truth'.

This was the logical end of his discipleship. He no longer subscribed to any world-view, whether Schopenhauer's or his own: and to him it was literally shattering. It meant the end of his 'mission'. Having nothing now to pit against his own inward division, he had nothing to pit against humanity's either: for humanity, he believed, no less than himself, had need of an all-embracing world-view. Only where men were united by a common purpose and ideal, could a culture spring up and thrive. In the absence of any such world-view, the passionate will, gushing forth like a mountain torrent, met with no power pure and strong enough to guide it towards the good and beneficial—turned therefore, inevitably, towards destruction.

This was what had happened in Europe since the disruption of medieval Christendom. Now that it was happening in him, Nietzsche's historical insight served only to deepen his despair, while despair in its

[1] H, II, Preface, 1.

turn invested his warnings with an urgency they could have drawn from
no other source:

'The hostile forces were practically held together in medieval times by
the Church, and in some measure assimilated by the strong pressure
which she exerted. When the bond broke and the pressure relaxed, they
rose once more against each other. The Reformation taught that many
things were "adiaphora"—departments requiring no guidance from
religion: this was the price it paid for its own existence. Christianity had
paid a similar one to secure its existence against the far more religious
antiquity: and from that time forward the gulf had widened steadily.
Nearly everything nowadays is directed by the coarsest and most
vicious forces, by the egoism of the money-makers and by the mili-
tarists. The State, in the hands of the latter, does attempt, as does the
egoism of the money-makers, to reorganize everything after its own
fashion, and to clamp together those opposing forces: in other words, it
desires of men the same idolatry as they paid to the Church. With what
result? We shall live to see. At all events, we find ourselves still on the
ice-floes in the stream of the Middle Ages; it is thawing fast and their
movement is ominous. Floe piles upon floe; all the banks are flooded
and threatened.'[1]

We shall meet with that telling image again before we have done.
Henceforward, precisely because he was aware of it in himself, the possibility of a catastrophic relapse into anarchy was never remote from
Nietzsche's mind. The haunting insecurity he suffered, the 'anxious
dread', attuned him to the insecurity of humanity. In *Schopenhauer as
Educator* this prospect of a world void of religion, a world given over
entirely to the anarchical interplay of contending interests and idolatries,
all at once wrings from his lips a great cry of desolation, so poignant and
arresting that it checks the very heart-beat of the hearer:

'There is a wintry sky over us, and we dwell on a high mountain, in
danger and in need. Short-lived is all our joy, and the sun's rays strike
palely on our white mountains. Music is heard; an old man grinds an
organ, and the dancers whirl around, and the heart of the wanderer is
shaken within him to see it: everything is so disordered, so drab, so
hopeless. Even now there is a sound of joy, of clear thoughtless joy! but
soon the mist of evening closes around, the note dies away, and the wanderer's footsteps are heard on the gravel; as far as the eye can reach there
is nothing but the grim and desolate face of nature.'[2]

[1] TS, III, 4.   [2] *Ibid.*

Where there is no vision, the people perish! It reminds one of *Ecclesiastes*. And there follow words sadder still, whose sombre significance the accident of time has only amplified, without distorting:

'There are certainly forces there, enormous forces; but wild, primitive, quite merciless. One looks on with chill expectancy, as though into the cauldron of a witch's kitchen; every moment there may arise sparks and vapour, to herald some fearful apparition. For a century we have been ready for a world-shaking convulsion; and though we have lately been trying to set the conservative strength of the so-called national state against the great modern tendency to volcanic destructiveness, it will only be, for a long time yet, an aggravation of the universal insecurity and foreboding. We need not be deceived by individuals behaving as if they knew nothing of all this anxiety: their own restlessness shows how well they know it. They think more exclusively of themselves than men ever thought before; they plant and build for their little day, and the chase for happiness is never greater than when the quarry must be caught today or tomorrow: the next day perhaps there is no hunting. We live in the age of the atom, of the atomistic chaos.'[1]

That may be called prophetic, in the fullest sense of that ill-used, overused word.

Total scepticism was a bitter pill for Nietzsche to swallow—there can be no doubt of that. Neither the lamentations of *Thoughts out of Season*, nor the despondency and self-distrust of his letters ('Shall I ever attain to inner freedom? It is very dubious')[2] need surprise us. There must have been times when he felt that his one highest aim had vanished, and he had no more.

Nevertheless, it would be a mistake to present even *Schopenhauer as Educator* as a pessimistic production. There were other times, and those not rare, when the very darkness of the prospect before him served to enhance his ambition. Nietzsche's sincerity was matched by his courage. He had a faculty for turning despair itself to advantage—which proves that it was not absolute despair; and this very polemic, as he afterwards boasted, contains a declaration of faith. 'My most secret history, my development, is written down in, "Schopenhauer as Educator". But above all the *vow* I made! *What* I am today, *where* I am today—at a height from which I speak no longer with words but with thunderbolts —oh, how far I was from all this in those days! But I saw the land—I did not deceive myself for one moment as to the way, the sea, the danger—*and* success!'[3]

[1] TS, III, 4.   [2] L, 1, 4, 74.   [3] EH, p. 81.

The nature of the vow, although not specified, is clear. If total scepticism lay ahead—very well then, he would grapple with total scepticism, and either fight his way through or else succumb in the attempt. If
no impregnable world-view lay to hand, in the work of Schopenhauer
or any other philosopher—*since* no such world-view lay to hand—he
himself would be the one to create it. *He* would give Europe that vision
for lack of which it was perishing!

*   *   *

But how far he was from all this in 1874! Hardly had Nietzsche grown
used to the thought that he would have to part company with Schopenhauer, than a still darker suspicion began to assail him: supposing he
had to part company with Wagner as well? It was not only the spectre
of total scepticism that was returning to haunt him, but also the spectre
of total isolation. What wonder if, once again, he tried to suppress his
misgivings?

'I know not what Wagner may have been for other men', he was to
write in *Ecce Homo*, 'but no cloud ever darkened *our* sky.'[1] That was
exaggeration. By 1888, distance and the misery of intervening years had
invested Tribschen with a light that never was on sea or land. Quite a
number of small clouds had darkened their sky from the first. The fact
remains, that throughout the years of their closest intercourse, he and
Wagner had been united by that strongest of masculine ties, allegiance
to a common cause. The hopes of both were centred on Bayreuth: at
once the symbol and source of German emancipation. It was not until
about 1872 that Nietzsche began to attach equal importance to his own
educational projects.

Thenceforward some change in his attitude was inevitable. Whatever
he might say, and say in all sincerity, Bayreuth was no longer *all*-im-
portant. He could no longer envisage it as more than one among several
forces making for the re-birth of Hellenism; nor prevent his mind, and
pen, from straying in other directions. Whereas formerly sacrifices had
come naturally—in other words, he had not felt them as sacrifices at all
—now it was only in obedience to an ideal of self-sacrifice that he could
reach up to Wagner's expectations. Accordingly, he began to feel his
very loyalty a constraint, to chafe against the obligations it imposed on
him—and suffer a bad conscience in consequence.

To make matters worse, the Wagners noticed the change, and, instead
of encouraging his own specific contribution to culture, let slip no
occasion to remind him of the difficulties they faced, or reproach him,
however mildly, with his failure to assist them to the utmost. Expecting

<hr />

[1] EH, p. 41.

him to act as their propagandist-in-chief, it was with unconcealed dis-appointment that they received a publication like *The Use and Abuse of History*, in which (as Cosima naively remarked) Wagner's name was not even mentioned. 'It has become plain', Nietzsche confided in his journal, 'that my only value lies in my being a Wagner commentator: I am to be nothing more. I am permitted to admire only *that* which is stamped with the seal of Bayreuth's approval.'[1] This alone would have been enough to set him wondering whether they were quite as dis-interested as he had always presumed.

Now, however, he had graver cause for doubt. How, after all, could Wagner be expected to enthuse over *The Use and Abuse of History*? To the very extent that it coincided with his earlier views, it clashed with his present ones. That 'super-historical' attitude, which Nietzsche had treated so cavalierly, was precisely the attitude that Wagner was now extolling as the ultimate of human wisdom. In his memorandum, *State and Religion*, the erstwhile revolutionary had taken pains to assure King Ludwig that, thanks to Schopenhauer's philosophy, he no longer believed in either progress or 'the people'.

Nietzsche had read and admired this memorandum during the first few weeks of their acquaintance. So full was it of 'Schopenhauerian earnest-ness',[2] he had exclaimed, that he would gladly have been a king in order to receive such exhortations! He was not ignorant of the change in Wagner's views; their common attachment to Schopenhauer had been the earliest bond between them. Sooner or later, therefore, the question was bound to arise: did Wagner, or did he not, genuinely subscribe to this philosophy? If he did, then there was reason to doubt his import-ance, as a torch-bearer of German culture; if he did not—there was still more reason to doubt his sincerity.

Nietzsche's devotion to Wagner, in fact, could not long outlast his devotion to Schopenhauer. The two were inseparable: and a quite trivial incident now was enough to bring his half-conscious suspicions to a head. Early in 1874, intelligence reached him that the whole Bayreuth plan was threatened with failure: funds were no longer forthcoming, either from the King or from private subscribers, to enable the *Fest-spielhaus* to be completed. This, if true, could mean one thing only: namely, that Wagner had misjudged both the time and the temper of the people—and how could such misjudgement be reconciled with the con-cept of genius?—'There is a very intimate relation between greatness

---

[1] Quoted: *The Nietzsche-Wagner Correspondence*, ed. E. Förster-Nietzsche, Duckworth, 1922.
[2] L, 17, 8,69.

and the instinct which knows the proper moment at which to act.'[1]
Immediately on receipt of this intelligence, Nietzsche settled down to a
reappraisal of his friend, not merely as philosopher, but as musician.

'I set to work,' he told Rohde, 'to investigate the reasons for the
failure of the undertaking; this I did in the most cold-blooded manner,
and in so doing, learned a great deal and arrived at a far better understanding of Wagner than I ever had before.'[2] The results of the investigation, in the shape of an assortment of notes, show that he reached
straight away nearly all the conclusions he was to divulge some fourteen
years later:

'One of Wagner's chief characteristics: lack of discipline and modera-
tion. Carries everything to the extreme limit of his strength and feelings.
... Wagner brings together all possible effective elements at a time when
popular taste is dulled and demands extremely crass and vigorous
methods. Everything is employed—the magnificent, the intoxicating,
the bewildering, the grandiose, the frightful, the clamorous, the ecstatic,
the neurotic. ... Himself possessing the instincts of an actor, he wishes
to imitate mankind only in the most effective and realistic manner. His
extreme nature sees only weakness and insincerity in any other methods.
Painting for effect is an extremely dangerous thing for artists. ... He makes
a determined effort to assert himself, and to dominate in an age antagonistic to all art. Poison is an antidote to poison. Every sort of exaggeration
is polemically arrayed against the forces hostile to art. Religion and
philosophical elements are introduced, aspirations for the idyllic—in
short, everything, everything.'[3]

Whether a just verdict or not, one pretty devastating to the author of
The Birth of Tragedy! For the second time within twelve months, the
soldier of culture had been made to turn the sword against himself.

I will not conceal my own opinion that it is, substantially, a just
verdict. The wonder to me is not that Nietzsche should have outgrown
his enthusiasm for Wagner's music, but that he should have succumbed
to it so completely in the first place, and remained its champion so long.
But perhaps the explanation is not far to seek. His initial response had not
been wholly unlike that of those English undergraduates, who, in the
1860's, would promenade the streets of Oxford chanting 'Dolores' and
'Faustine' (they, too, were sadly disillusioned when Swinburne became
a Putney imperialist, and *Songs before Sunrise* turned out to have been
songs after sunset). Genuine ecstasy was mingled with cruder sensations:
'Our youth was up in arms against the *soberness* of the age. It plunged

[1] TS, IV, I.   [2] Quoted: *The Nietzsche-Wagner Correspondence.*   [3] *Ibid.*

into the cult of excess, of passion, of ecstasy, and of the blackest and most austere conception of the world.'[1] As for his long adherence to the cause, that was due, in part at least, to his loneliness: 'I had no-one save Richard Wagner.'[2] His relation to the Master, in this respect, was not unlike Shelley's to that other great *histrio* (the first European 'star'), Lord Byron.

It was due to this cause, at all events, that even after writing these notes, Nietzsche did his best to conceal his misgivings. He confided only in Overbeck. To the rest of his friends he appeared, and sought to appear, just what he had always been, the foremost Wagnerian of all. Only on one occasion did his 'better knowledge' betray itself: when, the following August, he went out of his way to display a brightly bound score of Brahms's *Song of Triumph* on Wagner's piano at *Wahnfried*, to catch the composer's eye as often as he entered the room. This was not merely self-assertion; it was a deliberate experiment on Wagner's nature—and the reaction was as conclusive as it was explosive. 'At that moment', he told his sister long afterwards, 'Wagner was *not* great.'[3]

By then the intervention of King Ludwig had saved the *Festspielhaus*. But it was too late to save Nietzsche's faith. All the King's horses and all the King's men could not put that together again. No wonder, therefore, that he experienced some difficulty when it came to making 'Richard Wagner at Bayreuth' the theme of the fourth *Thought out of Season*! Unlike its predecessors, this work was abandoned and resumed time after time, between 1875 and 1876. In the end, he was forced to solve the problem, much as he had solved that of *Schopenhauer as Educator*, by attaching the name of Wagner to a full-length portrait of 'the artistic genius'. It was a procedure the more successful in this case, in that he had adopted it once before—on his first acquaintance with Wagner.

Thus, the fourth *Thought out of Season*, like the third, is of almost exclusively autobiographical interest. To the extent that it deals specifically with Wagner, it reflects Nietzsche's views of ten years before. Only to the extent that it deals with the artistic genius does it reflect his views at the time of writing. Considered from this angle, however, it represents another declaration of faith—and reads at times like a synopsis of his own future history.

* * *

The artistic, as we should expect, is blood-brother to the philosophical genius, being characterized no less by loyalty to the 'higher self'. He is a man whose knowledge is dominated by the 'plastic power' of life, and whose stature is proportionate to this power: so that the

[1] CW, p. 89.   [2] CW, p. 73.   [3] Quoted: *The Nietzsche-Wagner Correspondence*.

greatest artist would be known by his capacity to assimilate all learning and turn it to sap. Of Wagner Nietzsche says, 'it was as a philosopher that he went, not only through the fire of various philosophical systems without fear, but also through the vapours of science and scholarship while remaining ever true to his higher self—a higher self which exacted of him *complete manifestations of his polyphonic being*, which bade him suffer and learn that he might achieve such manifestations'.[1] In this respect he is comparable to Goethe.

Since the artist must express his synthesis symbolically, what distinguishes the productions of genius is above all their architectonics. Throughout the longest composition, whether it be a poem, a symphony or a musical drama, the whole never ceases to dominate the parts; multiplicity is reduced to unity: and this unity is not artificial or superimposed, but rather natural and organic: 'all one is conscious of is the great *necessity* of it all'.[2] In this, Nietzsche claims, lies the secret of style; and it is with this pre-eminently that he accredits Wagner: 'Wagner is never more himself than when he is overwhelmed with difficulties and can exercise power on a large scale with all the joy of a lawgiver. To subdue restless and contending masses to simple rhythmic movement, and to exercise one will over a bewildering host of claims and desires— these are the tasks for which he feels he was born, and in which he finds his freedom.'[3]

It is the Greek ideal; and, epitomising once more his variant of the Romantic Myth, Nietzsche interprets the history of Europe as a dialogue between the Hellenic and the Oriental spirits. Since the time of Alexander the Great, he writes, the Oriental has tended to predominate: knowledge, in the guise of religion and science, has been cultivated at the expense of life. 'It is now necessary that a generation of *anti-Alexanders* should arise', capable of appropriating the fruits of this spirituality for the further enrichment of mankind. 'In the person of Wagner I recognize one of these anti-Alexanders'.[4] The terms 'Hellenic' and 'Oriental' here are equivalent to 'Dionysian' and 'Apollonian'; and the 'Anti-Alexander', of course, is none other than the 'music-practising Socrates'. He is that great and powerful nature who recapitulates in himself the history of European man, and passes beyond it, thereby anticipating and inaugurating a new epoch.

Wagner's own development, accordingly, Nietzsche represents as a similar dialogue—between an unprecedented will to power, on the one hand, and an unlimited capacity for learning on the other. (This is the first occasion in his work on which the intuitive side of man's nature is

[1] TS, IV, 3.   [2] TS, IV, 9.   [3] *Ibid.*   [4] TS, IV, 4.

identified with power, rather than love.) From the interplay, the rivalry and ultimate reconciliation, of these two forces, sprang the glorious sequence of musical dramas extending from *Rienzi* to *The Ring*:

'Observed from its earliest beginnings, the development of his art constitutes a most magnificent spectacle, and—even though it was attended with great suffering—reason, law, and intention mark its course throughout. Under the charm of such a spectacle the observer will be led to take pleasure even in this painful development itself, and will regard it as fortunate. He will see how everything necessarily contributes to the welfare and benefit of a talent and a nature fore-ordained, however severe the trials may be through which it may have to pass. He will realize how every danger gives it more heart, and every triumph more prudence; how it partakes of poison and sorrow and thrives upon them. The mockery and antagonism of the surrounding world only goad and spur it on the more. Should it happen to go astray, it but returns from its wanderings and exile loaded with the most precious spoil; should it chance to slumber, "it does but recoup its strength".'[1]

Not only science and scholarship, be it noted, but equally his most personal experience, serve as nutriment to the creative personality. All things work together for good to him who remains loyal to his higher self.

Thus, one of the crucial events in Wagner's life, we are given to understand, was the reception of *Lohengrin* and *Tannhäuser*. Whereas, in *Rienzi*, the musician's devouring ambition had gained the upper hand, employing all Meyerbeer's tricks for winning the applause of the mob, 'in these operas he looked about him for his equals—the anchorite yearned for the number. But what were his feelings withal? Nobody answered him. Nobody had understood his question. . . .'[2] Faced with this blank incomprehension, Wagner 'staggered and vacillated':

'The possibility of a complete overthrow of all things presents itself to him, and he no longer shrinks from the possibility. Maybe, beyond that upheaval and desolation, a new hope will arise—maybe not: anyway, better Nothing than so repellent a Something! Shortly afterwards, he was a political exile and in dire distress.'[3]

It was through this very humiliation, however, that Wagner rose to his greatest heights: 'then only, with this terrible change in his outward and inward destiny, there begins that period of the great man's life over which as a golden reflection there is stretched the splendour of the highest mastery'.[4]

[1] TS, IV, 6.   [2] TS, IV, 8.   [3] *Ibid.*   [4] *Ibid.*

By what steps Wagner freed himself from this nihilistic phase, Nietzsche forebears to recount—they would, he says, be unintelligible! But the inference is clear enough. Having looked for a lie in everything, he was rewarded with a marvellous disillusioning. His encounter with Schopenhauer was associated with a mystical experience, from which he emerged re-born, 'the desire for supreme power, the inheritance of former conditions, now directed wholly into creative art'.[1] He was now the perfected dithyrambic dramatist. And, in an eloquent passage, Nietzsche presents once again his Dionysian ideal:

'In a dance, wild, rhythmic yet gliding, and with ecstatic gesture, the born dramatist makes known something of what is going on within him, of what is taking place in nature: his dithyrambic movements are as eloquent of shuddering comprehension and exuberant penetration as of tender approach and voluptuous surrender. Intoxicated speech follows the course of this rhythm; melody resounds coupled with speech, and in its turn melody projects its sparks into the realm of images and ideas. A dream-apparition, like and unlike the image of Nature and her wooer, hovers forward; it condenses into more human shapes; it spreads out in response to an heroically triumphant will, and to a most blissful collapse and cessation of will: thus tragedy is born.'[2]

The first-fruits of this rebirth of Wagner's art were *Tristan und Isolde* and *Die Meistersinger*—'that clear golden and thoroughly fermented mixture of simplicity, deeply discriminating love, observation and roguishness'.[3] But the crowning glory, of course, was *The Ring*. And while Wagner was still at work on *The Ring*, 'something happened, which caused him to stop and listen: *friends* were coming . . . the nucleus and first living source of a really human community which would reach perfection in some age still remote'.[4]

* * *

The friends, of course, were Rohde, von Gersdorff, before all, Nietzsche himself: and they were coming to Bayreuth that summer. August 1876 had been appointed for the opening of the *Festspielhaus*. 'For us', Nietzsche writes, 'Bayreuth is the consecration of the dawn of the combat'[5]—the combat of the heroic few against the massed ranks of German Philistinism—and he seems, in the very act of composing his panegyric, to have half convinced himself of its truth. At all events, he was as thrilled by the prospect of Wagner's triumph as any of his companions-in-arms.

'Does it not seem almost like a fairy-tale to be able to come face to

[1] TS, IV, 8.   [2] TS, IV, 7.   [3] TS, IV, 8.   [4] *Ibid.*   [5] TS, IV, 4.

face with such a personality? Must not they who take any part whatsoever, active or passive, in the proceedings at Bayreuth, already feel
altered and rejuvenated, and ready to introduce reforms and to effect
renovations in other spheres of life?'[1] To us, who know the sequel, the
irony of these declamations is excruciating. As if that were not enough,
'it is certain', he adds, 'that in Bayreuth even the spectator is a spectacle
worth seeing.'[2] And indeed he was. Twelve years afterwards Nietzsche
was to say that a genuine Bayreuthian ought to be preserved in spirit for
the edification of posterity.

He arrived at the beginning of August, stopping with Wagner's
friend Malwida von Meysenbug; sat through the first rehearsal of *The
Ring*; and then, without a word of explanation—with only a brief,
'fatalistic telegram'[3] of apology—fled into the recesses of the Böhmer-
wald. The awakening, like the dream, is best conveyed in his own words:

'He who has any notion of the visions which even at that time had
flitted across my path, will be able to guess what I felt when one day I
came to my senses in Bayreuth. It was just as if I had been dreaming.
Where on earth was I? I recognized nothing that I saw; I scarcely recognized Wagner. It was in vain that I called up reminiscences. Tribschen—
remote island of bliss: not the shadow of a resemblance! The incomparable days devoted to the laying of the first stone, the small group of
the initiated who celebrated them, and who were far from lacking
fingers for the handling of delicate things: not the shadow of a resemblance! *What had happened?*'[4]

What had happened? The question was to haunt Nietzsche for years.
Sometimes he believed it was Wagner who had changed: and assuredly
it was in adversity that Wagner's character had shone. In victory he
scarcely contrasted with the wealthy subscribers and sycophants whose
favour he so sedulously cultivated. 'The Wagnerite had become master
of Wagner,'[5] therefore, was one of the answers Nietzsche found: 'since
Wagner had returned to Germany, he had condescended step by step
to everything that I despise—even to anti-semitism'.[6]

That this was not the whole truth, however, nor even a principle part
of it, is proved by the single fact that Wagner had been a brazen anti-
semite at least as long as Nietzsche had known him. It was he himself
who had changed. It was Nietzsche who had become, or was in process
of becoming, master of Nietzsche: and the extremity of his revulsion was
a measure of the distance he had travelled. Perhaps the best thing he ever
said on the subject was also the simplest: 'I realized that Wagner was no

[1] TS, IV, 4. [2] TS, IV, 1. [3] EH, p. 85. [4] *Ibid.* [5] EH, p. 84. [6] CW, p. 73.

longer indispensable.'[1] He could dispense with the Master now, because he had in fact already dispensed with him. His awakening was merely the end of an illusion that had outlived its service.

It was a bitter awakening for all that. Schopenhauer and Wagner between them had been his guarantors of the 'German genius'. With his faith in them, his faith in that vanished too—and *Thoughts out of Season* ended abruptly. Nietzsche the Idealist, Nietzsche the Romantic, died and was buried at Bayreuth.

[1] Quoted: *The Nietzsche-Wagner Correspondence.*

Second Movement

THE CONQUEST
OF NIHILISM

'Strange! I am continually possessed by this thought: that my history is not solely a personal history, that in living as I do live, forming myself and setting myself on record, I am serving the interests of many.'

V

THE SCEPTIC

Nietzsche's great contemporary, and aberrant disciple, Bernard Shaw, once entertained the fancy that all men of genius are fated to a serious illness in their late thirties—a few, like Raphael, Mozart and Byron, having taken it all too seriously. . . . Nietzsche was nearly one of those few: so nearly, that he remained persuaded to the end of his days that he had inherited from his father a predisposition to early death.

Nowadays, there is little reason to doubt that the disease which nearly killed him in his thirty-sixth year was syphilitic in origin. The myopia that embittered his suffering was certainly a paternal legacy, aggravated by incessant reading and writing; the dysentery and diphtheria he had contracted during the campaign of 1870 may have helped to undermine what Elizabeth curiously calls 'his hitherto splendid digestive organs'— thenceforward he was seldom free long at a time from painful gastric disorders. But these were subsidiary causes. A powerfully built man, a capable rider and tireless walker, as little suited by physique as by temperament to an exclusively sedentary existence, he would have recovered quickly, but for the virulent heritage of Bonn.

To what extent this disease directly affected his mind, prior to the final breakdown of 1889, is impossible to ascertain. Probably very little. At all events, the seemingly abrupt twists and turns of his thought are no stranger than those of other thinkers whose health has never been in doubt. The most that can plausibly be said is that it may have intensified his moods of exaltation and depression.

His own belief that psychological factors contributed to his illness, on the other hand, is incontestable. Apart from everything else (and we shall have occasion to revert to the topic), there is nothing like an uncongenial occupation for impairing even the soundest constitution. 'The man who is bed-ridden often perceives that he is ill of his position, business or society, and through them has lost all self-possession.'[1] Already, by 1872, Nietzsche was quite literally sick of his job. He had reached the end of his interest in philology; whatever attraction his professorship might once have held had evaporated entirely. If he continued

[1] H, I, 289.

to discharge his duties as well as circumstances allowed, that was only because no other course lay open to him. He could not afford to retire; the few alternative occupations for which he was qualified would have carried the same, or worse, liabilities. There may even have been times when he felt a little thankful to his illness for giving him a chance to do what he wanted. 'As my bodily constitution is now very good,' he had written to Hans von Bülow during a temporary rally, 'my literary future seems to be well-nigh hopeless.'[1]

Even what he wanted to do, moreover, was often not what he wanted: that is to say even his services to the Wagnerian cause had come to be performed from a sense of duty rather than from genuine inclination. To a greater extent than he was aware at the time, his literary work itself was indentured labour. On a man of his integrity, the strain imposed by the last two *Thoughts out of Season* must have been severe; it is hardly surprising that his health should so far have deteriorated by the summer of 1876 that he was compelled to solicit a year's leave of absence from Basle.

This respite came none too soon. His 'coming to his senses' at Bayreuth was the occasion, if not the cause, of a general physical collapse. It was with heartfelt relief, as well as gratitude, that he accepted Malwida von Meysenbug's invitation to spend the winter with her at Sorrento. There, at long last, he was able to bid farewell to past preoccupations. There too, by a curious chance, he bade his final farewell to Wagner.

The story of their last meeting is familiar: how Wagner, still unconscious of the change in his quondam disciple, expounded the theme of *Parsifal*; how he dwelt on his own religious experiences—remorse, repentance, absolution—as the true source of its inspiration; and how Nietzsche, walking beside him in silence, could master his feelings only so far as to mutter a few broken words of apology—and slip away into the darkness.

Years afterwards, no doubt with this incident in mind, he was to conclude that Wagner had succumbed to 'the *typical velleity* of the artist':[2] in other words, that he had grown weary of having (as Keats said the poet should have) no identity or determined character, and, not content with entering imaginatively into the experiences of a medieval Christian, had tried to make out that he was one. But it was Schopenhauer who had made smooth the way for this deception, and what Nietzsche was chiefly conscious of at the time was the danger he himself had escaped. So this was where Romanticism ended—at the foot of the Cross!

[1] L, 2, 1, 75.   [2] GM, III, 4.

'The unexpected event illumined for me in one lightning-flash the
place that I had abandoned, and also the great horror that is felt by
everyone who is unconscious of a great danger until he has passed
through it. As I went forward alone, I shuddered, and not long afterwards I was ill, or rather more than ill—weary: weary of my ceaseless
disappointment about all that remained to make us modern men enthusiastic, at the thought of the power, work, hope, youth, love, flung
to all the winds: weary with disgust at the effeminacy and undisciplined
rhapsody of this romanticism, at the whole tissue of idealistic lies and
softening of conscience, which here again had won the day over one of
the bravest of men: last and not least, weary from the bitterness of inexorable suspicion—that after this disappointment I was doomed to
mistrust more thoroughly, to despise more thoroughly, to be alone
more thoroughly than ever before. My task—whither had it flown?
Did it not look now as if my task were retreating from me and as if for
a long future period I should have no more right to it? What was I to
do to endure this terrible privation?'[1]

* * *

The breach with Wagner was one of the most painful episodes in
Nietzsche's life. 'Something', he was to predict truly enough in his
autobiography, 'will always keep our names associated in the minds of
men, and that is, that we are two who have suffered more deeply,
even at each other's hands, than most men are able to suffer nowadays.'[2]
Whether or not this was true of Wagner, it was certainly true of himself.
Henceforth he was veritably alone.

It would be a serious mistake, all the same, to overrate its importance
in his development. As we have seen, it was at least as much the consequence as the cause of a change in his outlook that had been proceeding a long while before. To any completely honest man—to any man,
that is, who values truth above all else—a time must come, sooner or
later, when he is alone: when the best friends cease to speak the same
language, and even to retain their friendship it is needful to wear a mask;
when he has either to face up to his destiny by himself or else pay the
penalty for evasion. 'That hidden masterful Something, for which we
have no name until at last it shows itself as our task—that tyrant in us
exacts a terrible price for every attempt that we make to escape him or
give him the slip, for every premature act of self-constraint, for every
reconciliation with those to whom we do not belong, for every activity,
however reputable, which turns us aside from our main purpose, yes,

---

[1] H, II, Preface, 3.   [2] EH, p. 44.

even for every virtue that would fain protect us from the cruelty of our most individual responsibility.'[1]

The penalty may not always be sickness, as Nietzsche supposed; it may merely be arrested development—of which the history of genius itself affords too many instances. The penalty for honesty, on the other hand, is invariably and inevitably isolation. Ninety-nine per cent of the whole of human society and intercourse, after all, is founded on the assumption that men do not value truth above all else—that truth is a secondary consideration, if indeed it is a consideration at all. Prejudice is the cement of society; the fact that this is rarely acknowledged but one more proof of its truth.

The views of the normal man are formed in adolescence; what minor alterations they undergo subsequently, are designed mainly to conceal the too obvious gaps between profession and practice. He models himself upon others; and perhaps this is just as well, since a single-minded dedication to truth is barely compatible with stability: 'the free spirit hates all rules and customs, all that is permanent and definitive, hence he painfully tears asunder again and again the net around him, though in consequence thereof he will suffer from numerous wounds, slight and severe; for he must break off every thread *from himself*, from his body and soul'.[2] It is a sound instinct that warns the family-man, in particular, against too close a concern for truth.

Nietzsche was never a normal man; and what made him abnormal was less the ability, which he shared with other writers of the first rank, to communicate his experience and findings in words (so that we, who lack such ability, may not lack the inspiration as well), than his unfaltering devotion to 'the true, the real, the non-apparent, the certain'. When he spoke of the will to truth as 'his innermost desire and profoundest need',[3] when he described it as having 'developed into a passion, which does not shrink from any sacrifice, and at bottom fears nothing but its own extinction',[4] he was not exaggerating. He was one of the most honest men who have ever lived, and consequently one of the loneliest.

It was not only Wagner's friendship that he lost at this time. His oldest confidant, Rohde, had married and settled down at Jena; he remained the Wagnerian and Schopenhauerian Nietzsche had made him, and by and by sank below the horizon. So likewise von Gersdorff, whom he estranged by his very efforts to retain him; it was years before they met again. In their place came new associates—Paul Rée, the Jewish philosopher, who happened to be staying at Sorrento, and Peter Gast, the composer, to whose loyalty he owed so much. But, although their

[1] H, II, Preface, 4.   [2] H, I, 427.   [3] JW, 2.   [4] D, 429.

intercourse revived Nietzsche's recurrent dream of a community of kindred spirits, neither then nor afterwards was he able to establish such intimate ties as formerly. There was always an element of pretence in his relationships; he had to stick to the surface of things, if he was to keep up the illusion—the necessary illusion—of a genuine affinity of spirit. It was the same necessity, he confessed, which had prompted his self-identification with Wagner and Schopenhauer in *Thoughts out of Season*, that led him to label *Human, All-too-Human* 'a book for free spirits'. In fact there were no such free spirits. 'There is not a soul who at heart is either well-pleased, or anxious, or distressed, or anything whatever, about the ''things'' that I hold dear.'[1]

That was the simple truth, and it was surely a hard one to bear. For Nietzsche, however fastidious, was not made for absolute isolation. He loved to converse freely, above all to laugh freely, in a small circle of men he could trust, and trust to understand. Small wonder that his letters from 1876 onwards are one long cry of loneliness; or that he should have dreamed repeatedly of Wagner himself—'and always in the spirit of our former intimate companionship':

'No words of anger have ever passed between us, not even in my dreams—on the contrary, only words of encouragement and good cheer, and with no-one have I ever laughed so much as with him. All this is now a thing of the past—and what does it avail that in many respects I am right and he is wrong? As if our lost friendship could be forgotten on that account! And to think that I had already suffered similar experiences before, and am likely to suffer them again! They constitute the cruellest sacrifices that my path in life and thought has exacted from me—and even now the whole of my philosophy totters after one hour's sympathetic intercourse even with total strangers! It seems to me so foolish to insist on being in the right at the expense of love, and *not to be able to impart* one's best for fear of destroying sympathy. *Hinc meae lacrymae.*'[2]

'It seems to me so foolish': and it seemed so foolish to Nietzsche's acquaintances too—for critics have never been wanting to charge him with wilful perversity. Yet it was by virtue of this foolishness that he was able to go on growing, and it is only because he went on growing that there are still critics who remember his name.

* * *

At Sorrento, he at first tried to resume work on 'We Philologists'—intended originally as the fourth, and later the fifth of the *Thoughts out of*

[1] L, 10, 12, 85.   [2] L, 20, 8, 80.

Season. But that proved impossible. For one thing, his illness put sustained composition out of the question; bed-ridden and practically blind, the most he could manage now was to commit short notes to paper, and await a more favourable season to dictate them. For another, the whole spirit and standpoint of *Thoughts out of Season* lay behind him. *We Philologists* is a fascinating document just because we can trace in it, step by step, his abandonment of old positions, and occupation—sometimes premature occupation—of new ones.

His 'task' had indeed retreated from him—or he had advanced beyond it. The confidence with which he had sallied forth as the 'soldier of culture' could not be recaptured. If he had been deceived in Wagner and Schopenhauer, what trust could be placed in anything he had hitherto stood for? 'Realities were all too plainly absent from my stock of knowledge, and what the "idealities" were worth the devil alone knew!'[1] There was nothing for it, he soon saw, but to reconstruct his philosophy from bedrock.

Accordingly, he plunged into the study of science—experiencing, like Goethe and Schweitzer, all the relief that physics can bring after an over-indulgence in metaphysics. Not that it was relief he was seeking: even biological problems he approached in the spirit of a philosopher, rather than of an 'employee of science'[2]—a particular and personal need directing the course of his research. But the humblest fact, definitely ascertained, now seemed fairer than the loftiest theory. This time, he was resolved, the foundations of his world-view should be irremovable; not a stone be used in the building but was proof against wear and tear. It was a very brave resolution, and the book that resulted from it is one of the bravest there is.

'The memorial of a crisis',[3] he himself called *Human, All-too Human*, and the definition is exact, whether applied to the manner or the matter: for, of course, Nietzsche being Nietzsche, a man all of a piece, the crisis is commemorated as conspicuously in the one as the other. The same two factors which had compelled the abandonment of *We Philologists*, his illness and his determination to print nothing but what he felt certain of, conspired to enforce a new literary form—the aphorism; and like the good craftsman he was, he made a virtue of necessity. Sensing its possibilities, he exploited them to the utmost, swiftly transforming himself into a master of concise, restrained, epigrammatic speech. The contrast between this and all his previous works is so marked that he once cited it as evidence that Bacon might have written Shakespeare.

The same French authors who served as his models, moreover, La

[1] EH, p. 86.   [2] H, III, 171.   [3] EH, p. 82.

Rochefoucauld and Chamfort in particular, exactly matched his mood. He was growing out of Romanticism; in order to reach bedrock, he had to submit every one of his preconceptions to the most rigorous scrutiny: 'lonely now and miserably self-distrustful, I took sides, not without resentment, *against* myself, and *for* everything that hurt me and was hard to me'.[1] What more natural than to turn to the pioneers of the Enlightenment? Already in the last two *Thoughts out of Season*, he had been paying tribute to that great denier of all that could be denied, Montaigne. *Human, All-too-Human* carried a motto from Descartes, and was published, deliberately, on the centenary of Voltaire's death.

When we speak of Nietzsche as 'growing out of Romanticism', however, it is well to be sure what we mean. So much nonsense has been talked on that subject. Romanticism itself, for example, is often represented as merely an emotional reaction against eighteenth-century formalism in art and rationalism in philosophy: and it is quite true that all the Romantics began with such a reaction. But only the minor ones ended with it. What the major Romantics sought, and in some cases found, was new artistic forms, no less exacting than the old, and new philosophical systems, no less logically coherent; and what inspired their quest was a religious experience which, owing to the activities of the Enlightenment, could no longer find adequate expression in terms of orthodox Christianity. The typical Romantic artist was not Berlioz but Beethoven; the typical philosopher, not Schlegel but Hegel.

The author of *The Birth of Tragedy* had been typical. For Nietzsche, therefore, 'growing out of Romanticism' did not mean merely growing out of an adolescent enthusiasm for the Romantics (a very necessary preliminary, but no more, to acquiring a mature appreciation of them)— that he had long since done. It could as little mean reverting wholeheartedly to eighteenth-century rationalism—that would have been pure retrogression. It meant, and could mean, one thing only: advance to a wholly new position.

He himself makes this very clear. 'In the period of rationalism', he writes for instance, 'justice was not done to the importance of religion, of that there is no doubt.'[2] The French free-thinkers had tended to deny, not merely such formulations of religious experience as a new science had rendered obsolete, but religious experience itself. They had either ignored it altogether, or else misrepresented it so crudely as to carry no weight with the initiate. Romanticism was justified insofar as it remedied this defect:

[1] H, II, Preface, 4.   [2] H, I, 110.

'It is certainly one of the greatest and quite invaluable advantages which we gain from Schopenhauer, that he occasionally forces our sensations back into the older, mightier modes of contemplating the world and man, to which no other path would so easily lead us. The gain to history and justice is very great—I do not think that anyone would so easily succeed now in doing justice to Christianity and its Asiatic relations without Schopenhauer's assistance, which is specially impossible from the basis of still existing Christianity. Only after this great *success of justice*, only after we have corrected so essential a point as the historical mode of contemplation which the age of enlightenment brought with it, may we again bear onward the banner of enlightenment, the banner with the three names, Petrarch, Erasmus, Voltaire.'[1]

What Nietzsche objects to in Romanticism is not that it exposed the superficiality of an earlier rationalism, but that 'in the reaction that followed this rationalism, justice was far over-stepped; for religions were treated lovingly, even amorously, and, for instance, a deeper, even the very deepest, understanding of the world was ascribed to them; which science has only to strip of its dogmatic garment in order to possess the "truth" in unmythical form.'[2] He differs, in short, from the rationalists, in that he acknowledges the fact of religious experience, and from the Romantics, in that he denies that this experience affords any revelation of a metaphysical reality. In *Human, All-too-Human*, he faces up at last to the issues raised in his notes of 1872 and the essay *On Truth and Falsity*. It is, before all else, a sustained critique of metaphysics.

* * *

The three volumes were compiled in the autumn of 1877, 1878, and the summer of 1879, respectively. The second and third appeared originally under separate titles, 'Miscellaneous Maxims and Opinions' and 'The Wanderer and his Shadow'. When Nietzsche reissued them all as one work, however, he was only undersigning the evident fact that they stand for a single phase in his development. Their temper is the same throughout; the arrangement of the material is the same, and so is the procedure adopted.

'War,' he called this later, 'but war without powder or smoke.'[3] In other words, he launches no frontal attack on metaphysical systems. What he does is to take, one by one, those experiences which have been held to necessitate recourse to metaphysics, and see whether they cannot be given a purely naturalistic explanation—'substituting, as is natural to a positive mind, for the improbable something more probable'.[4] It is

---

[1] H, I, 26.   [2] H, I, 110.   [3] EH, p. 83.   [4] GM, Preface, 4.

the procedure he admired in Epicurus. The particular experiences, ethical, religious and aesthetic, are, of course, those by which he himself had been drawn to Schopenhauer; and Schopenhauer, whether mentioned by name or not, is his sparring partner throughout.

Thus, the pangs of conscience had been pronounced by Schopenhauer inexplicable apart from the postulate of free will; and since, in the phenomenal world, the will was not free, he had been compelled to accept a noumenal world in which it was. To a young man, Nietzsche observes, such an argument is very seductive, because, 'when he recognizes the innermost world-puzzle or world-misery in that which he so strongly disapproves of in himself',[1] he feels relieved of responsibility. Yet what, in reality, does it amount to? Exceedingly little. When Schopenhauer said 'inexplicable', all he really meant was 'unjustifiable': and what reason is there for assuming that the pangs of conscience must be justified? We have, in fact, only to admit that they may be unjustifiable in order to see that they are perfectly capable of being explained without recourse to metaphysics at all. With this, he proceeds to offer his own, naturalistic explanation.

It is fairly familiar nowadays. Conscience, he suggests, was not responsible for morality; morality was responsible for conscience—and morality originated in purely utilitarian considerations. Such actions were originally labelled 'good' as helped to preserve the community, such 'bad' as tended to endanger it. It was only when this fact was lost sight of that the epithets came to be transferred, first from the actions to their motives, and then from the motives to those who entertained them —so that we speak now of good and bad men; and it was only then, when obedience to a moral code was enjoined from earliest childhood without any explanation being offered, that the phenomenon of conscience arose: 'the sum-total of our conscience is all that has regularly been demanded of us, without reason, in the days of our childhood, by people whom we respected or feared. . . . The belief in authority is the source of conscience; which is therefore not the voice of God in the hearts of man, but the voice of some men in man.'[2]

This hypothesis is confirmed by the fact that conscience has enjoined quite different conduct in different times and places. Indeed, much that is now called 'good', since it has established its utility, was formerly considered 'bad'—even by the innovator himself. All good things had conscience against them at first; and it is only because this has been forgotten that conscience now appears so mysterious and terrible a thing as to demand a supernatural interpretation and sanction. 'A poet might say

¹ H, I, 17.   ² H, III, 52.

that God has placed forgetfulness as doorkeeper in the temple of human dignity.'[1]

This is typical of Nietzsche's procedure; and it will be seen that with regard to ethical experience itself, he shows just as much sympathy for the Romantics as he does for the earlier rationalists. If he is as cynical as Hobbes or Chamfort, in his estimate of the primitive, and normal, motivation of human beings ('one will seldom go wrong, if one attributes extreme actions to vanity, average ones to habit, and petty ones to fear'),[2] he is as insistent as Schopenhauer himself that conscience is actually the determining factor on some occasions. He will not allow himself to be confused with those moralists, such as La Rochefoucauld, who have maintained that it is always and everywhere a mere stalking-horse for egoism. The following passage, one among several like it, deserves to be borne in mind:

'NOT TO BE CONFUSED.—There are moralists who treat the strong, noble, self-denying attitude of such beings as the heroes of Plutarch, or the pure, enlightened, warmth-giving state of soul peculiar to truly good men and women, as difficult scientific problems. They investigate the origin of such phenomena, indicating the complex element in the apparent simplicity, and directing their gaze to the tangled skein of motives, the delicate web of conceptual illusions, and the sentiments of individuals or groups, that are a legacy of ancient days gradually increased. Such moralists are very *different* from those with whom they are most commonly *confounded*, from those petty minds that do not believe at all in these modes of thought and states of soul, and imagine their own poverty to be hidden somewhere behind the glamour of greatness and purity. The moralists say, "Here are problems", and these pitiable creatures say, "Here are impostors and deceptions". Thus the latter *deny* the *existence* of the very things which the former are at pains *to explain*.'[3]

What Nietzsche denies is not that conscience may be the determining impulse in a particular situation, but that it is anything other or more than an impulse. The prompting of conscience, he holds, is not different in kind from the prompting of hunger or thirst.

For this very reason, however, it is nonsense to talk of 'absolute disinterestedness' in Schopenhauer's sense. About even the most impressive act of self-sacrifice there is nothing miraculous. The mother who gives up everything for her child, the soldier who lays down his life for the Fatherland, simply gratifies one desire or inclination at the expense of

[1] H, I, 92.   [2] H, I, 74.   [3] H, III, 20.

another and weaker. Nietzsche may not always be happy in the expressions he finds for this view, but to those acquainted with the theory he is combating, there will be nothing far-fetched in his paradox, that a God of perfect love would be incapable of a single disinterested act.

* * *

With regard to religious experience, his procedure is exactly the same: to propound a purely naturalistic explanation, without subtracting from the reality of what is to be explained. Religious experience, as he understands it, results directly from the interweaving of ethics with the notion of a supernatural being—the latter dating back to animistic times.

Every man, he submits, is aware of impulses that conflict with customary morality, and is liable, accordingly, to the pangs of self-contempt. The criminal and the innovator—the one behind, the other ahead of, his time—find such impulses all-powerful. The saint, on the other hand, wages incessant war on them. Measuring himself against the standard of absolute altruism, he thinks of himself as wholly corrupt; consumed by the conviction of sin, he despairs, and in every trivial event reads warnings of the wrath to come. Since, however, not even the most miserable sinner can remain miserable all the time, there must come, even to the saint, moments of relative well-being: and then, just as he has misinterpreted, and thereby intensified, his pain, so he misinterprets and intensifies his relief. Knowing himself actually no better than he was, he can only conceive it as something miraculous—as a totally undeserved afflatus of heavenly grace, an earnest of forgiveness, a foretaste of ultimate redemption.

Nietzsche shows scant respect now for the ascetic. Although this holy man, he declares, may be compounded of many motivations, none of them are superhuman, and most are all-too-human:

'Sometimes the saint practises that defiance of himself, which is near relative of domination at any cost, and gives a feeling of power even to the most lonely; sometimes his swollen sensibility leaps from the desire to let his passions have full play into the desire to overthrow them like wild horses under the mighty pressure of a proud spirit; sometimes he desires a complete cessation of all disturbing, tormenting, irritating sensations, a waking sleep, a lasting rest in the lap of a dull, animal, and plant like indolence; sometimes he seeks strife and arouses it within himself, because boredom has shown him its yawning countenance.'[1]

The ascetic owed his ascendancy, Nietzsche opines, to the widespread

[1] H, I, 142.

craving for cruelty of the degenerate classical world: the spectacle of his self-lacerations was 'the last pleasure that antiquity invented after it had grown blunted even at the sight of beast-baiting and human combats';[1] and nothing more than this ascendancy is required to explain why 'even in our own age, which no longer believes in God, there are still thinkers who believe in the ascetic'.[2]

For all that he generously allows that other types of holiness have been known—for example, Jesus of Nazareth—it must be acknowledged that this account of religious experience is as crude as anything perpetrated by the eighteenth century. Nietzsche's own experience, at this point, was unequal to the task he had set himself; only his approach is of interest. Much later, in *The Genealogy of Morals*, he was to refine the interpretation.

The approach, however, is what matters; and even here, it is to be noted, he attempts to correct the historical mode of contemplation which the age of enlightenment brought with it. He does allow that the religious life has immeasurably enlarged man's emotional and intellectual capacities. He is as ready as the Romantics, in fact, to admit the reality of those exalted states of consciousness which they made the keystone of their philosophies. Where he departs from them is in his insistence that even these states, which seem to differ so absolutely, not merely in degree but in kind, from anything we ordinarily know, have been produced by the sublimation of faculties we have in common with the brutes. To take a concrete example (the example he himself took in *The Genealogy of Morals*), Schopenhauer the 'pure, passionless subject of knowledge', belonged as much to the natural world as Schopenhauer the libidinous misogynist.

* * *

It cost Nietzsche little, we may believe, to say goodbye to the ascetic. He had never been congenial company. But what of the genius? Nowhere is his taking sides against himself more apparent than in the sections of *Human, All-too-Human*, 'Concerning the Soul of Artists and Authors'.

Since the first primitive poets and painters entertained their compatriots with representations of weddings, victories and hunts, he writes, many different kinds of pleasure have been bestowed by the arts at different stages of human development. For instance (and here he anticipates present-day theories on the motivation of children's drawings) in symmetry and regularity, the artist may express his taste for an ordered existence, whereas, at other times, it is the violation of rules that awakens his keenest delight. 'He who pursues this speculation still fur-

[1] H, I, 141.   [2] H, I, 143.

ther will know *what kind of hypotheses* for the explanation of aesthetic phenomena are hereby fundamentally rejected.'[1]

To the hypothesis that art portrays the Platonic Idea, Nietzsche had, of course, never subscribed; so it is not surprising to find this dismissed as 'a vain imagination and delusion'.[2] Even the characters in a drama, we are told, are only bundles of characteristics, and superficial characteristics at that: 'art starts from the natural *ignorance* of man about his interior condition (in body and character): it is not meant for philosophers or natural scientists.'[3] With the poet as portrayer of the Idea, however, goes now the musician as spokesman of the Will. 'No music is deep and full of meaning in itself, it does not speak of "will", of the "thing-in-itself"; that could be imagined by the intellect only in an age which had conquered for musical symbolism the entire range of inner life.'[4] Music, he submits, has acquired its emotional significance only through its long association with verse, thanks to which certain combinations of sounds automatically suggest certain states of mind. It is therefore by no means 'a universal language for all time, as is often said in its praise, but corresponds exactly to a particular period and warmth of emotion which is the inner law of a quite definite culture'.[5] Palestrina would have meant nothing to a Greek; to a future generation, Wagner may be equally unintelligible. Thus summarily is *The Birth of Tragedy* dismissed. It is hardly a shock after this to learn that the Greeks developed the magnificent type of the Bacchanal out of St. Vitus' dance, or that Socrates' *daimon* was probably an affection of the ear! Nietzsche rends himself.

To be sure, his abandonment of metaphysical hypotheses has definite compensations. We have only to recall that cancelled fragment of *The Birth of Tragedy*, 'On Music and Words', to realise what contradictions and perplexities they had involved. Now at least he is free to judge many different varieties of art on their own merits; and in 'The Wanderer and his Shadow' he makes the most of this freedom. It is packed with masterly *aperçus* on individual musicians, painters and poets. While 'that barbaric, if ever so delightful, outpouring of hot and highly coloured things from an undisciplined, chaotic soul, which is what we understood by "art" in our youth', provokes, indeed, only his disgust, he is equally well able to appreciate the 'wiser and more harmonious'[6] productions of classical or neo-classical taste, and the major achievements of Romanticism. The latter, he states, communicate directly those exalted states of consciousness that proceed from the religious life; and 'how strong the

[1] H, II, 119.   [2] H, I, 160.   [3] *Ibid.*
[4] H, I, 215.   [5] H, II, 171.   [6] H, II, 173.

metaphysical need, and how hard to the last nature makes our parting from it may be seen from the fact that even in the free spirit, when he has cast off everything metaphysical, the loftiest effects of art can easily produce a resounding of the long-silent, even broken, metaphysical string—it may be, for instance, that at a passage in Beethoven's Ninth Symphony he feels himself floating above the earth in a starry dome with the dream of *immortality* in his heart.'[1]

Nevertheless, we must not be deceived. We know the derivation of that metaphysical need; it can no longer be invoked as witness to a metaphysical reality, let alone to a mystical intuition. The artist is not 'inspired', whatever he himself may think; and if he is loth to relinquish a superstition that has redounded so long to his glory, that only goes to prove him an instance of arrested development, who would, if he could, arrest the development of mankind—an enemy of enlightenment, a dispenser of narcotics and stimulants, valuing ideas in proportion to their emotive force. What he likes to call inspiration is at most a sudden release of productive power, suspended over a long period. It betokens no peculiar insight into the nature of things; neither do the thoughts associated with it spring from any more reliable source than previous hearsay or research.

As for the cult of 'genius': though this may serve a useful purpose, by predisposing the young man to wholehearted apprenticeship to a master, it is of questionable benefit to the master himself, whom it seduces into extravagant claims and robs of the faculty for self-criticism. 'The slow consequences are: the feeling of irresponsibility, of exceptional rights, the belief that mere intercourse with him confers a favour, a frantic rage at any attempt to compare him with others'[2]—as, for example, by placing Brahms's *Song of Triumph* on his piano. There would be no mistaking the particular bearing of these passages, even if we did not happen to know that the word 'artist' had been substituted, at the last moment, for 'Wagner'.

What importance, then, can be attached to art henceforward?

'Above all, for centuries it has taught us to look upon life in every shape with interest and pleasure and to carry our feeling so far that at last we exclaim, "Whatever it may be, life is good". This teaching of art, to take pleasure in existence, and to regard human life as a piece of nature, without too vigorous movement, as an object of regular development—this teaching has grown into us; it reappears as an all-powerful need for knowledge. We could renounce art, but we should not there-

[1] H, I, 153.   [2] H, I, 164.

with forfeit the ability it has taught us—just as we have given up religion, but not the exalting and intensifying of temperament acquired through religion. As the plastic arts and music are the standards of that wealth of feeling really acquired and obtained through religion, so also, after a disappearance of art, the intensity and multiplicity of the joys of life which it had implanted in us would still demand satisfaction. The scientific man is the further development of the artistic man.'[1]

We cannot expect to gather the fruits of all seasons at once, Nietzsche concludes. We may be thankful that we ourselves still live in a time when the joys of art, and of many varieties of art, are still accessible. But the future belongs to the scientist—'the artist will soon come to be regarded as a splendid relic'[2]—and only a retrograde mind could wish it otherwise. Never, one is tempted to comment, was art dismissed so artistically.

*   *   *

Thus Nietzsche takes, one by one, the ethical, the religious and the aesthetic experience, granting its reality, and at the same time proposing a completely naturalistic explanation. The most exalted states of mind, he submits, can be derived, at one or more remove, from the simple instinct of self-preservation—from the pursuit of pleasure and avoidance of pain. They are 'only sublimations in which the fundamental element appears almost evaporated, and is only to be discovered by the closest observation'.[3]

But what, it may be asked, of the 'intellectual conscience' itself? What of that pure, disinterested will to truth which he has so often extolled in the past, and exhibits so pre-eminently in the course of this very analysis? Does even that admit of no loftier origin?—His answer to these questions is implicit in what has been written, and explicit in the passage just quoted: 'the scientific man is the further development of the artistic man'. The will to truth is the offspring and heir of morality, religion and art. It is, in fact, their historical justification.

That this conclusion also was painful to Nietzsche hardly needs stressing. In *Thoughts out of Season* he had drawn up a long, ironical catalogue of the real motives actuating the university scholar, as distinct from the philosophical genius. It is with a visible effort that he now cites this very catalogue as a further instance of youthful idealism: 'for, if it be true that for the making of a scholar "a number of very human impulses and desires must be thrown together", that the scholar is indeed a very noble but not a pure metal, and "consists of a confused blending of very different motives and attractions", the same thing may be said

---

[1] H, I, 222.   [2] H, I, 223.   [3] H, I, 1.

equally of the making and nature of the artist, the philosopher and the moral genius—and whatever glorified great names there may be in that list. *Everything* human deserves ironical consideration with respect to its *origin*.'[1]

The intellectual conscience originated, like conscience itself, in purely utilitarian considerations. A man prefers (if he does prefer it) the true to the untrue, '*now* from habit, heredity and training, *originally* because the true, like the fair and the just, is more expedient and reputable than the untrue'.[2] What is more, if it has been disciplined by religion and directed by art, it has likewise been reinforced from another and still more dubious quarter. The philosopher, Nietzsche asserts, in an aphorism significantly headed, 'FROM THE MOST INTIMATE EXPERIENCE OF THE THINKER', desires immortality: 'it is his immeasurable pride that will only employ the best and hardest stones for the work—truths, or what he takes for such'.[3] The Greek philosophers themselves were one and all tyrants of the mind, insatiably eager to impose their systems on others— indeed, to be accepted as legislators, since 'to be a lawgiver is a sublimated form of tyranny'.[4]

Nietzsche is as ruthless with his former idols as he was with the scholar, and as ruthless with himself as with them. No more than the saint or the artist does the philosopher derive his light from heaven; no more than the will to goodness or beauty, does the will to truth necessitate a recourse to metaphysics.

What the metaphysicians have persistently done, he concludes, is to treat certain habits of mind implanted by the religions of the past as though they were an irreducible datum, and to erect their systems upon them. No wonder these systems bear a striking resemblance to the original Jewish, Christian or Hindu cosmogonies! It is a resemblance 'such as children often bear to their parents, only that in this case the fathers were not clear about that motherhood, as happens sometimes'.[5] Noticing the resemblance, they have then, instead of deriving the 'metaphysical need' from those religions, proceeded to derive those religions from the 'metaphysical need', completing a vicious circle:

'A lack of historical sense is the hereditary fault of all philosophers; many, indeed, unconsciously mistake the very latest variety of man, such as has arisen under the influence of certain religions, certain political events, for the permanent form from which one must set out. They will not learn that man has developed, that his faculty of knowledge has developed also; whilst for some of them the entire world is spun out of

[1] H, I, 252.   [2] H, II, 26.   [3] *Ibid.*   [4] H, I, 261.   [5] H, I, 110.

this faculty of knowledge. Now everything *essential* in human development happened in prehistoric times, long before those four thousand years which we know something of; man may not have changed much during this time. But the philosopher sees 'instincts' in the present man and takes it for granted that these pertain to what is unalterable in mankind, and, consequently, can furnish a key to the understanding of the world; the entire teleology is so constructed that man of the last four thousand years is talked of as an *eternal* being, towards which all things in the world have from the beginning a natural direction. But everything has evolved; there are *no eternal facts*, as there are likewise no absolute truths. Therefore historical philosophizing is henceforth necessary, and with it the virtue of diffidence.'[1]

The criticism is radical, and applies not only to the Idealist, but equally to the type of Romantic who, having constructed a system of his own, discovers that it already exists and rejoins the Christian Church.

The upshot of the whole matter follows inevitably. Not, of course, that metaphysical systems are untrue; but certainly that they are unverifiable—and therefore of no account. For, no matter how questionable the particular naturalistic explanation so far advanced, its mere existence as a plausible alternative to the metaphysical makes distrust of the latter inescapable; and 'where there is distrust of metaphysics, there are on the whole the same results as if it had been directly refuted and *could* no longer be believed in'.[2] The only attitude permissible to an honest mind, respecting the existence or nature of a metaphysical reality, becomes one of unqualified scepticism. Its possibility, indeed, must always be conceded: 'but there is nothing to be done with it, much less is it possible to let happiness, salvation and life depend on the spider-thread of such a possibility'.[3] The conclusion is also Epicurus's. In *Human, All-too-Human*, Nietzsche emerges, for the first time, as a thoroughgoing atheist.

* * *

Nietzsche always spoke of himself as an atheist. He never used the term 'agnostic'—and with good reason. He knew nothing of purely theoretical problems. His philosophy was something to be lived: and agnosticism, however plausible in theory, is impossible to put into practice. There is no half-way house between living as though God exists and as though He does not. If earlier free-thinkers thought there was, that was only because they never realized how profoundly their minds were still swayed by theistic assumptions. They lived as believers unbeknown.

Nietzsche, on the contrary, was as single-minded in his unbelief as

[1] H, I, 2. [2] H, I, 21. [3] H, I, 9.

ever he had been in his belief. No sooner had he disposed of metaphysics than he went on to draw the ultimate consequence of the step. It is this, more even than his attempt to do justice to metaphysics, that establishes his claim to have advanced to a wholly new position.

To begin with, he realized clearly that, if neither ethical, religious nor artistic experience could be invoked to justify metaphysics, no more could metaphysics be invoked to justify them. Their value had to be called in question; they had to be judged anew, and that by the only criterion acceptable to the intellectual conscience—truth. No indulgence could henceforth be permitted to any attitude, no matter how venerable, that was based on an incorrect appraisal of facts. A sense of right and wrong reflecting merely the opinions of primitive legislators, a religious sense fostered by erroneous interpretations, an aesthetic sense harnessed to the religious, would have either to establish new titles to esteem or else make ready for supersession. History left no doubt that they could be superseded: 'the needs which have been met by religion and are now to be met by philosophy are not unchangeable; these themselves can be *weakened* and *eradicated*'.[1]

With respect to art and religion, we have already seen, he accepted this conclusion unflinchingly; it would not be long before he passed the same verdict on morality. At the very moment of acknowledging their historical justification, he was compelled to deny them all other justification. The intellectual conscience is a parricide.

But that was not all. The question now arose once more: what of the intellectual conscience itself? As the offspring and heir of those three, was not this likewise required to produce its credentials? Now that its metaphysical sanction was gone, what proof could it cite of its own ability to ascertain truth, even with regard to the physical world? That was the question which, at one stroke, set Nietzsche clean apart from earlier free-thinkers: since, as he was to point out later, 'our belief in science still always rests on a *metaphysical belief*—even we knowers of today, we godless foes of metaphysics, even we take *our* fire from that conflagration which was kindled by a thousand-year-old faith, from that Christian belief, which was also Plato's, that God is truth, that truth is *divine*'.[2]

The eighteenth-century *philosophes*, while they disclaimed all knowledge of a metaphysical world, never doubted that the physical could be known. However sceptical they might be towards the supernatural, they were confident that reason could comprehend the natural. With rare exceptions, they were not greatly concerned with epistemology. Con-

[1] H, I, 27.   [2] GM III, 24.

tent with the traditional distinction of 'primary' and 'secondary' qualities, they took the objectivity of objects for granted; and if they heard,
did not seriously heed, the paradoxes of Bishop Berkeley. For the most
part, they were simple, down-to-earth materialists. The world, as they
saw it, could be explained in terms of the predetermined motion, in
absolute space and time, of particles of differing mass: it was the 'one
huge, dead, immeasurable steam-engine' of Carlyle.

Nietzsche, however, had submitted to the *Critique of Pure Reason*; and
while he could not, with Kant, 'erect the Cross on the appalling background of the impossibility of knowledge',[1] neither could he recapture
the naive assurance of a Laplace. Resolved as he was to 'distrust of anything and everything',[2] he adopted, not only a Materialist view of
Idealism, but an Idealist view of Materialism.

* * *

His critique of knowledge, unfortunately, was never systematically
presented. Perhaps that is why it has been systematically ignored. He
scarcely more than alludes to it in *Human, All-too-Human* itself. It is only
when we turn to his posthumous papers that we realize how incessantly
it preoccupied him, or what pains he lavished upon it. Yet it was a
natural sequel to his critique of metaphysics—his point of departure, as
we should expect, being widely removed from Kant's. It was an extension of his 'historical philosophizing', which could only have come into
being after the theory of evolution had established itself. How closely
the two critiques were related can be seen from the following note:

'A morality—a mode of life *established* by long experience and trial—
comes to be felt in the end as a law, as *sovereign*. . . . Simultaneously, the
whole assemblage of related values and determinations fuses with it. It
becomes something venerable, unassailable, sacrosanct, true; a condition of its development being that its origin should be *forgotten*. . . .
This is a sign that it has become sovereign. . . .

'It is possible that the same thing has taken place in connection with
the *categories of reason*. It may be that they, after much groping and
fumbling, were eventually established by virtue of their relative utility.
. . . a time came when they were fused into one, when man became
conscious of them as a whole—and ordained them: that is to say, when
they acquired the force of ordinances. . . . From that time forward they
passed as *a priori*, as independent of experience, as ineluctable. And for
all that they may only represent the usage appropriate to certain races
and certain species—their "truth" is merely their utility.'[3]

[1] H, II, 8.   [2] H, III, 213.   [3] WP, 514.

Briefly, then, what Nietzsche contends is that the habits of mind implanted by morality, religion and art are only the latest of a long series acquired in the course of evolution, the earlier of which are now so deeply ingrained that they could no longer be weakened or eradicated, even if this were desirable; and that, like our sense of right and wrong, our sensations of time, space and causality, for instance, may have only subjective validity. Indeed, he insists, the more we know (or think we know) about the motivation of evolution, the less likely it does appear that these should be absolutely 'true'. They are 'seen to be but an idiosyncrasy of one particular species of animals.'[1]

Suppose that an organism is activated exclusively by the instinct of self-preservation, that it virtually *is* this instinct: all it can know of an object is its strength in relation to itself; the idea it forms of this object, therefore, is the projection of an evaluation in terms of pleasure or pain. The projection may increase in complexity with the organism; it does not on that account change its nature. On the contrary, every step towards differentiation is accompanied by a step towards simplification —in effect, towards falsification.

Thus, Nietzsche intimates, we should have to descend to the inorganic world at least, in order to discover an immediate reaction to an external force. At every subsequent level, the force is construed by comparison with previous forces, 'memorized' in the structure of the sense-organ. Again, where several sense-organs are co-ordinated, the machinery of co-ordination embodies a similar 'memory', modifying the image (*Gestalt*) of the object. At each stage, what Kant would have called the 'synthesis of apprehension' comes into play: so that the knowledge an organism acquires of the external world is virtually an artistic creation, formed through the selection of what is relevant from what is irrelevant to the purpose of survival, and the introduction of a unity into the former, expressive of the personality of the creator. A body of knowledge resembles the body of a living creature; and each living creature occupies a world of its own contrivance:

'The entire organic world consists of an assemblage of beings each surrounded by a little universe which they have created by projecting their strength, their desires, their habitual experiences outside themselves, thereby contriving their *external world*. The aptitude for creation (for modelling, discovering, inventing) is their primary aptitude; naturally they have only a similar falsified, invented, simplified idea of themselves.

[1] WP, 515.

' "A being accustomed to a kind of rule in its dreams"—that is the living being. Vast masses of such customs have ended up by congealing to a point at which entire *species* live by them. They are probably propitious to the conditions of existence of such beings.'[1]

Our own world of every day, Nietzsche infers, is only one among the infinite number of such little universes. We have, quite literally, no eyes for what has not, at one time or another, favoured our existence. It is the product of a process of selection and falsification, starting in the dark backward and abysm of time, and still continuing unabated. It is no more definitive or final than that of the grass or the green-fly:

'The sublimity of nature, all those impressions of grandeur, of nobility, of grace, of beauty, of goodness, of austerity, of power, of rapture, which we register in the contemplation of nature, history and mankind, are not *immediate sensations*, but the aftermath of innumerable, deep-rooted *errors*; everything would appear cold and lifeless to us were it not for this long schooling. The firm lines of the mountain, the delicacy of the shades, the particular pleasure conferred by each colour, are already heirlooms. At some time, one colour served less than another to suggest some threatening phenomenon, and little by little it has acquired a soothing effect (blue, for example).'[2]

So much seems relatively sure. But, Nietzsche submits, it is only by virtue of the same process of instinctive selection that we have arrived at the percept, thence at the concept, of the 'thing identical with itself'. We could never have imagined a discrete and stable entity, did we not habitually overlook the continuous interaction of everything known to us, and the uninterrupted sequence of small insignificant changes: 'that is *enduring* whose variations are too gradual and subtle for us to perceive'.[3] And it is only by virtue of this fiction, of the 'thing identical with itself', that we have arrived at our percepts and concepts of space and time. Of space, because 'human spatial laws presuppose the reality the permanence of images, forms and substances, and their endurance, that is, space as we know it belongs only to an imaginary world';[4] of time, because ' "time" will not serve to distinguish rapid movement from slow. In absolute Becoming, no force ever comes to rest, it can never be other than a force: its "more or less rapid movement" cannot be measured, because we lack any static term of reference. . . .'[5] The mechanistic notion of casuality derives from the same fundamental fiction. The framework of the mechanistic universe is thus reduced to the

---

[1] N, XIII, 81.   [2] N, XII, 37.   [3] N, XII, 29.   [4] N, XII, 31.   [5] N, XII, 32.

frame of mind appropriate to a certain species at a certain stage of development. The Newtonian picture of the world is shown to be as 'subjective' as that of everyday. Its 'truth' is merely its utility.

Perhaps it took his partial blindness so to wrest Nietzsche from his artist's immersion in the visible world as to enable him to undertake this critique. One pictures him lying in his darkened room avenging himself, so to speak, on his defective eyesight by indicting it as a deceiver—and then, on stepping out into the sunlight, being dazzled anew by the bright reality of the mirage. One of his posthumous notes happens to corroborate this picture—and, as a summary of his argument, surely merits translation at last?

'When I go out into the open air, I am always astonished at the admirable solidity of all our impressions—the forest appears to us under such and such a form, the mountain under such and such another; there is no confusion, no groping, no hesitation in us with respect to any of our impressions. And yet the greatest uncertainty, a sort of chaos, must once have reigned; long periods of time must have elapsed before all that could have been *settled* by heredity. Those whose perceptions of distance, of light, of colours, etc., were essentially different, were elbowed aside and could only with difficulty perpetuate their species. For thousands of years the different way of feeling must have been suspect and shunned as "*madness*". Mutual understanding was impossible; the "exceptional" was left on one side to perish. From the very beginnings of organic life a horrifying cruelty has eliminated everything that "felt otherwise". *Science*, perhaps, represents only a continuation of this process of elimination, being absolutely impossible unless it acknowledges the "normal man" as the highest standard, to be preserved at all cost. We live within the residue of our ancestors' impressions, embedded, so to speak, in petrified feelings. They invented and created imaginatively—but what decided whether such poems and fantasies should live on was the fact, discovered by experience, of whether they made for life or death. Errors or truths—it was all one, provided life was possible with them. An impenetrable network was woven little by little. We come into a world already *enmeshed* in this network, and science itself cannot extricate us.'[1]

There is no need to emphasize today the force of Nietzsche's critique of Materialism. Now that the conclusions of science itself have, as he foretold, come into collision 'with the erroneous original suppositions,'[2]

[1] N, XII, 38.   [2] H, I, 19.

every one of Kant's synthetic propositions *a priori*, has been super-seded. No educated man will attempt any longer to refurbish the immeasurable steam-engine. It has become as obsolete as the stage-coach.

Nietzsche, however, does not stop at this point. The fundamental propositions of pure mathematics, he goes on to claim, themselves derive from the same fiction as absolute space and time. Mathematics is a species of logic, and the simplest sum, like the simplest syllogism, depends on the assumption, not merely of things identical with them-selves, but of things identical with each other. In reality there are no such things—nor could there be. 'The co-existence of two perfectly *identical* things is impossible', since 'it would presuppose an absolutely identical *origin*', which, in its turn, would presuppose 'the absolutely identical origin of *everything*, that is to say, that everything else would have to be absolutely identical throughout time'.[1] The most we can look for in nature is similar things: 'even in chemistry we ought to speak of "simi-lar" qualities, and not of "the same". . . Nothing repeats itself; in truth every atom of oxygen is unique.'[2] It follows that 'logic (like geo-metry and arithmetic) only applies to *imaginary entities, created by us*. Logic is an attempt to *comprehend the world in accordance with a scheme of Being which we ourselves have drawn up*; *or, more exactly, to make it formulable and predictable to us*'.[3] The reality of becoming is insusceptible to precise formulation, even in mathematical terms.

Here again Nietzsche shows himself well in advance of his time. Fif-teen years later, H. G. Wells was to advance this same criticism, ques-tioning the physicist's assumption that the ultimate unit of nature corre-sponded to the mathematical unit; and, thirty years later still, to point the relevance of his criticism to contemporary discoveries—when the individuality which the physicists had ignored at the outset returned to plague them at last, in the guise of atoms and molecules that obstinately refused to conduct themselves identically.[4] Perhaps it is easier for an artist than it is for a scientist to realize how much is, and must necessarily be, discounted in any purely mathematical exploration of nature. (It was Wells also who once startled his readers by announcing that 'the human mind is as much a product of the struggle for survival as the snout of a pig, and may be as little equipped for the unearthing of fundamental truth'.)

Whatever else it may be, Nietzsche deduces, reality is not logical— 'the world *appears* logical to us because we have begun by *making* it

[1] N, XII, 29.   [2] N, XII, 28.   [3] WP, 516.
[4] 'The Rediscovery of the Unique', *Fortnightly Review*, July, 1891.

logical'.[1] What we might call the post-mechanistic interpretation, therefore, is no less subjective than the mechanistic: 'When Kant says, "the
understanding does not derive its laws from Nature, but dictates them
to her", it is perfectly true with regard to the idea of Nature which we
are compelled to associate with her (Nature = World as representation,
that is to say as error), but which is the summing-up of a number of
errors of the understanding. The laws of numbers are entirely inapplic-
able to a world which is not our representation—these laws obtain only
in the human world.'[2] The 'truth' of this interpretation, too, is merely
its utility.

'In the last analysis, there are only *practical* sciences, founded on the
basic errors of mankind, the admission of things and identical things.'[3]
The most that physics and chemistry can hope to achieve is a 'common
language of signs, enabling us more easily to *calculate*, and so to *control*,
nature'.[4] And that, of course, is a wonderful achievement. The intellectuality which enables man to master an ever-growing mass of facts by
means of signs is his 'highest power'.[5] But, let us never forget, first,
that the facts comprise only the limited selection available to us; secondly
that we can never arrive at more than an approximate (as we might say
nowadays, a statistical) formulation; thirdly, and most important of all,
that even this '*explains nothing*'.[6] The actual reality of the nature, or
nature of the reality, thus calculated and controlled, remains what it has
always been, a *qualitas occulta*.

Having watched the protagonists of mechanistic and atomic theory at
close quarters, Nietzsche concludes, he is persuaded that they too, in the
end, will have to acknowledge the creation of the most concise and comprehensive system of signs as their ultimate aim, and 'renounce explanation'.[7] They too will find that the essence of things eludes their grasp
to the last. 'In short, science is laying the road to *sovereign ignorance*'.[8]
His prediction has been amply fulfilled.

* * *

Although some of the notes just quoted belong to a later date,
Nietzsche's theory of knowledge was complete by 1878 at latest. It is,
therefore, quite incorrect to speak of a 'positivist phase' in his philosophy. Notwithstanding his respect for Comte and anticipations of
'logical positivism', he himself was at no time a positivist. 'In opposition to positivism', he wrote, 'which halts at phenomena—"There are
only *facts*"—I would say: No, facts are precisely what is lacking, only
interpretations.'[9]

[1] WP, 521.   [2] H, I, 19.   [3] N, XII, 33.   [4] N, XIII, 83.
[5] N, XIV, 46.   [6] N, XIII, 84.   [7] N, XIII, 85.   [8] WP, 608.   [9] WP, 481.

On the other hand, of course, neither was he a neo-Idealist like Eddington, whose well-known pronouncements his own so often recall. He had already blocked every peep-hole but one in the *principium individuationis*. The conclusion he ultimately draws, therefore, is as distinctive as it is disconcerting. It is presented, summarily, in the sixteenth aphorism of *Human, All-too-Human*.

Science, he states here (indicating his own science), 'celebrates its greatest triumph in a *history of the origin of thought*', which exposes the world we know as 'a host of errors and fantasies which arose gradually in the general development of organic being, which are intergrown with each other, and are now inherited by us as the accumulated treasure of all the past—as a treasure, for the value of our humanity depends upon it'. In so doing science may 'lift us, at least for moments, above and beyond the whole process'; but it cannot do more; it can never liberate us from the errors and fantasies. What we learn from these moments, indeed, is precisely that no liberation is possible: 'perhaps we shall then recognize that the thing-in-itself is worth a Homeric laugh; that it *seemed* so much, indeed everything, and *is* really empty, namely empty of meaning.'

The wheel has turned full circle. Nietzsche had plunged into the study of science determined to reach bedrock at last, only to find that science itself rules out the possibility of reaching it. There is no bedrock. 'The fact that one can *enumerate* certain phenomena, such as many chemical phenomena, and likewise predict them, gives no warrant for the supposition that one has thereby touched on "absolute truths".'[1] The nearer we approach to the realization that reality is a flux, the more apparent it becomes that absolute truth is unattainable: indeed, that it is a solecism, since there is neither a subject unconditioned by the object and capable of estimating it objectively, nor an object unconditioned by the subject with reference to which it could be estimated. 'Knowledge' is active valuation; 'truth', in the only sense in which it can be retained, a creation:

'The will to truth is a *fixing*; it is a *making* true and lasting, a total elimination of that *false* character, a conversion of it into *what is*. Thus, "truth" is not something which would be there to seek out, to discover, but something *which is to be created* and which lends its name to a *process*, or rather, to a will to overcoming that in itself has no end: introducing truth as a *processus in infinitum*, an *active* determining,—*not* a becoming conscious of something which, in itself, were fixed and determined.'[2]

[1] N, XIV, 34.   [2] WP, 552.

That only is 'true' which bears no relation to ourselves, and for this very reason is meaningless; that only is meaningful which bears some relation to ourselves, and for this very reason is false.

In which case, it may be said, must not even the idea of reality as a flux also be pronounced untrue? Nietzsche concurs. He has arrived back at the point from which he started, at 'the belief that *there is no truth*, the nihilistic belief':[1] and nihilism, of course, is the name for his wholly new position:

'ADVANCE IN FREETHINKING.—The difference between past and present freethinking cannot better be characterized than by that aphorism for the recognition and expression of which all the fearlessness of the eighteenth century was needed, and which even then, if measured by our modern view, sinks into an unconscious naïveté. I mean Voltaire's aphorism, "*croyez-moi, mon ami, l'erreur aussi a son mérite*".'[2]

'Error also has its merit'—as if there were anything other than error!

It is this, the shattering despair of truth itself, that sets Nietzsche finally apart from rationalist as from Romantic—and for him it was truly shattering. We do not have to look far to see that the 'Homeric laugh' was actually an exceedingly hollow one. For, if all that makes life worth living, if the very continuance of life, depends upon error and fantasy— if 'we are from the beginning illogical, and therefore unjust beings, *and can recognize this*'[3]—does not the intellectual conscience stand convicted, by its own testimony, of irrelevance at best, even of parasitism? Is it not destined, after all, to be more of a curse than a blessing to mankind?

Nietzsche's own innermost desire, his profoundest need, has, it seems, come into collision with the nature of things; and the will to truth, which began as a parricide, looks likely to end as a suicide:

'But does not our philosophy thus become a tragedy? Does not truth become hostile to life, to improvement? A question seems to weigh upon our tongue and yet hesitate to make itself heard: whether one *can* consciously remain in untruthfulness? or, supposing one were *obliged* to do this, would not death be preferable? For there is no longer any "shalt"; morality, in so far as it had any "shalt", has been destroyed by our mode of contemplation, just as religion has been destroyed. Knowledge can only allow pleasure and pain, benefit and injury to subsist as motives; but how will these motives come to terms with the sense of truth? They also contain errors (insofar as, as already said, inclination and aversion, and their very incorrect determinations, really decide our

<hr>

[1] WP, 598.   [2] H, II, 4.   [3] H, I, 32.

pleasure and pain). The whole of human life is deeply immersed in untruthfulness; the individual cannot draw it up out of this well without thereby conceiving the deepest distaste for his whole past, without finding his present motives—those of honour, for instance—absurd, and without opposing scorn and disdain to the passions which conduce to happiness in the future. Is it true that there remains but one sole way of thinking which brings after it despair as a personal experience, as a theoretical result, a philosophy of destruction?'[1]

With this we are left face to face with the question, 'What is the value of truth, or the will to truth?'—unanswered, and seemingly unanswerable.

* * *

The average educated man, Nietzsche observes, in *Human, All-too-Human*, tends within the first thirty years of his life to recapitulate a whole epoch of earlier history. Thus, in the nineteenth century, he may grow out of traditional Christianity at an early age, pass through a phase of enlightenment, and come to rest finally in Romanticism—for, after the age of thirty, he is usually 'disinclined for new mental turnings.'[2]

The further progress of culture, however, depends on those with sufficient 'elasticity' to go on developing beyond this point—it is they who set the standard for the next generation; indeed, if they go on long enough, they may actually anticipate the outlook of several succeeding generations. 'Men of great elasticity, like Goethe, for instance, get through almost more than four generations in succession would be capable of; but then they advance too quickly, so that the rest of mankind only comes up with them in the next century, and even then perhaps not completely.'[3] Pre-eminently a man of this type, Nietzsche himself anticipated a scepticism that was to come into its own only fifty years after *Human, All-too-Human* was published.

His foreknowledge of this was, as it happens, one of his great consolations, and was destined, as time went on, to play an ever larger part in his speculations. The more extreme his isolation, the more he needed a reassurance that it was not for nothing—that it was the inevitable price to be paid for a prophetic mission; and already by 1877 the note of exaltation is occasionally audible. For instance, 'Forward upon the path of wisdom, with a firm step and a good heart!'[4] he adjures his readers (and himself) at the close of the fifth Division:

'However you may be situated, serve yourself as a source of experience! Throw off the displeasure at your nature, forgive yourself your

[1] H, I, 34. [2] H, I, 272. [3] *Ibid.* [4] H, I, 292.

own individuality, for in any case you have in yourself a ladder with a hundred steps úpon which you can mount to knowledge. . . . Can you not, with the help of these experiences, follow immense stretches of former humanity with a clearer understanding . . .? And inasmuch as you wish with all your strength to see in advance how the knots of the future are tied, your own life acquires the value of an instrument and means of knowledge. It is within your power to see that all that you have experienced, trials, errors, faults, deceptions, passions, your love and your hope, shall be merged wholly in your aim. This aim is to become a necessary chain of culture-links yourself, and from this necessity to draw a conclusion as to the necessity in the progress of general culture. When your sight has become strong enough to see to the bottom of the dark well of your nature and your knowledge, it is possible that in its mirror you may also behold the far constellations of future cultures. Do you think that such a life with such an aim is too wearisome, too empty of all that is agreeable? Then you have still to learn that no honey is sweeter than that of knowledge, and that the overhanging clouds of trouble must be to you as an udder from which you shall draw milk for your refreshment.'

It is bravely and beautifully spoken; and from this passage, the first of many like it, we see one reason why Nietzsche did not despair absolutely. Only a man in love with the truth can experience the shattering despair of truth, and to such a man despair is impossible. It is impossible because he will always want to know the truth about despair itself. He is that 'Don Juan of knowledge', who, at the last, even 'feels a longing for hell, for this is the last knowledge which seduces him'.[1]

There is no escape: he can no more surrender his ambition to learn from all experience, no matter how bitter it may be, than he can help finding in that very ambition an incentive to go on living. It may be, it is, illogical: but man is from the beginning an illogical and unjust being. Were he not so, there would be no cause for despair; since he is so, despair is not the result.

Nevertheless, in *Human, All-too-Human*, Nietzsche comes as near to despair as any true philosopher can; for it is a shadowy consolation, at best, to be the pioneer of an epoch of nihilism; and he could no longer, as in *Thoughts out of Season*, simply dismiss the illusoriness of ideals. Then he had been able to 'leave the super-historical men to their loathings and their wisdom' with a scarcely concealed relief—'we wish rather today to be joyful in our unwisdom'. Now, identified as he is with wis-

[1] D, 327.

dom, he finds himself joyless in it. The tone of the book as a whole is one of unrelieved gloom.

Even the attempts he makes—and they are many—to find compensations for his disillusionment, only serve in the end to reinforce this impression: since, as he afterwards confessed, it was his exacerbated pride that revolted against the logical consequences of pessimism. He refused to give way to an argument that might be attributed to his physical infirmity: 'in this state of mind we take up a bitter stand against all pessimism in order that it may not appear to be a consequence of our condition, and thus humiliate us as conquered ones'.[1] The artificiality of these silver linings reveals itself every time.

To take one example: it is only, he affirms, when the belief in divine Providence has been discredited that man can begin to take his own future seriously in hand; it is only when his attention has at last been diverted from remote things to things of this world—those everyday matters of health and hygiene, for instance, which the vanity of philosophers has treated as beneath their attention—that further progress becomes possible. At first sight, to be sure, it may seem as though science, unlike metaphysics, is incapable of providing the firm foundations upon which a civilization may be built, 'and as a matter of fact it does need doubt and distrust as its most faithful auxiliaries. Yet, in the course of time, the sum of inviolable truths—those, namely, which have weathered all the storms of scepticism, and all destructive analysis—may have become so great (in the regimen of health, for instance), that one may determine thenceforth to found "eternal" works'.[2] Accordingly, Nietzsche continues, the task of the free spirit resolves itself for the present into a patient accumulation of such truths—a humble, steady winnowing-out of 'little hard grains'[3] of fact from the chaff of theoretical speculation—and with this he professes himself content.

But was he? Three years is long for a man of his temperament to go on 'piling stone upon stone, pebble upon pebble';[4] and towards the end of 'The Wanderer and his Shadow' his impatience becomes unmistakable. 'THE GREAT DANGER OF THE SAVANT' is plainly self-questioning. What, he asks, if the fascination of things close to hand should end by absorbing him completely? What if he should wake up one day and find that time had transformed even him into a 'dexterous dwarf', *unable* any longer to rise above himself? 'He grows anxious as to whether mastery in small things may not be a convenience, an escape from the summons to greatness in life and form.'[5]

Again, in the 'Miscellaneous Maxims and Opinions', Nietzsche turns

[1] D, 114.   [2] H, I, 22.   [3] H, III, 213.   [4] H, I, 37.   [5] H, III, 179.

scornfully on the author of *Thoughts out of Season*: 'only he who can do nothing better should attack the world's evils as the soldier of culture',[1] and only a retrograde mind will find so much evil to attack. True, much that was precious in the past has gone beyond recall—'for instance, circumscribed, primitive national cultures':[2] but, for those who have eyes to see, the very science which has banished these holds out the prospect of still finer things. It is only now that men 'can *consciously* resolve to develop themselves towards a new culture; while formerly they only developed unconsciously and by chance, they can now create better conditions for the rise of human beings, for their nourishment, education and instruction; they can administer the earth economically as a whole, and can generally weigh and restrain the powers of men'.[3] There follows somewhat later a 'vision' which owes more to Comte than to Wagner:

'A VISION.—Hours of instruction and meditation for adults, even the most mature, without compulsion but in accordance with the moral injunction of the whole community; the churches as the places most worthy and rich in memories for the purpose; at the same time daily festivals in honour of the reason that is attained and attainable by man; a newer and fuller budding and blooming of the ideal of the teacher, in which the clergyman, the artist and the physician, the man of science and the sage, are blended, so that their individual virtues should emerge as a collective virtue in their teaching itself, in their discourses, in their method—this is my ever-recurring vision, of which I firmly believe that it has raised a corner of the veil of the future.'[4]

That is noble enough; and the vision was destined to recur in Nietzsche's writings. But could an exclusively scientific culture really satisfy him? Could he finally reconcile himself to the elimination of art?

The evidence speaks for itself. At one moment, we find him toying with the idea that, since an excessive cultivation of science might tend to make men too cold, they would need to be heated up from time to time with 'illusions, one-sidedness, passions',[5] that a higher culture might even have to 'give man a double brain, two brain-chambers, so to speak, one to feel science and the other to feel non-science, which can lie side by side, without confusion, divisible, exclusive'.[6] Surely the oddest defence of the arts ever penned by a writer of genius! At another moment—'supposing', he muses, 'someone were living as much in love with the plastic arts or music as he was carried away by the spirit of science, and that he was to regard it as impossible for him to end this

[1] H. II, 183.   [2] H, I, 24.   [3] *Ibid.*
[4] H, II, 180.   [5] H, I, 251.   [6] *Ibid.*

contradiction by the destruction of one and complete liberation of the other power'[1] . . . What then?

What indeed? Once only does the idea flash upon him that a new kind of artist is conceivable: one who will take as his subject-matter, not the phantasmagoria of mythology, but the reality of science itself; who 'will divine those cases where, in the midst of our modern world and reality (which will not be shirked or repudiated in the usual artistic way) a great, noble soul is still possible, where it may be embodied in harmonious equable conditions, where it may become permanent, visible and representative of a type, and so, by the stimulus to imitation and envy, help to create the future'.[2]

But this glimpse of 'science and art welded into a new unity'[3] is only a glimpse. Nietzsche pursues the idea no farther. And the reason is all too apparent. At this stage, he could not conceive of the true as the beautiful. His knowledge, so far from inspiring, terrified him. In *Human, All-too-Human*, wherever the façade of optimism cracks, it is to disclose a deeply divided mind.

* * *

Nietzsche's mind and body preyed on each other. To make matters worse, in the autumn of 1877 he had to resume his duties at Basle; and if these had been irksome before, they were an unspeakable burden now, persuaded as he had grown in the interval that the first pre-requisite of further progress was a clean sweep of everything savouring of mythology or metaphysics.

Philology, he had concluded in his abandoned polemic, as soon as it attains its goal, condemns itself to death, for its goal 'is to describe ancient culture itself as one to be abolished'.[4] The study of antiquity had become 'superfluous for the training of our youth', and ought to be superseded 'by the science of the *future*'.[5] Small wonder that within three months of his return his precarious health showed signs of giving way once again.

He hung on until the spring of 1879. Then neither he nor the university authorities could dissemble any longer his incapacity to shoulder his responsibilities. Nothing remained but to hand in his resignation. In grateful acknowledgement of past services, they awarded him an annual pension of a thousand francs, to be renewed for the ensuing six years.

At the time, it hardly looked as though Nietzsche would need it so long. Free though he now was to go where he liked and do what he wanted, his disease only gained upon him. From Basle he fled to Berne, from Berne to Wiesen, from Wiesen to St. Moritz (it was in the course

[1] H, I, 276.   [2] H, II, 99.   [3] *Ibid.*   [4] TS, V, 184.   [5] *Ibid.*

of these wretched wanderings that 'The Wanderer and his Shadow' was compiled)—all to no avail. The quest for health proved as fruitless as the quest for truth. At last, a beaten man, he retreated to his point of departure—to Naumburg.

'Here', he wrote to Peter Gast, 'I *will* have no thoughts.'[1] He had resolved to follow out Voltaire's injunction literally—to 'cultivate his garden'. On a plot of land near the city wall, 'I have ten fruit trees', he continued with pathetic pride, 'roses, lilies, carnations, strawberries, gooseberries and currants. In the spring my work will be extended to ten beds of vegetables. It is all my own idea and gives me great pleasure.'

But even Voltaire failed him. The pleasure did not last. Try as he might to ward off the raging attacks of migraine, Nietzsche could no more escape his problems than his shadow; and, as the year drew to an end—'the most dreadful of my life'[2]—he began to prepare for his own end also. Only his 'hero-will' remained unbroken. 'I shall depart,' he told Gast, 'without bitterness and unbowed.'[3]

[1] L, 30, 9, 79.   [2] L, 31, 12, 79.   [3] *Ibid.*

VI

THE PHYSICIAN

Yet Nietzsche did not die. Instead, to his own and everyone else's amazement, the opening weeks of 1880 saw the beginnings of a slow recovery. He had survived the worst of his illness, as he had the worst of his despair. By February, notwithstanding severe relapses, he was able once more to shake the dust of Naumburg from his feet, and head for his beloved Italy.

He had never liked Naumburg. It was not only the fogs and cold winds that made him cry out against 'this terrible gloomy North';[1] the atmosphere was saturated with the pietism that had so much oppressed his childhood. His mother's anxieties were a continual irritant. Though she could understand neither him nor his books, nothing could prevent her from reading them, and what she read filled her with dismay. How could her Fritz have turned out so unlike his father? She could only put it down to some wilful perversity, and, when her own remonstrances proved futile, the opinions of uncles, aunts and neighbours were enlisted to persuade him of the error of his ways.

We can find something comic, as well as pathetic, in the spectacle of Nietzsche, at the very height of his powers, still being subjected to these sorrowful dissuasions. He could not. He hated giving his mother pain; hated the feeling of guilt it gave him; hated her for causing this feeling, and himself for harbouring such hatred. There is ample evidence that he never suffered the stings of a bad conscience more acutely than when engaged in uprooting conscience.

At Sorrento, on the other hand, he had learned to admire a way of life warmer, richer and more carefree than anything he had known in Germany. In his vocabulary, the word 'southern' stands for all these qualities. Italy had been a revelation to him, as it has to so many other men of letters, German, French and English, who have fled the Philistinism of their compatriots. If he could not himself capture the spontaneity of a people untouched by puritanism or prosperity, he could at least, among them, escape the necessity of acting a part in order to avoid giving offence, and the resentment this necessity occasioned. He was not thrown perpetually onto the defensive: after his own fashion, he could

[1] L, 1, 80.

relax and breathe freely. Once, comparing Byron with Rousseau, he remarked that 'he too screwed himself up to sublime attitudes and to revengeful rage—a sign of vulgarity; ater on, when Venice restored his equilibrium, he understood what *alleviates more* and does *more good . . . l'insouciance.*'[1]

It was to Venice that Nietzsche repaired in the early spring of 1880, to rejoin the congenial Gast; and there, almost at once, his spirits too began to revive. He did not stay long: the heat of summer sent him up to the Engadine; the following winter found him alone at Genoa. He was still subject to frequent and painful recurrences of the old disorder, still wretchedly lonely at times. But the formidable, if heroic, tension of *Human, All-too-Human* is absent from the new collection of aphorisms compiled in January 1881, and its very title tells a tale: *The Dawn of Day.*

Two closely related aphorisms point the contrast. In the last of the 'Miscellaneous Maxims and Opinions', he had drawn a sombre likeness between himself and Odysseus:

'I too have been in the Underworld, even as Odysseus, and I shall often be there again. Not sheep alone have I sacrificed, that I might be able to converse with a few dead souls, but not even my own blood have I spared. There were four pairs who responded to me in my sacrifice: Epicurus and Montaigne, Goethe and Spinoza, Plato and Rousseau, Pascal and Schopenhauer. With them I have come to terms. When I have long wandered alone, I will let them prove me right or wrong; to them will I listen, if they prove each other right or wrong. In all that I say, conclude, or think out for myself and others, I fasten my eyes on those eight and see their eyes fastened on mine.—May the living forgive me if I look upon them at times as shadows, so pale and fretful, so restless and, alas! so eager for life.'

In one of the last aphorisms of *The Dawn of Day*, Nietzsche reverts to this simile (adding, significantly, 'the mother of Odysseus died of grief and yearning for her child').[2] The Free Spirit, he declares, is compelled to break the hearts of his stay-at-home friends by his long and lonely voyaging in strange seas. But—having found in the companionship of the dead a compensation for the loss of the living—he returns in the end from the Underworld with a new courage and hope.

* * *

This return, it need hardly be said, was not accomplished without exertion, setbacks, and frequent relapses into despair. 'The habits of our senses have wrapped us up in a tissue of lying sensations', he cries at

[1] WP, 100.   [2] D, 562.

one moment, 'which in their turn are the basis of all our judgements and "knowledge"—there is no exit or escape to the *real world*!'[1] The heading of that aphorism is 'IN PRISON'—and in prison Nietzsche still often felt himself to be. It is, therefore, no surprise to find him still seeking ways of escape.

One way there was which he had not as yet explored: one that Schopenhauer had taken before him, and Eddington was to take after-wards—the way of introspection. Might not the psychologist solve the riddle which the physicist could only propound? Might not that essence of things which eluded, and was bound to elude, the investigator of the objective world, yield to an investigation of the subjective? 'The answer to the riddle,' Schopenhauer had affirmed, 'is given to the subject of knowledge who appears as an individual, and the answer is—will.' The will is the man-in-himself; by analogy we may conclude that it is the thing-in-itself. 'Surely,' Eddington was to claim, 'that mental and spiritual nature of ourselves, known in our mind by an intimate contact transcending the methods of physics, supplies just that interpretation of the symbols which science is unable to give.' This emergency exit was at least worth consideration, and in *The Dawn of Day* Nietzsche turned to it.

By this time, however, he was a far more critical psychologist than Schopenhauer had ever been. Already, in *Human, All-too-Human*, he had pointed out that the propensity of men to deceive themselves, so important in Schopenhauer's eyes, had been a commonplace among moralists for centuries (which is true, notwithstanding that some of our contemporaries suppose it an even more recent discovery): and all that those moralists had written about 'rationalization', his own observation had confirmed. He was, indeed, too honest an introspective not to doubt the possibility of honest introspection, and this doubt damped his hope from the start.

Is it really 'an immediately certain truth' (and not a mere tautology) 'that every voluntary motion is the manifestation of an act of will'? Does our self-knowledge really justify such an affirmation, to say nothing of the far-reaching conclusions Schopenhauer bases upon it? Nietzsche expressed his misgivings, as his habit was, antithetically: 'what men have found it so difficult to understand from the most ancient times down to the present day is their ignorance in regard to themselves, not merely with respect to good and evil, but something even more essential. The oldest of illusions lives on, namely, that we know, and know precisely, in each case, *how human action is originated*.'[2]

[1] D, 117.   [2] D, 116.

Schopenhauer had confidently assumed that we can tell what motives govern our actions, and so pronounce judgements on character. But can we? Before any conclusions could be reached, it was necessary to examine this premise; and it would be hard to find a better illustration of Nietzsche's own dictum, 'original minds are distinguished, not by being the first to see a new thing, but by seeing the old, well-known thing, which is seen and overlooked by everyone, as something new',[1] than the succession of pregnant aphorisms in which he demolished nineteenth-century psychology. For the starting-point of his investigation was—dreams.

They had always preoccupied him. Scattered up and down his writings may be found a small armoury of observations on this subject. For example, in *Human, All-too-Human*, he advises his readers to consult their dreams if they want to know how they really feel towards their relatives and friends. And dreams, he now intimates, are alone sufficient to betray the existence in ourselves of motives and impulses to action, of which we not merely take no account, but are totally unaware. Indeed, he says, the very fact that men are unanimous in disowning these particular works of art (and works of art they surely are, these 'symbolic concatenations of scenes and images')[2] is eloquent of their self-revelatory nature:

'You would be responsible for everything—except only your dreams! What miserable weakness, what lack of logical courage! Nothing is *more* your own than your dreams! Nothing is more your own work! Substance, form, duration, actor, spectator—in these comedies you are everything yourself. And yet it is just here that you are ashamed of yourselves, and already Oedipus, the wise Oedipus, was drawing consolation from the thought that we cannot be blamed for what we dream. From this I conclude that the great majority of men must be conscious of some horrifying dreams.'[3]

In the light of a more developed psychology, we may detect, in this very association of ideas, an illustration of Nietzsche's thesis.

The dream-world, he goes on to suggest, is a compensatory world. It is those cravings which happen to have been frustrated by day that seek an imaginary fulfilment by night, the fact that virtually identical stimuli are invested with such diverse interpretations being due to the difference of interpreter: 'another instinct wished to play a part, to show itself, to exercise itself and be refreshed and discharged'.[4]

If this is the case, however, may we not, even when awake, be in-

[1] H, II, 200.   [2] H, III, 194.   [3] D, 128.   [4] D, 119.

fluenced more than we suppose by unconscious needs and desires? It is unlikely, to say the least, that they should be wholly in abeyance by day. May we not, to take an example, react to the same event or person in such different ways at different times simply because different instincts happen to be craving for outlet? We attribute the variations in our reactions to variations in the events or people provoking them, but in doing that we may, again, merely be acting like the dreamer—inverting cause and effect. For 'everyone knows from experience how quickly the dreamer weaves into his dream a loud sound that he hears . . . that is to say, explains it from *afterwards*, so that he first *thinks* he experiences the producing circumstances and then that sound'.[1]

Of course not all our motives are unconscious. Sometimes we envisage a situation beforehand and determine our conduct accordingly. We experience what we call a 'conflict of motives', and have to decide, more or less painfully, between alternative courses of action. But how often, when the moment actually arrives, we are still betrayed by some unforeseen impulse into doing the very opposite of what we planned! It is a safe conjecture that the real 'conflict of motives' has been proceeding all the while unknown to us, and that the total effect of our conscious deliberations has been merely to set one 'very necessary motive in the line of combat with the other motives'.[2] Even when we do act as we have planned, moreover, there is no proof that our conscious deliberations have been the decisive factor: 'I am as little able to draw up this battle-line as to see it: the battle itself is hidden from my sight, as likewise is the victory, as victory; for I certainly know what I finally *do*, but I do not know which motive has actually proved to be the victor.'[3]

In short, unconscious impulses probably play some part in all our actions—and the possibility must not be ruled out that they play the whole part. It is, at all events, conceivable that the ends we consciously postulate have no effect whatsoever: 'why could not an "end" be merely an *accompanying feature* in the series of changes among the active forces which bring about the action—a pale stenographic symbol stretched in consciousness beforehand, and which serves as guide to what happens, even as a symbol of what happens, *not* as its cause . . . ? Are not all conscious phenomena only final phenomena—the last links in a chain, but apparently conditioning one another in their sequence within the plane of consciousness?'[4]

These words are taken, not from *The Dawn of Day*, but from a note written several years later. But it is clear that Nietzsche had already

<hr />

[1] H, I, 13. [2] D, 129. [3] *Ibid.* [4] WP, 666.

entered upon what he was then to call 'the phase of *modesty of conscious-ness*'—when 'we learn not to make ourselves responsible for our self, since *we*, as conscious, purposive beings, are but the smallest part of it'.[1] We have grown accustomed, he writes in *The Dawn of Day* itself, to believe in two separate kingdoms—the human kingdom of purposes and volition, and the non-human of accident and chance, which so often scatters our best-laid plans; in mythological language, the domains of the dwarfs and the giants. It now appears that chance may be the single sovereign over both.

But does not such a conclusion cast doubt on the very argument that leads to it? If all rational thought is merely the reflection of irrational forces, proceeding unknown to the thinker, what title has Nietzsche's own thought to command our confidence? Manifestly, none whatever: he grimly admits it. It is exactly what he suspected from the start: intro-spection does indeed establish the futility of introspection as a means of arriving at truth:

'Let us learn then, for it is time we did so, that even in our supposed separate domain of aims and reason the giants likewise rule. And our aims and reason are not dwarfs, but giants. And our own webs are just as often and as clumsily rent *by ourselves* as by the slate. And not everything is purpose that is called purpose, and still less is everything will that is called will. And if you come to the conclusion, "Then there is only one domain, that of stupidity and hazard?" it must be added that possibly there is only one domain, possibly there is neither will nor aim, and we may only have imagined these things. Those iron hands of necessity that shake the dice-box of chance continue their game in-definitely: hence, it *must* happen that certain throws perfectly resemble every degree of appropriateness and good sense. It may be that our own voluntary acts and purposes are merely such throws, and that we are too circumscribed and vain to conceive our extremely circumscribed state! that we ourselves shake the dice-box with iron hands, and do nothing in our most deliberate actions but play the game of necessity. Possibly! To rise beyond this "possibly" we should already have to have been guests in the Underworld, away from all that is of the surface, and to have played at dice and betting with Proserpine at the table of the goddess herself.'[2]

And so the portcullis rings down on the last gateway to the 'real world'. Nietzsche's scepticism with regard to the objective is completed by a scepticism, no less absolute, with regard to the subjective. 'We have

[1] WP, 666.   [2] D, 130.

taken great pains to learn that external things are not as they appear to us.—Well! It is the same with the inner world. Moral acts are in reality "something different",—we cannot say more, and all acts are essentially unknown.'[1] The inner world, as much as the outer, is a world of appearances. Our knowledge of the universe is conditioned from first to last by the instrumental role of the intellect; and from this role there is no evidence that it can ever break free. 'Misery and disgust!'[2]

* * *

Nietzsche had reached the point at which Christianity of a certain persuasion calls for the 'leap of faith'. If—so runs the argument—reason can never bring certainty, then there must be a revelation: for to live in absolute scepticism is intolerable. From this it is a short step to submission, to either the Church or the Bible. He himself was aware of the call: that was one reason why his eyes were so often fastened on Pascal. Pascal is his sparring-partner in *The Dawn of Day*, as Schopenhauer had been in *Human, All-too-Human*.

But Nietzsche could not respond to the call: if only because he saw that the leap of faith itself presupposed a faith, and his scepticism extended even to that. Why, he had already asked, this assumption that the nature of things is so ordered as to be tolerable to us?—'There is no pre-established harmony between the promotion of truth and the welfare of mankind.'[3]

That he called a 'fundamental insight', and it is nothing less. Only when we have grasped it, can we see what he meant, when he defined Pascal's religion as 'a continuous suicide of reason'.[4] The definition has been criticized on the ground that Pascal was a very great reasoner, indeed, a great mathematician, and always eager to establish the rationality of faith itself. But Nietzsche, far from disputing this, stressed it. The great French free-thinkers, he said, owed much of their superiority to that of the Christians they were matched against—Fénélon, Mme. de Guyon, the leading Huguenots and 'that foremost of all Christians in his combination of ardour, intellect and honesty, Pascal'.[5] Still, he insisted, even Pascal's argumentation started out from the one 'capital error' or assumption: 'he believed that he could prove Christianity true on the ground that it was necessary: and that presupposes the existence of a true and righteous providence which sees to it that everything *necessary* is also true'.[6]

Of course, even if we grant this assumption, Pascal's further deductions remain questionable. It does not follow, for instance, because a revelation is necessary, that the Christian Church is its vehicle. The

[1] D, 116. [2] D, 483. [3] H, I, 517. [4] BGE, 46. [5] D, 192. [6] N, XI, 320.

benefits alleged to have been conferred by the Church no more sub-
stantiate its veracity than the acquittal of a criminal in the dock does that
of defending counsel. Neither the joyfulness of the believer nor the
inflexible courage of the martyr proves more than the strength of their
faith: a madman may derive both from his *idée fixe*. 'We do not deny',
Nietzsche was to write later, 'that "faith brings joy": *for that very
reason* we do deny that faith *proves* anything; a strong faith, which
brings joy, causes suspicion of the object of that faith; it does not establish its "truth", it does establish a certain probability of—*illusion*.'[1]

Nevertheless, it was upon Pascal's initial assumption that he concentrated his fire—and rightly, for it is upon this that the leap of faith
depends:

'How many are there who still come to the conclusion: "Life would
be intolerable were there no God!" Or, as is said in Idealist circles:
"Life would be intolerable if its ethical significance were lacking."
Hence there must be a God—or an ethical significance of existence! In
reality the case stands thus: He who is accustomed to conceptions of this
sort does not desire a life without them, hence these conceptions may
be necessary for him and his preservation—but what a presumption to
decree that everything necessary for my preservation must actually
be there! As if my preservation were something necessary!'[2]

From scepticism of this sort, the 'leap of faith' offers no escape.

If such scepticism is really intolerable, therefore, we must frankly
conclude that the intellectual conscience is hostile to life—there is no
a priori reason why it should not be—and resign ourselves to the consequences: the extinction either of honesty or of mankind:

'My brothers! let us not conceal it from ourselves: science, or more
plainly speaking, the *passion for science*, is here—a formidable, new,
growing power, the like of which has never yet been seen, with eagle's
wings, owl's eyes and the feet of a dragon—yes, it is already so strong
that it grasps itself as a problem and asks: "how am I even possible
among *mankind*! How will mankind be possible *with me*!"'[3]

* * *

In *Human, All-too-Human*, as we saw, Nietzsche did all but resign
himself to this conclusion: and the gloom of it still recurs in his writing.
By the time of *The Dawn of Day*, however, he is by no means so fully
persuaded that to live in absolute scepticism is intolerable. Atheism itself,
he is beginning to find, has a compensation: and it is in opposition to
Pascal that he formulates this as well.

[1] GM, III, 24.   [2] D, 90.   [3] N, XII, 6.

Pascal's ambition, as Nietzsche saw it, was to track human egoism down to its last hiding-place, drag it out to the light of day, and so expose once and for all the total depravity of man's nature. To this end he had bent his incomparable powers of psychological analysis, sparing the self-deceptions of others as little as Schopenhauer, and his own as little as theirs. He had 'made an attempt to find out whether it was not possible, with the help of the very subtlest knowledge, to drive everybody to despair'[1]—in order that everybody should fling himself at the foot of the Cross. And, if 'he failed—to his second despair',[2] that was only because men were as dishonest as he had portrayed them: his failure was the measure of his success.

On anyone honestly convinced that egoism was sinful, and conscience the voice of an outraged deity, Nietzsche believed, the effect of Pascal's critique must be devastating. In the first place, he would be overcome by the terror of Hell—a terror which has embittered the deaths of countless thousands of men, and the whole lives of others who have witnessed these death-bed agonies. In one indignant aphorism, he asserts that no torments inflicted by man upon man have exceeded those endured as a result of this superstition, and possibly he was right. Though it is soft-pedalled by the Churches today, we have only to recall what Kierke-gaard suffered through his father's persuasion that he had sinned against the Holy Ghost, to see how real it has been in the past. (It is regrettable that Nietzsche never came to know Kierkegaard. He would certainly have rated him highly, and his comments on a psychologist with whom he had still more in common would have been of the deepest interest.)

In the second place, the believer would have no option but to seek, by every refinement of self-mortification, to extirpate his passions entirely: for every passion is inescapably egoistic; the effect of Pascal's critique is to bring the whole of man's life under the rubric 'sin'. It was because Pascal himself drew this conclusion, and, unlike Schopenhauer, acted upon it, that Nietzsche pronounced him 'the one logical Christian'.[3] If he not merely read but loved the author of *Pensées*, he said, it was 'as the most instructive sacrifice to Christianity, slowly done to death, first bodily, then mentally, according to the terrible consistency of this most appalling form of inhuman cruelty.'[4]

Pascal was a great psychologist and Nietzsche, like the free-thinkers, had learned from him. 'When,' he writes again, 'trained in this Christian school of scepticism, we now read the moral books of the ancients, for example those of Seneca and Epictetus, we feel a pleasurable superiority, and are full of secret penetration,—it seems to us as if a child talked

[1] D, 64.   [2] *Ibid.*   [3] L, 20, 11, 88.   [4] EH, p. 38.

before an old man, or a pretty, gushing girl before La Rochefoucauld: we know better what virtue is!¹'

If Pascal was great, however, he himself was greater still: for we free spirits, he goes on, 'have applied this same scepticism to all *religious* states and processes, such as sin, repentance, grace, sanctification, and have allowed the worm to burrow so well, that we now have the same feeling of subtle superiority and insight even in reading all Christian books: we know also the religious feelings better!'²

Nietzsche, in other words, had gone a stage further even than Pascal (or Kierkegaard), having tracked down conscience itself, including the intellectual conscience prompting the *Pensées*, to egoism. And if the first result of *this* critique was, by destroying the evidence for a supernatural world, to plunge whoever submitted to it into the depths of intellectual despair, a second result, as he now saw, was to lift him clean out of moral despair: for with the supernatural sanction for conscience went all that Pascal had deduced from it.

If sentiments, impulses and actions motivated by conscience differ only in degree, not in kind, from those of which conscience disapproves, then indeed, there are 'no moral actions at all'³—in the sense of actions freely or disinterestedly performed. If, on the other hand, absolute altruism is a fiction, and a self-contradictory fiction at that—then neither are there any immoral! The very ejaculation, 'human, alas! all-too-human',⁴ bespeaks a continued adherence to the absolute, whose logical basis has been destroyed. If 'nothing is true, everything is allowed'.⁵

Nietzsche had won a glimpse of this in *Human, All-too-Human* itself. There had been moments, even then, when he had been able, in a kind of ecstasy, to rise above his own life 'and look down into the depths of reason and unreason';⁶ when, pressing home to his soul the defeat of his innermost desire, he had experienced in that very anguish the throes of a new birth.

Thus, 'the complete irresponsibility of man for his actions and his nature',⁷ he had written, 'is indeed the bitterest pill which he who understands must swallow, if he has been accustomed to see the patent-of-nobility of his humanity in responsibility and duty.' To recognize that all our actions are determined; that what we experience as choice is only the rivalry of conflicting impulses and the victory of the strongest; that the single craving for self-gratification satisfies itself in every situation; that what we call good is but a sublimation of what we call evil, and what we call evil a degradation of what we call good: 'to recognize all

---

¹ JW, 122.   ² *Ibid.*   ³ D, 148.   ⁴ EH p. 83.
⁵ GM, III, 24.   ⁶ D, 114.   ⁷ H, I, 107.

this may be deeply painful, *but consolation comes after—such pangs are the pangs of birth*'.[1] Out of this very knowledge is born a habit of mind that precludes despair:

'Everything is necessity—so says the new knowledge, and this knowledge itself is necessity. Everything is innocence, and knowledge is the road to insight into this innocence. . . . Even if the inherited habit of erroneous valuations, love and hatred, continue to reign in us, yet under the influence of growing knowledge it will become weaker; a new habit, that of comprehension, of not loving, not hating, of overlooking, is gradually implanting itself in us upon the same ground, and in thousands of years will perhaps be powerful enough to give humanity the strength to produce wise, innocent (consciously innocent) men, as it now produces unwise, guilt-conscious men,—*that is the necessary preliminary step, not its opposite.*'[2]

It is, indeed, no small thing to be rid of 'the goading of the thought that one is not only nature or more than nature'[3]—of the illusion, in Spinoza's words, of an *imperium in imperio*. In this passage, as in that which adjures us to become necessary chains of culture-links, there is an authentic gleam of Spinoza's *amor intellectualis*—and Spinoza, it will be recalled, was one of those Shades who had responded to Odysseus's sacrifice.

In *Human, All-too-Human*, it had still been no more than a gleam, 'The butterfly wants to break through its chrysalis: it rends and tears it, and is then blinded by the unaccustomed light. . . . The sun of a new gospel throws its rays upon the highest point of the soul . . . then the mists gather thicker than ever, and the brightest light and the dreariest shadow lie side by side.'[4] Now, however, what he had glimpsed at those moments, Nietzsche saw face to face: and there can be no doubt at all that it brought him an immense personal relief.

* * *

He himself had never, except as a child, been touched by the terror of Hell; nor, at any rate after 1866, had he made any consistent effort to live up to the ascetic ideal. As a boy, however, and perhaps as a man, he certainly had been afflicted with feelings of guilt regarding his sexual nature. There is no mistaking the personal accent of a passage such as the following:

'The passions become evil and malignant when regarded with evil and malignant eyes. It is in this way that Christianity has succeeded

[1] H, I, 107.   [2] *Ibid.*   [3] H, I, 34.   [4] H, I, 107.

in transforming Eros and Aphrodite—sublime powers, capable of idealization—into hellish genii and phantom goblins, by means of the pangs
which every sexual impulse was made to raise in the conscience of
believers. Is it not a dreadful thing to transform necessary and normal
sensations into a source of inward misery, and thus arbitrarily to render
interior misery necessary and normal *in the case of every man?* Furthermore this misery remains a secret, with the result that it is all the more
deeply rooted; for it is not all men who have the courage, which Shakespeare shows in his sonnets, of confessing to their Christian gloom on
this point.'[1]

It reminds one of Blake's indignant, 'Children of a later age . . .' And in
his autobiography Nietzsche was to express himself still more violently.
One clause of his own moral code, he says there, would read as follows:
'Preaching of Chastity is a public incitement to unnatural practices. All
depreciation of the sexual life, all sullying of it by means of the concept
"impure", is *the* crime against life—is the veritable sin against the Holy
Spirit of Life.'[2]

Long before it became such common knowledge as it is today
(though still far from common enough), Nietzsche saw that the very
branding of sexuality as evil served to make it evil. In effect, he pointed
out, it could never be extirpated—the Christian 'who thinks he has
killed his sensuality is wrong, for his sensuality still lives in an uncanny
vampire form, and torments him in hideous disguises'[3]—and the attempt
to extirpate it could have only the direst consequences to humanity.
What generations of children might have suffered directly from being
conceived in a sense of sin could never be known; what European culture had suffered was manifest on every hand:

'We couple the generation of human beings with a bad conscience!
The final outcome of this diabolization of Eros is a farce: the "devil"
Eros has gradually become of greater interest to mankind than all the
angels and saints, thanks to the mumbo-jumbo and mystification of the
Church in all things erotic: it is thanks to the Church that the *love-story*
has become, down to our own time, the one real interest common to all
circles—with an exaggeration which would have been incomprehensible
to antiquity, and which will provoke roars of laughter in the future. All
our poetizing and thinking, from the highest to the lowest, is marked,
and more than marked, by the excessive importance bestowed on the
love story as the principal item. Posterity may perhaps, on this account,

[1] D, 76.   [2] EH, p. 66.   [3] H, III, 83.

judge the entire legacy of Christian culture to be something narrow and insane.'[1]

What would he have written, if he had lived on into the age of the cinema? The posterity he anticipated is still very far from sight.

Not only had Nietzsche suffered directly the consequences of a puritan upbringing, but, as we know, the guilt attendant upon his excesses at Bonn had contributed largely to his conversion by Schopenhauer. Schopenhauer, in fact, had done for him precisely what Pascal aimed to do (he was, Nietzsche said, 'a modern Pascal, with Pascalian judgements of value'[2])—and the effect of that conversion had been, not to mitigate but to exacerbate, his guilt. In all probability—such was his revulsion of feeling at the time—he had suppressed his sexuality altogether; and it was not merely a vocational frustration that set him seeking a 'drug' or 'intoxicant' in metaphysics and Wagnerian music.

'The worst disease of mankind has arisen from the struggle against diseases, and the apparent remedies have in the long run brought about something worse than it was intended to remove by their use. In their ignorance, men believed that the momentarily effective, stupifying and intoxicating means, the so-called consolations, were the true healing powers; they did not even observe that they often had to pay for their immediate relief by a general and profound worsening of their pain, that the sick had to suffer from the after-effects of the intoxication, then from the absence of the intoxication, and later still from an oppressive feeling of disquietude, nervous starts and general ill-health. Men whose sickness had reached a certain stage never recovered from it—those physicians of the soul, universally accredited and revered, saw to that. It has justly been said of Schopenhauer that he was one who again took the sufferings of humanity seriously: where is the man who will at length take the antidotes to these sufferings seriously, and pillory the unheard-of quackery with which men, even up to our own age, and under the most high-sounding names, have been wont to treat the illnesses of their souls?'[3]

To Nietzsche, at this moment, Christianity seemed little more than a systematic exploitation of the sense of sin. He even went so far as to intimate that guilt-consciousness, in the form he knew it, had been deliberately instilled by the priest, in order that he might thereafter step in with his pharmacopœia of quack remedies, securing undisputed ascendancy. And once again, he may have been right: some missionaries could be invoked in witness. 'Alas, how much superfluous cruelty has

[1] D, 76.   [2] WP, 1017.   [3] D, 57.

been brought about by those religions which invented sin! and by those men who, by means of such religions, desired to reach the highest enjoyment of their power!'[1]

The love of power, he adds, has been 'the demon of mankind'.[2] Born originally of the 'feeling of impotence and fear'[3] besetting man in primitive times, it has gradually 'become his strongest propensity, and the means he has discovered for gratifying it form almost the entire history of culture'.[4]

So—the truth now becomes plain to us—in tracing the way in which mankind had seized on supernatural explanations for conscience, Nietzsche, in *Human, All-too-Human*, had been doing nothing more nor less than retrace his own procedure of ten years before. He had been using history to illuminate his own experience—gazing, as he afterwards put it, 'over the broad and dangerous territory through which my mind had up to that time wandered'.[5] In taking sides against himself, he had accomplished—perhaps he was the first to accomplish—a virtual self-analysis. And now he was tasting the fruits. If psychological factors had, as he believed, contributed to his breakdown, their removal undoubtedly contributed to his recovery.

Here indeed was a compensation for the loss of 'an ethical significance of existence'! It was almost a justification in itself—and all the greater by virtue of his persuasion that, in liberating himself, he was paving a way for the liberation of others. Not that he supposed—or, if he did suppose it, he was speedily undeceived—that the sense of sin would vanish as soon as its origin was known. The evil that men do lives after them, and guilt-consciousness was too firmly established in men of his generation to be exorcised quite so easily. But he did believe that it could no longer be systematically exacerbated and exploited, that it might, on the contrary, be very materially eased: 'to soothe the imagination of the patient, in order that at least he does not have to suffer more from his thoughts concerning his illness than from the illness itself, which has been the case hitherto—that, it seems to me, is something! and it is by no means a trifle! And now do you understand our task?'[6]

Nietzsche believed, in short, that he had alighted on the one true remedy for that moral despair which Pascal, like Schopenhauer, had striven to induce with the help of the very subtlest knowledge: it was a knowledge even subtler. The cure for a partial analysis was a complete one. Consequently, as in *Human, All-too-Human*, so in *The Dawn of Day*, he pictures the emergence of a new type of physician, combining

[1] D, 53.   [2] D, 262.   [3] D, 23.   [4] *Ibid.*   [5] GM, Preface, 2.   [6] D, 54.

the roles of doctor and priest—an ideal physio- and psycho-therapist. No doubt he thought of himself as a rudimentary specimen of the type— and if so, he was not deluded. To Pascal's '*le moi est toujours haissable*', he opposed the contrary maxim: 'Love yourselves through Grace, and you will no longer find your God necessary, and the entire drama of the Fall and Redemption of mankind will reach its last act in yourselves.'[1]

* * *

On the first stage of his journey from the Underworld, Nietzsche arrived at what Sigmund Freud called 'the psychological ideal, the primacy of the intellect'. His cryptic statement, in *The Dawn of Day*, of most of the premises of psycho-analysis, presents a striking (and much neglected) instance of the almost-simultaneous formulation, by two or more men, of the same scientific theory.

Nevertheless, this was only the first stage. In a preface written six years later, he was to warn his readers that his aphorisms were meant to be read slowly, and we do well to bear the warning in mind. Many of them have a deceptive simplicity; their arrangement, too, appears more casual than it is. We may be sure that he knew what he was about when he set the following sentences at the opening of Book IV:

'We have considered, and finally established that there is nothing good, nothing beautiful, nothing sublime, nothing evil, in itself, but rather that there are states of soul in which we bestow such epithets on things outside ourselves and in us. We have taken back the predicates from things, or at all events remembered that we have *lent* them these predicates. Let us take care lest, with this insight, we lose the faculty of lending and become at the same time *wealthier* and *more avaricious*.'[2]

Nietzsche saw (more clearly than Freud) that 'the greatest freedom of the conscious intellect'[3] spelt the abrogation, not merely of ancestral, but also of contemporary, prejudices. If conscience could not be taken on trust, much less could convention. For a man to adapt himself to society, therefore, would be as irrational as to adapt himself to the Church. This freedom spelt a new obligation: to decide what was 'good' or 'bad' for oneself. And here, of course, a new and far-reaching question arose: by what criterion were his judgments to be formed, on things outside himself and in him? To put it another way, what 'condition of soul' was he to adopt as his norm?

To this question Nietzsche now addressed himself; and although, in a sense, he had already assumed an answer, in his discussion of sexual repression, it was my no means so easy to formulate. A hint of the direc-

[1] D, 79. [2] D, 210. [3] H, III, 212.

tion his thought took is supplied by a note jotted down: 'One no longer chooses one's food for moral reasons; in the same way, one will one day cease to "do good" for moral reasons.'[1]

When we speak nowadays of food as 'good' or 'bad', we do not impute any moral qualities to it. It may have been otherwise in Biblical times, but we have recollected that we have merely lent the things these predicates. All we infer is that the dish in question is good or bad *for us*, in other words that it conduces to our health or the reverse: and health we assess by the (very subjective) criterion of happiness. He began therefore by simply extending the concept 'health' to embrace mental as well as physical well-being, declaring that whatever made for his happiness the individual was entitled to call 'good', whatever militated against it, 'bad'. To evaluate for oneself meant to ask on every occasion, not 'is this right or wrong?' but 'will this conduce to my pleasure or pain?'

Put in that way, the answer sounds like a passport to anarchy: and Nietzsche was the first to admit it. He knew quite well that his theory, were it ever to be popularized, would add yet another flake to the impending avalanche of nihilism. 'Inevitably! or at any rate for a fairly long time, as long as the scale of valuations remains under the reacting influence of former mistakes',[2] men would make the non-existence of moral absolutes an excuse for revenging themselves on morality. But that did not greatly disturb him. For one thing, he thought, no misery accruing from anarchy could exceed that inflicted by the bad conscience of the past; for another, the goal of happiness would itself prescribe restraints—and, if merely the repression of men's passions had hitherto made them so unmanageable, such restraints would not be hard to enforce:

'You hypochondriacs, you philosophical blindworms talk of the formidable nature of human passions, in order to inveigh against the character of the whole world-structure. As if the passions were always and everywhere formidable! As if this sort of terror must always exist in the world! Through a carelessness in small matters, through a deficiency of observation of self and of the rising generation, you have yourselves allowed your passions to develop into such unruly monsters that you are frightened now at the mere mention of the word "passion"! It rested with you and it rests with us to divest the passions of their formidable character and so to dam them that they do not become devastating floods. We must not exalt our errors into eternal fatalities. Rather shall we

[1] N, XIII, 130.   [2] D, 148.

honestly endeavour to convert all the passions of humanity into sources of joy.'[1]

If Nietzsche was not unduly disturbed by the possible effect of his teaching, however, it was, above all, because he knew that this thing which sounded so easy—the single-minded pursuit of one's own happiness—was actually the hardest in the world. This freedom was veritably a burden—so heavy that men recoiled from it. For to know what constitutes *our* happiness means first of all to know ourselves.

'A valuation of our own,' he writes in *The Dawn of Day*, 'that is, the judgement of something by the amount of pleasure or displeasure it causes just us, and no-one else, is something very rare.'[2] In the last analysis, indeed, it is unattainable, since not merely our moral judgements, but all our likes and dislikes have been conditioned by heredity, example and precept—'trusting in our feelings simply means obeying our grandfather and grandmother and their grandparents more than the gods within *ourselves*: our reason and experience.'[3] But even if these, our most deeply-rooted proclivities, be left out of account, the fact remains that 'the great majority of people, whatever they may think and say about their "egoism", do nothing for their ego all their life long, but only for a phantom of this ego which has taken shape in the heads of their acquaintance and communicated itself to them.'[4]

Our ideas of ourselves, as of most other things, are nine-tenths second-hand. Often we do not even know what we enjoy. Certain occupations have been distinguished as 'enjoyable', and it is quite possible for an individual to go on pursuing them year after year before waking up to the fact that he does not enjoy them at all. It is equally possible for him (if he happens to be puritanically disposed) to go on shunning them year after year, with an expenditure of will-power that would do credit to a gymnast or dictator, and is, as a single relapse would show, redundant from beginning to end.

'How few really examine the questions: *why* do you live here? Why do you associate with so-and-so? How did you come by this religion? What effect has this or that diet on you? Was this house meant for you? etc. Nothing is rarer than an ascertainment of the *ego* for ourselves. The *prejudice* prevails that we know *the ego*, it *never fails* to operate: but we devote next to no labour or intelligence to getting to know it—as if, in the matter of self-knowledge, intuition could take the place of research'![5]

It is, as Nietzsche points out, the accumulation of these second-hand

[1] H, III, 37. [2] D, 104. [3] D, 35. [4] D, 105. [5] N, XII, 117.

ideas that has given rise to the concept 'man'—'all men who do not know themselves believe in a bloodless abstraction called "man"'. And unfortunately it is not only a concept—since as long as men do believe in it, the bloodless abstraction exists in the flesh; true individuality never makes its appearance. It is necessary, therefore, to make a holocaust of all these ideas, as well as of moral presuppositions, if we are to discover what really constitutes our own happiness: 'we must learn anew in order that at last, perhaps very late in the day, we may be able to do something more: *feel anew*'.[1]

Thus, it is clear, the individual who trusts to the gods within himself is not in for an easy time: 'how difficult this *science of the individual* is!'[2] Neither a voluptuary nor a conformist, he will inevitably, in a society like our own, appear both eccentric and suspect. It is no surprise to find Nietzsche inveighing anew against the cult of normality: 'the unconventional, who are so often productive and inventive, must no longer be sacrificed: it must never again be considered a disgrace to depart from morality either in actions or in thought; many new experiments must be made with life and society, and the world must be relieved from a huge weight of bad conscience.'[3]

Many new experiments must be made. But where were the experimenters? Nietzsche found himself practically alone. For the present, he insisted therefore, there was no possibility of arriving at any generalizations with respect to health or happiness. The data were not yet available. It was up to each to find out for himself—and refrain from dogmatism. 'We should not give the individual, insofar as he desires his own happiness, any directions as to the road leading to happiness; for individual happiness arises from particular laws that are unknown to anybody, and can only be hindered or obstructed by directions emanating from outside.'[4] One day it might be otherwise; one day a consensus of opinion might be formed; and then, provided mankind was willing to make the happiness of health its goal, it might 'impose a new moral law on itself'.[5] But that was a distant dream. Meanwhile there was nothing to be done but lead the hard life of the pioneer:

'Who is now in a position to describe that which will one day *supplant* moral feelings and judgements!—however certain we may be that all these are founded upon errors, and that the structure is beyond repair: their obligation must diminish from day to day, provided the obligation of reason does not diminish! For the task of reconstructing the laws of life and action our sciences of physiology and medicine,

[1] D, 103.   [2] N, XI, 243.   [3] D, 164.   [4] D, 108.   [5] *Ibid.*

society and solitude, are as yet insufficiently sure of themselves: and it is only from them that we can borrow the foundation-stones of new ideals (though not the ideals themselves). Thus we live a prospective or retrospective existence, according to our tastes and talents, and the best we can do in this interregnum is to be as much as possible our own *reges*, and to establish small *experimental states*. We are experiments—if we want to be!'[1]

* * *

The second stage of Nietzsche's journey from the Underworld began with his establishment of such a small experimental state. Elsewhere he speaks of 'the day on which the great liberator broke my fetters, the thought that life may be an experiment of the thinker, not a duty, not a fatality, not a deceit!'[2]—and this liberation is clearly reflected in *The Dawn of Day* itself. Two little aphorisms, 'FREED FROM SCEPTICISM' and 'SATIATED WITH MANKIND' (both couched in the form of a dialogue between those time-honoured personages A and B) actually make game of his nihilism, contrasting the exhilaration of discovery, even in the relative and irrational, with the hopeless pursuit of certainty.

For Nietzsche's theories, of course, were immediately translated into practice. They were always working hypotheses—and nothing could more pointedly illustrate the prevalence of the 'bloodless abstraction called "man"' than the charge, so often brought against him (it is sometimes expressed as a compliment), of inconsistency in this respect.

He called himself an 'immoralist', we are told, and *The Dawn of Day* a campaign against morality: yet all the time he was leading a life so austere that well-wishers took pity upon him, while the Genoese peasants he lodged with would call him *il piccolo santo* and present him with candles for his devotions! It never occurs to those who find this incongruous, that there may be other kinds of happiness than their own (whatever that may be), and that 'a philosopher, for example, in the midst of the most abstract, the most icy and hyperborean gymnastics, may feel as happy as a fish in water.'[3]

Nietzsche, however, was a philosopher: and if his philosophy was to organize his life for happiness, his happiness was to organize it for philosophy. That was what he was now doing. Down there at Genoa, lonely and sick though he often was, he was discovering day by day the conditions of his own optimum productivity; and this productivity, naturally enough, often takes the form of a record of these conditions. Some of the later aphorisms, indeed, are little more than songs in praise

[1] D, 453.　　　[2] JW, 324.　　　[3] WP, 917.

of the *vita contemplativa* itself: the charming 'LIVING CHEAPLY', for instance, or the more significantly headed 'IDEAL SELFISHNESS'—which because of its momentous sequel, must be quoted here almost entire:

'Is there a more sacred state than that of pregnancy? To perform every one of our actions in the silent belief that in one way or another it will benefit that which is growing within us—that it must *enhance* its mysterious value, the thought of which fills us with rapture! At such a time we refrain from many things without having to force ourselves to do so: we suppress the angry word, we grasp the hand forgivingly; our child must be born of all that is best and kindest. We shun our own brusqueness and harshness, in case it should instil a drop of unhappiness into the cup of the beloved unknown. Everything is veiled, in suspense; we know nothing of what is going on, but simply wait and try to be *prepared*. At the same time we experience a pure and purifying feeling of profound irresponsibility, rather like that felt by a spectator before a drawn curtain—*it* is growing, *it* is coming to light; we have nothing to do with determining its value, or the hour of its arrival. We are thrown back altogether upon indirect, beneficent and defensive influences. "Something greater than we are is growing here"—such is our most secret hope: we prepare everything with a view to its most auspicious entry into the world—not only everything useful, but the noblest gifts of our souls. So sacredly should we live—can we live! Whether what we are expecting is a thought or a deed, our relationship to every essential achievement is none other than that of pregnancy, and all our vainglorious talk of "willing" and "creating" should be cast to the winds! This is the true *ideal selfishness*: always to watch over and possess the soul in patience, that our productivity may *come to a beautiful termination*! . . .'[1]

Necessity, in the shape of his illness, had first imposed this way of life upon Nietzsche. But for that blessing in disguise, he reflected, he might never have escaped the frustrations of Basle and Bayreuth—surroundings into which he had fallen 'thanks to my ignorance and youth, and in which I had afterwards remained owing to inertia—the so-called "sense of duty"'.[2] Now he was committed to it of his own free will: and even if the siren-song of 'duty' had once again made itself heard, he would not have given way to it—would, indeed, have felt it his duty to resist. Odysseus's one obligation was to hold fast to his chosen course. This was the result of the long, painful 'course of anti-romantic self-treatment'[3] initiated in *Human, All-too-Human.* As he told Rohde a few

[1] D, 552.   [2] EH, p. 87   [3] H, II, Preface, 2.

months later, 'in every respect I have been my own physician, and as everything in me is one, so I had to treat my soul, my mind and my body simultaneously and with the same remedies. I admit that others would have *perished* from my treatment, but that is why I am so eager in *warning* people against myself.'[1]

This was the result—this 'ideal selfishness', with the access of health it betokened. And so, at long last, the momentous thought was born (it follows immediately upon the foregoing aphorism): Suppose this access of health had been, all along, the hidden purpose of his philosophy? Suppose that, at the very time when he was taking sides with his intellect against his emotions, with no other conscious aim than to re-establish his world-view upon an immoveable foundation, he had really been obeying the *fiat* of something deeper, stronger and wiser than either intellect or emotion; something that simply made use of his conscious self, with all its willing and striving, to achieve an end of which he was unconscious?

'CIRCUITOUS ROUTES.—Where does all this philosophy mean to end with its circuitous routes? Does it do more than transpose into reason, so to speak, a continuous and strong impulse—a craving for a mild sun, a bright and bracing atmosphere, southern plants, sea breezes, short meals of meat, eggs and fruit, hot water to drink, quiet walks for days at a time, little talking, rare and cautious reading, living alone, pure, simple, and almost soldier-like habits—a craving, in short, for all things most well suited to my own personal taste? a philosophy which is in the main the instinct for a personal regimen—an instinct that longs for my air, my height, my temperature, and my kind of health, and takes the circuitous route of my head to persuade me to it?

'There are many other and certainly more lofty philosophies, and not only such as are more gloomy and pretentious than mine—and are they perhaps, taking them as a whole, nothing but intellectual circuitous routes of the same kind of personal impulses?—In the meantime I look with a new eye upon the mysterious and solitary flight of a butterfly high on the rocky banks of the lake where so many flowers are growing: there it flies hither and thither, heedless of the fact that its life will last only one more day, and that the night will be too cold for its winged fragility. For it, too, a philosophy might be found, though it might not be my own.'[2]

That thought is enough. The Underworld is left behind for ever. The great question which has been tormenting Nietzsche so long is answered

[1] L, 15, 7, 82. [2] D, 553.

—as all great questions are, almost by-the-way. The will to truth, far from being hostile to life, is revealed as the servant of life—as the servant of that deeper, or higher, Self, which now, for the first time, attains to consciousness of itself. In this lucid, profound, and subtly beautiful aphorism, one can all but feel the sudden-sweet emergence of a new mode of knowledge, whereby the groping, aspiring, despairing Nietzsche we know is relegated wholly to the world of nature, and contemplated there with the same tender and whimsical detachment as the plants and the butterfly.

This time, indeed, the butterfly has shattered its chrysalis; the sun of a new gospel throws its ray upon the highest point of the soul. This time his pregnancy has issued in the birth, not of a new thought only, but of a new man: for to know the Self is to be the Self. His science has ended by acknowledging the sovereignty of the unconscious, and therewith abrogated its own; the man of understanding is united with the man of heart and man of body.

Mark how the very subjects of his despair become now the objects of his delight. The profound irresponsibility of man for his actions and his nature, the instrumental role of the intellect, secluding it from absolute truth: nothing is denied—and yet everything is transformed. 'The knowledge even of the ugliest reality is beautiful', he exclaims: 'The happiness of those who can recognize augments the beauty of the world, bathing everything that exists in a sunnier light: discernment not only envelops all things in its own beauty, but in the long run permeates the things themselves with its beauty—may ages to come bear witness to the truth of this statement!'[1]

Now, at last, Nietzsche can be joyful in his wisdom—can, in his own deeply spinozistic phrase, 'look on the world as on a god we love'.[2] Moreover, and in consequence of this, he can no longer overlook the possibility of a new kind of art. 'Music in former times attended upon the *Christian savant*, transforming his ideas into sounds: why cannot it likewise find in the end that brighter, more cheerful and universal sound which corresponds to the *ideal thinker?*'[3]

Why not, indeed? It was during this spring of 1881, as he recollected afterwards, that his taste in music, so long denied altogether, underwent a sudden and decisive change. At Recoaro, he and Gast, 'also one of the "reborn", discovered that the phoenix music hovered over us in lighter and brighter plumage than it had ever worn before'.[4] The spirit of music had risen again from its ashes—the birth of tragedy was at hand.

[1] D, 550.   [2] D, 497.   [3] D, 461.   [4] EH, p. 97.

VII

THE VISIONARY

The life of Nietzsche, every biographer has to admit, amounts to little more than the history of his thought. It does not lend itself to dramatization. The history of his thought, on the other hand, amounts to little less than the life of the man, and since his inward development was as rich in 'fatalities and convulsions'[1] as his outward was destitute of them, it is one of the most dramatic on record.

Whether or not this is to his advantage as a thinker is a point on which opinions differ widely. Most critics regard it as a disadvantage. A philosopher, they say, should be 'objective'; he should not allow his personality to shape his ideas—or, presumably, his ideas to shape his personality. They find it hard to attach any importance to one who not merely changed his mind every six years, but pronounced diametrically opposite judgements with the same dogmatic vehemence.

This point of view, however, is open to at least two objections. In the first place, as Berdyaev insisted, 'objectivity' is a will o' the wisp. Philosophy, like science, proceeds from a personal need, to educe some intelligible order out of the chaos of experience. The very decision to philosophize is a personal decision; so is the decision to philosophize impersonally. Every philosophy, in consequence, bears the stamp of its author's personality; and if objectivity is the criterion of truth, truth is unattainable in this world. In the second place, since this was what Nietzsche himself contended, it is impossible to decide whether his thought merits serious attention without first having given it the serious attention it merits.

As a matter of fact, the dramatic character of his philosophy was not due to any peculiar subjectivity—still less to any lack of intellectual rigour or exactitude—but, on the one hand, to the intensity and diversity of the experience he strove to co-ordinate, and on the other, to his persistence in putting his theories to experiment, his preference for the empirical method. The only worthwhile method of criticizing a philosophy, he had declared as early as *Schopenhauer as Educator*, is to see whether one can live by it; from this principle he never deviated. 'One must be willing to *live* the great problems, in body and soul',[2] he was

[1] D, 481.   [2] N, XIII, 115.

still repeating in 1885. In the last resort, therefore, our estimate of his importance will depend on the store we set by this experiential (or 'existential') approach.

That he himself should have seen it as an advantage goes without saying. Towards the end of *The Dawn of Day*, contrasting Kant and Schopenhauer with Plato, Spinoza, Pascal, Rousseau and Goethe, 'with respect to their souls and not their intellects',[1] he observes of these two that 'their thoughts do not constitute a passionate history of their souls —we are not led to divine in them romance, crises, catastrophes or death-struggles. Their thinking is not at the same time the involuntary biography of a soul, but in the case of Kant merely of a head; and in the case of Schopenhauer merely the description and reflection of a character.' Kant, he adds, 'had not come through many experiences', while Schopenhauer 'lacked development'. The presence of fatalities and convulsions, was in Nietzsche's view, a sign that the philosopher was living his problems; and that, in turn, a sign that his solutions deserved attention; for, he asks, 'is it likely that the man who contradicts himself a thousand times over, who explores many ways, who adopts many masks and discovers in himself neither finality nor horizon, should be less acquainted with "truth" than a virtuous stoic, who, having taken up his position once and for all, like a pillar, remains as impenetrable as a pillar?'[2]

Whether we share this view or dispute it, it is absolutely essential to understand it, if we wish to understand Nietzsche; and the moment we do understand it, we understand also that his very inconsistencies were the outcome of a fundamental consistency. It was just because he never ceased to regard his theories as so many working hypotheses, to be modified or discarded as soon as they conflicted with facts, that he was never afraid of contradicting himself; and, it may be added, because he was not afraid of contradicting himself, he was far less dogmatic in fact than his style might lead one to infer. 'We should not let ourselves be burned for our opinions,' he once said, 'we are not so certain of them as all that. But we might let ourselves be burned for the right of possessing and changing our opinions.'[3]

A philosophy of this sort, obviously, defies systematization beyond a certain point. It is not merely useless, but betrays an incomprehension of his purpose, to try and harmonize his earlier and later views completely. Being a philosophy of life, Nietzsche's is a living philosophy, which, like other living and growing things, must be apprehended genetically. Its unity is 'dialectical', rather than logical. It is a real unity nonetheless.

[1] D, 481.   [2] N, XIII, 34.   [3] H, III, 333.

The seed cannot be dissociated from the fruit; even his abruptest *volte faces* are not so abrupt as they appear at first sight; and that pertinacious Frenchman, who once compiled an anthology of his self-contradictions, might have been more profitably employed in pondering the following maxim, also from *Human, All-too-Human*: 'however strongly man may develop upwards and seem to leap from one contradiction to another, a close observation will reveal the dovetails whence the new building grows out of the old. This is the biographer's task: he must reflect upon his subject, on the principle that nature takes no jumps.'[1] We have now reached a point in our own biographical, or genetical, approach to Nietzsche's philosophy at which we may verify this maxim.

*   *   *

On 10 April 1888 he wrote to George Brandes:

'What you say about "Schopenhauer as Educator" gives me infinite pleasure. That little performance serves the purpose of a distinguishing mark; he for whom it does not contain much that is personal has in all probability nothing in common with me. The whole scheme according to which I have ever since lived is drawn up in it. It is a rigorous fore-shadowing.'

In *Schopenhauer as Educator*, as we know, Nietzsche had elaborated a declaration of faith. The man who wished to 'find himself again', he had there declared, ought first to hold fast to that instinct which tells him where his food is to be found; and secondly make use of his intellect to deny uncompromisingly whatever can be denied. He had added, in Cromwell's words, 'a man has never risen higher than when he knew not whither his road might yet lead him'.[2]

We may be sure that Nietzsche himself had no idea whither his road might yet lead him when, a couple of years after this, he turned avidly to the study of physiology, medicine and natural science; and, taking sides against himself, proceeded to dismantle from top to bottom the meta-physical framework of *Thoughts out of Season*. Yet, as we can now see, throughout the three volumes of *Human, All-too-Human*, he was doing nothing other than practise the precept he had already laid down—and in the event, his faith was vindicated. He did find himself again. Having looked for a lie in everything, he experienced a marvellous disillusioning.

This act of self-discovery is not easy to describe. 'After all,' as he himself confessed ruefully, 'no-one can hear more in things, books included, than he already knows. A man has no ears for that to which experience has given him no access.'[3] The aphorisms, 'IDEAL SELFISH-

---

[1] H, III, 198.   [2] TS, III, 1.   [3] EH, p. 57.

NESS' and 'CIRCUITOUS ROUTES', come nearest to the heart of the matter.

Essentially, it was an act of self-transcendence—or, to use the term he preferred, for its freedom from 'transcendentalist' associations, of 'self-surpassing' (*Selbstüberwindung*). Some time in the winter of 1880–1, Nietzsche passed 'beyond good and evil'; that is to say, he acquired a new capacity for envisaging his own development, above all his mental development, with all its fatalities and convulsions, as something belonging wholly to the natural order—as something, therefore, that neither possessed nor required any moral justification, and for which, in the last resort, he was no more responsible than the butterfly is responsible for its wings. By virtue of this, he was relieved simultaneously of the long inward division that had been exhausting him body and mind, and of the strain imposed by his pride. He experienced an immense liberation, and a correspondingly immense access of energy and power.

He was, so to speak, taken out of his own hands. From that time forward his development ceased to be a purely unconscious process, retarded rather than advanced by whatever deliberate aims he may have set himself, and became the object of his conscious dedication. He learned to watch, and watch over, his continued exfoliation with the same detached and yet solicitous attention as a botanist bestows on a rare plant. He knew that nothing he did could alter the nature of the plant, which would declare itself in due course: he enjoyed, accordingly, a feeling of profound irresponsibility. At the same time, he knew that it was for him to discover and provide the conditions of its finest flowering; and beside the sense of responsibility this conferred, all his previous willing and striving looked like child's play. Perhaps it is in *Ecce Homo*, where he essays 'a direct answer to the question, *how one becomes what one is*',[1] that we have the finest representation of this way of life.

'The fact that one becomes what one is,' be begins here (in words reminiscent of Cromwell's), 'presupposes that one has not the remotest suspicion of what one is':[2]

'Meanwhile the organizing "idea", which is destined to become master, grows and grows into the depths; it begins to command, it leads slowly *back* from deviations and aberrations, it prepares *individual* qualities and aptitudes which will one day prove themselves indispensable as means to the whole; step by step it cultivates all the serviceable faculties, before ever it lets out a word as to the dominant task, the "goal", the "object", and the "meaning" of it all. Seen from this standpoint, my life

---

[1] EH, p. 49.   [2] *Ibid.*

is simply amazing. For the task of *transvaluing values*, more faculties were perhaps needful than have ever dwelt side by side in one individual: and above all, faculties that are antagonistic without being allowed to disturb or destroy one another. A hierarchy of faculties; distance; the art of separating without creating hostility; to confuse nothing; to "reconcile" nothing; enormous multifariousness, which is yet the reverse of chaos—all this was the precondition, the long secret work and artistry of my instinct. Its superior guardianship manifested itself with such strength that not once did I ever dream of what was growing within me —so that all my capacities suddenly burst forth one day, ripe and in their full perfection. I cannot recall ever having exerted myself, I can point to no trace of *wrestling* in my life; I am the reverse of a heroic nature. To "will" something, to "strive" after something, to have an "aim" or a "desire" in my mind—I know none of these things from experience. Even at this moment I look out upon my future—a *broad* future!—as upon a smooth sea: no sigh of longing ripples its surface. I have not the slightest wish that anything should be otherwise than it is: I myself would not be otherwise.'

That is a retrospective account, and in one particular it is demonstrably inaccurate. Nietzsche had known, all too well, what it meant to will and strive. But for his 'hero will', he might never have survived the winter of 1879–80. It was only with the summer of 1881 that he was able to confess, 'to myself, I, as a whole, often seem little more than the scratching upon a piece of paper made by an unknown power with the object of trying a *new pen*'.[1] But it was true from that time forward; and what is so hard to describe is happily less hard to divine: the book he wrote immediately afterwards is redolent of this new energy and power.

The Joyful Wisdom, as he said, is 'really nothing but a revel after long privation and impotence; the frolicking of returning energy, of newly awakened belief in a tomorrow and after-tomorrow; of sudden sentience and prescience of a future, of near adventures, of seas open once more, and aims once more permitted and believed in.'[2] The concluding section in particular, 'Sanctus Januarius', veritably has the crispness, clarity and sparkle of a January morning, when the ground is still hard underfoot and crusted with last year's leaves, and yet one can all but feel the upsurge of sap in the trees. Indeed—if I may be allowed to be personal— it was this book, more than any other, that first drew me to the study of Nietzsche. Though I understood but little of it then, and do not believe

---

[1] L, 8, 81.   [2] JW, Preface, 1.

now (any more than he did) that it *can* be fully understood until we have accompanied the author through the long darkness of *Human, All-too-Human* and still twilit solitudes of *The Dawn of Day*, here, if anywhere, was the incentive to undertake that march.

Since, however, the whole purpose of *The Joyful Wisdom* is just to proclaim Nietzsche's liberation, and since that liberation amounts to a vindication of his earlier faith, the philosophy that begins to take shape in it bears a distinct affinity to that of *Thoughts out of Season*. The 'aims once more permitted and believed in' of 1881 are not wholly at variance with that 'task' which, five years earlier, seemed to have retreated beyond recall. Everything that can be denied has been denied—and everything includes the metaphysical integument of *Thoughts out of Season*—but something has remained undeniable; something which had, so to speak, been hidden and preserved by that integument until it was strong enough to dispense with it. He himself acknowledges this. 'Schopenhauer's man,' he says, 'drove me to scepticism towards everything that was revered, esteemed, hitherto defended (also towards Greeks, Schopenhauer, Wagner) genius, saint, pessimism of knowledge. By this *roundabout way* I came to the *summit*.'[1]

Nietzsche's thought has described a spiral. In retrospect, *Human, All-too-Human* and *The Dawn of Day* take on the appearance of a vast *reculer pour mieux sauter*. 'Be thyself! all that thou doest and thinkest and desirest is not—thyself!'[2]—Such, according to *Schopenhauer as Educator*, was the message of every man's conscience if he would but give heed to it. 'What saith thy conscience?' Nietzsche demands in *The Joyful Wisdom* (in one of those 'granite sentences at the end of the third book')[3] and the answer is his first commandment: 'Thou shalt become what thou art' (*Du sollst der werden, der du bist*).[4]

* * *

The 'conscience' which makes this demand, needless to say, is not the same that Nietzsche has described as the voice of our parents and grandparents. He has discovered (or thinks he has discovered) a new conscience. This use of one and the same word to denote different, and sometimes contradictory, things, is unfortunately persistent in his writings—we shall meet with further instances as we proceed—and may have contributed to his reputation for inconsistency. Yet it is hard to see how it could have been avoided, except by the adoption of some esoteric, and ultimately more baffling, terminology, such as Blake had recourse to; and provided only we are prepared to tread warily, to take pains, and if need be revise our conceptions again and again, as he did,

[1] N, XI, 120.   [2] TS, III, 1.   [3] EH, p. 96.   [4] JW, 270.

it constitutes no insurmountable obstacle to an understanding of his thought.

The conscience which demands that a man become what he is, is the 'higher self' of *Thoughts out of Season*, the 'organizing idea'. It is that, in the sick or divided man, which impels towards health—and by health we must now understand the condition of spontaneous growth depicted in *Ecce Homo*. In the whole or healthy man, it is that which manifests itself as his 'task'. The 'task of *transvaluing values*', which Nietzsche saw as his own, was nothing other than to declare this: to declare whatever made for health to be 'good', whatever militated against it, 'bad'.

Health, he still insists, is individual: 'what appeared as health in one person might appear as the contrary in another'.[1] To the time-honoured medical formula, 'Virtue is the health of the soul', he opposes 'Thy virtue is the health of thy soul', since, he explains, 'it is necessary to know thy aim, thy horizon, thy powers, thy impulses, thy errors, and especially the ideals and fantasies of thy soul, in order to determine *what* health implies even for thy *body*'.[2] Not only, therefore, may one man's meat be another man's poison, but what is meat for one and the same man today may be poison tomorrow. There can be no general prescriptions. Each must find out by experiment what is good or bad for *him*; and this, in *The Joyful Wisdom*, he himself proceeds to do.

Here, on a larger canvas than *The Dawn of Day*, he resumes that record of conditions favouring his own optimum productivity. It is one of the charms of the book. From beginning to end, he is engaged, delightfully engaged, in defining his personal 'tastes'—in scenery, in art, in solitude, in society, in everything under the sun—so that, as he told Rohde, 'it contains a portrait of myself',[3] one of the most candid self-portraits ever penned. And his express desire is that others should go and do likewise, imitating neither him nor the next man, but thinking back to their own true necessities, letting all sham necessities go:

> 'Attracted by my style and talk
> You'd follow, in my footsteps walk?
> Follow yourself unswervingly,
> So—careful!—shall you follow me.'[4]

Although Nietzsche purports to formulate no general prescriptions, however, although indeed he talks on occasion as if none were formulable, and no two healthy men would ever agree upon anything, this precept of his ought not to be pressed too far. It betrays a lurking confusion of thought, which was destined to have far-reaching consequences.

[1] JW, 120. [2] *Ibid.* [3] L, 15, 7, 82. [4] JW, Prelude, 7.

Quite obviously certain valuations must be common to all. They must, at the very least, share a 'taste' for health as such—and a distaste for what frustrates it.

The cult of normality, for instance, must clearly be distasteful to all. Nietzsche puts this cult down to fear—'the social instinct of fear, which thus assumes an intellectual disguise'.[1] It is the craving for security, he opines, that issues in suspicion of the individual who thinks and chooses for himself. Men sense in his existence a threat, and exalt the 'tool-like nature' in defence. Tolerant though he was, he would certainly have distrusted any man who, professing to have become what he was, yet dissented from him over this.

In fact, the main object of *The Joyful Wisdom* is precisely to determine the values inherent in health as such. And it is here that we meet with the first great difference between its teaching and that of *Thoughts out of Season*. Among the dispositions to be discarded, Nietzsche now includes, not merely the cult of normality, but many that he himself had formerly honoured. His first commandment is completed by a second like unto it: 'What dost thou believe in?—In this: That the weights of all things must be determined anew.'[2]

In the previous chapter we saw what misunderstandings his way of life has occasioned among biographers: how hard they have found it to believe that he could really have been happy in the single-minded pursuit of truth. These misunderstandings, as it happens, are not new. They beset Nietzsche during his own lifetime; and if he was sometimes amused by them—knowing so well that, for him, it would be 'a renunciation, a melancholy destruction of his own self, to be obliged to continue in the *vita practica*'[3]—he was also, on occasion, annoyed. He was annoyed, because they put him in a quandary. Whether he gave way to the solicitude of his well-wishers, breaking into his fruitful meditations, or rebuffed it, hurting their feelings, the result was exactly the same: his experiment was disorganized, his temper ruffled and frayed.

In *Ecce Homo*, he recalls that it was this obtrusiveness of his well-wishers, their everlasting anxiety to spare him his happiness, that first set him questioning the value of pity, and thus of altruistic sentiments in general: 'my experience gave me a right to feel suspicious with regard to all so-called "unselfish" instincts, with regard to the whole of "neighbourly love", which is ever ready and waiting with deeds or with advice'.[4] And once that suspicion was aroused, a stone was dislodged that was destined to bring down much—for, if Schopenhauer was right, pity or sympathy (*Mitleid*) was the very keystone of ethics. While,

[1] D, 174.   [2] JW, 269.   [3] D, 440.   [4] EH, p. 17.

therefore, 'this problem of the *value* of pity and pity-morality . . . seems at first blush a mere isolated problem, a note of interrogation for itself, he who once halts at this problem, and *learns* how to put questions, will experience what I experienced: a new and immense vista unfolds itself before him, a possibility seizes him like a vertigo, every species of doubt, mistrust and fear springs up, the belief in morality, in all morality, totters. . . .'[1]

In the name of health, Nietzsche had found himself challenging, first the repression of the passions, then the cult of normality. Now it was dawning upon him that *all* the sentiments, impulses and actions currently labelled 'good' might be open to doubt. What if those early legislators, to whom we owed our scale of values, had been wrong about *everything*? A new demand voiced itself in him: 'let us speak out this *demand*: we need a *critique* of moral values, the *value of these values* is itself *for the first time to be called in question*.'[2]

It is in *The Joyful Wisdom* that this critique begins to emerge. It is here that Nietzsche opens his sustained enquiry into pity. Not only into pity, of course—'one should consider from the same standpoint the virtues of obedience, chastity, piety and justice'[3]—but into pity first and foremost: partly because he shared Schopenhauer's estimate, and partly for another reason, which we shall have occasion to revert to. 'Where are thy greatest dangers?' reads a third of the granite sentences: 'In pity'.[4]

Nowhere, in fact, does Nietzsche define so clearly as here his own attitude towards this equivocal virtue: and since his 'transvaluation' turns largely upon it, since he himself is unintelligible apart from it, it is all-important to understand. In one aphorism 'THE WILL TO SUFFERING AND THE COMPASSIONATE' he deals with both aspects of the question: 'Is it to your advantage to be above all compassionate? And is it to the advantage of the sufferer when you are so?'[5]

Nietzsche knew, only too well, that it was not to his own advantage to be above all compassionate. He had a mission to discharge, a mission laid on him by his 'most personal conscience', to betray which now would amount to self-violation: and it was in the form of a temptation to betrayal that the cry for pity most often assailed him:

'How is it at all possible for a person to keep to *his* path! Some cry or other is continually calling one aside: our eye then rarely lights on anything without it becoming necessary for us to leave for a moment our own affairs and rush to give assistance. I know there are hundreds of

[1] GM, Preface, 6.   [2] *Ibid.*   [3] JW, 21.   [4] JW, 271.   [5] JW, 338.

respectable and laudable methods of making me stray *from my course*, and in truth the most "moral" of methods! Indeed, the opinion of present-day preachers of the morality of compassion goes so far as to imply that just this, and this alone, is moral: to stray from *our* course in this manner and to run to the assistance of our neighbour. I am equally certain that I need only give myself over to the sight of one case of actual distress, and *I, too, am* lost! And if a suffering friend said to me, "See, I shall soon die, only promise to die with me"—I might promise it, just as—to select for once bad examples for good reasons—the sight of a small mountain people struggling for freedom, would bring me to the point of offering them my hand and my life. Indeed, there is even a secret seduction in all this awakening of compassion, and calling for help: our "own way" is a thing too hard and insistent, and too far removed from the love and gratitude of others,—we escape from it and from our most personal conscience, not at all unwillingly, and, seeking security in the conscience of others, we take refuge in the lovely temple of the "religion of pity". As soon now as any war breaks out, there always breaks out at the same time a certain secret delight precisely in the noblest class of the people: they rush with rapture to meet the new danger of *death*, because they believe that in the sacrifice for their country they have finally that long-sought-for permission—the permission *to shirk their aim*:—war is for them a detour to suicide, a detour, however, with a good conscience.'

This, surely, is profoundly true. The gravamen of Nietzsche's charge against contemporary morality is that it sets the seal of its approval on all those sentiments, impulses and actions which make for the comfort, security and prosperity of society, never doubting that these constitute the highest good. He called it, for this reason, 'herd morality'; and believed it to be at once a cause and symptom of that bourgeois industrial civilization which, in general, is 'the vulgarest mode of existence that has ever been'.[1]

The true end of man, on the contrary, is to discover and obey his own most personal conscience, to 'become what he is'; and whoever undertakes to do that will learn, not merely that comfort, security and prosperity are things of secondary importance, but that their very opposites, pain, danger and deprivation, may be the quickest beast to carry him to perfection. For the sufferer's sake as much as for his own, therefore, he will hesitate before obtruding his sympathy:

'The compassionate person . . . wishes to *succour*, and does not reflect

[1] JW, 40.

that there is a personal necessity for misfortune; that terror, want, impoverishment, midnight watches, adventures, hazards and mistakes are
as necessary to me and to you as their opposites, yea, that, to speak
mystically, the path to one's own heaven always leads through the
voluptuousness of one's own hell. No, he knows nothing thereof. The
"religion of compassion" (or "the heart") bids him help, and he thinks
he has helped best when he has helped most speedily! If you adherents
of this religion actually have the same sentiments towards yourselves
which you have towards your fellows, if you are unwilling to endure
your own suffering, even for an hour, and continually forestall all
possible misfortune, if you regard suffering and pain generally as evil, as
detestable, as deserving of annihilation, and as blots on existence, well,
you have then, besides your religion of compassion, yet another religion
in your heart (and this is perhaps the mother of the former)—*the religion
of smug ease*. Ah, how little you know of the *happiness* of man, you com-
fortable and good-natured ones!—for happiness and misfortune are
brother and sister, and twins, who grow tall together, or, as with you,
remain small together!'[1]

Only the sufferer, perhaps, has a right to say that: but, if so, Nietzsche
had earned it.

*   *   *

In this evaluation of suffering, we meet with a second great resemblance between the teaching of *The Joyful Wisdom* and that of *Thoughts
out of Season*. That pain, danger and deprivation are as necessary to
existence as their opposites; that, far from constituting an objection to
life, they may be means to life's elevation; that 'the poison by which the
weaker nature is destroyed is strengthening to the strong—and he does
not call it poison':[2] these ideas are the keynote of *Richard Wagner at
Bayreuth*.

What he had divined in Wagner's development, Nietzsche now
discerned in his own. By virtue of the act of self-transcendence, he himself could now welcome all experience, the bitterest no less than the most
benign; and this it is that lifts him again and again above all negation
and contention, justifying his account of *The Joyful Wisdom* as 'yea-
saying' to an even higher degree than *The Dawn of Day*. Indeed, it is
in the noble New Year's Resolution at the outset of 'Sanctus Januarius'
that he propounds, for the first time, his famous formula for such an
affirmation:

'Today everyone takes the liberty of expressing his wish and his

[1] JW, 338.   [2] JW, 19.

favourite thought: well, I also mean to tell what I have wished for myself today, and what thought first crossed my mind this year,—a thought which shall be the basis, the pledge and the sweetening of all my future life! I want more and more to perceive the necessary characters in things as the beautiful:—I shall thus be one of those who beautify things. *Amor fati*: let that henceforth be my love! I do not want to wage war with the ugly. I do not want to accuse, I do not want even to accuse the accusers. *Looking aside*, let that be my sole negation! And all in all, to sum up: I wish to be at any time hereafter only a yea-sayer (*Ja-sagender*).'[1]

'FOR THE NEW YEAR' was written in January 1882—'the most wonderful month of January through which I have ever lived'.[2] But, like the whole of 'Sanctus Januarius', it harks back to the previous August. It was then that Nietzsche first became fully aware of the pattern being woven out of his life—a pattern over which his conscious calculations had little or no control, of which, indeed, they formed but a single thread among others, and to which, as it now appeared, not one of his miseries or misfortunes was irrelevant. All through that August he was in a state of ecstasy, shedding, as he told Peter Gast, 'tears of joy and exultation'.[3]

Then it was, too, that he alighted on the hamlet of Sils Maria, in the Engadine, destined henceforth to be his summer resort. With its austere surrounding peaks and larch-wooded, flowering valleys, this unfrequented spot matched his temperament so well that he was soon a familiar figure to the inhabitants, climbing the slopes or lying beside the lake, singing aloud to himself: and, like the author of 'The Everlasting Yea' at a similar climax in his life, he doubtless saw in this chance also the workings of a destiny that shapes our ends.

That he actually was tempted at this time to believe in a special Providence, is as certain as it is understandable. He owns up to it in the aphorism immediately following the New Year's Resolution:

'There is a certain climax in life, at which, notwithstanding all our freedom, and however much we may have denied all directing reason and goodness in the beautiful chaos of existence, we are once more in great danger of intellectual bondage, and have to face our hardest test. For now the thought of a personal Providence first presents itself before us with its most persuasive force, and has the best of advocates, appearance, in its favour, now when it is obvious that all and everything that happens to us always *turns out for the best*. The life of every day and

<hr>

[1] JW, 276.   [2] EH, p. 95.   [3] L, 14, 8, 81.

of every hour seems to be so anxious for nothing else but always to prove this proposition anew: let it be what it will, bad or good weather, the loss of a friend, a sickness, a calumny, the non-receipt of a letter, the spraining of one's foot, a glance into a shop-window, a counter-argument, the opening of a book, a dream, a deception: it shows itself immediately, or very soon afterwards, as something "not permitted to be absent",—it is full of profound significance and utility precisely *for us*! Is there a more dangerous temptation to rid ourselves of the belief in the Gods of Epicurus, those careless, unknown Gods, and believe in some anxious and petty Divinity, who knows personally every little hair on our heads, and feels no disgust in rendering the most wretched services?'[1]

However, Nietzsche will not give way. Scepticism, pushed to its furthest limits and held there in the teeth of despair, has been the condition of his self-discovery; he cannot go back on it now. Firmly, in the following sentences, he pronounces his *retro me*:

'Well—I mean in spite of all this! we want to leave the Gods alone (and the serviceable genii likewise), and wish to content ourselves with the assumption that our own practical and theoretical skilfulness in explaining and suitably arranging events has now reached its highest point. We do not want, either, to think too highly of this dexterity of our wisdom, when the wonderful harmony which results from playing on our instrument sometimes surprises us too much: a harmony which sounds too well for us to dare to ascribe it to ourselves. In fact, now and then there is one who plays *with* us—beloved Chance: he leads our hand occasionally, and even the all-wisest Providence could not devise any finer music than that of which our foolish hand is then capable.'[2]

Nietzsche will not have it that the 'unknown power' of which he is the instrument is other than his own higher self. The whole man—or at any rate, a very large part of him—is in those lines: his pride, his humility, his pathos, above all, the strength of his intellectual conscience.

Here, indeed, is where we meet with the second great difference between *The Joyful Wisdom* and *Thoughts out of Season*. Thanks to his patient dismantling of metaphysics, Nietzsche's philosophy now has no place for a 'metaphysical end'. He has rejected, not merely morality, but also its offspring and heir, the belief in absolute truth. 'God is dead':[3] this famous pronouncement likewise sounds for the first time here.

In an earlier aphorism he has defined the conflict which came to a head in himself: the conflict between the will to truth, on the one hand,

[1] JW, 277.   [2] *Ibid.*   [3] JW, 108.

and on the other the conclusion it leads to—that absolute truth is un-attainable. 'In comparison with the importance of this conflict', he has written, 'everything else is indifferent; the final question concerning the conditions of life is here raised, and the first attempt is here made to answer it by experiment.'[1]

By 1881, Nietzsche had resolved that conflict. *The Joyful Wisdom* opens with the triumphant affirmation that nothing we know or think can now prove hostile to life, not even our realization that life is ulti-mately meaningless. He had accepted the defeat of his innermost desire and profoundest need, and found in that acceptance his peace. But to accept a conclusion is not the same as to refute it, any more than—to take a more familiar situation—to reconcile ourselves to a bereavement is the same as to have the beloved restored to us. To see that the meta-physical thirst is merely a creaturely instinct, and that to indict the nature of things for failing to assuage it is folly and presumption—'how could we presume to blame or praise the universe!'[2]—is not the same as to arrive at a metaphysical certainty after all.

Nietzsche, therefore, was committed to the belief that even the sig-nificance he discerned in everything that summer was only 'appearance'. It did not belong to the world as such; it belonged to it only for him. It was the secret work of his ancestors' instincts and his own, apart from which all would have been cold and lifeless to his gaze. That the value of things is always a human value, prescribed by one generation and in-herited from it by another, was the contention he had pitted against the metaphysicians: he could not relinquish it now, and at bottom he did not want to relinquish it. This is what constitutes his unique distinction. In no other philosopher is mysticism of so high an order combined with absolute scepticism.

Rightly or wrongly, he will not allow that even his self-transcendence reveals any transcendent truth, that even his own standard of values possesses any absolute value—though future generations may come to think that it does, may, indeed, find it as inescapable as we do our categorical imperatives. In the last resort, his own mission is no *com*-mission: the new gospel he is to enunciate is, like all its predecessors, ultimately only a mirage, whereby the avid will detains its creature in life:

'THE CONSCIOUSNESS OF APPEARANCE.—How wonderfully and novelly and at the same time how awfully and ironically, do I feel myself situated with respect to collective existence, with my knowledge! I

---

[1] JW, 110.   [2] JW, 109.

have *discovered* for myself that the old humanity and animality, yea, the collective primeval age, and the past of all sentient being, continues to meditate, love, hate, and decide in me,—I have suddenly awakened in the midst of this dream, but merely to the consciousness that I just dream, and that I *must* dream on in order not to perish; just as the sleep-walker must dream on in order not to tumble down. What is it that is now "appearance" to me! Verily, not the antithesis of any kind of essence,—what knowledge can I assert of any kind of essence whatsoever, except merely the predicates of its appearance! Verily not a dead mask which one could put upon an unknown X, and which to be sure one could also remove! Appearance is for me the operating and living thing itself; which goes so far in its self-mockery as to make me feel that here there is appearance, and Will o' the Wisp, and spirit-dance, and nothing more,—that among all these dreamers, I also, the "thinker", dance my dance, that the thinker is a means of prolonging further the terrestrial dance, and in so far is one of the masters of ceremony of existence, and that the sublime consistency and connectedness of all branches of knowledge is perhaps, and will perhaps, be the best means of *maintaining* the universality of the dreaming, the complete, mutual understandability of all these dreamers, and thereby *the duration of the dream.*'[1]

In that powerful aphorism, we touch the very quick of Nietzsche's philosophy. This, indeed, *is* the joyful wisdom: this half-solemn, half-amused recognition of man as 'a visionary animal', distinguished from other animals by his need to believe that he knows the why and wherefore of existence: of the thinker as the type of man who temporarily meets this need; and of himself as such a thinker. Perhaps, he writes, 'when access stands open to everyone at all times to this ultimate emancipation and irresponsibility . . . then laughter will have united with wisdom, perhaps then there will be only "joyful wisdom".'[2]

* * *

This brings us to the third and last major difference-in-resemblance between the teaching of *The Joyful Wisdom* and that of *Thoughts out of Season*. The resemblance is clear enough. Nietzsche's earlier works are characterized, one and all, by a contradiction: between theoretical pessimism and practical optimism; between the Schopenhauerian view of life as a meaningless phantasmagoria, and a passionate devotion to the furtherance of art and culture.

He had been uneasily conscious of this at the time. He had even tried

¹ JW, 54.   ² JW, 1.

to excuse it, by means of a curious casuistry: claiming that one had no right to condemn life before one had seen it at its best—in other words, that the denial of the Will could only succeed upon its maximum affirmation. 'Behind my *first period*,' he confesses, 'there is the leer of jesuitism: I mean to say, illusion is consciously kept up, and forcibly posited as the *foundation of culture*'.[1] When, in *The Joyful Wisdom*, we come on the old phrase of *The Birth of Tragedy*, 'as an aesthetic phenomenon existence is still *endurable* to us',[2] it looks as though the contradiction has returned.

And so, in a sense, it has. Illusion *is* still consciously kept up, and posited as the foundation of culture. Art is, once again, justified as a prophylactic against despair, against the 'longing for nothingness' that would ensue upon a naked confrontation with 'reality'; 'if we had not approved of the Arts and invented this sort of cult of the untrue, the insight into the general untruth and falsity of things now given us by science—an insight into delusion and error as conditions of intelligent and sentient existence—would be quite unendurable. *Honesty* would have disgust and suicide in its train. Now, however, our honesty has a counterpoise which enables us to escape such consequences—namely, Art, as the *good-will* to appearance.'[3]

Nevertheless, the difference between Nietzsche's earlier and later standpoints is no less marked than the resemblance. He himself sums this up too: 'In place of the philosopher, I have put the free spirit . . . who acknowledges and plumbs the irrational nature of existence, without becoming jesuitical.'[4] The very completeness of his nihilism has now obviated all need for excuses. He can now affirm the will with a clear conscience—because nothing whatever is left in whose name it could be denied.

His 'criticism of all pessimism down to the present day' has, in effect, ended by making it look like optimism: 'books that are written against life are strong means of attraction to life'.[5] Schopenhauer was no pessimist, he exclaims, for he still believed that life had an aim, even if a negative one (had Nietzsche himself not imbibed *The World as Will and Idea* with a new sense of dedication?). Schopenhauer was no pessimist—much less was he a free spirit: 'for some time past there have been no *free* spirits, *for they still believe in truth*'.[6]

Schopenhauer denied life in the name of morality: Nietzsche denies morality in the name of life: and 'this *pessimism of strength* issues also in a *theodicy*, that is to say in a total *yea-saying* to the world'.[7] Far from

---

[1] N, XII, 212.   [2] JW, 179.   [3] *Ibid.*   [4] N, XII, 215.
[5] H, II, 16.   [6] GM, III, 24.   [7] WP, 1019.

extenuating this now, therefore, he glories in it: 'no longer the modest expression, "it is all *only* subjective", but "it is all *our* work! let us be proud of it"'.[1] He positively exults in the thought that he, even he, is in a position to prescribe the values that future generations shall inherit, that the *vis contemplativa* is likewise the *vis creativa*.

Finally, as though to emphasize the contrast, it is Schopenhauer's own terms that he adopts to define his standpoint. For, though the fact has escaped notice, Schopenhauer himself had foreseen the possibility of such an affirmation (it was a possibility, he said, to which the philosophy of Spinoza might lead), and these were the words he had used to describe its protagonist: 'A man who had thoroughly assimilated the truth we have already advanced, but had not come to know, either from his own experience or from a deeper insight, that constant suffering is essential to life, who found satisfaction and all that he wished in life, *and could calmly and deliberately desire that his life, as he had hitherto known it, should endure for ever or repeat itself ever anew* . . .'

Nietzsche was that man. Whether or not he consciously recalled this passage, it was in terms reminiscent of it that he now presented his vision:

'THE HEAVIEST BURDEN.—What if a demon crept after thee into thy loneliest loneliness some day or night, and said to thee: "This life, as thou livest it at present, and hast lived it, thou must live once more, and yet innumerable times; and there will be nothing new in it, but every pain and every joy and every thought and every sigh, and all the unspeakably small and great in thy life must come to thee again, and all in the same series and sequences—and similarly this spider and this moonlight among the trees, and similarly this moment, and I myself. The eternal sand-glass of existence will ever be turned once more, and thou with it, thou speck of dust!"—Wouldst thou not throw thyself down and gnash thy teeth, and curse the demon that so spake? Or hast thou once experienced a tremendous moment in which thou wouldst answer him: "Thou art a God, and never did I hear aught more divine!" If that thought acquired power over thee, as thou art, it would transform thee and perhaps crush thee; the question with regard to all and everything—"Dost thou want this once more, and also for innumerable times?"—would lie as the heaviest burden upon thy activity! Or, how wouldst thou have to become favourably inclined to thyself and to life, so as *to long for nothing more* than for this last eternal sanctioning and sealing?—'[2]

[1] WP, 1059.   [2] JW, 341.

This is the penultimate aphorism of *The Joyful Wisdom*, and the germ of that doctrine of Eternal Recurrence which has been such a stone of offence to Nietzsche's interpreters.

In essence, it is perfectly simple. It is exactly what he called it, 'the highest formula for a Yea-saying to life that can ever be attained';[1] and nobody who has once discerned the pattern being woven out of his suffering, and found in that discernment its own reward, will misconstrue his subsequent confession: 'the moment in which I begot Recurrence is immortal, for the sake of that moment alone I will endure Recurrence'.[2]

Nietzsche, we know, experienced that tremendous moment in August 1881: 'that day I happened to be wandering through the woods alongside the Lake of Silvaplana, and I halted not far from Surlei, beside a huge rock that towered aloft like a pyramid. It was there that the idea struck me.'[3] For him it was the moment of 'the Great Noon', which finally dispelled the 'shadows of God', as of his own despair: and it was at or about this same hour that he begot the figure of Zarathustra, to be at once the exemplar and spokesman of his new gospel:

'When Zarathustra was thirty years old, he left his home and the Lake of Urmi, and went into the mountains. Here he enjoyed his spirit and his solitude, and for ten years did not weary of it. But at last his heart changed,—and rising one morning with the rosy dawn, he went before the sun and spake thus. . . .'

So begins the ultimate aphorism of *The Joyful Wisdom*—entitled, 'INCIPIT TRAGOEDIA'.

* * *

Like *The Dawn of Day*, and just a year later, *The Joyful Wisdom* was completed at Genoa. It was the last aphoristic work for some time to come. Both the physical and the mental factors that had forced this form on Nietzsche now belonged to the past. In 'Sanctus Januarius', he had recaptured the exaltation of the previous summer, and already confidently anticipated the new form appropriate to his new purpose. It looked as though nothing stood in the way of his launching out on *Thus Spake Zarathustra* forthwith.

Actually, another year had to elapse before the first Part was composed, making eighteen months in all between its conception at Sils Maria and eventual deliverance at Genoa (a fact, he remarked, which 'might suggest, at least to a Buddhist, that I am at bottom a female elephant').[4] Why this long interval?

[1] EH, p. 96.   [2] NZ, 62.   [3] EH, p. 96.   [4] EH, p. 97.

There were two reasons. In the first place, knowledge, that is not purely theoretical, takes time to digest and assimilate: nearly all his books, he observed, were retrospective. In the second place, as Elizabeth Förster-Nietzsche records,[1] 'just as he was beginning to recuperate, an unkind destiny brought him a number of most painful experiences'. Hardly had he finished *The Joyful Wisdom*, in fact, than his new-found philosophy was submitted to a test as severe as any that could have been devised; and since the repercussions of this extended throughout the succeeding three years, it may be as well at this stage to re-tell the one incident in his life with an appeal for the present-day biographer.

By the age of thirty-seven, Nietzsche had seemingly abandoned the idea of marriage. Although he had toyed with it in the past—even, on one occasion, to the extent of a half-hearted proposal—he believed himself generally unsuited to it. At an age when, reasonably enough, quite different passions usually possess the soul, his own had been focussed on art, and the problems set by art. By the time he began to contemplate it seriously, he was already so deeply committed to the *vita contemplativa* that, like Kierkegaard, he could only see in domestic ties a threat to his spiritual independence. 'I shall certainly not marry,' he told von Gersdorff in May 1876: 'on the whole, I hate the limitations and obligations of the whole civilized order so very much that it would be difficult to find a woman free-spirited enough to follow my lead.'

It is highly probable, moreover, that this intellectual persuasion was reinforced from another quarter. 'Perhaps it not infrequently happens,' he states in one of his aphorisms, 'that noble men with lofty aims have had to fight their hardest battles in childhood; by having perchance to carry out their principles in opposition to a base-minded father addicted to feigning and falsehood, or living, like Lord Byron, in constant warfare with a childish and passionate mother. He who has had such an experience will never be able to forget all his life who has been his greatest and most dangerous enemy.'[2]

Nietzsche had certainly suffered in childhood from 'the caprices and whims of a melancholy temperament';[3] he had had to assert at every step his right to take risks and learn for himself. There can be little doubt that the revulsion against maternal care and security, which so often finds expression in his writing, had roots in this early experience:

'The free spirit will always feel relieved when he has finally resolved to shake off the motherly care and guardianship with which women surround him. What harm will a rough wind, from which he has been so

[1] Introduction to Z.   [2] H, I, 422.   [3] D, 341.

anxiously protected, do him? Of what consequences is a genuine disadvantage, loss, misfortune, sickness, illness, fault, or folly more or less
in his life, compared with the bondage of the golden cradle, the peacock's-
feather fan, and the oppressive feeling that he must, in addition, be grateful because he is waited on and spoiled like a baby? Hence it is that the
milk which is offered him by the motherly disposition of the women
about him can so readily turn into gall.'[1]

As he showed when a riding-accident damaged his chest at Naumburg,
Nietzsche would endure almost any pain in secret, rather than expose
himself to the ministration of a nurse. He felt humiliated by sympathy:
and since, 'in all feminine love something of maternal love also comes to
light',[2] this alone would have been enough to put him on his guard
against women.

Not that he was a mysogynist, or anything like one. Only the in-
fatuated believers in stage-properties like 'feminine intuition' will confound his realistic outlook with Schopenhauer's. But this initial recoil
from women must have been partially responsible for the sublimation of
his passions; and once that sublimation had been achieved, he was
determined to perpetuate it. For, naturally, he was quite aware of the
part it played in his work: 'it is the same force that expends itself in
artistic conception and in the sexual act; there is only one kind of force.'[3]
It was for this reason, as he often insisted, that 'a certain asceticism, a
grimly gay renunciation, is . . . one of the favourable conditions for the
highest intellectualism'.[4] *The Genealogy of Morals* contains an admirable
dissertation on the theme.

However, the letter to von Gersdoff was written at a moment of
confidence, that is to say, when his hopes and plans for his 'ultimate
spiritual emancipation' were 'in full bloom'; his books also commem-
orate such moments. There were other times, and those not infrequent,
when philosophy lost its hold on him; when he could no longer write
as he wished, and was consumed with doubt as to whether his mission
was, after all, so important as to justify the sacrifice of every normal
fulfilment:

'One day the wanderer shut the door behind him, stood still, and
wept. Then he said: 'Oh, this inclination and impulsion towards the
true, the real, the non-apparent, the certain! How I detest it! Why does
this gloomy and passionate taskmaster follow just *me*? I should like to
rest, but it does not permit me to do so. Are there not a host of things

<hr>

[1] H, I, 429.   [2] H, I, 392.   [3] WP, 815.   [4] GM, III, 9.

seducing me to tarry! Everywhere there are gardens of Armida for me, and therefore always fresh separation and bitterness of heart! I must set my foot forward, my weary wounded foot: and because I must, I often cast grim glances back at the most beautiful things which could not detain me—*because* they could not detain me!"'[1]

At such times—and, for obvious reasons, many of his letters were written at such times—Nietzsche's passionate nature rebelled against the loneliness to which he was condemned, a loneliness of body and heart as well as mind and spirit. Everything seemed trifling compared with the love he had missed; he was haunted by the faces of women. And was it really impossible to imagine one who would not clip the wings of his aspirations—who, on the contrary, would give him the encouragement he craved? At the back of his mind, there hovered the image of Cosima Wagner. Why should not he, the true Dionysus, likewise meet with his Ariadne?

Nietzsche's friends, as we have seen, seldom understood his 'dominant instinct'.[2] They had no entry to the world of ideas in which he habitually lived, nor could they appreciate his horror of exclusion from it. To them, his aversion to earning a living appeared almost culpable; his premonition that, if he married, his taste for solitude would occasion estrangement, a fine-drawn fantasy. They saw (and in view of his letters, they can be excused for seeing) only the lonely bachelor, in sad need of a woman's solicitude. Malwida von Meysenbug, in particular, was full of concern for his plight; and when, in the winter of 1881-2, she fell in with a girl who was not only charming but clever, the moral seemed obvious.

Nietzsche was introduced to Lou Salome at Rome. The circumstances happened to be propitious. Having just finished *The Joyful Wisdom*, he was enjoying, or trying to enjoy, a period of relaxation. He was stronger, in mind and body, than he had been for many years past; even his eyesight was better. Lou, moreover, did really display some of the qualities required of his Ariadne. A Russian, only twenty years old, but intellectually precocious, she was genuinely interested in his ideas. It was thanks to this that he warmed to her at once. When she agreed to their meeting again at Lucerne, the omens must have looked auspicious indeed. Lucerne, in his mind, was indelibly associated with the Wagners. He himself stood now on the threshold of his highest mastery. Had the moment arrived at last?—How verdant, and yet how delicate, his hopes were during that spring, is revealed by a letter to Lou: 'now the skies are

clear above me. . . . From now onwards, now that you will advise me,
I shall be well-advised, and need not be afraid. . . . I do not want to be
lonely any more. I want to learn how to be a human being once again.
Oh, I still have everything to learn in this respect! . . .'[1]

There is something deeply pathetic about these lines, even apart from
the sequel. Truly, Nietzsche still had everything to learn! For Lou, of
course, never for a moment considered him as a husband. Why should
she? He was thirty-seven, a recluse, an invalid, not even famous as yet,
what is more, as backward a suitor as his admired Stendhal—he actually
proposed by proxy. She, not yet twenty-one, might be intrigued by his
theories and sorry for his sufferings, but her life lay in front of her, and
she wanted to make the most of it. Gently, but firmly—and certainly
wisely—she declined the offer. Had she not done so, she might have
shared the fate of Regina Olsen.

The blow was nevertheless a cruel one to Nietzsche—and worse was
to follow. Before their acquaintance, he had grown so accustomed to
solitude that it no longer held any terrors; now it was hard to return to.
Instead of cutting himself adrift from her, therefore, he prolonged their
association—it was then that he set her *Hymn to Life* to music—and this
was the cause of a still more bitter dispute with his family.

The instrument of unkind destiny was Elizabeth herself—who, having
conceived a violent jealousy of Lou, now set out by every means to
poison his mind against her. Not content with insinuations, she even sent
reports home to Naumburg, calculated to enlist Frau Nietzsche's pious
and possessive fears in the cause: the immediate upshot being that he
broke off relations with mother and sister alike. But by then the damage
had been done. Notwithstanding Elizabeth's engagement soon afterwards to the professional anti-semite, Förster—a reaction, so Nietzsche
believed, against everything he himself stood for—her insinuations had
gained a foothold in his mind. It was not very long before he was
quarrelling with Lou as well, and even his old friend Rée, writing letters
to both of which he was afterwards heartily ashamed.

Consequently, when at long last he did find himself alone again at
Genoa, he had touched a nadir of misery. To his feeling of isolation was
added the bitterness of seeing himself, at the age of thirty-eight, an in-
effectual and rejected, perhaps a ridiculed, suitor. He was utterly consumed with loathing for his family and all that it stood for, 'Naumburg
respectability', which had not only ruined his personal relationships,
but, in so doing, robbed him of the fruitful peace of mind he had been
enjoying in these very surroundings a year before. The drugs he was

[1] Letter, 2.7.82.

taking to combat insomnia further exasperated his nerves. 'My whole life has disintegrated before my eyes', he cried to Overbeck.[1] More than once he was within sight of suicide.

That was in January 1883. By March *amor fati* had reasserted itself. 'The sky looks unbrokenly clear and pure,' he was able to tell Overbeck, 'and in me, too, everything is more ordered and contented. I see a certain necessity in having suffered so much—I have, in this way, cut out of my soul three or four wishes, wishes for happiness, wishes of a personal nature, which I still entertained, and am again much freer than I was before. The separation from my family is taking the shape of a true blessing for me.'[2] Five months later still, he was telling Elizabeth herself that it was 'absolutely *necessary*' that he should be misunderstood, and 'the fact that those "nearest to me" should be the first to do this was what I realized last summer and autumn, and by that alone I became filled with the glorious consciousness of being on the right road'.[3]

That traditional morality was embodied in those who were 'nearest him', however, was not the worst of the discoveries Nietzsche had made that year. Another is betrayed by the very fact that he was once again in touch with his family: even in himself it was ineradicable. Try as he might, he could not remain loyal to his own most personal conscience without suffering the pangs of the impersonal, and in the end the latter had proved the stronger. 'I am certain,' he had written, 'that I need only give myself over to the sight of one case of actual distress, and *I, too, am* lost!' The sight of his mother's distress had been more than he could endure.

'WHAT BELONGS TO GREATNESS.—Who can attain to anything great if he does not feel the force and will in himself to *inflict* great pain? The ability to suffer is a small matter: in that line, weak women and even slaves often attain masterliness. But not to perish from internal distress and doubt when one inflicts great anguish and hears the cry of this anguish—that is great, that belongs to greatness.'[4]

Nietzsche was unequal to his own philosophy. As he confessed to Overbeck, 'I am not hard enough for such things.'[5] Rather than say once and for all, 'Woman, what have I to do with thee?' he preferred to act a part: inwardly boiling with resentment, to keep up a façade of cheerful affection. And, of course, he *was* lost. No sooner was he reconciled with his family than the whole dreary cycle began again: fresh recriminations with Lou and Rée, succeeded by renewed antagonism towards mother

---

[1] Letter, 11.2.83.   [2] *Ibid.*   [3] L. 8, 83.

[4] JW, 325.   [5] Letter, to Overbeck, Summer 1883

and sister. It is hardly surprising that during the summer of 1883, his detestation of Naumburg and all that it symbolized—bourgeois-Christian civilization—should have touched a pitch of almost insane intensity.

On 26 August we find him writing to Gast, 'For a year I have been incited to emotions of a kind I have abjured with the best will. I really think I have mastered them, at least in their grosser aspects of vengefulness and resentment.' But only a couple of days later, his desperation breaks out anew, in a letter to Overbeck:

'Dear friend, the parting from you threw me back into the deepest melancholy, and during the whole of my return journey, I could not shake off my black and evil feelings, one of which was a veritable hatred of my sister, who, by being silent at the wrong moment and by talking at the wrong moment throughout a whole year, has deprived me of the fruits of the best victories I have won over myself, so that I have, in the end, become the victim of a ruthlessly revengeful sentiment, although my innermost mind has foresworn revenge and punishment. This inner conflict is bringing me step by step nearer madness (could you, perhaps, do something drastic to make my sister appreciate this point?) and I feel it in the most terrible manner. Nor do I know how a journey to Naumburg would diminish the danger. On the contrary, horrible moments might ensue, and my long-nourished hatred might emerge in speech and action. And in that case I, far more than the others, would be the victim. Even now it is inadvisable for me to write anything to my sister, except letters that are quite harmless (one of the last I sent her was full of cheery verses). Perhaps my reconciliation with her was the most fatal step in the whole affair—I now realize that it led her to believe that it gave her a right to be revenged on Fräulein Salome.'[1]

Although, six months afterwards, Nietzsche told Elizabeth directly, 'this much is certain, that you and no-one else have endangered my life three times in one twelve-month', it was not until the very end of his days that he was able to renounce his family finally—and then it was too late. They proved devoted keepers.

Elizabeth took pains to suppress these letters, and nothing could demonstrate more clearly than her idealized portrait of her brother how incapable she was, not only of comprehending, but even of respecting, his principles. Their survival, despite her efforts, throws some light on the suffering he endured as a result of a Christian upbringing—and thus on the magnitude of his achievement in surmounting his hatred of

[1] Quoted: E. H. Podach, *The Madness of Nietzsche.*

Christianity. For surmount it he did. 'Behind almost every word' of *Zarathustra* stands 'an act of self-overcoming of the highest order.'[1] It was in the very midst of these afflictions that his greatest work came into being—a work in which science and art are welded into a new unity, and the passion aroused, but never fulfilled, by his contact with Lou Salome, is directed wholly into creative art: 'the most detached of all my productions'.[2]

[1] L, 8, 83.   [2] L, 19, 2, 83.

VIII

THE PROPHET

(1)

The first three parts of *Thus Spake Zarathustra* were the fruit of three bursts of inspiration, in February 1883, June–July 1883, and January 1884, respectively. Parts I and II complement one another; Part III stands somewhat apart. With these the poem, as originally designed, was complete. Part IV, composed in February 1885, was an afterthought; and of the yet further instalments projected at various dates, nothing remains but an assortment of cryptic notes and the untranslatable 'Dionysus Dithyrambs'. It is the first three Parts that will concern us mainly in this chapter.

The inspiration of each of these lasted exactly a fortnight—a space of time that seems incredibly small for compositions of such length, breadth and height. But most of the thoughts had been ripening in Nietzsche's mind for months or years; it required only a strong wind to bring them down—and the wind arose. In after-years he was fond of referring to the exaltation he had experienced on those occasions, when rhythm, image and idea flooded his brain simultaneously, and his steps, as he walked or danced, kept time to the music of the verse. To find another who had known such an *afflatus*, he said, one would have to go back thousands of years,—to the age of the Greek tragedians.

Here, of course, he was mistaken. One would have to go back at most a hundred. His nearest-of-kin, indubitably, was not Aeschylus, but William Blake: and there is something very Blake-like in the assertion, 'length, the need of a wide-embracing rhythm, is almost the measure of the force of an inspiration'.[1] Isolated though he was, Nietzsche was never driven into total esotericism; *Zarathustra* is more intelligible than even the earliest of the 'Prophetic Books', and considerably more restrained: his native eloquence, while it reinforced, did nothing to replace, that command of lucid, succinct expression he had acquired by years of training in the aphorism. The affinity, both of style and substance, between *Zarathustra* and *The Marriage of Heaven and Hell* is none the less obvious (where else shall we find such a 'clear golden and thoroughly

[1] EH, p. 102.

180

fermented mixture of simplicity, deeply discriminating love, observation and roguishness'?): and it is easy to imagine the delight that Blake might have taken in illustrating Nietzsche's poem.

The experience he enjoyed was by no means so rare as he supposed. Several of the English Romantics had known it at one time or another. There is not a single word in these lines of Keats'—'given' to him, as he said, 'in a sort of inspiration'—that does not correspond exactly to Nietzsche's account of the 'Dionysian':

> 'Knowledge enormous makes a God of me.
> Names, deeds, grey legends, dire events, rebellions,
> Majesties, sovran voices, agonies,
> Creations and destroyings, all at once
> Pour into the wide hollow of my brain,
> And deify me, as if some blithe wine
> Or bright elixir peerless I had drunk,
> And so become immortal . . .'

By an odd coincidence, moreover, Nietzsche's exact contemporary, Edward Carpenter, was engaged during the self-same months on that quaint, refreshing, undeservedly forgotten rhapsody, *Towards Democracy*, in 'a mood of exaltation and inspiration—a kind of super-consciousness—which passed all that I had experienced before, and which immediately harmonized all those other feelings, giving to them their place, their meaning, and their outlet in expression.'[1] With respect to the uniqueness of his experience, Nietzsche was often at fault.

The explanation he gave for it, on the other hand, is as original as it is important, for, unlike Carpenter (who was a disciple of the *Bhagavadgita*), he could no longer attribute the 'musical mood', as he had done in *The Birth of a Tragedy*, to a rupture of the *principium individuationis* and re-absorption into the Primordial Unity. 'If one had the smallest vestige of superstition left in one,' he confessed, 'it would hardly be possible completely to set aside the idea that one is the mere incarnation, mouthpiece or medium of an almighty power';[2] but by this time he was too humble (or, as he preferred to put it, too proud) to lay claim to any such status. His chief purpose was to reclaim for man the powers he had lent his divinities—to establish as 'his own creation, his noblest adornment and justification, all the beauty and sublimity we have lent to things, real and imaginary.'[3]

Once again, therefore, he set firmly aside the temptation of super-

[1] Carpenter, *My Days and Dreams*, Allen & Unwin, 1921.
[2] EH, p. 101.   [3] N, XII, 170.

naturalism. 'Music,' he wrote, 'is an echo of states, the conceptual expression of which was *mysticism*: a feeling of transfiguration and illumination on the part of the individual. Or rather, the reconciliation of internal antinomies in something new, *the birth of a third reality*.'[1] In other words, it was the natural speech of the reintegrated man; what took possession of the poet at the moment of inspiration was his own deeper, or higher, self.

But what is this 'higher self'? It is clear from his notes that Nietzsche had long felt the need for some more exact definition. He had been going into the question intensively; and since much depends on the answer he found to it—since *Zarathustra* itself is scarcely intelligible apart from it—it behoves us to retrace his thought.

* * *

In *The Joyful Wisdom*, as might have been expected, he had undertaken a brief review of Schopenhauer's philosophy in the light of his own. It is here that he repudiates Schopenhauer's 'undemonstrable doctrine of *one will*' and 'his *denial of the individual*', as the '*extravagances* and vices of the philosopher'.[2] At the same time he singles out for praise, besides 'the strength of his intellectual conscience, which *endured* a lifelong contradiction of "being" and "willing", and compelled him to contradict himself on almost every point', Schopenhauer's 'immortal doctrines of the intellectuality of intuition, the *a priority* of the law of causality, the instrumental nature of the intellect, and the non-freedom of the will'.[3] These, it appears, were the tenets he still found acceptable. It was Schopenhauer's name, accordingly, that he retained for the deeper self—the will.

It had many advantages, and few drawbacks. It had no metaphysical penumbra, such as surrounds the word 'soul'; it put consciousness in its place; above all, it served to underline the dynamic character of the self, which, as Schopenhauer insists, has no existence apart from its actions and reactions. On the other hand, 'to will' on its own is meaningless: *what* is willed must also be specified. As Nietzsche wrote later, 'the character of will has been cancelled owing to the fact that its content, its "whither", was subtracted from it: in Schopenhauer this is so to the highest degree; what he calls "will" is merely an empty word.'[4] When he himself came to try and restore the content, however, difficulties began to arise.

Schopenhauer had referred to the will as a 'will to live'. This was clearly unsatisfactory. Apart from all other objections, and they were manifold, it did not correspond to Nietzsche's own experience. True, he

[1] N, XIV, 139.   [2] JW, 99.   [3] *Ibid.*   [4] WP, 692.

was alive and hoped to remain so; but life was not an end in itself. Had that been all that he needed, he could have secured it without any such dangerous exertion as he lavished day by day on his work. Further, if it had come to a choice between living on and pursuing his mission, he would unhesitatingly have chosen to die.

Was it a 'will to happiness', then? At the time of *The Dawn of Day*, he might almost have subscribed to this definition. He had, at any rate, made happiness the criterion of good. But even then the term had been strained to bursting-point by the meanings he was trying to pump into it. Inseparable from happiness, as he understood it, was the willing acceptance of unhappiness; it was happiness of a very particular kind——the happiness of health.

Why not a 'will to health', then? That certainly came nearer the mark; and nearer still a 'will to wholeness': for this will, of course, which 'gradually disciplines one's whole being into unity', is none other than the 'plastic power' of *The Use and Abuse of History*. Yet neither health, nor wholeness, nor even growth, would serve to carry the point he most wished to drive home—namely, that the end is attained, not in contemplation (as Spinoza had taught), but in action; that self-creation is the prelude only to creation.

What, then, is the common denominator of wholeness, growth and creation? For a time, Nietzsche seems to have settled on 'possession'. Finally, taking his courage in both hands, he answered, 'the feeling of power'!

' "He certainly did not hit the truth who shot at it the formula: 'Will to existence': that will—doth not exist!

"For what is not, cannot will; that, however, which is in existence—how could it still strive for existence!

"Only where there is life, is there also will: not, however, Will to Life, but—so I teach thee—Will to Power!

"Much is reckoned higher than life itself by the living one; but out of the very reckoning speaketh—the Will to Power!"

Thus did Life once teach me: and thereby, ye wisest ones, do I solve you the riddle of your hearts.'[1]

There is no call, for the present, to criticize this definition. The important thing is to know what Nietzsche signified by it, and what it signified to Nietzsche. Until we know that, we are not in a position to criticize. It has been the besetting sin of his interpreters, that they have set out to judge him by some preconceived standard, comfortably un-

[1] Z, 34.

aware that it was precisely this standard that he was calling in question, and that they were first summoned to vindicate. In point of fact, the resistance this definition commonly arouses is of the same kind as Freud encountered, when he characterized the basic human impulse as erotic. It is a moral prejudice; and unless we are prepared to have all our prejudices, moral and intellectual, shattered by Nietzsche's critique, his works will always be lost on us. 'I am not writing for the feeble,' he said, 'who want to obey, and fall with outstretched arms into slavery.'[1]

On the other hand, the exuberance with which his definition has been received in certain other quarters is no less suspect: for, if he was not writing for the feeble, neither was he writing for the self-styled strong—the petty officers of all ranks, who have made capital out of his name. The passage quoted continues:

'I have found strength where nobody looks for it, among simple, kind and gentle people, without the least taste for domination—and conversely, the taste for domination has often appeared to me a sign of inner weakness: they are afraid of their slave's soul, and deck it out in regal attire (they end up by becoming the slaves of their supporters, their reputations, etc.). The powerful natures *rule* of necessity, without so much as lifting a finger—even though they bury themselves all their lives in some garden-house.'

What Nietzsche signified by the Will to Power was that basic human impulse which, in his earlier works, he had tended to identify with love. What the definition signified to him is not difficult to conjecture: probably, when it first occurred to him, it had as great an effect as the formula 'Reverence for Life' had on Albert Schweitzer. In a flash it co-ordinated all the seemingly unrelated psychological observations of *Human, All-too-Human, The Dawn of Day* and *The Joyful Wisdom*; it brought a new order into the chaos of his experience.

It explained, for example, why the love of power was in truth 'the demon of mankind'. There was no need to have recourse to a primitive 'feeling of impotence and fear'. Thus, when 'the conscientious one'—the representative of science at its best, 'severe, rigorous, restricted, cruel and inexorable'[2] in the pursuit of learning, preferring the humblest fact to the loftiest theory—pronounces fear 'man's original and fundamental feeling', Zarathustra retorts: 'why, *fear*—is an exception with us. Courage, however, and adventure, and delight in the uncertain, in the unattempted—*courage* seemeth to me the entire primitive history of man.'[3] Assuredly it was easier to attribute the deformities of history

[1] N, XI, 251.   [2] Z, 64.   [3] Z, 75.

to the perversion of a Will to Power than to fear—let alone to love.

The wonder, indeed, is not that Nietzsche should have embraced this definition with relief, but that he should have hesitated so long before doing so. After all, he had already anticipated it in *Richard Wagner at Bayreuth*. There he had interpreted the life-history of the artistic genius in terms of a dialogue, between the Will to Power on the one hand, and an unlimited capacity for learning on the other; whilst in *Human, All-too-Human* he had derived the appetite for knowledge itself from the craving for immortality. Perhaps it took the immense access of power supervening upon his own self-transcendence finally to convince him.

Be that as it may, the Will to Power is henceforward his definition of the deeper self; and it is the triumph of this Will over inward division that issues, as he thinks, in 'inspiration'. In *Zarathustra*, therefore, to an even greater extent than in *The Use and Abuse of History*, the explicit is also the implicit. It is a manifestation of the Will, and it is all about the Will; it is the chant of a reborn man, and it is all about rebirth—the rebirth of the individual, the rebirth of humanity at large. For this reason, the first two Parts, at least, constitute an organic unity, exemplifying to an outstanding degree the quality he denoted by 'style': 'all one is conscious of is the great *necessity* of it all'.

For the same reason, the doctrine of these Parts is both simple and hard to expound. Simple, because, the entire work being the steady unfolding of a single idea, and everything leading back to that, it is almost a matter of indifference where one begins; hard, because to isolate any one thought is immediately to impoverish it. The only commentary really required is provided by Nietzsche's earlier works, particularly *The Joyful Wisdom*—and if many interpreters have gone astray, it is because of their inveterate habit of reading his books backwards.

* * *

Perhaps the best point of departure is supplied by one of the earliest of the Discourses, in which Nietzsche seeks to safeguard his idea from the start against the most obvious misconstruction. His purpose being, as we have seen, to reclaim for the natural all that has hitherto been classed as supernatural, it is of fundamental importance that the Self should not be imagined as a soul distinct from the body:

' "Body am I, and soul"—so saith the child. And why should one not speak like children?

But the awakened one, the knowing one, saith: "Body am I entirely, and nothing more; and soul is only the name of something in the body."

The body is a great wisdom—a plurality with one sense, a war and a peace, a flock and a shepherd.

An instrument of thy body is also thy little wisdom, my brother, which thou callest "brain"—a little instrument and plaything of thy big wisdom.

"Ego," sayest thou, and art proud of that word. But the greater thing—in which thou art unwilling to believe—is thy body with its big wisdom; it saith not "ego", but doeth it.

What the sense feeleth, what the spirit discerneth, hath never its end in itself. But sense and spirit would fain persuade thee that they are the end of all things: so vain are they.

Instruments and playthings are sense and spirit: behind them there is still the Self. The Self seeketh with the eyes of the senses, it hearkeneth also with the ears of the spirit.

Ever hearkeneth the Self, and seeketh; it compareth, mastereth, conquereth, and destroyeth. It ruleth, and is also the ego's ruler.

Behind thy thoughts and feelings, my brother, there is a mighty lord, an unknown sage—it is called Self; it dwelleth in thy body, it is thy body.'[1]

In these lines Nietzsche comes as near as anywhere to a direct statement of his central idea. The body, he affirms, is a thing far greater than we ordinarily understand. It comprehends mind as well as the other organs, and has a will of its own, over and above their particular wills. Mind is not, as the vulgar materialist supposes, subservient to stomach and genitals; neither are stomach and genitals subservient to mind; but senses, passions, intellect, are all alike subservient to the Self, which, in their totality, they constitute.

Not only are all subservient, all are necessary to it. For its own purpose it brought them into being; to the fulfilment of this purpose all must co-operate. In the title of the succeeding Discourse, *Freuden- und Leidenschaften*, Nietzsche reverts to a play upon words he had introduced in *Human, All-too-Human*, when claiming that all the passions of humanity could be converted into sources of joy: and this thought, of course, is no new one. As early as 1871, he had extolled the Greek genius for sublimating even the most dangerous impulses: envy and rage in their athletic contests, homosexuality in the education of the adolescent, the defensive hauteur of the individual in Apollonian art, the orgiastic relapses of the people in Dionysian.

Now, however, that he had derived all the so-called higher emotions from the lower, it took on a still greater significance. He saw that, unless

[1] Z, 4.

the latter were powerful, nothing could be expected from the former: that 'all the *inferior* instincts must be present and in fresh force, if the superior are to flourish with a will; only it takes a firm hand to control the whole'.[1] This is the insight he condenses in Zarathustra's epigram, 'Man must become better and more evil';[2] and this, too, he now expands in a succession of images:

'Once hadst thou passions and calledst them evil. But now hast thou only thy virtues: they grew out of thy passions.

Thou implantedst thy highest aim into the heart of those passions; then became they thy virtues and joys.

And though thou wert of the race of the hot-tempered, or of the voluptuous, or of the fanatical, or of the vindictive;

All thy passions in the end became virtues, and all thy devils angels.

Once hadst thou wild dogs in thy cellar; but they changed at last into birds and charming songsters.

Out of thy poisons brewedst thou balsam for thyself; thy cow, affliction, milkedst thou—now drinkest thou the sweet milk of her udder.

And nothing evil groweth in thee any longer, unless it be the evil that groweth out of the conflict of thy virtues.'[3]

Note how love and learning do co-operate in the very expression of this insight.

That man is fortunate, Nietzsche adds, who is possessed of only one powerful passion. He then sees things from one angle only, and his path through life is easy. Where there is more than one, and the balance between them is even, conflict is unavoidable, since each, having its share of the Will to Power, demands unqualified allegiance: 'Lo! how each of thy virtues is covetous of the highest place; it wanteth thy whole spirit to be *its* herald, it wanteth thy whole power, in wrath, hatred and love.'[4] So it had been with himself, when he was living as much in love with the arts as he was carried away by the spirit of science, and had seen no end to the conflict. Now, however, even this 'evil' is known to be the condition of growth, this mutual jealousy of the passions, the very means to man's self-surpassing:

'He whom the flame of jealousy encompasseth, turneth at last, like a scorpion, the poisoned sting against himself.

Ah! my brother, has thou never seen a virtue backbite and stab itself?

[1] N, XIII, 123.   [2] Z, 73, 5.   [3] Z, 5.   [4] *Ibid.*

Man is something that hath to be surpassed: and therefore shalt thou love thy virtues,—because thou wilt succumb by them.'[1]

There is a subtle piece of psychology, beyond the reach of most present-day analysts: for Nietzsche's wisdom begins where theirs ends; where psycho-analysis gives way to psycho-synthesis; where the intellect, in the act of discovering its true relation to the Self, *surrenders* its primacy.

The will of the Self, he declares, is to 'create beyond itself'.[2] For this purpose alone it brought all the organs into being. This Will to creation, therefore, is Virtue, and there is no other. Yet, since no two Selves are identical, neither are any two Virtues. Virtue—'the health of thy soul'—is always unique, inimitable, indescribable: and this insight he likewise conveys, in language itself unique, inimitable and indescribable:

'My brother, when thou hast a virtue, and it is thine own virtue, thou hast it in common with no-one.

To be sure, thou wouldst call it by name and caress it; thou wouldst pull its ears and amuse thyself with it.

And lo! Then hast thou its name in common with the people, and hast become one of the people and the herd with thy virtue!

Better for thee to say: "Ineffable is it, and nameless, that which is pain and sweetness to my soul, and also the hunger of my bowels."

Let thy virtue be too lofty for the familiarity of names, and if thou must speak of it, be not ashamed to stammer about it.

Thus speak and stammer: "That is *my* good, that do I love, thus doth it please me entirely, thus only do *I* desire the good.

Not as the law of a God do I desire it, not as a human law or a human need do I desire it; it is not to be a guide-post for me to celestial realms and paradises.

An earthly virtue is it which I love: little prudence is therein, and still less of worldly wisdom.

But that bird built its nest beside me: therefore, I love and cherish it—now sitteth it beside me on its golden eggs."

Thus shouldst thou stammer and praise thy virtue.'[3]

In these lines, if anywhere in the poem, a Virtue manifests itself, with all that perfection of imagery which is the birthright of the re-born—and which, be it noted, veritably breaks through the barrier of concepts.

Such a Virtue as this, which is simply the expression of a man's integral Self—of that 'third reality', which emerges from the reconciliation of antinomies—is, of course, in the highest degree natural and spontaneous. It involves no stress or strain, no iron self-discipline or

[1] Z, 5.   [2] Z, 4.   [3] Z, 5.

self-watchfulness. These qualities, Nietzsche asserts, are attributes of the heroic, the sublime, the domineering—but never of the re-born. The mark of re-birth is an effortless beauty and grace.

So, 'I do not like those strained souls',[1] Zarathustra exclaims,' ungracious is my taste towards all those self-conscious ones'; and, confronted with a virtuous stoic, who has conquered all his vices and keeps himself under rigid control, he bursts out laughing:

'To be sure, I love in him the shoulders of the ox, but now do I want to see also the eyes of the angel.

Also his hero-will hath he still to unlearn: exalted shall he be, and not only sublime: the ether itself should raise him, the will-less one!

He hath subdued monsters, he hath solved enigmas. But he should also redeem his monsters and enigmas; into heavenly children should he transform them.

As yet hath his knowledge not learned to smile, and to be without jealousy; as yet hath his tumultuous passion not become calm in beauty.

Verily, not in satiety shall his longing submerge and be silent, but in beauty! Gracefulness belongeth to the munificence of the magnanimous.

His arm across his head: thus should the hero repose; thus should he also surmount his repose.

But precisely to the hero is *beauty* the hardest thing of all. Unattainable is beauty to all violent wills.'[2]

It reminds one of Keats's description of poetry: "'tis the supreme of power; 'tis might half-slumbering on its own right arm'; and truly Zarathustra's precept is matched by his practice. From this alone it should be obvious how far removed from Nietzsche's ideal was that Henleyesque posturing with which he is so often accredited. 'Let thy goodness be thy last self-conquest', Zarathustra adjures the stoic in conclusion: 'for this is the secret of the soul: when the hero hath abandoned it, then only approacheth it in dreams—the super-hero.'[3]

* * *

This condition of animal spontaneity at the human level, which Nietzsche both proclaims and exemplifies, is the touchstone of his revaluation. It manifests itself as creativity. Whatever helps creation, therefore, is 'good', whatever hinders it, 'bad'.[4] He calls it also 'the bestowing virtue', and sees it exemplified to the utmost in the very bestowal of these epithets—that is, 'the creation of values'.

Originally, he gives us to understand, they were bestowed by peoples, or 'herds', upon whatever helped or hindered their Will to Power:

[1] Z, 35.   [2] *Ibid.*   [3] *Ibid.*   [4] Z, 22.

'A table of virtues hangeth over every people. Lo! it is the table of their triumphs; lo! it is the voice of their Will to Power.

It is laudable, what is hard to them; what is indispensable and hard they call good; and what relieveth in the direst distress, the unique and hardest of all,—they extol as holy.

Whatever maketh them rule and conquer and shine, to the dismay and envy of their neighbours, they regard as the highest and foremost thing, the measure, the meaning of all else.'[1]

In this way, he accounts for the thousand moral codes which have regulated the lives of different peoples. Though the 'good' of one was often the 'evil' of another, each regarded its own as absolute—so long as it accorded with its needs.

What helps at one stage, however, may very well hinder at another. Consequently (it has happened time after time) a moral code may come to be felt as a fetter, only the more oppressive for being riveted in conscience itself—for 'almost in the cradle are we dowered with heavy words and values: "good" and "evil"—so calleth itself this dowry.'[2] Then dawns the day of the individual: the individual, that is, whose own Will to Power is so strong that it can no longer endure this constriction and fights itself gradually free.

In the opening Discourse of *Zarathustra*, Nietzsche records the stages of this emancipation—his 'path of wisdom',[3] as he calls it elsewhere. Such an individual must first have been a camel, 'the strong, load-bearing spirit in which reverence dwelleth';[4] next, a lion, able in the loneliest wilderness to fight the great dragon, 'Thou Shalt'; finally—a child. The camel would be the author of *Thoughts out of Season*, still devoted to Schopenhauer and Wagner; the lion, 'forced to find illusion and arbitrariness even in the holiest of things, that it may capture freedom from its love',[5] the author of *Human, All-too-Human*; the child is Zarathustra himself, who, having recovered his innocence, can do what even the lion could not—create new values:

'Innocence is the child, and forgetfulness, a new beginning, a game, a self-rolling wheel, a first movement, a holy Yea.

Aye, for the game of creating, my brethren, there is needed a holy Yea unto life: *its own* will, willeth now the spirit; *his own* world winneth the world's outcast.'[6]

Zarathustra, indeed, is the triumphant paean of such a man, and one of its glories is the *benedicite* which, ever and again, bursts from

---

[1] Z, 15.   [2] Z, 55.   [3] N, XIII, 39.   [4] Z, 1.   [5] *Ibid*.   [6] *Ibid*.

Nietzsche's lips as he celebrates his emancipation; the chant of gratitude for all change and suffering, birth-throes and death-throes, now revealed as the conditions of his Yea-saying:

'All the imperishable—that's but a simile, and the poets lie too much.

But of time and becoming shall the best similes speak: a praise shall they be, and a justification of all things that pass away!

Creating—that is the great salvation from suffering, and life's alleviation. But for the creator to appear, suffering itself is needed, and much transformation.

Yes, much bitter dying must there be in your life, ye creators! Thus are ye advocates and justifiers of all things that pass away.

For the creator himself to be the new-born child, he must also be willing to be the child-bearer, and endure the pangs of the child-bearer.

Verily, through a hundred souls went I my way, and through a hundred cradles and birth-throes. Many a farewell have I taken: I know the heartbreaking last hours.

But so willeth it my creating Will, my fate. Or, to tell you it more candidly: just such a fate—willeth my Will.

All *feeling* suffereth in me, and is in prison: but my *willing* ever cometh to me as my emancipator and joy.

Willing sets free: that is the true doctrine of will and freedom—so teacheth you Zarathustra.'[1]

It is no abstract theory that Nietzsche is enunciating, but a wisdom bought at the price of experience. And his hope is, that by defining anew as 'good' what actually helps creation, as 'bad' what hinders it, he may succeed, as others have succeeded, in giving his chosen people a new lease of life.

But, of course, to those still enslaved to the old moral code, his teaching is bound to sound criminal. What is 'moral' to him is 'immoral' to them, and *vice versa*. To them, he must seem to be preaching sheer selfishness—as indeed he is, the selfishness of the Self: 'healthy and holy call I this selfishness'.[2] Knowing nothing of the Self, however, they know nothing of such selfishness either. All they know is 'the selfishness of the sick, the sickly selfishness'[3]—and if they could, they would send him to the stake.

These are the pharisees, the 'monsters of virtue'[4] ('fiends of righteousness', Blake called them), whose Will is too weak to emancipate itself, and therefore wills its own demise. Their values are symptomatic of this

[1] Z, 24. [2] Z, 22, 1. [3] *Ibid.* [4] WP, 425.

weakness. It is their very incapacity to accept time and becoming that prompts them to invent a 'beyond', and to pit this against the here-and-now; and it is with them in mind that Zarathustra utters that noble caution, 'Remain true to the earth, my brethren, with all the power of your virtue! Let your bestowing love and your knowledge be devoted to the meaning of the earth.'[1] Creation, or generation, being now the touchstone of good, such degeneration must be the touchstone of bad: 'Tell me, my brother, what do we think bad, and worst of all? Is it not *degeneration?*'[2]

These are 'the good and the just', with whom, Zarathustra reiterates, lies 'the greatest danger to the whole human future'.[3] Yet even with them, he is not always indignant. How could he be, seeing that they are no more responsible for their weakness than he is for his strength? 'Gentle is Zarathustra to the sickly. Verily, he is not indignant at their modes of consolation and ingratitude. May they become convalescent and triumphant over their weakness, and create higher bodies for themselves!'[4] From time to time he will even plead with them, admonish them to hear in his words the very voice of their own true conscience: 'That your virtue is your Self, and not an outward thing, a skin, or cloak: that is the truth from the basis of your souls, ye virtuous folk!'[5]

It is of no avail. To them, such words are only a further blasphemy. They purse their lips and raise their brows: 'so you think we should do just as we will?' Yes, Zarathustra replies—but first of all you have to find out who 'you' are!—and remembering what his own self-knowledge has cost, what wonder if a note of exasperation creeps into his cry: 'Ah, that ye understood my word: "Do ever what ye will—but first be such as *can will*".'[6]

Ultimately, Nietzsche's table still bears only one commandment: Thou shalt become what thou art. Hence his words in 'that decisive chapter entitled, "Old and New Tables"':[7]

'Willing setteth free: for willing is creating: so do I teach. And *only* for creating shall ye learn!

'And also the learning shall ye *learn* only from me, the learning well! He who hath ears to hear, let him hear!'[8]

To become what one is: that is the precondition of creation. What the individual creates thereafter will depend on his personal aptitudes.

All the same, as we have seen, there are values inherent in health; values which, though each may discover them independently, all will

[1] Z, 22, 2.   [2] Z, 22, 1.   [3] Z, 56, 26.   [4] Z, 3.
[5] Z, 27.   [6] Z, 49, 2.   [7] EH, p. 104.   [8] Z, 56, 16.

inevitably share: and these Nietzsche hopes to establish. One by one, in these first two Parts, he redefines the traditional virtues—pity, obedience, chastity, piety, justice—assigning to each, as he supposes, a new content. His revaluation of pity we know. There is no space here, nor is it needful, to enlarge upon all the others. It will suffice to consider briefly his standpoint regarding three of the most important human relationships: discipleship, friendship and marriage. In each case it will be found to derive directly from that first commandment.

* * *

That Nietzsche should have written well on discipleship was only to be expected. He himself had been a disciple: and a 'true disciple' he claimed to be still, not only of Schopenhauer, but of Wagner—by virtue of being their 'true opponent'.[1] In the aphorism quoted above, in which he reviews what remains of their teaching, when all that can be denied has been denied, he states that even from Wagner it is possible to learn one thing undeniable: namely—and here he cites his own words from *Richard Wagner at Bayreuth*—that 'all who wish to be free must become so through themselves'. Let us therefore, he concludes, 'remain loyal to what is true and original in Wagner, particularly in this, that we, his disciples, remain loyal to ourselves, to what is true and original in us.'[2]

Loyalty to ourselves: that, in Nietzsche's view, was the only lesson really worth learning from any master. True discipleship, accordingly, though it might be inspired, could never be demanded; and though it might assume many forms, could never be expressed in imitation. There was no book that irritated him more—perhaps mainly on account of its title—than *The Imitation of Christ*.

His mind was made up on this subject in conscious opposition to Wagner's—or what he supposed to be Wagner's. Whether Wagner had, in truth, demanded unqualified submission from his disciples, or whether they had simply been carried away by the magnetism of a stronger personality, Nietzsche, at least, had had to fight for his independence, and the experience was not to be forgotten. His letters to Gast reflect a touching anxiety not to be a second Wagner. If he wished to impose his will on others, as he did, his will was always that they too should become such as *could* will.

To a true master, he maintained, nothing could be more acceptable than his disciples' growing independence. If they challenged him, so much the better: that would be the soundest tribute to his teaching. He had longed that Wagner himself could have seen things in this light—

[1] D, 542.   [2] JW, 99.

there is an aphorism in 'Sanctus Januarius', 'STELLAR FRIENDSHIP', in which this longing finds exquisite expression—and in the beautiful farewell Discourse at the close of Part I of *Zarathustra*, he shows how he himself would have wished to act, had the opportunity ever come his way:

'I now go alone, my disciples! Ye also now go away, and alone! So will I have it.

Verily, I advise you: depart from me, and guard yourselves against Zarathustra! And better still: be ashamed of him! Perhaps he hath deceived you.

The man of knowledge must be able not only to love his enemies, but also to hate his friends.

One requiteth a teacher badly if one remain merely a pupil. And why will ye not pluck at my wreath?

Ye venerate me; but what if your veneration should some day collapse! Take heed lest a statue crush you!

Ye say, ye believe in Zarathustra! But of what account is Zarathustra? Ye are my believers: but of what account are all believers!

Ye had not yet sought yourselves: then did ye find me. So do all believers; therefore all belief is of so little account.

Now do I bid you lose me and find yourselves; and only when ye have all denied me, will I return unto you.

Verily, with other eyes, my brethren, shall I then seek my lost ones; with another love shall I then love you.

And once again shall ye have become friends unto me, and children of one hope: then will I be with you for the third time, to celebrate the great noontide with you.'

Strangely enough, these lines were written 'precisely in the hallowed hour when Richard Wagner died in Venice'.[1]

Somewhat later, Nietzsche was to say that he owed it to Schopenhauer and Wagner that he was able 'as it were, to make them take sides against themselves.'[2] So it is always with the true disciple: his gratitude is manifest in antagonism, his reverence in betrayal; 'it cannot be helped—every master has but one pupil, and *he* becomes disloyal to him, for he also is destined for mastery'.[3] The 'Nietzschean' will always be a solecism.

True discipleship is consummated in friendship: a relation between equals. The love of friends is that 'other love' referred to by Zarathustra; and in one of his notes for the poem, Nietzsche states tersely

[1] EH, p. 97.   [2] CW, p. 102.   [3] H, II, 357.

what he meant by it: ' "Love thy neighbour"—this would mean first and foremost: "Let thy neighbour go his own way"—and it is precisely this kind of virtue that is the most difficult.'[1]

Difficult or not, it is certainly the rarest kind. The last thing most people wish for their friends (let alone their relations) is that these should go their own way, more especially if it happens to be a way that leads through hardship and danger. The very hallmark of neighbour-love is taken to be an unremitting effort to spare us from going our own way—to spare us from becoming what we are. In the last analysis, it is themselves that such people wish to spare—even when their solicitude is genuine, and not, as it often is, a pleasurable indulgence in emotion, an attempt to place the other under an obligation, or a means of acquiring the reputation of 'one who sympathises and understands'. The more genuine it is, the more it bespeaks a petty nature, for which hardship and danger are the worst of evils.

The true love, the love of the Self, is unsparing. 'Woe unto all lovers who have not a loftiness which is still above their pity,'[2] cries Zarathustra:

'But attend also to this word: All great love is above all its pity: for it seeketh still—to create what is loved!

"Myself do I offer unto my love, *and my neighbour as myself*"—such is the language of all creators.

All creators, however, are hard.'[3]

Rather than mitigate hardship, the creator will even augment it, if, by that means, he can the better enable his friend to become what he is. He will destroy his illusion, for example, at the risk of destroying his consolation. It is this that Zarathustra means by his saying, 'in one's friend one shall have one's best enemy. Thou shalt be closest unto him with thy heart when thou withstandest him.'[4]

Such love is sometimes called 'disinterested'. Nietzsche, of course, shunned the word. It smacked of Romanticism, of idealistic talk about 'renunciation' and the supersession of the individual by 'spirit'. He held that it was nothing impersonal; that even self-sacrifice was a sacrifice to the Self; that, in the art of friendship as in every art, the Self alone was creative. He held likewise that, if we should so act as to enable the man who delights us to blossom forth, it is by blossoming forth ourselves that we do most to promote this: 'thou canst not adorn thyself fine enough for thy friend'.[5] The joy of the creator is itself the best medicine for the uncreated: 'physician heal thyself: then wilt thou also heal thy

[1] N, 2, 15.   [2] Z, 25.   [3] Z, 22, 2.   [4] Z, 14.   [5] *Ibid.*

patient. Let it be his best cure to see with his eyes him who maketh himself whole.'[1]

Terminology apart, however, the essence of friendship, in his view, as of discipleship, is respect for the other's personality. Friendship, in fact, differs from discipleship only in being a relation of *mutual* purgation and creation: since, of course, illusions and weaknesses will never be all on one side. In what Blake called 'the severe contentions of friendship', it is as likely that one's own conviction will succumb as the other's—and just as desirable. 'A friend of truth,' Nietzsche said, 'that is, an enemy of deception, that is a friend of independence, ought, when refuted, to exclaim, "I have escaped a great danger: I was all but strangled in my own shoe-laces!"'[2] He never had any patience with the 'paternal vanity'[3] of thinkers.

It was part of Nietzsche's tragedy that he never met personally anyone who would so contend with him for the truth. He was driven to realize in imagination the satisfaction that life denied him: in *Zarathustra*, 'the mythopoeic instinct goes forth in quest of a friend'.[4] But his loss was our gain. Few men, at least in modern times, have written so well on friendship.

Like the Greeks, he rated it higher than married love. He was, we know, suspicious of marriage. He had witnessed *mésalliances* enough to rid him of romantic illusions: 'laugh not at such marriages: what child hath not had reason to weep over its parents?'[5] From his own standpoint, moreover, many a 'successful' match was no better than a *mésalliance*, since it spelt the end of the man's concern for ideals, his abandonment of his 'task'. Yet the all-too-celebrated saying about the whip (so provocative to the literal-minded) should not mislead us. On this subject, too, Nietzsche had thought long and earnestly, and his conclusions deserve respect.

He was, of course, no feminist. 'The happiness of man is, "I will"; the happiness of woman is, "He will"':[6] that is the atheist's transcription of 'He for God only, she for God in him.' He adhered to the traditional belief that woman aspires to a fulfilment, and perfection, different from those of man; and that, though it was in her nature to put a man's power to the proof, there was no-one she despised more than him who attracted without being able to overpower her. She wished to believe in a man, and the only man she could believe in was one who believed in himself. A marriage that spelt the husband's abandonment of his task, therefore, spelt frustration to her: and it was for the woman's sake as much as the man's that Nietzsche deplored such matches.

He believed, indeed, that the militant feminism of his day had its roots

[1] Z, 22, 2.   [2] N, XI, 161.   [3] *Ibid.*   [4] N, XII, 123.   [5] Z, 20.   [6] Z, 18.

in such frustration: 'of man there is little here, therefore do their woman become like men: for only he who is man enough will *save the woman* in woman'.[1] And naturally this disgusted him. Not because he doubted the qualification of some women for so-called masculine professions; still less because he disputed that all women could, if so minded, change their traditional character (no characters being unchangeable): but because he was persuaded that any such change would be for the worse. He did not so greatly admire the man of the present day as to think him a desirable model: '*Masculinisation of women*, that is what "the emancipation of women" really means. In other words, that they should model themselves on the man of the present day and claim the same rights as he. I see in this a *degeneration* of the present-day women's instincts; they ought to realize that in this way they are ruining their powers.'[2]

For the sake of both men and women, therefore—above all, for their children's sake—Nietzsche was opposed to precipitate marriage. Zarathustra advises couples to live together experimentally before they commit themselves finally. Only the man with a task, and the strength to sustain it, was *worthy* of wife or child. Of marriage as it might be, however, not Kierkegaard himself has entertained a more exalted idea: for it might be, Nietzsche declared, a lifelong dedication, not merely to mutual, but to joint creation:

'I have a question for thee alone, my brother: like a sounding-lead, cast I this question into thy soul, that I may know its depth.

Thou art young, and desirest child and marriage. But I ask thee: Art thou a man *entitled* to desire a child?

Art thou a victorious self-conqueror, the ruler of thy passions, the master of thy virtues? Thus do I ask thee.

Or doth the animal speak in thy wish, and necessity? Or isolation? Or inner discord?

I would have thy victory and freedom long for a child. Living monuments shalt thou build to thy victory and freedom.

Beyond thyself shalt thou build. But first of all must thou be built thyself, four-square in body and soul.

Not only onward shalt thou propagate thyself, but upward! For that purpose may the garden of marriage help thee!

A higher body shalt thou create, a first movement, a spontaneously rolling wheel—a creator shalt thou create.

Marriage: so call I the will of the twain to create the one that is more than those who created it. The reverence for one another, as those exercising such a will, call I marriage.'[3]

[1] Z, 49, 2.   [2] N, XIV, 243.   [3] Z, 20.

Marriage, like friendship and discipleship, is revalued from the stand-point of the creator.

* * *

It is not only Nietzsche's virtues that derive directly from his first commandment; so likewise does his ideal. For no ethical system is com-plete without an ideal, least of all one whose keynote is creative activity. Neither discipleship, friendship nor marriage, it will be noted, has its end in itself. The deepest bond between man and woman is the child; between man and man, allegiance to a common cause. ' "We wish to create a Being" '—so runs another of his notes—'we all wish to have a hand in it, to love it. We all want to be pregnant—and to honour and respect ourselves on that account. We must have a goal in view of which we may all love each other!'[1]

Nietzsche desires that men should be 'warriors', that is to say, neither centred upon one another, nor merely reacting passively to circum-stances, but actively taking the initiative, united in a task that transcends themselves. The Will to Power is by nature aggressive; it goes forth in search of obstacles, it seeks to compare, master, conquer, and destroy. In olden times, this Will found expression in the struggle of people with people and the foundation of States and Empires. Now, though raised to a higher level, it still demands equivalent action: 'war', therefore, 'but without powder, between different thoughts and the hosts who support them'.[2] It is to this 'spiritual warfare', for the sake of ideas and their consequences, that he summons men in the celebrated lines:

'If ye cannot be saints of knowledge, then, I pray you, be at least its warriors. They are the companions and forerunners of such saintliness.

I see many soldiers; could I but see many warriors! "Uniform" one calleth what they wear; may it not be uniform what they therewith hide!

Ye shall be those whose eyes ever seek for an enemy—for *your* enemy. And with some of you there is hatred at first sight.

Your enemy shall ye seek; your war shall ye wage, and for the sake of your thoughts! And if your thought succumb, your uprightness shall still shout triumph thereby!

Ye shall love peace as a means to new wars—and the short peace more than the long.

You I advise not to work, but to fight. You I advise not to peace, but to victory. Let your work be a fight, let your peace be a victory!

One can only be silent and sit peacefully when one hath bow and arrow; otherwise one prateth and quarreleth. Let your peace be a vic-tory!

[1] NZ, 51.   [2] NZ, 54.

THE PROPHET　　　　　　　

Ye say it is the good cause which halloweth even war? I say unto you: it is the good war which halloweth every cause.

War and courage have done more great things than charity. Not your sympathy, but your bravery hath hitherto saved the victims.'[1]

Once more the explicit is implicit: and let us hope it is no longer needful to dwell on the fate of these lines at the hands of those who (in Blake's phrase) 'for ever depress Mental and prolong Corporeal War'. There was surely a twofold irony in the spectacle of Britain, prostrate in admiration for the soldier, being invited to see in them a witness to German infamy!

But what is to be the cause in which these warriors will unite, the goal they will aim at, the Being they will wish to create? The answer is contained in Zarathustra's words: 'Your highest thought, however, ye shall have it commanded unto you by me—and it is this: man is something to be surpassed.'[2] To be inherent in health, the ideal can be one thing only: the elevation of humanity itself to a new level of creativity; the raising of a generation, which shall not have to struggle, as ours must struggle, against the tyranny of good and evil, but be free from the start to follow the dictates of its Will. On the soil of a generation so raised, Nietzsche surmised, a finer type of man might spring up than any the world has seen yet, a type beside which the healthiest of those who have had to reconquer their health will appear but forerunners and foreshadowings. It was for the loftiest representative of this type that he adopted the name 'Superman' (*Übermensch*).

With this conception, the grand spiral of Nietzsche's thought reaches its apex. The analogy with *Thoughts out of Season* is manifest. There he had proclaimed a new educational principle, which should permit the next generation to realize its full potentialities, and spare the man of genius in particular that conflict with the spirit of his age which had so often been his undoing. He had called for a hundred 'soldiers of culture' to initiate the new renaissance—not in the belief that they themselves could enter the Promised Land, but in the determination that their children, at least, should not be crippled by the unnatural education in vogue. He had issued his summons in *The Use and Abuse of History* —and not a soul had responded. Wholly appropriate, therefore, is the haunted and haunting 'Grave-Song', recalling that phase of his life, and the disillusion that had brought it to an end:

'How did I ever bear it? How did I survive and surmount such wounds? How did my soul rise again out of those sepulchres?'

[1] Z, 10.　　　　　　[2] *Ibid.*

Yea, something invulnerable, unburiable is with me, something that would rend rocks asunder: it is called *my Will*. Silently doth it proceed, and unchanged throughout the years. . . .'[1]

Nietzsche's underlying purpose has, indeed, remained unchanged. One by one, in *Zarathustra*, reappear the threads of his earlier thought: his criticism of the 'objective' in 'The Immaculate Perception', of the philologists in 'Scholars', of the Hegelian State-worshippers in 'The New Idol', of the Culture-Philistines in 'The Land of Culture'. It is in the last of these that we hear, for the first time, that proud and poignant affirmation, 'unto my children will I make amends for being the child of my fathers: and unto all the future—for *this* present day.'[2]

Thus, in imagination, the childless Nietzsche, the master without pupils, the professor without students, shoulders the responsibility for an entire succeeding generation; and once more appeals for a band of dedicated souls—'lonely ones of today, seceding ones'[3]—to share the responsibility with him. 'Ye could well create Superman,' he exhorts them: 'not perhaps ye yourselves, my brethren! But into fathers and forefathers of the Superman could ye transform yourselves: and let that be your best creating!'[4] This will be the cause in which his warriors will unite. 'May I bear Superman', will be the prayer of their women; 'May we create Superman', their own.[5]

* * *

The idea of the Superman dominates the first two Parts of *Zarathustra*. '*I teach you the Superman*'[6] are almost the prophet's opening words. Though the name was not of Nietzsche's coining, it was he who first gave it currency, and even today he is known more by this than by anything else. The bare fact that 'he believed in the Superman' has sufficed to establish the conventional portrait (*vide* Bertrand Russell *et alios*), of one who sought in an earthly hereafter compensation for the evils of the present, and staked his faith on the 'progress of the species'.

That this portrait has not even the verisimilitude of a caricature must, by this time, be obvious. *Amor fati* is the keynote of *Zarathustra*. It was always the uncreative, Nietzsche averred, who were compelled 'to place the value of life in a "life after death", or in the progressive development of ideas, or of mankind, or of the people, or of man to super-man.'[7] The creative, on the contrary, would find their America here or nowhere; and only when they had found it, would they be capable of sharing his ideal. The Superman is *amor fati* incarnate.

As for the 'progress of the species', faith in that is possible only to a

[1] Z, 33.   [2] Z, 36.   [3] Z, 22, 2.   [4] Z, 24.
[5] Z, 18.   [6] Z, Prologue, 3.   [7] WP, 666.

theist. Evolution, as Nietzsche saw it, had no inherent goal; it was precisely because it had none, that man was summoned to choose his own. God being dead, 'man becomes responsible for all that lives'.[1] The advent of Superman, therefore, far from being inevitable, depends entirely upon our volition. 'The danger of a reversion to *animality* is real.'[2]

Europe, Nietzsche saw, was living in a moral interregnum. A thawing wind had blown, the ice was giving way: 'O my brethren, is not everything *at present in flux?*'[3] Though the idealism of the past still lived on, its ideals were perishing daily. 'We possess a powerful store of moral *feelings*, but we have no goal for them all. They mutually contradict each other: they have their origin in different tables of values.'[4] This state of affairs could not last. Unless that idealism was given a goal, it too would be dissipated: the alternative to generation was degeneration:

'And thus spake Zarathustra unto the people:

It is time for man to fix his goal. It is time for man to plant the germ of his highest hope.

Still is his soil rich enough for it. But that soil will one day be poor and exhausted, and no lofty tree will any longer be able to grow thereon.

Alas! There cometh the time when man will no longer launch the arrow of his longing beyond man—and the string of his bow will have unlearned to whizz!

I tell you: one must still have chaos in one to give birth to a dancing. star. I tell you: ye still have chaos in you.

Alas! There cometh the time when man will no longer give birth to any star. Alas! There cometh the time of the most despicable man who can no longer despise himself.

Lo! I show you *the Last Man*.'[5]

The Last Man is the antipodes of the Superman—he projected them simultaneously, Nietzsche said. He is the culmination of the present-day 'mass-man', born of industrialism, living on newspapers, dying in the dregs of Christianity; a man incapable of evil, because all his passions will have been atrophied; happy, because happiness, for him, will mean comfort, security, incessant mass-produced entertainment; content, because no longer eager to create, but only to consume; at one with his neighbours and himself, because indifferent to all that makes for truth: the perfect end-product of utilitarianism.

Nietzsche was acquainted with the 'mass man'; he had fled from Germany—much as, forty years later, Lawrence fled from England—to

[1] N, XII, 168.   [2] N, XII, 360.   [3] Z, 56, 8.   [4] NZ, 2.   [5] Z, Prologue, 5.

escape him. He knew his destiny too, and believed that if once it were
realized, all hope for the future would be lost. Even the inspiration of
history would perish: not merely because the memory of the mob goes
back at most a couple of generations, but also because 'a great potentate
might arise, an artful prodigy, who with favour and disfavour could
strain and constrain all the past until it became for him a bridge, a harbinger, a herald and a cock-crow'.[1] Humanity would be robbed of its
history, and history of its meaning. The lives of the dead can be given
a meaning, and the whole of past time a goal, he writes in one of his
notes, only 'if out of *this* material we shape the Superman':[2] only, that
is, if we seize the opportunity while it lasts, to posit a loftier goal and
will the conditions of its realization.

This opportunity, however, if it is irrecoverable, is also unprecedented: for the very forces, above all the force of science, which have
undermined past ideals, have, at the same time, placed in our hands the
means of realization:

'The conditions for the emergence of a *stronger* type, which have been
reached here and there, partly by necessity, partly by chance, we can
now understand and *will* consciously: we can create the conditions under
which such an ascent is possible. Up till now "education" has had the
good of society in view: *not* the greatest possible good of the future,
but the good of just the existing society. "Tools" for it were what was
wanted. Were the *resources of energy increased*, it is possible to see how
part of these resources might be diverted from the good of society to a
future good.'[3]

Always in the past, Nietzsche insists, the aim of morality has been
the supremacy of the people, indirectly of the race. Though 'genius to
Zarathustra seems like the incarnation of his thought',[4] even genius,
hitherto, has been no more than a lucky chance. Though 'the Greeks
were wonderful',[5] their whole life being so organized as to favour the
flowering of genius, even the Greeks hardly knew what they were
about, and, if they had known, would still have been unable, with their
rudimentary science, to plan the future more effectively than they did.
Only now is it possible deliberately 'to bring forth creatures which stand
sublimely above the whole species man, and to sacrifice "one's neighbours" and oneself to this end.'[6] Only now can the many moralities with
their many restricted goals give way to one morality with one goal, in
the pursuit of which humanity itself will, for the first time, be one:

[1] Z, 56, 11.   [2] N, XII, 360.   [3] WP, 898.   [4] NZ, 53.   [5] NZ, 57.   [6] NZ, 46.

'A thousand goals have there been hitherto, for a thousand peoples have there been. Only the fetter for the thousand necks is still lacking; there is lacking the one goal. As yet humanity hath not a goal.

But pray tell me, my brethren, if the goal of humanity be still lacking, is there not also still lacking—humanity itself?—

Thus spake Zarathustra.'[1]

A time like the present, Nietzsche believed, a moral interregnum, was a time of great danger—but of still greater potentialities. The decay of the old ideals was final; they would never regain their hold on humanity; the saint, whether Christian, Buddhist or Hindu, had had his day. But it was only for want of an alternative that the will was turning towards destruction: and an alternative ideal was conceivable. In *Zarathustra* he was trying to supply it. His hope was that men would be so enthused by it, that they would never rest until they had realized the conditions of its fulfilment.

But *what*, it may be asked, are these conditions, and *how* are they to be realized? To such questions, he has no answer. Or rather, he has many answers, which the curious may find in his notes, and to some of which we shall have to return. But they are not to be found in *Zarathustra*, and it is wrong to read them into it: first, because it is essential to his approach that the answers are to be discovered by experiment—experiment on ourselves first of all; and secondly, because it is just to this task that he wishes to direct all the courage, devotion and energy of his warriors.

Even the groundwork, he points out in *The Joyful Wisdom*, has yet to be laid. 'He who wants to make moral questions a subject of study has an immense field of labour before him. . . . The observation alone of the different degrees of development which the human impulses have attained, and could yet attain, according to the different moral climates, would furnish too much work for the most laborious; whole generations, and regular co-operating generations of the learned would be needed in order to exhaust the points of view and the material here afforded.'[2] Scientists and economists, educationists and artists, doctors, historians and statesmen, have all their contribution to make, before the great venture can even begin—'a process of experimenting in which every kind of heroism could satisfy itself, an experimenting for centuries, which could put into the shade all the great labours and sacrifices of previous history.'[3]

Nietzsche's task is not to prescribe the conditions, but simply to pro-

----

[1] Z, 15.   [2] JW, 7.   [3] *Ibid.*

claim the goal, that 'nobler ideal of action' to which, he had always maintained, science must be subordinated, if it is not to prove disastrous to mankind. On this alone, his heart and mind are at one. This, however, he does proclaim, with all the splendour of language at his command: and what is explicit in Zarathustra's Discourses is implicit in the figure of the prophet—a Nietzsche without Nietzsche's infirmities, without that bad conscience which, he now knew too well, he himself could never hope to outlive.

'I had to render homage to Zarathustra, a Persian,' he was to write later, 'the Persians being the first to have seen history as a great whole. A succession of cycles, each presided over by a prophet. To each prophet his *hazar*, his empire of a thousand years.'[1] Before his mind's eye there floated that 'ever-recurring vision' of a civilization more comprehensive, more purposive and humane, than any the world had seen heretofore; of festivals in honour of the future, arenas for athletic contests, theatres for the enactment of tragedies, temples where men would re-dedicate themselves to the generation of Superman—and, of all this civilization, *Thus Spake Zarathustra* would be the Gospel!

It was the same vision that glowed and coruscated in the electric air of Turin, on the eve of his final breakdown:

'I am such a harbinger of joy as there never was; I know tasks so lofty that the very idea of them has hitherto been wanting, only after me do hopes exist again. Thus I am necessarily also the man of fate. For when truth enters the lists against the lies of millennia, we shall have shocks, a spasm of earthquakes, a transposition of mountain and valley, the like of which has never been dreamed. The concept Politics is then raised wholly to the plane of spiritual war.'[2]

* * *

It is always easy to smirk at ideals and idealists, especially when they express themselves as incautiously as this. Indeed, it is a principal occupation of writers, who have generally tended to be sycophants, and are just as obsequious towards their present-day patron, the people, as they used to be towards the nobility. To flatter our little weaknesses, to present them as delightful and endearing—what more is required of the successful essayist? 'Man is something to be surpassed!' Such an exhortation is hardly a passport to popularity.

Yet those who hear in these words no more than the ravings of a madman are not merely wanting in imagination, but ignorant of contemporary history. There was nothing extravagant in Nietzsche's claim

[1] N, XIV, 303.   [2] EH, p. 132.

to have given the Germans their profoundest book; nothing megalomaniac even in his persuasion that he was thereby inaugurating a new
epoch. Books, and much shallower books than *Zarathustra*, have
decided the fate of peoples. Not twenty years had then elapsed since
another had been published in German, which has already replaced the
Bible, the Koran and the Analects over half the surface of the world, and
whose author is even now hailed as the Messiah with whom 'pre-history
ends and human history begins'.

Why is it, then, that Marx has had such titanic effect, whilst Nietzsche
still rests in comparative obscurity? There are many reasons; but one,
and by no means the least important, we have touched on already in
these pages: Marx was swimming with the current. That is the proudest
boast of his following—that he knew which way history was going, and
went with it. Nietzsche, on the contrary, who also knew which way
history was going, for that very reason swam against it with all his
might. It was going in the direction of the Last Man:

'Therefore, O my brethren, a *new nobility* is needed, which shall be the
adversary of all mob and tyrant rule, and shall inscribe anew the word
"noble" on new tables.

For many noble ones are needed, and many kinds of noble ones, *for
a nobility*! Or, as I once said in parable: "That is just divinity, that
there are Gods, but no God."' [1]

Nietzsche, not being a theist, not believing in the divine purpose of the
world, called on an *élite* to rise against the tyranny of the actual, to submit to laws that were not the laws of fickle history—and no such *élite*
was forthcoming.

In the first part of *Zarathustra*, indeed, he recaptured all the confidence with which he had issued *The Use and Abuse of History*. His
Will, as the 'Grave Song' tells us, was once more buoyed with hope.
Like many great prophets in the first flush of their illumination, he seems
to have fully believed that a message so self-evident and urgent could
not fail to awake an immediate response, in his friends at the very least;
and the reception it actually did meet with staggered him: 'the case of
Zarathustra proves that one can speak with the utmost clearness, and
yet be heard by no-one'. [2] His sister says that he resolved for a moment
to write no more; and though it would have been as impossible for him
to stop writing as for a fountain to stop overflowing, the beautiful
'Night-Song', composed at Rome in the spring of 1883, gives poignant
expression to his disappointment, his longing for genuine readers. A

[1] Z, 56, 11.   [2] Quoted: E. Förster-Nietzsche, Introduction to Z.

mystic, he wrote the following year, could be defined as one 'who has enough and too much of his own happiness, and seeks out a language for his happiness because he wishes to *give away*.'[1]

Above all, Nietzsche was horrified to see his message construed as one of hatred and revenge. It is this realization, that his '*doctrine* is in danger', that 'mine enemies have grown powerful and have disfigured the meaning of my doctrine, so that my dearest ones have to blush for the gifts that I gave them',[2] that impels Zarathustra's return to his disciples at the beginning of Part II; and he makes more than one attempt to safeguard it: 'rather will I be a pillar-saint than a whirl of vengeance!'[3]

In the Discourse, 'On Passing By', for example, Zarathustra is made to encounter a Fool, whom the people called "the ape of Zarathustra": for he had learned from him something of the expression and modulation of language, and perhaps liked also to borrow from the store of his wisdom.'[4] This Fool takes up his own cry against the effeminacy of men and the masculinization of women, against democracy as the rule of the trader and mediocrity sanctified as virtue—and Zarathustra descends on him like a sandstorm. 'Floweth there not a tainted, frothy swamp-blood in thine own veins, when thou hast learned to croak and revile?' he cries:

'What was it that first made thee grunt? Because no-one sufficiently *flattered* thee:—therefore didst thou seat thyself beside this filth, that thou mightest have cause for much grunting.—

That thou mightest have cause for much *vengeance*! For vengeance, thou vain fool, is all thy foaming; I have divined thee well!

But thy fool's-word injureth *me*, even when thou art right! And even if Zarathustra's word *were* a hundred times right, thou wouldst ever— *do* wrong with my word!'[5]

Any fool can denounce, and win an audience by denouncing, evil: by so doing he only duplicates it. The creator alone can annihilate, and he annihilates by creating: 'out of love alone shall my contempt and my warning bird take wing'.[6] Therefore Zarathustra gives the Fool this parting precept: 'where one can no longer love, there should one— *pass by*!'[7]

The nobility Nietzsche looked for was a nobility of yea-sayers, of men who had become what they were, the new, the unique, the inimitable. That is what he meant by the saying, 'there are Gods, but no God'. Such men alone either could or would transform themselves into fathers and forefathers of the Superman. It is one of the crowning ironies of philo-

[1] N, XIII, 297.   [2] Z, 23.   [3] Z, 29.   [4] Z, 51.   [5] *Ibid.*   [6] *Ibid.*   [7] *Ibid.*

sophical history that the only time he has seemed to exert an influence comparable to Marx's, was the time when he himself was invoked by an artful prodigy as the prophet of revenge and the Last Man.

Nietzsche tried to safeguard his doctrine. So far his attempt has proved unavailing. Europe, indeed, has neglected its prophets so long that now the very survival of the species hangs in the balance—it was by no means so secure as he thought. Whereas he could look forward at least to *a* future, today we write our books, great and little, in the knowledge that within a few years or months, they, we and every possible reader may well have been exterminated. 'The Last Man liveth longest,'[1] he predicted. The Last Man may prove to be the shortest-lived of all; he may prove literally the last.

Still, the issue is not decided; and this much, at all events, is certain: that if ever the West does rear a generation great enough for discipleship—great enough, that is, to listen and learn from the genius when he appears, as men still sometimes do in the East, instead of sneering at him during his lifetime, and sniggering after his death—that generation will find in *Zarathustra* a perennial fountain of inspiration.

(2)

Contrary to a common impression, the first three Parts of *Thus Spake Zarathustra* were planned as a whole, and executed according to plan. Nietzsche was aiming at a classical perfection of form, and though he failed to achieve it, he failed less completely, and for other reasons, than most of his critics have alleged.

Parts I and II are devoted to a revaluation of ethics, and to proclaiming the goal towards which this revaluation points. The ideal of the Superman, let it be repeated, springs from the idea of the Self, or Will to Power, and cannot be understood apart from it. Unless that leading idea is grasped, the unity of these two Parts is lost.

One value there is, however, which Nietzsche has so far left untouched. In neither of these Parts does he more than allude to what, we know, he considered his most significant achievement, the revaluation of truth. It would be surprising if, in a work which he considered his most important, this achievement were not represented. In fact, the whole of Part III was reserved for its exposition.

Here, as elsewhere, artistic went hand in hand with philosophical necessity. It was not only dramatically appropriate that the revaluation

[1] Z, Prologue, 5.

of truth should constitute the climax of the poem: the teaching of Parts
I and II formed an indispensable prolegomenon. 'It was chiefly a matter
of climbing onto the second *rung*, in order from this position to reach the
third, the title of which is "Midday and Eternity".'[1] *Zarathustra* has, so
to speak, both an exoteric and an esoteric doctrine, and the esoteric can
only become intelligible to those who have made the exoteric their own.

This is indicated in the poem itself. Zarathustra is represented as
deliberately concealing his 'highest thought' from his disciples, until
such time as they shall be ready to receive it:

'Still are my children verdant in their first spring, standing nigh one
another, and shaken in common by the winds, the trees of my garden
and of my best soil.

And verily, where such trees stand beside one another, there *are*
Happy Isles!

But one day will I take them up, and put each by itself alone! that it
may learn loneliness and defiance and prudence.

Gnarled and crooked and with flexible hardness shall it then stand by
the sea, a living lighthouse of unconquerable life.

Yonder where the storms rush down to the sea, and the snout of the
mountain drinketh water, shall each on a time have his day and night
watches, for *his* testing and recognition.

Recognized and tested shall each be, to see if he be of my type and
lineage: if he be master of a long will, silent even when he speaketh, and
giving in such wise that he *taketh* in giving:

—So that he may one day become my companion, a fellow-creator
and fellow-enjoyer with Zarathustra.'[2]

These disciples are still at the initial stage on the path of wisdom, when
it is needful before all else 'to revere more (and obey more and *learn*
more) than anybody; to receive into oneself whatsoever things are
worthy of veneration and let them fight it out among themselves; to bear
every burden . . . the time of community.'[3] To expose them at this stage
to the full blast of scepticism, would be, not to strengthen, but to
weaken, them.

That is one reason for Zarathustra's reticence: and it should be
remembered that his disciples are Nietzsche's imaginary readers. But
there is another, also indicated in the poem, which may have been more
intimately his own. 'The gentleness and mildness of the first and second
Parts', reads one of his notes, 'are both signs of a power not yet self-
reliant.'[4]

[1] L, 13, 1, 83.   [2] Z, 47.   [3] N, XIII, 39.   [4] NZ, 76.

Zarathustra is represented as himself unready to face the ultimate consequence of his scepticism: to face, that is, all that is implied in the idea of a meaningless universe—a universe in which even he, the thinker, is but one more means of prolonging the terrestrial dance.

Hence the singular effect produced on him, towards the close of Part II, by the Soothsayer's lamentation, ' "All is empty, all is alike, all hath been!" '[1] Instead of rebutting this with a glorification of life, as we should expect, Zarathustra is overwhelmed by it: 'sorrowfully did he go about and wearily'; and soon afterwards, falling asleep, he dreams the dream of death: 'All life had I renounced, so I dreamed. Night-watchman and grave-guardian had I become, aloft, in the lone mountain-fortress of Death.'[2]

His disciples, naturally, can make nothing of this. To them, Zarathustra is one who has long since vanquished pessimism. And he refuses to enlighten them. In the ensuing Discourse, on 'Redemption', he lets fall a hint of the truth—'not backward can the Will will; that it cannot break time and time's desire, that is the Will's most lonely tribulation'[3] —only to stop short with a look of terror. When one of them offers a consolatory interpretation of the dream, he responds with a shake of the head.

To us, the bearing should be clear. It is not, indeed, the old pessimism of Schopenhauer and Leopardi that has overwhelmed Zarathustra, but a new one, beside which theirs appears child's-play—and one which he has not yet dared face. He has in truth been 'suppressing something', not only from his disciples, but from himself: and now he can suppress it no longer. He must either wrestle with it till the going down of the sun, or else succumb before his final test.

Part II ends accordingly with two solemn Discourses, 'The Wisdom of Man' and 'The Great Silence', in which the prophet is overheard praying that this cup may pass from him:

'Then was there spoken unto me without voice: " *Thou knowest it, Zarathustra?* "

And I cried in terror at this whispering, and the blood left my face: but I was silent.

Then there was once more spoken unto me without voice: "Thou knowest it, Zarathustra, but thou dost not utter it"!—

And at last I answered, like one defiant, "Yes, I know it, but I will not utter it!". . .

[1] Z, 41.   [2] *Ibid.*   [3] Z, 42.

And there was spoken unto me for the last time: "O Zarathustra, thy fruits are ripe, but thou art not ripe for thy fruits!

So must thou go again into solitude".'

These Discourses form a transition from the second movement to the third.

When Part III opens, Zarathustra is already alone. Notwithstanding his shrinking from the silence and the abyss, he has no real desire to escape his destiny. He is actually in one of those moods when all that takes place shows itself as something not permitted to be absent—'the time is now past when accidents could befall me'[1]—and nerved for his final test:

'Before my highest mountain do I stand, and before my longest wandering: therefore must I first go deeper than I ever ascended.

Deeper into pain than I ever ascended, even into its darkest flood! So willeth my fate. Well! I am ready.'[2]

There can be no doubt that these developments are autobiographical. Nietzsche himself had been shunning the ultimate consequence of his scepticism, and in order to write the third Part, he had to confront it anew. His intention required that the ethical system he had proclaimed should be completed by the equivalent of a metaphysical. One of his letters to Gast, written in the interval between the second and third Parts, throws a flood of light on his intention. Here, after comparing their own relationship to that of a writer of comedy with a writer of tragedy ('I remember telling you that Wagner saw in me a writer of tragedy in disguise'), he confides:

'This Engadine is the birthplace of my *Zarathustra*. Only a moment ago I found the first draft of the thoughts incorporated in it. And one of the notes reads as follows: "The beginning of August 1881 in Sils Maria, 6,000 feet above the sea, and at a much higher altitude above all human affairs."

'I wonder how the pain and confusion of my spirit affected the tone of the first two Parts! (for the thoughts and the aims were already fixed). How strange, dear old friend! Quite seriously, I believe that *Zarathustra* turned out to be more cheerful and happier than he would otherwise have been. I could prove this almost "documentarily".

'On the other hand: I should not have suffered, nor should I suffer still a quarter as much as I have done, if during the last two years I had

[1] Z, 45.   [2] *Ibid.*

not fifty times over applied the themes of my hermit theories to practical life, and owing to the evil—yea! terrible results of this exercise—
driven myself to doubts concerning my very self. To this extent did
Zarathustra wax cheerful at my expense, and at his expense did I grow
overcast with gloom.

'By-the-by, I must inform you, not without regret, that now with the
third Part, poor *Zarathustra* is really going to be plunged in gloom—so
much so, that Schopenhauer and Leopardi will seem like children and
beginners beside *his* "pessimism". But the plan of the work requires it.
In order, however, to be able write this Part, what I shall need, in the
first place, is profound Heavenly cheerfulness—for I shall succeed with
the pathos of the highest kind only if I treat it as play. (In the end
everything becomes bright).'[1]

The notes referred to at the beginning of this passage (they have been
preserved) were those that Nietzsche had jotted down at that 'tremendous moment' when the idea of the Eternal Recurrence first came to him,
as 'the highest formula for a Yea-saying to life'. Before he could compose Part III, he had to recover the ecstasy of that summer. Part III is
the record of the recovery.

Hence the striking contrast between this and the preceding Parts. If
it lacks their unity—the unity that goes with evaluation from a fixed
standpoint—it is notably more dramatic. There is progress throughout,
towards a foreseen *dénouement*. It is also, however, more obscure. This
Part, indeed, would be practically unintelligible without recourse to
other sources: for, by 1883, Nietzsche's recovery of the standpoint of
1881 had become intensely difficult. It involved a twofold self-conquest.
In the interests of clear exposition, it will be needful to treat the two
aspects of this self-conquest separately: but we should remember that,
in his own experience, as in the poem itself, they were inextricably bound
up with each other. Both are conveyed by the single symbol of Zarathustra's fitting himself to be 'teacher of the eternal return'.

* * *

The Eternal Recurrence is a thought so fantastic to most of us, so
remote from human experience, that there has been a natural tendency
among Nietzsche's critics to underplay it. They have inclined to treat it
as he himself treated Schopenhauer's 'undemonstrable doctrine of *one
will*' as 'a vice and extravagance of the philosopher'. It has even been
suggested that he was really in two minds about it, and for this reason
substituted the idea of the Superman as the theme of Parts I and II.
That this suggestion is untenable, we have seen. It stands to reason,

[1] L, 3, 9, 83.

in fact, that an idea to which Nietzsche attached such tremendous significance will not be lightly apprehended, and that if we think we have apprehended it lightly, we have in all probability misapprehended it. He himself has warned us: 'you must have experienced every form of scepticism and must have wallowed in ice-cold baths, otherwise you have no right to this thought.'[1] It stands to reason, equally, that the 'highest thought' of a philosopher whose ideas were invariably experiential can be neither so fantastic nor so remote as it may appear at first sight.

That in origin, at least, it was not so remote, we have already had occasion to note. In *The Joyful Wisdom*, the Recurrence is presented simply as the award of some fairy or demon, which, *if* it were offered, would be as rapturously embraced by the man who says Yea to life as it would be violently repelled by the Schopenhauerian Nay-sayer. It stands for the assertion of the Will.

As long as we are bound to morality, Nietzsche contends, we are bound to condemn the universe, because the universe is fundamentally immoral—and the heart's desire for absolute truth is a heritage of morality. The moment, on the other hand, surrendering our heart's desire, we pass beyond good and evil, we are free to affirm the universe, if only because there is nothing left in whose name it can be denied.

In actual experience, the joy of this self-transcendence is such that we cannot help affirming the universe: 'for nothing exists for itself alone, either in ourselves or in things; and if our soul has but once vibrated and resounded as a chord for joy, all the eternities have conspired to bring this about—and in this single moment all eternity finds itself approved, redeemed, justified, affirmed.'[2] To say Yea to anything is to say Yea to everything—and whoever is capable of saying Yea to everything would be capable of welcoming its perpetual return.

From this angle, the Recurrence may be regarded as a touchstone of *amor fati*: and it is still from this angle that Nietzsche presents the idea in *Beyond Good and Evil*, which shows that whatever development it may have undergone in the interval, its primary significance remained unchanged:

'Whoever, like myself, prompted by some enigmatical desire, has long endeavoured to go to the bottom of the question of pessimism and free it from the half-Christian, half-German narrowness and naivety in which it has finally presented itself to this century, namely, in the form of Schopenhauer's philosophy: whoever, with an Asiatic and super-

[1] ER, 43.   [2] WP, 1032.

Asiatic eye, has actually looked inside, and into the most world-renouncing of all possible modes of thought—beyond good and evil, and no longer like Buddha and Schopenhauer, under the dominion and delusion of morality—whoever has done this, has perhaps just thereby, without really desiring it, opened his eyes to behold the opposite ideal: the ideal of the most world-affirming, exuberant and vivacious man, who has not only learned to accept and come to terms with what was and is, but wishes to have it again *as it was and is*, for all eternity, insatiably calling out *da capo*, not only to himself, but to the whole piece and play; and not only to a play, but actually to him who requires just this play—and makes it necessary; because he always requires himself anew—and makes himself necessary.'[1]

The Recurrence, like *amor fati*, is a formula for that Yea-saying to life which is attained by the man who has overcome, not indeed his absolute scepticism, but the despair and revolt engendered by such scepticism. It stands for the conquest of nihilism.

Now at such a moment of total affirmation, the activity of valuation is suspended. That is why no man can live beyond good and evil—living being dependent upon valuation. That is why, also, the realization, *omnis existentia est perfectio*, can never, truly possessed, absolve a man from the effort to alter existence. Whether he wants to or not, he is bound to alter it: every action presupposes a judgement, every breath he draws bears consequences to the remotest time. The most he can do is live in the knowledge that there *is* a beyond good and evil; and that amounts, in effect, to making the acquisition of this knowledge, and the health conferred by it, his highest good. Thus the supersession of moral imperatives issues in a new imperative: 'Thou shalt become what thou art'.

Nietzsche, however, not infrequently offended against this distinction. He offended against it in two opposite ways—both of which, oddly enough, led to the same destination. This can be studied in *The Joyful Wisdom*, where as often as his vision grows dim, the New Year's Resolution is forgotten.

In the first place, recollecting that beyond good and evil there veritably is no qualitative distinction between the sick and the healthy, the divided and the whole, he will relegate his own 'taste' for health or wholeness to the same status as his taste for this or that diet, weather or scenery; in other words, he will confuse the prescription, 'become what thou art' with those purely personal and private prescriptions which the individual is required to draw up when once he has become what he is.

[1] BGE, 56.

In the aphorism, 'ABOARD SHIP', for example, he suddenly exclaims, 'the evil man, also, the unfortunate man, and the exceptional man, shall each have his rights, his philosophy, his sunshine!'[1]—which sounds like the very breath of toleration, until we realize what it implies: namely, that certain men, and presumably certain distinguishable classes of men, either cannot, or need not, or ought not, to attain to health at all, and consequently to a philosophy of health.

Translated into practice, this exclamation would imply, at best, a total indifference to the welfare of others: and there are occasions when Nietzsche virtually draws this conclusion. Whereas, in 'THE WILL TO SUFFERING AND THE COMPASSIONATE', he makes it clear that the healthy will seek, if not to spare their friends, at least to help them master their distress—to 'make them more courageous, more enduring, more simple, more joyful'—elsewhere he not infrequently talks as though individuality and community must always and everywhere be at odds, and every man's hand be raised against his brother's.

In the second place, swinging to the opposite extreme, he will arrogate to his own 'good' the status of an absolute; he will fall into the very error he has charged upon every other morality: 'it demands that there should be only one morality, it admits of no comparison, no criticism: it claims unconditional belief in itself.'[2] In other words, he will confuse the perfection of health, as opposed to sickness, with that perfection which, *sub specie aeternitatis*, belongs inalienably to both.

It was peculiarly easy for Nietzsche to fall into this error, inasmuch as contemporary morality was equally opposed to the 'ideal selfishness' that constituted his 'good' and to the realization that all 'goods' are ultimately relative. But the result was catastrophic. Having identified his 'good' with 'beyond good and evil' itself, he could only see in the opposition it encountered something absolutely satanic, to be eradicated at no matter what cost. He was carried away, again and again, on a tide of sheer negation; he became, for all his protests to the contrary, a 'naysayer'.

One instance of this may be cited. Wisely, in the aphorism, 'A NEW PRECAUTION', he counsels us not to 'struggle in direct conflict' with the enemy: 'let us rather see to it that our own influence on *all that is to come* outweighs and overweighs his influence.'[3] Yet, such is the intensity of his loathing for bourgeois morality, within a few pages of this we find him declaring, not merely that even a military civilization would be preferable to the industrial, seeing that the soldier does at least repudiate the religion of smug ease, but that war itself would be the greatest of

[1] JW, 289.   [2] N, XIII, 114.   [3] JW, 321.

blessings, as a means of eradicating it: 'I greet all the signs indicating that a more manly and warlike age is commencing, which will, above all, bring heroism again into honour! For it has to prepare the way for a yet higher age, and gather the force which the latter will one day require—the age which will carry courage into knowledge, and *wage war* for the sake of ideas and their consequences.'[1]

It has quite escaped Nietzsche's notice at this moment (although, as we have seen, he recollected it soon afterwards) that the soldier—he whose every action is dictated from above, who performs his duties effectively in proportion as his individuality is submerged in the unit, whose most characteristic, indeed symbolic, property is the uniform—is the perfection of the 'tool-like nature'; and, however well-equipped to destroy, about the last person on earth to create. 'We, however, *would seek to become what we are,*—the new, the unique, the inimitable, making laws for ourselves and creating ourselves.'[2]

These inconsistencies show how easily Nietzsche could lend himself to the abuse of his teaching on pity. Only squeeze that a little, and the 'self-concentration' of the artist becomes an excuse for the callousness of the slave-owner, the resolute independence of the thinker for the insensibility of the drill-sergeant.

By the summer of 1883, the reception of the first two Parts of *Zarathustra*, combined with the 'terrible results' of his attempt to apply its theories, had exacerbated his loathing of bourgeois morality to a pitch of almost insane extravagance. The resistance his gospel had encountered, more especially within his own circle, had all but extinguished the vision informing it. Never had he been further from *amor fati* than at the time of that letter to Gast, written on the eve of departure for Naumburg. Not a week had gone by since he had depicted himself to Overbeck as the 'victim of a ruthlessly revengeful sentiment'.

In order to write Part III, therefore, he had first of all to conquer this loathing. To recover the ecstasy of 1881, he had to accept, not merely his personal affliction, but the resistance responsible for it: for 'in approving all things, one approves equally all the *approbations* and *reprobations* of the present and past'.[3] And this is one aspect of the experience symbolized by Zarathustra's acceptance of the Recurrence.

* * *

There is, however, another, and more important, aspect. By 1883, Nietzsche had long ceased to see in the Recurrence *merely* a formula for Yea-saying. He had come to believe in it as a reality—at all events as a possibility—and one which, for him, opened up momentous vistas.

[1] JW, 283. [2] JW, 335. [3] N, XIII, 184.

His reason for this belief is not to be found in the various 'scientific' proofs scattered among his posthumous papers. These are of no importance. Had he believed that science could establish such a truth, he would not have been the sceptic he was. It was precisely because he was such a sceptic, that the conclusion was forced upon him. He had discovered—what any man may discover, who ponders the problem long enough—that every *objection* to his hypothesis sprang from a moral presumption. It sprang from 'the old habit of thinking of some purpose in regard to all phenomena, and of thinking of a directing and creating deity in regard to the universe':

'Although the world is no longer a God, it must still be capable of the divine power of creation and everlasting transformation; it must arbitrarily *forbid* itself to relapse into one of its previous forms; it must have, not only the intention, but also the *means* of *guarding* itself against any repetition: so, every instant, it must *direct* every one of its movements to the avoidance of goals, final states, repetitions—and whatever else may be the result of such an unpardonably insane mode of thought and desire. This is still the old religious mode of thought and desire, a sort of longing to believe that *in some way or other* the world yet resembles the old, beloved, infinite, unlimitedly creative God—that in some way or other "the old God still lives": that longing of Spinoza's which finds expression in the term, *deus sive natura*.'[1]

For all that he called the Recurrence 'the most scientific of all hypotheses',[2] this was the argument that really weighed with Nietzsche: 'He who does not believe in a *circular movement* of the universe must believe in an *arbitrary* God'.[3] The demonstration was negative, but not the less persuasive for that. So long as God could not be proved, neither could the Recurrence be disproved. If not a certainty, it was at least a glorious, gloomy or grotesque possibility—and 'even supposing the recurrence of the cycle to be only a probability or a possibility, even a thought, even a possibility, can shatter us and transform us. It is not only feelings and definite expectations that do that! See what effect the thought of eternal damnation has had!'[4] The idea of the Recurrence, in fact, *was* the ultimate consequence of nihilism—and it was as such that it became, in his eyes, 'the great *disciplinary* thought'.[5]

Since, he surmised, only those who could realize that 'nihilism, in that it is the *negation* of a real world, of a Being, might be a *divine mode of thinking*',[6] would be in a position to welcome 'the thought of

---

[1] WP, 1062.   [2] WP, 55.   [3] N, XII, 57.
[4] ER, 30.   [5] WP, 1056.   [6] WP, 15.

thoughts', once it was promulgated it would serve as a flail to thresh the wheat from the chaff among mankind. Those to whom a meaningless universe was repugnant, would find it unendurable. Seeing in the prospect of 'existence as it is, without either a purpose or a goal, but inevitably recurring, without an end in nonentity' only 'the extremest form of nihilism: nothing ("meaninglessness") eternal',[1] they would fall into utter despair and lose all inclination to live. Thus, the proud would inherit the earth, and 'among such as these a state will be possible of which the imagination of no utopist has ever dreamed!'[2]

Here, of course, Nietzsche was being singularly naïve. He ought to have realized that only a man in love with truth can ever despair of truth: that the uncreative, therefore, far from succumbing to the thought of the Recurrence, would merely dismiss it from their minds, or, if they were serious at all, embrace the alternative hypothesis of God. For once in a way, he overrated the integrity of the common mortal. Nevertheless, we must be on our guard against belittling his whole conception. When he spoke of its effect on the creative, he was speaking from experience: there cannot be any doubt that it did both shatter and transform him.

That is why he was undisturbed by the obvious objection: that if all that we do we have already done innumerable times, and nothing we do can introduce the slightest alteration into the predestined cycle, this thought must paralyse, rather than fortify, the will. The same objection, he pointed out, could be levelled against any determinist system, even Spinoza's or Calvin's, and was just as irrelevant to the one as to the others—the knowledge of our determination being itself an inescapable factor in the process: 'if thou assimilatest the thought of thoughts, it will also alter thee'.[3]

That, too, is why he believed himself to have found in the Recurrence a perfect counterpoise to the belittling of life, which has supervened upon the decay of supernaturalism. 'Religious belief is declining', he writes, 'and man is learning to regard himself as ephemeral and unessential . . . he does not exercise so much effort in striving or enduring';[4] the result is a vulgar hedonism. Without distracting our attention from the things of this world, as the old religious had done, the idea of the Recurrence would yet enable us 'to stamp the impress of eternity upon our lives'.[5] It would solve, in short, that problem which the late George Orwell (one of the acutest observers of his time) likewise regarded as crucial: 'how to restore the religious attitude while accepting death as final.'

'My doctrine is this: Live so that thou mayest *desire* to live again,— that is the task,—for *in any case* thou wilt live again!'[6] Heaven and

[1] WP, 55.   [2] ER, 32.   [3] ER, 28.   [4] ER, 26.   [5] ER, 35.   [6] ER, 27.

earth will pass away, and with them all that prolongs the terrestrial dance; but sooner or later—and what matter how much later, if we, non-existent meanwhile, know nothing of the lapse of millennia?—all will reconstitute itself: heaven and earth, the immeasurable process of evolution, the creator and his creation. Freed and exalted by this thought, the creative, Nietzsche affirms, will strive as never before to make their lives such as they can *wish* to be immortalized.

Knowing that 'one's every action exerts an unlimited influence on all that is to come',[1] they will feel that they are building, not for the moment only, but for all eternity: *non alia sed haec vita sempiterna*. More, knowing that, just as the present is the source of the future, so the future is the source of the past, they will exult in the godlike conviction that even the past is in some degree subject to their will—that man is his own creator! 'I myself am the *fatum*, and *throughout eternity, it is I who condition existence.*'[2] With this, Nietzsche reclaims for man the last prerogative of deity; and, as often as he reverts to the theme, his own work rises to such a pinnacle of unearthly eloquence, that it is impossible, for a moment at least, not to participate in his vertiginous ecstasy.

However, most of these notes belong to the late summer and autumn of 1881, when, as we know, he was living in a state of continuous exaltation, 'filled with a new vision which I had seen in advance of the rest of mankind'.[3] It was not long before this vision, too, began to reveal 'that Janus face which all great knowledge possesses'.[4]

The sequel might have been predicted. Since he himself could not always remain a Yea-sayer—since, that is, he himself could not always conquer nihilism—the very possibility which, in his moments of strength, had seemed an antidote to metaphysical anguish, served to magnify that anguish to infinity. It was not only his loathing for the 'small man' that returned at these times to plague him. No sooner was he now revisited by the thought of the meaninglessness of existence, than, to his horrified recollection, this became 'meaninglessness eternal'. The Recurrence recoiled on his own head. He it was now who could see in it only the extremest form of nihilism; he it was who was driven to utter despair! What wonder that he confided his ideas to Lou Salome 'as though they were a mystery unspeakably hard to tell!' He spoke of them, she recalled, 'in a low voice, with every appearance of the most profound horror: and truly life had been for him such bitter affliction, that he suffered from the eternal recurrence as from an atrocious certainty'.

So long as we envisage the Recurrence only as an abstract, and more

---

[1] N, XIII, 74.   [2] N, XII, 399.   [3] L, 14, 8, 81.   [4] EH, p. 91.

or less dubious, scientific hypothesis, this horror of Nietzsche's is bound to be unintelligible. It will appear to us, as it did to Overbeck (in whom he likewise confided), a symptom of impending insanity. It is only when we experience it, as he did, as the *nec plus ultra* of nihilism, that its real significance comes home to us. Then, on the contrary, even its probability ceases to be of concern: it becomes, as Berdyaev has said, the most powerful symbol ever devised for a universe emptied of God, of even the 'shadows of God'.

'If we do not make the *death of God* a magnificent *renunciation*, and a constant *victory over ourselves*', Nietzsche had written, 'we shall have to support this deprivation.'[1] It proved to be true of himself. He was one who, having pushed scepticism to its furthest limit, all at once finds nothing above him any longer; for whom the heavens have become empty as they never were to a living creature before; who cries out in all the agony of a child awakening from a nightmare in a deserted house, only to hear the echo of his own cry reverberate back on him, ages afterwards. The wonder is, not that he should have shrunk from the very recollection of this experience, but that he should have borne it as long as he did. He was the first atheist, and if there has been another one since, we have yet to hear of his name.

Nowadays, one does not like to think of the solitude he must have endured. To live with the 'thought of thoughts' for a night even, or for an hour, can be an overwhelming experience; and he lived with it constantly, never knowing when it might grip him again by the throat. He must have walked about among men like a ghost among the living, or like one of those spectral heroes who haunt the pages of Dostoievsky (Ivan Karamazov, too, had glimpsed the thought in his delirium). Nor is the impression he made on Rohde surprising, when, after an interval of nearly ten years, they met for the last time in 1886: 'an atmosphere of indescribable strangeness surrounded him, something wholly unknown to me in former times. . . . *It was as though he came from a country where no-one lived.*' One is more disposed nowadays to see in this horror a cause than a symptom of insanity.

Yet, even if insanity is, as it may be, the ultimate consequence of atheism, that still does not constitute any refutation of atheism: since, as Nietzsche continued to insist (and Berdyaev unaccountably ignores), 'there is no pre-established harmony between the promotion of truth and the welfare of mankind'. If man as he is cannot tolerate meaninglessness eternal, therefore, and every retreat is cut off, the only hope that remains is a new kind of man who can:

[1] N, XII, 167.

'Suddenly the terrible chamber of truth is opened; an unconscious self-protectiveness, caution, ambush, defence keeps us from the gravest knowledge. Thus have I lived heretofore. I suppress something; but the restless babbling and rolling down of stones has rendered my instinct over-powerful. Now I am rolling my last stone, the most appalling truth stands close to my hand. . . .

'We fight with it,—we find that our only means of enduring it is to create a creature who is able to endure it:—unless, of course, we voluntarily dazzle ourselves afresh and blind ourselves in regard to it. But this we are no longer able to do! We it was who created the gravest thought,—let us now create a being to whom it will be not only light but blessed.'[1]

It is strange that Berdyaev himself should have been one of those who detected an inconsistency between the idea of the Superman and that of Eternal Recurrence. This note alone should show how intimately related they were. The Superman, as Nietzsche finally conceived him, was a being so completely divested of even the last heritage of morality, the desire for absolute truth, so world-affirming, exuberant and vivacious, that he would be able not merely to endure, but to rejoice in, meaninglessness eternal: a being for whom even this would represent a divine mode of thinking. 'Now that there is no longer a God, solitude has become intolerable; it is *necessary* that a higher man should set his hand to the task.'[2] The Superman stands for that necessity.

But does he also stand for a possibility? That was precisely the problem that Nietzsche was driven to solve, and solve in the only way that could prove anything at all—by experiment. If *he* could surmount his horror, for no matter how short a time, he believed, then there would be reason to think that mankind might surmount it for good. The story of Part III of *Zarathustra* is the story of that experiment. It depicts 'the self-overcoming of Zarathustra as the prototype of mankind's self-overcoming for the benefit of Superman':[3] and this is the second aspect of Zarathustra's acceptance of the Recurrence.

The bare fact that the poem was composed, however, tells us the solution to the problem. Had the extremity of Nietzsche's isolation not given way, at some point or other, to a corresponding extremity of communion, his inspiration would never have been renewed. As it was, not only did he surpass himself anew, but, by virtue of this very self-conquest, the idea of the Eternal Recurrence underwent yet a further, and final, metamorphosis. Without ceasing to be 'the highest formula for a

[1] NZ, 42.   [2] N, XIV, 336.   [3] NZ, 20.

yea-saying to life ever attained', it became—and here we reach the
climax of his dialectic—at once a symbol and a ratiocination of that
quality of 'eternity' which is revealed in all things at the instant of self-
transcendance—the instant when, as Dostoievsky put it, 'it seems to me
that I understand the extraordinary phrase of the apostle, "There will
no longer be any time"'.

Blake used to speak of such instants as 'eternal moments'; and perhaps it would be fitting to set his presentation of the thought side by side
with Nietzsche's own. Here is Blake, speaking through the lips of his
reborn Milton:

> 'I am that Shadowy Prophet, who, Six Thousand Years ago,
> Fell from my station in the Eternal bosom. Six Thousand Years
> Are finish'd. I return: both Time & Space obey my will.
> I in Six Thousand Years walk up and down; for not one moment
> Of Time is lost, nor one Event of Space unpermanent;
> But all remain; every fabric of Six Thousand Years
> Remains permanent: tho' on the earth, where Satan
> Fell and was cut off, all thing vanish & are seen no more,
> They vanish not from me & mine; we guard them, first & last.
> The generations of men run on in the tide of Time,
> But leave their destin'd lineaments permanent for ever & ever.'

And here is Nietzsche, speaking through the lips of his reborn Zarathustra:

> 'I, however, am a blesser and a Yea-sayer, if thou be but around me,
> thou pure, thou luminous heaven! Thou abyss of light!—into all
> abysses do I then carry the Yea-saying of my blessing.
>
> A blesser have I become and a Yea-sayer: and therefore strove I long
> and was a wrestler, that I might one day get my hands free for blessing.
>
> This, however, is my blessing: to stand above everything as its own
> heaven, its round roof, its azure bell and eternal security: and blessed is
> he who thus blesseth!
>
> For all things are baptized at the font of eternity, and beyond good
> and evil; good and evil themselves, however, are but fugitive shadows
> and damp afflictions and passing clouds. . . .'[1]

In most of his last notes on the theme, the Eternal Recurrence
becomes for Nietzsche virtually a synonym for the *species aeternitatis* of
Spinoza: and that no doubt is why, recalling in *Ecce Homo* the occasion
when the idea first sprang to his mind, he substituted for the words of

[1] Z, 48.

his letter to Gast, '6,000 feet above the sea, and at a much higher altitude above all human affairs', the words, '6,000 feet *beyond man and time*'.[1] This was not, as appears at first sight, a mere hyperbole—he meant it. Only, he was reading back into his earlier experience the thought of a later date.

* * *

The 'argument' of *Zarathustra*, Part III, is stated at the outset, in the Discourse headed, 'The Vision and the Enigma'. Here the prophet tells how, of late, walking through a corpse-coloured twilight, he was tormented by his Spirit of Gravity in the guise of a dwarf, reminding him continually that in the end it would all be the same, that even his mission was nothing more than a means of prolonging the terrestrial dance. ' "O Zarathustra," it whispered scornfully, syllable by syllable, "thou stone of wisdom! Thou threwest thyself high, but every thrown stone must—fall!" '

At last, goaded beyond endurance, he had turned on this nagging spirit: ' "Halt dwarf!" said I. "Either I—or thou! I, however, am the stronger of the two: thou knowest not mine abysmal thought! *It*—couldst thou not endure".' So saying, he had proceeded to evoke this thought, though falteringly, in a low voice, for he himself was still terrified of it. It was that of 'THE HEAVIEST BURDEN'.

The charm worked: the dwarf vanished. Hardly, however, had he completed the incantation before he was startled by the howling of a dog, and there before him lay a young man, a shepherd, 'writhing, choking, quivering, with distorted countenance, and with a heavy black serpent hanging out of his mouth'. In a frenzy of horror, Zarathustra had adjured the victim, 'Bite! Bite! Its head off! Bite!'—and now, recalling the spectacle, he turns to his auditors:

'Ye daring ones around me! Ye venturers and adventurers, and whoever of you have embarked with cunning sails on unexplored seas! Ye lovers of mysteries!

Solve unto me the mystery that I then beheld, interpret unto me the vision of the lonesomest man!

For it was a vision and a foresight:—*what* did I then behold in the parable? And *who* is it that must come some day?

Who is the shepherd into whose throat the serpent thus crawled? *Who* is the man into whose throat all the heaviest and blackest will thus crawl?

—The shepherd, however, bit as my cry had admonished him; he bit

[1] EH, p. 96.

with a strong bite! Far away did he spit the head of the serpent:—and sprang up.—

No longer shepherd, no longer man—a transfigured being, a light-surrounded being, that *laughed*! Never on earth laughed a man as *he* laughed!

O my brethren, I heard a laughter which was no human laughter—and now burneth a thirst in me, a longing that is never assuaged.

My longing for that laughter burneth in me: oh, how can I still endure to live! And how could I endure to die at present!—

Thus spake Zarathustra.'

The shepherd, of course, is Zarathustra himself; the serpent, 'the serpent of eternity';[1] the laughter for which he thirsts, that joyful wisdom, that ultimate emancipation and irresponsibility, which will be his once again, when he has conquered his loathing and horror.

The Discourses that follow take up the tale of this self-conquest. 'All unrest and violent longing, all loathing, should be presented in the third Part, and be overcome',[2] Nietzsche had written in another of his notes; and we may suspect, though we cannot be certain, that these Discourses constitute a faithful record of his own struggles between the autumn of 1883, when he told Gast that Zarathustra was about to be plunged in gloom, and January 1884, when he at last recovered the 'profound, Heavenly cheerfulness' necessary to composition.

It may be argued, indeed, that they constitute too faithful a record. The plan of the work required that he 'demonstrate through Zarathustra the ideal of the sacrifices involved: abandonment of one's birthplace, one's family, one's country; life under the contempt of the prevailing morality; the torment of trials and reverses':[3] but the emotion aroused by these memories is too seldom recollected in tranquillity. Nietzsche, the passionately inflamed, loving and hating man, gets the better of Nietzsche the genius; he is carried away, once more, on a tide of sheer negation:

'O my brethren, am I then cruel? But I say: What falleth, that shall one also push!

Everything of today—it falleth, it decayeth; who would preserve it! But I—I wish also to push it!

Know ye the delight which rolleth stones into precipitous depths?—Those men of today, see just how they roll into my depths!

A prelude am I to better players, O my brethren! An example! *Do* according to my example!

[1] N, XII, 426.   [2] NZ, 76.   [3] N, XIV, 102.

And him whom ye do not teach to fly, teach I pray you—*to fall faster!*'[1]

It is a far cry from this to the wisdom of 'Passing-by'.

'Divine suffering is the substance of the third Part'[2]—and even the divinest of sufferers has been known to wax acrimonious where the good and just are concerned. The plan of the work required that Nietzsche should reveal nihilism in both its forms, theoretical and practical—for 'nihilism is not a mere meditating over the "in vain"—not only the belief that everything deserves to perish; one actually takes a hand, one *drives to destruction*'[3]—but lines like the following, even while they show how inextricably, in his experience, metaphysical horror was bound up with emotional recoil, tremble on the brink of bathos:

'The great disgust of man—*it* strangled me and had crept into my throat: and what the Soothsayer had presaged: "All is alike, nothing is worth-while, knowledge strangleth".

A long twilight limped before me, a fatally weary, fatally intoxicated sadness, which spake with yawning mouth.

"Eternally he returneth, the man of whom thou art weary, the small man"—so yawned my sadness, and dragged its foot and could not go to sleep.'[4]

With rare exceptions, such as 'Before Sunrise', these Discourses are among the weakest in the book.

Nevertheless, in the end the reader is richly rewarded. For, in the end, the 'vision and foresight' is fulfilled. Zarathustra does 'become master even of his loathing of man':[5] and no sooner is his transfiguration effected, in 'The Convalescent', than the poetry not merely recovers, but rises to unprecedented heights—first in that lovely antiphon, in which his animals rehearse the burden of his newly-won doctrine, hailing him 'teacher of the eternal return'; then in those three magnificent chants, 'The Great Longing', 'The Second Dance-Song' and 'The Seven Seals', which together form the climax of the poem.

In 'The Great Longing', Nietzsche's verse mounts to a crescendo of ecstasy reminiscent of the second Isaiah, as he invokes his own Will in such terms as the prophets of old reserved for the Spirit of the Lord:

'O my soul, every sun shed I upon thee, and every night and every silence and every longing:—then grewest thou up for me as a vine.

O my soul, exuberant and heavy dost thou now stand forth, a vine with swelling udders and full clusters of golden-brown grapes:—

[1] Z, 56, 20.   [2] NZ, 77.   [3] WP, 24.   [4] Z, 57.   [5] EH, p. 113.

—Filled and weighted by thy happiness, waiting from super-abundance, and yet ashamed of thy waiting.

O my soul, there is nowhere a soul which could be more loving and more comprehensive and more extensive! Where could future and past be closer together than with thee?'

In 'The Second Dance-Song', wild, rhythmic yet gliding, an image like and unlike the image of Nature and her wooer hovers forward. It is an ode to Life—Life as she is and must be, inclusive of Death—in his worship of whom all the poet's passions are exalted and etherialized. He pursues her, he woos her; and, when she reproaches him with the intention of leaving her, whispers in her ear the secret she thought she alone knew—the secret of everlasting renewal.

Finally, in 'The Seven Seals or the Yea and Amen Lay', we catch an echo of that superhuman laughter by which Zarathustra has been haunted and beguiled—'for in laughter is all evil present, but it is sanctified and absolved by its own bliss'. Here the whole world of chance and change—not excluding the many who repudiate chance and pine for a respite from change—is caught up and baptized anew at the font of eternity:

'If ever a breath hath come to me of the creative breath, and of the heavenly necessity which compelleth even chances to dance star-dances:

If ever I have laughed with the laughter of the creative lightning, to which the long thunder of the deed followeth, grumblingly but obediently:

If ever I have played dice with the Gods at the divine table of the earth, so that the earth quaked and gaped apart, and snorted forth fire-streams:—

—For a divine table is the earth, and trembling with new creative dicta and dice-casts of the Gods:

Oh, how could I not be ardent for Eternity, and for the marriage-ring of rings—the ring of the return?

Never yet have I found the woman by whom I should like to have children, unless it be this woman whom I love: for I love thee, O Eternity!

For I love thee, O Eternity!'

This Eternity is no barren abstraction, but Life once again, perceived in all the beauty of her divine particularity: and it is here, if anywhere, that we must look for the living testimony to Nietzsche's ultimate conquest of nihilism. In dithyrambs such as these—resembling nothing in German literature, unless it be Goethe's *Rhapsody on Nature*—he emerges at last as the Dionysian chorist of his dreams. Perhaps we shall now understand why he called *Richard Wagner at Bayreuth* 'a vision of my own future'[1] and *Thus Spake Zarathustra*, 'a new "Ring"?'[2]

It is from this time forward, indeed, that the term 'Dionysian' begins to feature anew in his writing: and to feature ever more frequently until, in *Ecce Homo*, every extract from the poem is succeeded by the refrain, 'but this is the very idea of Dionysus!'

'The psychological problem presented by the type Zarathustra is, how can he, who to an unprecedented degree says no, *acts* no, to all that has been hitherto affirmed, be nevertheless the reverse of a nay-saying spirit? how can he, who bears the heaviest of destinies and the most fateful of tasks, yet be the lightest and most transcendental of spirits—for Zarathustra is a dancer? how can he who has the hardest and most terrible grasp of reality, and who has thought the most "abysmal thoughts", nevertheless avoid conceiving these things as objections to existence, or even as objections to the eternal recurrence of existence?—how is it that, on the contrary, he finds cause *to be himself* the eternal Yea to all things, "the tremendous and unlimited saying of Yea and Amen"? ... "Into every abyss do I bear the benediction of my yea-saying" ... But this, once more, is precisely the idea of Dionysus.'[3]

Some of Blake's comments on his *Milton* sound a strain not dissimilar—and perhaps with equal justice.

Be that as it may, it will hardly be denied that *Zarathustra* is the pinnacle of Nietzsche's actual achievement, and the conclusion of 'The Second Dance-Song' the pinnacle of the poem. For Part IV, an afterthought (he himself called it 'an interlude'),[4] is also an anticlimax. Diffuse, where the others are concise, allegorical where they are figurative, it took far longer than they to write, and the reason is all too plain: it is uninspired.

Zarathustra corresponded to, and commemorated, a particular climacteric in Nietzsche's development; his attempt to make it the vehicle of later speculations, however understandable, was misconceived. He was composing, he believed, a new Gospel. At every stage, Zarathustra is pitted against Jesus, Dionysus against Christ, the tragic view of life against the Christian. To complete the parallel—or parody, as he sometimes called it—it was necessary that the hero should suffer martyrdom. But, try as he might, Nietzsche could not depict that consummation, even to himself; and his failure to do so—more eloquent than any success—lay in the nature of things. Try as he might, he would never succeed in writing a tragedy: he would only succeed in living one.

[1] EH, p. 81.   [2] L, 1, 2, 83.   [3] EH, p. 109.   [4] L, 8, 1, 88.

Third Movement

THE TRANSVALUATION
OF ALL VALUES

'My master-quality is the quality of self-mastery. But nobody has greater need of it than I: I am incessantly skirting the abyss.'

IX

THE MYTHOLOGIST

Nietzsche has been called 'the greatest European event since Goethe'. I believe that this estimate will command more and more assent from the thinking minority as time goes on—if time is allowed to go on, and minorities are allowed to think. His centenary in 1944 occasioned little comment, compared with Goethe's five years later; but that may be due, in part at least, to Europe's not having had time to catch up with, let alone overtake, his thought. He called himself a 'firstling of the twentieth century',[1] and with good right. Every important trend of twentieth-century philosophy is anticipated in his works. For this reason, it will not be before the twenty-first that they can be justly assessed.

'Believe me,' he wrote to his sister in 1881, 'all the moral struggles, all the speculation of Europe, and much else besides, have now come to a head in me.'[2] By then, the New Enlightenment lay as far behind him as Romanticism lay behind that; and, though he could sometimes exult in the thought of the distance he had travelled, he had also to pay the price of his 'elasticity'. From the time of *Zarathustra* onwards, his isolation was complete.

Much of the bitterness, and also the exaggerated self-esteem, of his later writings must be put down to this. A sense of prophetic mission is only natural to a prophet; but one who is incessantly confronted with the question, 'Am I wrong, or is everybody else?' can hardly avoid eccentricity. He himself was aware of this, and tried, unavailingly, to avoid it. 'The inability to communicate one's thoughts is in very truth the most terrible of all kinds of loneliness', he cried on one occasion: 'A deep man needs friends. All else failing, he has at least his god. But I have neither god nor friends . . .! Get me a small circle of men who will listen to me and understand me—and I shall be cured!'[3]

Unhappily it was not until another year had elapsed—not until 1887— that 'friends began to come', Brandes, Taine, Strindberg; and by then it was too late. As he told Burckhardt 'the exceedingly spiritual and painfully complex life I have led hitherto (and thanks to which my bodily constitution, *which is at bottom a strong one*, has been shattered) has

[1] JW, 343.   [2] L, 29, 11, 81.   [3] L, 8, 7, 86.

gradually led me into a state of lonely isolation for which there is now no cure'.[1] The fame he had pined for in earlier years, for the sake of the disciples it might bring, when at last it did overtake him, served only to hasten his breakdown.

It is the height of folly, therefore, to invoke this breakdown as a reason for neglecting his philosophy. If anything, it should be additional reason for studying it. For those issues, problems and conflicts that set him so completely apart from his contemporaries were the very ones which weigh upon all of us today, and which we, too, must now either come to terms with or perish. To an extent still unascertainable, his private world was our public one.

That, indeed, is the outstanding fact about Nietzsche, beside which even the rightness or wrongness (in our view) of the particular solutions he found is a matter of secondary importance. We can learn as much from the negative as from the positive results of an experiment, and learn we must. One of his last notes reads as follows: 'To have travelled round the whole circumference of the modern soul, and to have sat in all its corners—my ambition, my torment, and my happiness. Veritably to *overcome* pessimism, and, as result, the glance of a Goethe—full of love and goodwill.'[2]

The way in which Nietzsche himself appeals continually to Goethe is noteworthy. Of the four men he named as his 'predecessors'[3]—Heraclitus, Empedocles, Spinoza and Goethe—the German, he undoubtedly felt, was his spiritual nearest-of-kin: and it is not hard to see why. Not only were both men of versatile genius—Nietzsche being as accomplished a psychologist, musician and prose-writer as Goethe was a biologist, painter and poet; not only were both pre-eminently endowed with that historical insight, which Nietzsche called a 'sixth sense';[4] but what enabled them to rear so many talents to maturity without being torn in pieces between them, and what, in all probability, contributed to their historical insight, was precisely that overmastering urge to continuous growth which thrust them forward into the future:

'Have we ever complained among ourselves of being misunderstood, misjudged, and confounded with others; of being calumniated, misheard, and not heard? That is just our lot—oh, for a long time yet! say, to be modest, until 1901—it is also our distinction; we should not have sufficient respect for ourselves if we wished it otherwise. People confound us with others—the reason of it is that we ourselves grow, we change continually, we cast off old bark, we still slough every spring, we

always become younger, higher, stronger, as men of the future, we thrust ,
our roots always more powerfully into the deep—into evil—while at
the same time we embrace the heavens more lovingly, more extensively,
and suck in their light ever more eagerly with all our branches and leaves.
We grow like trees—that is difficult to understand, like all life!—not in
one place, but everywhere, not in one direction only, but upwards and
outwards, as well as inwards and downwards. At the same time our
force shoots forth in stem, branches, and roots; we are really no longer
free to do anything separately, or to *be* anything separately. . . . Such is
our lot, as we have said: we grow in *height*; and even should it be our
fatality—for we dwell ever closer to the lightning!—well, we honour
it none the less on that account.'[1]

It was precisely this urge to continuous growth that made the man, in
either case, more significant than even the sum of his individual achievements, and his philosophy the very articulation—one might say, the
secretion—of a personality.

'It is certain,' Nietzsche writes elsewhere, 'that one's inmost nature
gradually disciplines one's whole being into unity; that passion for
which for ages one can find no name saves us from all digressions and
dispersions, that *mission* whose involuntary custodian we are'[2]—and
Goethe would emphatically have endorsed this. Indeed, rightly or
wrongly saluting a kindred spirit in Napoleon, Goethe coined his own
name for the type of man who, by virtue of his submission to the
artistic mastery of the Will, emerges as a creative-destructive force of
nature—*Eine Natur*.

The gradual emergence of such a personality constitutes one of the
most magnificent spectacles nature has to offer. Observed from its
earliest beginnings, it is fascinating; and the fascination increases tenfold
when it is shared, as it is in both these instances, by the man himself. For
Goethe and Nietzsche are further distinguished, above all others perhaps,
by the extent of their awareness of what was taking place in them.
There came a point in the life of each when his development ceased to be
a purely unconscious process and became the object of his conscious
dedication.

There is no need to cite evidence for this. In the case of Nietzsche, his
letters, the preface to *The Genealogy of Morals*, his introductions to the
1887 editions of *Human, All-too-Human, The Dawn of Day* and *The
Joyful Wisdom*—to say nothing of *Ecce Homo* itself, are all alike
eloquent witnesses: so much so, that there are times when even his

[1] JW, 371.   [2] L, 14, 12, 87.

claim to have entered 'a state of such profound self-consciousness as perhaps no man has ever attained before'[1] scarcely strikes one as exaggerated. Moreover, as we have seen, that 'transvaluation of values', which eventually revealed itself as his own special mission, amounted to nothing less than a proclamation of this condition of growth as the healthy, and therefore the 'good'. 'It is a sign of well-constitutedness when a man like Goethe clings with ever greater heartiness to "the things of this world"—in this way he holds firmly to the grand concept of mankind, which is that man becomes *the glorifier of existence* when he learns to glorify himself.'[2]

In *Thus Spake Zarathustra*, Nietzsche did proclaim, and not merely proclaim but display, this health, this 'good': and therewith his mission, as originally conceived, was fulfilled. The remainder of his writing represents a sustained attempt to work out the implications of the new gospel—historical, philosophical, political and religious; an attempt to which he was driven, as always, by the simple need to make sense of his experience. No sooner, however, had he addressed himself to this undertaking, than the mission itself began to assume still grander, and more grandiose, proportions: it became, in effect, a 'transvaluation of *all* values' (*Umwertung aller Werte*). And, in consequence, the outline of yet a further great work began to take shape in his mind, of which this was to be the title.

The books he published from 1884 onwards may be considered as so many by-products of this work. Hence the impression they make, of being drawn from a vast potential of knowledge and experience. The aphorisms of *Beyond Good and Evil* and 'We Fearless Ones' (Book V of *The Joyful Wisdom*, added in 1887), cold, abrupt, crystalline, stand like icebergs for much more than appears on the surface; the three polemics of *The Genealogy of Morals* well forth like torrents of lava from an inexhaustible reservoir. All these, in his own view, were 'so much bait',[3] thrown out to allure collaborators to his side.

It follows that the remainder of *this* book will represent an exposition and criticism of 'the transvaluation of all values'; and also that it will no longer be possible to adopt a rigidly chronological approach. Instead, we shall glance at Nietzsche's historical, philosophical, political and religious conceptions in turn, beginning, in this chapter, with the historical. It is necessary to begin with this, because it is only when we have understood the historical perspective in which he placed *Zarathustra* that we are in a position fully to realize either the scope or the aim of his

---

[1] L, 11, 88.   [2] WP, 820.   [3] EH, p. 115.

magnum opus. Beyond Good and Evil and *The Genealogy of Morals*
between them provide most of the data.

* * *

Nietzsche, naturally, did not suppose that health, as he understood it,
had entered the world for the first time in the persons of Goethe and
himself. On the contrary, that condition of spontaneous, all-round, tree-
like growth seemed to him so pre-eminently natural that normality
looked pathological beside it. Already in *The Joyful Wisdom*, he had surmised that formerly 'these qualities were usual, and were consequently
regarded as common: they did not distinguish people';[1] it was only
nowadays that a man had 'to foster them in face of a different, opposing
world', and 'either become a great man thereby, or a deranged and
eccentric person, unless he should altogether break down betimes'.[2]
Even then, accordingly, he had pictured it as 'a species of atavism'.[3]
In *Beyond Good and Evil* this surmise is stated as a fact.

Wherever history affords the spectacle of a fresh, uncorrupted people,
Nietzsche now asserts, no matter how primitive or barbarous at first, we
find these same qualities in evidence. Look, for example, at the half-
savage conquerors of the Mediterranean basin in the eighth and ninth
centuries B.C. They accepted all their passions—indeed, they deified
them; they rejoiced in the world as it is, in spite of, or even because of,
its harsh and terrible features—the Homeric hero would rather be a
bondslave in the house of his enemy than a Shade in the Underworld;
they despised nearly all that modern men desire—security, comfort,
consideration; they glorified nearly all that modern men fear—danger,
hardship, independence. They sought before all things life, and life
more abundant. The Will to Power subdued them to its purpose; and
it was because it did so that they themselves were able to subdue 'old
mellow civilizations in which the final vital force was flickering out in
brilliant fireworks of wit and depravity':[4] and not only that, but also, in
the fullness of time, to assimilate, without being overwhelmed by, the
learning these civilizations had amassed. Were they not the forebears of
Aeschylus and Sophocles, Heraclitus, Thucydides and Pericles?

Nietzsche had a nickname for these conquerors, which has become
notorious—'magnificent blond brutes'.[5] Contrary to professorial
assumption, he did not hold them up as models for modern Europeans,
any more than Rousseau did the primitive Amerindians. If they were
'natural', they were also 'naive'; if they were 'more complete men' than
their adversaries, 'that at every point also implies more complete
beasts'.[6] He did, nevertheless, like Rousseau, contend that they pos-

[1] JW, 10.   [2] *Ibid.*   [3] *Ibid.*   [4] BGE, 257.   [5] GM, I, 11.   [6] BGE, 257.

sessed, without even knowing it, something which we are none the better for lacking—namely, health, wholeness, spontaneity. Between what they were and what they would be, there was no persistent contradiction. 'Sexuality, the lust for power, the delight in appearance and dissimulation, the great and joyous gratitude for life and its fundamental realities are the essence of the pagan cult, and have the good conscience on their side.'[1]

Philology supported him at this point. In all the Aryan languages, he discovered, creations as they were of those nordic conquerors, the word 'good' was originally a synonym for the 'powerful'. Everywhere, he points out in *The Genealogy of Morals*, ' "aristocrat", "noble" (in the class sense), is the root-idea out of which have necessarily developed "good" in the sense of "with aristocratic soul", "noble", in the sense of "with a soul of high calibre", "with a gentlemanly soul"—a development which invariably runs parallel with that other by which "vulgar", "plebeian", "low" are made to change finally into "bad".'[2] Whatever else these men may have been, who thus made what they actually were the criterion of human worth, they were assuredly no Pascals!

In *Beyond Good and Evil* and *The Genealogy of Morals*, therefore, Nietzsche declares that his own idea of the 'good', so far from being something new and unique, was actually the original idea. The predicate 'good' was not, after all, bestowed in the first place upon such actions as happened to benefit the individual or community—he and his rationalistic models in *Human, All-too-Human* had been at fault—it had been created by healthy men to designate the qualities of health. 'Spontaneous pleasure in oneself and one's own activities is the *source* of all judgements of value—faith in one's self'.[3] It follows that, just as they, the noble, distinguished themselves as the good, so may we, the good, distinguish ourselves as the noble: and this is how Nietzsche defines the 'noble' in a crucial aphorism:

'The noble type of man regards *himself* as a determiner of values; he does not require to be approved of; he passes the judgement: "What is injurious to me is injurious in itself"; he knows that it is he himself only who confers honour on things; he is a *creator of values*. He honours whatever he recognizes in himself: such morality is self-glorification. In the foreground there is the feeling of plenitude, of power, which seeks to overflow, the happiness of high tension, the consciousness of a wealth which would fain give and bestow: the noble man also helps the un-

_____
[1] WP, 1047.   [2] GM, I, 4.   [3] N, XIV, 65.

fortunate, but not—or scarcely—out of pity, but rather from an impulse generated by the superabundance of power. . . .'[1]

The likeness to Aristotle's Μεγαλόψυχος ἀνηρ is not accidental.

Forgetfulness, Nietzsche had written in *Human, All-too-Human*, is the doorkeeper in the temple of human dignity. In *The Genealogy of Morals*, this verdict is explicitly reversed. Memory, the historical memory, is the doorkeeper: since, if we go far enough back, we find that the 'moral man' was first of all the creator and commander of moralities.

If this is the case, however, how are we to account for the fact that 'good' has come to designate the very opposite qualities, and the very opposite type of man? Nietzsche replies: a scale of values so radically unnatural as that of present-day Europe could only have come into existence in radically unnatural conditions: but those conditions are provided for on his theory—by slavery. Our morality has been derived, not from the rulers of the Mediterranean world, but from the peoples they subdued—and it has been derived precisely from their reaction against these rulers. In origin and essence alike, it is a 'slave-morality'. By the same token, Nietzsche's own can be defined as a 'master morality'. This is the solution he proffers, briefly in *Beyond Good and Evil*, at length in the first polemic of *The Genealogy of Morals*.

'Master morality', be it noted, is simply the natural morality of man. It does not presuppose slavery—it was, we are given to understand, the morality of all the roving nordic, hamitic and semitic tribes, before ever the Mediterranean fell to their swords. Its motive-force is a triumphant affirmation, of life and self: 'it acts and grows spontaneously, it merely seeks its antithesis in order to pronounce a more grateful and exultant "yes".'[2] Slave morality, on the other hand, is bound up with repression, and could never have come into existence apart from it—being the product of what Nietzsche distinguishes as the 'reactive feelings': hate, envy, mistrust, jealousy, suspicion, rancour, revenge. Its motive-force is a negation: 'the slave-morality says "no" from the very outset to what is "outside itself", "different from itself" and "not itself": and this "no" is its creative deed. . . . Its action is fundamentally a reaction.'[3]

This is essential to grasp; and there can be no doubt that Nietzsche has alighted here on a very important distinction. The two attitudes he defines are real, and have certainly played a large part in history, whether or not it was the part he himself assigned them. If we wish to study slave morality at close quarters, he says, we cannot do better than observe our

----

[1] BGE, 260.   [2] GM, I, 10.   [3] *Ibid.*

own anarchists and anti-semites. I myself have had occasion to observe both, and my conclusions accord with his.

There are notable exceptions, of course, at any rate among anarchists. As Brandes, who knew the Russians, was quick to point out, the name of Kropotkin alone should be a warning against hasty generalization. Nietzsche had Dühring in mind—a 'higher man', so he believed, 'ruined by isolation'.[1] But the majority answer to Dühring's description. They are men and women who know what they hate, and have never learned what they love: what they profess to love being merely the opposite of what they hate. The hatred comes first. They are men and women who can unite only in opposition to something: as soon as they have nothing to oppose, they either have to invent something, or fall into mutual recriminations and purges. They are, indeed, the purest representatives of the 'progressive' mentality—progress being invariably measured not by the whither, but the whence. 'The creed of revenge,' wrote Dühring, 'has run through all my works and endeavours like the red thread of justice': and he was only a little more candid than the majority of his kidney. As for the anti-semites—their very name gives them away. Like anti-fascists, anti-communists, anti-militarists, they are distinguished first to last by negation: their action is fundamentally a reaction.

Credit the Graeco-Roman slave population with such sentiments as these, Nietzsche intimates, and you already have a sufficient explanation of that reversal of values to which modern morality bears witness. The slave would very soon have professed, and in the end come, to love just the opposite type of man to his master, and the opposite human qualities —all those qualities, indeed, that distinguish the 'tool-like nature'. 'It is here that sympathy, the kind, helping hand, the warm heart, patience, diligence, humility and friendliness attain to honour: for here these are the most useful qualities, and almost the only means of supporting the burden of existence. Slave-morality is essentially the morality of utility'.[2] It is here also, he infers, that the antithesis 'good and evil' emerges, by contrast with the noble 'good and bad'—the noble preserving always a certain respect for his enemy: 'aristocratic morality knows nothing of "evil"; the "bad" always evokes some respect or pity.'[3]

Throughout his discussion of this subject, Nietzsche was drawing on his own experience. When he declared, in opposition to Dühring, that justice only began with the conquest of the reactive feelings, he must have remembered how he himself had had to conquer a ruthlessly revengeful sentiment in order to write *Zarathustra*. 'Oh, how *instruc-*

[1] NZ, 72.   [2] BGE, 260.   [3] N, XIII, 149.

tive it is to live in such an extreme state as mine!' he cries in one of his letters: 'only now do I understand history.'[1]

While the resentful hostility of the slave may account for the reversal of values, however, it cannot, by itself, account for the extraordinary ascendancy achieved by slave-morality. For this something further is needed. In his second polemic, accordingly, he plunges into the question, how resentment acquired an ideology of its own. For this, he maintains, not the slave himself, but the priest, was responsible.

* * *

The priest, according to Nietzsche, is primarily a weak strong man—or a strong weak one. That is to say, he is a type who, while sharing the slaves' resentment against the aristocracy, and appearing to make common cause with them, in fact exploits their sentiment in order to secure his own power. Thus, it is he who elaborates the compensatory dream of an after-world, in which the proud shall be put down from their seats, and the humble and meek exalted—at the same time taking good care to reserve this exaltation for those who perform his bidding. (Some telling passages are cited from Tertullian and Aquinas, to show how strongly this dream appealed to the appetite for revenge.) He also it is who trades on the bad conscience of the oppressed.

At this point *The Genealogy of Morals* links up with *The Dawn of Day*, only, of course, Nietzsche's theory is now incomparably more subtle. The origin of the bad conscience, in particular, he now attributes directly to the fact of repression—and this leads him on to conclusions which are wholly novel in his writings:

'At this juncture-I cannot avoid trying to give a tentative and provisional expression to my own hypothesis concerning the origin of the bad conscience: it is difficult to make it fully appreciated, and it requires long meditation, attention, and sleeping upon. I regard the bad conscience as the serious illness which man was bound to contract under the stress of the most radical change which he has ever experienced—that change, when he finally found himself imprisoned within the pale of society and of peace. . . .'[2]

Imagine, Nietzsche says, the plight of a newly-subjugated population: of barbarians and semi-barbarians, 'perfectly adapted as they were to the savage life of war, prowling and adventure',[3] now suddenly deprived of every natural outlet. What must the effect on them be of this absolute frustration?—His answer is: introversion. 'All instincts which do not find a vent without, *turn inwards*.'[4] In this way, the Will to Power becomes a

[1] L, 1, 2, 88. [2] GM, II, 16. [3] *Ibid.* [4] *Ibid.*

will to self-torture—and for this the priest provides a *rationale*, by adapting the time-honoured notion of a debt owing to the gods.

Originally, the gods were ancestors; the debt was conceived more or less as a legal obligation, contracted between two generations, and discharged by periodical sacrifices. As the various tribes coalesced, however, so did the tribal deities—until the establishment of a single *Imperium* was reflected in the sovereignty of a single God; and as the God became greater, so did the debt that was owing him—until, finally, no merely human sacrifice could be conceived sufficient to discharge it. It was this idea, of an inexpiable guilt (the German word *Schuld* means both 'debt' and 'guilt') that became, in the hands of the priest, a justification at once for the bad conscience itself, and for all the extremities of self-laceration it prompted. In this lies the origin of the self-sacrificial ideal, considered as the very acme of holiness. 'Alas for this mad melancholy beast man! What fantasies invade it, what perversity, paroxysms of senselessness and *mental bestiality* break out immediately, at the very slightest check on its being the *beast of action*!'[1]

In thus baldly summarizing Nietzsche's theory, we are, of course, doing it injustice. It requires, as he says, continuous meditation, attention and sleeping upon. This was a subject he had brooded for years, and 'rather with the necessity with which a tree bears fruit, so do our thoughts, our values, our Yes's and No's and If's and Whether's, grow connected and interrelated, mutual witnesses of *one* will, *one* health'.[2] Not only is the argument presented in a highly concentrated form, impossible to master at a single reading; but it is the prototype, if not the actual progenitor, of every later attempt to interpret the history of religion as that of a racial neurosis. Indeed, the expression 'religious neurosis'[3] probably originated with Nietzsche.

It is interesting to note the resemblance between his interpretation and Freud's in particular. Freud, to be sure, put the bad conscience down to the inherited memory of a drama, which, so he imagined, must have been enacted time after time in the early history of mankind—the murder of a father by his sons; but his account of its subsequent development runs closely parallel to Nietzsche's. Both psychologists saw in asceticism an attempt to expiate an imaginary guilt; both saw in Christianity a partial alleviation—attained, according to Freud, through the thought of God sacrificing his own son; according to Nietzsche, through the thought of 'God himself sacrificing himself for the debt of man'.[4] Both, moreover, were persuaded that, by bringing the true facts to light, they were paving the way for a lasting cure.

[1] GM, II, 22.   [2] GM, Preface, 2.   [3] BGE, 47.   [4] GM, II, 21.

Only on one point are they notably at variance. Whilst both were keenly alive to the part played by the Jews in the creation of Christianity, they differed as to the reason. Freud suggested that the Jews were more than ordinarily tormented by the repressed memory, since it was none other than the semi-divine Moses whom their fathers had slain in the wilderness. For Nietzsche, with his eyes on the class-struggle, it was enough that the Jews, in Roman times, were the nation of priests and slaves *par excellence*, their warrior and peasant classes having been virtually eliminated by the Captivity. This, he believed, was the reason why they, in particular, should have proved capable of originating an ideology dynamic enough to bear slave-morality to victory over the classical world:

'Modern men, with their obtuseness as regards all Christian nomenclature, have no longer the sense for the terribly superlative conception, which was implied to an antique taste by the paradox of the formula, "God on the Cross". Hitherto there had never and nowhere been such boldness in inversion, nor anything at once so dreadful, questioning, and questionable as this formula: it promised a transvaluation of all ancient values.—It was the Orient, the *profound* Orient, it was the Oriental slave who thus took revenge on Rome and its noble, light-minded toleration, on the Roman "Catholicism" of non-faith: and it was always, not the faith, but the freedom from the faith, the half-stoical and smiling indifference to the seriousness of the faith, which made the slaves indignant at their masters and revolt against them. "Enlightenment" causes revolt: for the slave desires the unconditioned, he understands nothing but the tyrannous, even in morals; he loves as he hates, without *nuance*, to the very depths, to the point of pain, to the point of sickness—his many *hidden* sufferings make him revolt against the noble taste which seems to *deny* suffering. The scepticism with regard to suffering, fundamentally only an attitude of aristocratic morality, was not the least of the causes, also, of the last great slave-insurrection which began with the French Revolution.'[1]

Thus, according to Nietzsche, our present unnatural morality is to be explained by two factors: on the one hand the long, slow slave-insurrection, which brought the classical world to an end; on the other, Christianity, that Judaic ideology under which the insurrection triumphed. Without that ideology, slave-morality would have been impotent. With it, it proved all-powerful. It prevailed, not merely against the degenerate aristocracy of Rome, but equally against the fresh, unsophisticated bar-

[1] BGE, 46.

barian tribesmen who overran the dissolving Empire—and who might, had they only escaped the contagion, have repeated the exploits of their Homeric forerunners, evolving a culture of their own even nobler than that of the Greeks. The Vikings themselves succumbed. For a thousand years the only type of 'higher man' acknowledged in Europe was the ascetic priest or saint.

* * *

Nietzsche, it need hardly be said, regretted bitterly this overwhelming triumph of Christianity. As often as he thinks of what might have been, his indignation bursts forth in a torrent. 'The worm of conscience is a thing for the rabble, it is sheer ruin to a noble soul.'[1] To the Romans, he admits, Christianity may have been a tonic; to the barbarians, it was *poison*—and his tirades on occasion are almost enough to excuse the assumption that he was preaching a reversal to barbarism.

Nevertheless, it was not so. 'Human history', he writes in *The Genealogy of Morals* itself, 'would be too fatuous for anything were it not for the cleverness imported into it by the weak';[2] and again, 'it can fairly be stated that it is on the soil of this *essentially dangerous* form of human existence, the sacerdotal, that man really becomes for the first time an *interesting animal*, that it is in this form that the soul of man has in a higher sense attained *depths* and become *evil*—and those are the two fundamental forms of the superiority which up to the present man has exhibited over every other animal'.[3] We have only to follow his argument closely to realize that Nietzsche was, in fact, very far from regarding the ascendancy of salve-morality as an unmitigated disaster.

The bad conscience, he reaffirms, is an illness—but only in the sense that pregnancy is an illness. It was the necessary pre-condition of the emergence of new human faculties. But for the introversion effected by tyranny, which has 'changed completely the naïf egoism of the animal',[4] the intellectual conscience, in particular, could never have come into being: for, he reiterates, 'we are heirs to the conscience-vivisection and self-crucifixion of two thousand years: there lies our longest practice, our mastery perhaps, anyway our refinement'.[5]

Morality, Christian morality, represents a domination of one part of the self over the rest; but this very domination, which finds expression in ascetic practices, may also find expression in the quest for truth. What, after all, had Nietzsche himself been doing, when he took sides, 'not without resentment', *against* himself, but following a path marked out by generations of Christian thinkers—a path sometimes known as "the way of the cross in the operations of the intellect"? It was no accident

[1] N, XIV, 78.   [2] GM, I, 7.   [3] GM, I, 6.   [4] N, XI, 236.   [5] WP, 295.

that the Nietzsche of *Human, All-too-Human* should have found Pascal
congenial.

The Will, he points out in one of the most revealing of his aphorisms,
has the same requirements as 'everything that lives, grows and multi-
plies': its aim is 'the incorporation of new "experiences"; the assortment of new things in the old arrangements—hence, growth; or more
properly the *feeling* of growth, the feeling of increased power'.[1] Even so,
if this procedure is not to result in a false simplification of experience,
it has to be complemented by an impulse which compels the spirit of the
thinker 'to perceive *against* its own inclination, and often enough against
the wishes of his heart'.[2]

What he was preaching was not a reversal to barbarism, but a *reconciliation*, of the spontaneity and completeness of the savage with this
newly-acquired intellectual mastery and subtlety. And such a reconciliation, he believed, had already been achieved more than once. It
had been achieved, for instance, in thirteenth-century France: 'perhaps
the Provençals already represented in Europe one such high point—
men *extremely rich*, multifarious, and yet ruled by themselves, who were
not ashamed of their instincts.'[3] It had been achieved again, still more
conspicuously, in fifteenth-century Italy. The Italian Renaissance, indeed, was the first great resurgence of master-morality in Europe.

Nietzsche's admiration for the outstanding figures of the Renaissance
was intense. If he had caught it in the first place from Burckhardt, his
long residence in Venice and Genoa had only increased it. He loved
Columbus (according to Burckhardt the only really great explorer).
Petrarch and Leonardo, Michelangelo, Raphael and Rubens, he rated
second only to the Greek tragedians and artists; and there can be no
doubt that Cellini's autobiography materially influenced his own, produced as that was 'with so much of the self-glorification of antiquity'.[4]
He saw in the fifteenth and sixteenth centuries the dawn of a new hellenic
day.

Proportionately intense, for this reason, was his hatred of the German
Reformation, which, so he imagined, had plunged all into darkness once
more. Again and again he indicts this 'crime against culture'.[5] He could
not forgive the Germans for producing Luther, nor forgive Luther for
either his failure or his success. Where Luther failed, he provoked the
Counter-Reformation; where he succeeded—he succeeded in reinstating precisely that morality of resentment out of which Christianity
had originally sprung. 'He, the impossible monk, repudiated the *rule*
of the *homines religiosi*; he consequently brought about precisely the

[1] BGE, 230. [2] BGE, 229. [3] N, XIV, 91. [4] L, 13, 11, 88. [5] EH, p. 124.

same thing within the ecclesiastical order that he combated so impatiently in the civic order—namely, a "peasant insurrection".[1]

It was Luther's catastrophic blunder, in Nietzsche's view, instead of assailing the ideal of the priest and championing a new type of 'higher man', to assail the ideal of the 'higher man' and go on championing the priest. 'Every man his own priest' was the watchword: and notwithstanding Luther's own (quite illogical) attempt to forestall its application to politics, his 'peasant insurrection of the spirit'[2] was in fact the precursor of every subsequent egalitarian movement, down to the French Revolution.

Here, once again, however, we must beware of being misled by Nietzsche's vehemence. He did not condemn the Reformation, any more than he did Christianity, root and branch. He was keenly alive to the impetus it had given to rationalism—and therefore to atheism. Although, in his view, rationalism was rooted in Catholic Christianity, it could never have flowered outside the purlieus of Protestantism—and for the rationalism of the Enlightenment, his respect was still very great. This too, he held, might have been reconciled with the spontaneity and completeness of the savage. This too, in fact, *had* been so reconciled—in Goethe. For what else made Goethe what he was, 'no mere German, but a European event: a magnificent attempt to overcome the eighteenth century through a return to nature, through an *ascent* to the naturalness of the Renaissance, a kind of self-overcoming on the part of the century in question'?[3]

'That to which he aspired was *totality*; he was opposed to the sundering of reason, sensuality, feeling and will (as preached with most repulsive scholasticism by Kant, the antipodes of Goethe); he disciplined himself into a whole, he *created* himself. Goethe in the midst of an age of unreal sentiment, was a convinced realist: he said yea to everything related to him in this regard—there was no greater event in his life than that *ens realissimum* surnamed Napoleon. Goethe conceived a strong, highly-cultured man, skilful in all bodily accomplishments, able to keep himself in check, having a feeling of reverence for himself, and so constituted as to be able to risk the full enjoyment of naturalness in all its rich profusion and be strong enough for this freedom; a man of tolerance, not out of weakness but out of strength, because he knows how to turn to his own profit that which would ruin a mediocre nature; a man to whom nothing is any longer forbidden, unless it be *weakness* either as a vice or as a virtue. Such a spirit, *become free*, appears in the

---

[1] JW, 358.   [2] *Ibid.*   [3] TI, p. 109.

middle of the universe with a feeling of cheerful and confident fatalism; he believes that only individual things are bad, and that as a whole the universe redeems and affirms itself—*He no longer denies*. . . . But such a faith is the highest of all faiths: I christened it with the name of Diony-sus.'[1]

This, the finest of all Nietzsche's tributes to his great predecessor, features, as it happens, not in *The Genealogy of Morals*, but in *The Twilight of the Idols*. In *The Genealogy of Morals* itself, it is Napoleon whom he salutes as representing another resurgence of master-morality—Napoleon, whose ascendancy had momentarily checked the saturnalia of the slaves. But to Nietzsche, as to Carlyle (and also to Goethe himself), Napoleon was always the poet's counterpart—elsewhere he calls them the '*two great attempts* that were made to overcome the eighteenth century'[2]—and for no very far-fetched reason. Just as Goethe had mastered the rationalism of the Enlightenment, so Napoleon had mastered the revolutionary results of this rationalism. Moreover, just as Goethe had envisaged a supra-national, European culture, so, Nietzsche believed (on the evidence of the *Mémorial de Sainte-Hélène*, which he ranked with Eckermann's *Conversations*), Napoleon had laid the foundations of a supra-national, European State. It was yet another of their crimes against culture, that 'the Germans, with their Wars of Independence, robbed Europe of the significance—the marvellous significance, of Napoleon's life.'[3]

Nietzsche looked on the rationalism of the Enlightenment as 'the awe-inspiring *catastrophe* of a two-thousand-year training in truth, which finally forbids itself *the lie of the belief in God*'[4]—and valued it accordingly. Still more highly on this account, did he value the achievement of Goethe, who, thanks to the extraordinary force of his Will, had digested and assimilated this rationalism: he was veritably *Eine Natur*.

Nevertheless, Nietzsche could not regard even this achievement as final: since, like the rationalists themselves, Goethe had still believed in truth. He had discovered the world-view he needed, in order to reconcile his internal antinomies, in the pantheism of Spinoza; he had 'deified' the world, much as Schopenhauer diabolized it. Not until scepticism had been pushed to its furthest limit, in nihilism, could 'the auto-suppression of morals'[5] be said to have been finally accomplished: '*radical nihilism* being the conviction that existence is absolutely insupportable, if measured by the highest values we accept; and furthermore that we have not the smallest right to postulate a beyond or a thing-in-itself which

[1] TI, p. 109.   [2] WP, 104.   [3] EH, p. 125.   [4] GM, III, 27.   [5] D, Preface, 4.

would be "divine", which would be the embodiment of morality. This admission it is that constitutes the fruit of a really adult "truthfulness",[1] and this admission had as yet been made by one man alone: 'what distinguishes our philosophical position is a conviction unknown to all previous ages: that of *not being in possession of the truth*. All our predecessors "were in possession of the truth", even the sceptics'.[2]

Consequently, not until the nihilism of *Human, All-too-Human* had been reconciled with the spontaneity and completeness of the savage, could master-morality be said to have won its final victory: and that victory, needless to say, could not be reflected in pantheism—or in any 'theism' whatever. For all that the man who won it would look on the world 'as on a god we love', he would not believe in it as a god—he would not believe in it at all. For all that his love for life would be real, it would not be of quite the same kind as expresses itself in the *Rhapsody on Nature*—it would, as Nietzsche said, be 'the love for a woman we doubt'.[3]

In *The Genealogy of Morals*, therefore, it is not even Goethe whom Nietzsche finally hails as him who is to come. 'This man of the future, who will thus redeem us from the old ideal, as he will from that ideal's necessary corollary of great nausea, will to nothingness, and nihilism; this tocsin of noon and the great decision, which renders the will again free, who gives back to the world its goal and to man his hope, this Antichrist and Antinihilist, this conqueror of God and of Nothingness'[4] —this Angel of the Apocalypse is, of course, none other than Nietzsche himself—'*Zarathustra, Zarathustra the godless!*'[5]

* * *

This, then, in summary outline, is Nietzsche's interpretation of history. And at this juncture, if not long before, the reader will have realized what it adds up to: nothing more nor less than a new, bold, extraordinarily plausible, and possibly true, presentation of the Romantic Myth, in the very form in which he had inherited it from Wagner. Just as in *The Birth of Tragedy* and *Thoughts out of Season*, so in *Beyond Good and Evil* and *The Genealogy of Morals*, the history of Europe is rendered in terms of a dialogue between the Hellenic and the Oriental spirit, the one being continually raised, through its antagonism to the other, to a new level of manifestation.

Only in a single obvious respect does this new version depart from the old. Now, instead of Wagner, it is Nietzsche who figures as the music-practising Socrates, the Aeschylus of the new dispensation. Instead of Siegfried, it is Zarathustra who stands for that anti-Alexander,

[1] WP, 3.   [2] N, XI, 159.   [3] JW, Preface, 3.   [4] GM, II, 24.   [5] GM, II, 25.

that great and powerful nature who recapitulates in himself the history of European man, and passes beyond it, anticipating and inaugurating a new epoch.

Of course, the elaboration of the myth is incomparably more brilliant and subtle than anything of which Nietzsche was capable in 1870. But, if, as he said, *The Birth of Tragedy* 'smells offensively of Hegel',[1] so, and no less, does *The Genealogy of Morals*. In fact, one could epitomize the argument in Hegelian terms. One could point to the blond brute as thesis and the moral man as antithesis, whilst 'synthesis, the suppression of the moral man'[2] is his own word for Zarathustra.

It can hardly be accidental that, in *Beyond Good and Evil*, he comes nearer than ever before to giving Hegel his due, not merely attributing Schopenhauer's dislike of him to want of historical sense, but bracketing him with Goethe as an opponent of 'the English mechanical stultification of the world'.[3] He actually characterizes Hegel and Schopenhauer together as 'the two hostile brother-geniuses in philosophy, who pushed in different directions to the opposite poles of German thought, and thereby wronged each other as only brothers will do'[4]—a judgement memorable alike for its fairness and insight.

It should be clear, however, that by 1885 Nietzsche had no need to look to Hegel for his dialectics. That growth proceeds through the surpassing of contradictions was something his own experience had taught him. 'All great things go to ruin by reason of themselves', he writes at the end of *The Genealogy of Morals*, 'by reason of an act of self-dissolution: so wills the law of life, the law of *necessary* self-mastery even in the essence of life':[5] and his own life had been one long exemplification of this. One after the other in his works, history, philology, and ultimately morality—morality 'in its latest and noblest form'[6] of science—had turned the sting against itself.

It was upon this discovery that he based his doctrine of 'the order of rank'. Growth being the measure of greatness, greatness, in his view, was proportionate to the number of seemingly antagonistic viewpoints a man could comprehend and master. 'Do you wish to acquire a just and catholic outlook? You can do so by being one who has traversed many personalities, and whose last personality *requires* all the earlier as functions.'[7] In this respect, he was Catholic rather than Protestant in his sympathies.

G. K. Chesterton once observed that nothing so infallibly denotes a subtle and superior mind as 'the power of comparing a lower thing with a higher, and yet that higher with a higher still, of thinking on three

[1] EH, p. 69.   [2] NZ, 7.   [3] BGE, 252.   [4] *Ibid.*
[5] GM, III, 27.   [6] GM, III, 23.   [7] N, XII, 14.

planes at once'. That was likewise Nietzsche's persuasion—except that he allowed for many more planes than three. The sectarian is never able to envisage a problem from more than one angle, because he himself has never occupied more than one; a delicate sense of *nuance*, of gradation, of hierarchy, distinguishes the 'noble' mind. Nietzsche exhibits it pre-eminently. 'The ladder upon which he ascends and descends is prodigious; he has seen further, he has willed further, and *gone* further than any other man. There is a contradiction in every word he utters, this most yea-saying of spirits. In him all contradictions are bound up into a new unity.'[1] The panegyric of Zarathustra in *Ecce Homo* is not unmerited.

Nietzsche's dialectical interpretation of history was a direct expression of this comprehensiveness. It was because he experienced such a compulsion to establish an order of rank among his multitudinous sympathies, that he was able to establish one among the men and movements with which he sympathized. Hence his sympathy for Hegel himself. But not only had he no need to turn to Hegel for his dialectics, but, unlike Hegel, he was conscious of the nature of this compulsion. He was conscious, that is to say, that his interpretation *was* an interpretation: 'it behoves us to recognize the extent to which we are the *creators* of our sentiments of value, and *capable* in consequence of introducing a "meaning" into history'.[2] Intrinsically, like everything else, history was meaningless.

This did not imply that the development he discerned was illusory, any more than his own development had been—though other interpreters, with other sympathies, would find yet others. But it did imply that the dialectic of history was the creation of men themselves—and first and foremost of those men who, in the past, had experienced a like compulsion to reconcile the conflicting values of their times; whom that very reconciliation had empowered to direct the course of events.

Such men had rarely, if ever, recognized their own creativity. All through history, Nietzsche declares, one encounters those 'who dare not accomplish their task unless they can represent it as ordained of God; for whom the legislation of values is *unbearable* as long as they are unable to put it down to an "inspiration".'[3] He himself was perhaps the first to dare. He was the first, at all events, to acknowledge and proclaim his daring. It was for this reason that he still denied most of these forerunners, Hegel included, the ultimate dignity of the philosopher:

'*The real philosophers, however, are commanders and lawgivers*; they

[1] EH, p. 106.   [2] WP, 1011.   [3] WP, 972.

say: "Thus *shall* it be!" They determine first the Whither and the Why of mankind, and thereby set aside the previous labour of all philosophical workers, and all subjugators of the past—they grasp at the future with a creative hand, and whatever is and was, becomes for them thereby a means, an instrument, and a hammer. Their "knowing" is *creating*, their creating is a law-giving, their will to truth is—*Will to Power*.—Are there at present such philosophers? Have there ever been such philosophers? *Must* there not be such philosophers?"[1]

It was for this reason also, as we know, that Nietzsche could put his faith in no historical 'inevitability'. If the Superman was desirable, the Last Man was no less possible. Whether, in the end, victory fell to the one or the other, depended upon the decision and determination of men —depended, therefore, first and foremost upon his own. For what, he asks in *Ecce Homo*, has been responsible for 'the formidable power of the ascetic ideal',[2] despite its hostility to life? Why has the ascetic priest or saint so long been the only type of higher man acknowledged in Europe?—'Reply . . . because it was a *faute de mieux*—because hitherto it has been the only ideal and has had no competitors. "For man would rather aspire to nonentity than not aspire at all." But above all, until the time of *Zarathustra* there was no such thing as a counter-ideal.'[3] Oddly enough, it was precisely because he did *not* believe in himself as the mouthpiece of God or the Idea, that Nietzsche was able to tell the incredulous Elizabeth, 'Speaking quite literally, I hold the future of mankind in my hand'.[4]

* * *

The Romantic Myth underlies all Nietzsche's works from 1884 onwards. As long as we fail to grasp it, both these and the claims he advanced for them are bound to remain largely unintelligible. As soon as we do grasp it, on the other hand, many things appear in a new light. It becomes clear, for example, why *The Genealogy of Morals* should have been succeeded by *The Case of Wagner*.

Nietzsche used to bewilder his friends, Malwida von Meysenbug in particular, by calling himself Wagner's 'heir'[5]—and their bewilderment is hardly surprising, seeing that he would asseverate in the same breath that Wagner and he were not to be compared, that they belonged to different species. Yet both allegations were meant in all seriousness, and neither was without foundation.

Insofar as *The Art-Work of the Future* had influenced his own development, and therefore, indirectly, his own presentation of the Myth, he was

[1] BGE, 211.　　[2] EH, p. 117.　　[3] *Ibid.*　　[4] L, 12, 88.　　[5] L, 19, 2, 83.

veritably Wagner's heir: and he always claimed that he had learned from Wagner what it meant to be 'master of a long will'. At the same time, he held that Wagner himself had betrayed his deepest insight: first of all, when he began to 'read Schopenhauer's doctrine between the lines of his characters';[1] finally, when he capitulated to the ascetic ideal. In *Ecce Homo*, he recalls how he received, in exchange for *Human, All-too-Human*, a splendidly bound copy of *Parsifal*, inscribed, 'To his dear friend Friedrich Nietzsche, from Richard Wagner, Ecclesiastical Councillor'—'did it not sound as if two swords had crossed?'[2]

It was this final capitulation that filled Nietzsche with pity and contempt—pity for the loneliness which, he supposed, was responsible; contempt for the weakness of will that had tolerated such a defection. There are many passages in his books bearing covert witness to the anguish it occasioned him; it may have been true that he did not dare visit Bayreuth for fear of the pain that might ensue, whether he succumbed to his sympathy, and thereby betrayed his own insight, or stuck to his course, and thereby grieved Wagner still more. 'It was hard', he confessed to Gast, when the news of Wagner's death reached him, 'for six years to be the opponent of the man one had most reverenced on earth, and my constitution is not sufficiently coarse for *such a position*. After all, it was Wagner grown senile whom I was forced to resist.'[3]

Even so, this capitulation would not by itself have been sufficient to provoke his polemic. In that there was nothing unique. What forced him finally to break silence was something more: it was the fact that Wagner had proclaimed his defeat as a victory, and—what was worst of all—as the very victory which he, Nietzsche, had won!

Wagner, in other words, had continued to propagate the Romantic Myth, whilst assigning to Parsifal the place that belonged to Zarathustra. And he had got away with it. By 1887 the estimate of his role set forth in *The Birth of Tragedy* had become the accepted estimate of a large part of musical Germany, if not of musical Europe. The situation of a psychologist, Nietzsche writes in *Beyond Good and Evil*, may grow so paradoxical that, 'precisely where he has learned *great pity*, together with *great contempt*, the multitude, the educated and the visionaries, have on their part learned great reverence—reverence for "great men" and marvellous animals, for the sake of whom one blesses and honours the fatherland, the earth, the dignity of mankind and one's own self, to whom one points the young, and in view of whom one educates them'.[4] He had just received a mournful reminder of this in the

---

[1] JW, 99.   [2] EH, p. 89.   [3] L, 19, 2, 83.   [4] BGE, 269.

person of young Heinrich von Stein, who, after making the impression of the long-sought disciple, had thrown in his lot with Bayreuth.

His attitude towards Wagner at this date may be likened to that of a sixteenth-century Protestant towards the Pope. It was not the paganism of the Curia that most inflamed a Luther or a Latimer, but the parading of this paganism as Christianity. Protestants used to refer to the Church of Rome as the Scarlet Woman; Nietzsche called Wagner 'a pious seducer'.[1] He could not sleep at nights until he had broken the image he himself had helped hoist on its pedestal.

This has been strangely misconstrued. Nietzsche has been charged, for instance, with petty disloyalty for attacking Wagner after his death. He ought, we are given to understand, either to have published his polemic earlier, or else have kept silent altogether. But earlier than 1883, Nietzsche could not even have composed it: partly, no doubt, because as long as Wagner was alive, he had to avert his eyes from a tragedy that might sap his resolution; but also because, until the first part of *Zarathustra* was written, he had not earned the right to criticize at all. It was only then that he felt charged with a mission of such importance as to override personal loyalties.

Again, he has been charged with want of taste, for suggesting, in particular, that Wagner's father was Jewish. Here the boot is on the other foot. This would hardly have occurred to Nietzsche as an insult. Elsewhere he contrasts Wagner unfavourably with Mendelssohn, and even with Offenbach. He advanced the suggestion, as it happens, precisely in order to account for an anti-semitism he deplored. He was scrupulous in drawing on his private acquaintance. Had it been his object to discredit a friend in the eyes of the mob, he could have brought heavier artillery to bear.

The strangest charge, however, and the one that betrays the most complete misconception of his motives, is that which, seizing upon just these unfavourable contrasts, his preference for Bizet in particular, cites them as proof that he was so carried away on a tide of emotional reaction as to be incapable of responsible judgement: since, it is said, no critic in his senses can deny that in point of sheer technical mastery, Wagner stood head and shoulders above all his contemporaries, Bizet included.

I call this the strangest charge because, in fact, so far from denying this supremacy, Nietzsche was the first to insist on it. Had Wagner been a mediocre technician, he would have felt no cause to 'annihilate'[2] him. In one of his letters to Gast, he waxes lyrical about the Overture to

[1] L, 12, 88.   [2] L, 4, 10, 88.

Parsifal itself. 'Apart from all irrelevant questions (as to what use this music can or *ought* to be) and on purely aesthetic grounds', he writes, 'has Wagner ever done anything better?'[1] But—and this is the all-important consideration—in *The Case of Wagner* itself, it was precisely those 'irrelevant questions', and those alone, that concerned him.

Nietzsche's aesthetics were formulated (as he said) from the standpoint of the creator, rather than the spectator. All artists, he claimed, may be divided into two classes: 'those who suffer from *overflowing* vitality, who wish for Dionysian art and a tragic insight into and outlook upon life; and those who suffer from *reduced* vitality, who need repose, peace, calm seas, or else intoxication, spasm, stupor.'[2] He regarded the smallest artist belonging to the first class as superior in kind to the greatest belonging to the second. This was the standpoint from which he ranked Bizet higher than Wagner.

Only in a single respect did the distinction correspond to one of technical proficiency. The ascendancy of the Will over the passions, Nietzsche always maintained, was reflected directly in the unity of a work of art: 'the greatness of a musician, in a word, is to be measured by his aptitude for the grand style'.[3] It was by this criterion that he had, in *Thoughts out of Season*, pronounced Wagner greatest of all; it is by the same criterion that he now pronounces him the *décadent par excellence*. For, he asks, how is decadence characterized?—'By the fact that in it life no longer animates the whole':[4] and Wagner is 'only worthy of admiration and love by virtue of his inventiveness in small things, in his elaboration of detail . . . as our greatest musical *miniaturist*'.[5] It is an odd reversal of judgement, and few would care to uphold it; but once his standpoint is known, it is evident that if *The Case of Wagner* is bad (and it is certainly his slightest production), it is not bad for the reasons generally advanced.

Nietzsche launched his attack on Wagner, not because he thought him a minor musician, but because he knew him to be a major one; and not because his mental faculties were weakened, but because he attached an importance to music inconceivable to the Philistine of Culture. His polemic actually bears witness to a higher estimate of Wagner than most of the rejoinders it provoked—and to an infinitely higher estimate of art. *Parsifal* and *The Ring* represented, in his eyes, a veritable apotheosis of decadence—an apotheosis such as only a great genius could have encompassed: and therein lay their danger, for what a genius is able to express, he is able also to transmit. Under cover of Dionysian professions, Wagner was playing the game of the priests—sapping, corrupt-

[1] L, 21, 1, 87.   [2] CW, p. 66.   [3] N, XIV, 145.   [4] CW, p. 19.   [5] CW, p. 21.

ing and perverting that Will to Power on which the future of Europe depended.

If decadence is contagious, so, of course, is overflowing vitality; and that is why Nietzsche set such store by Rossini, Bizet, and even his friend Peter Gast (whom, in his solitude, he consciously or unconsciously idealized). In them, he believed, a restorative influence was at work. In their hands music was re-assuming its proper function, to be 'a stimulus to life',[1] and in that sense 'sublimely practical'.[2] According to their several capacities—would they had been equal to Wagner's! — these three did respond to the aspirations of the hale, instead of ministering to the needs of the sick. They taught no moral sentiments or sentimentalities; they quickened the impulse that might carry a man beyond morality.

Nevertheless—need it be said?—it was not the writer of comedy but the writer of tragedy whom he placed at the head and top of all whose art proceeded from the 'bestowing virtue': and not even Bizet could be described as a genuine tragedian. For tragedy at its highest, Nietzsche held (in conscious opposition to Schopenhauer), stood for 'a Yea-saying free from all reserve, applying even to suffering, and guilt, and all that is questionable and strange in existence';[3] it compelled the spectator to perceive against his inclinations, and against the wishes of his own heart, in order, at the last, to reward him with a foregleam of *amor fati*:

'The overwhelming artists, who make a harmony ring out of every conflict, are those who benefit even things by their own stature and self-redemption: they declare their inmost experience through the symbolism of each work of art—their creating is gratitude for their being. The *depth* of the tragic artist lies in this, that his aesthetic instinct surveys the remoter issues, that he does not halt short-sightedly at what is nearest, that he affirms the *economy* as a whole, which justifies the *terrible*, the *evil*, the *questionable*, and not only—justifies.'[4]

While, therefore, in *The Case of Wagner*, Nietzsche pitted *Carmen* against *The Ring*, he left his readers in no doubt as to who was really Wagner's 'antipode'[5]—or antipope. The titles of his last two collections of aphorisms would have made it clear to the blind: *The Twilight of the Idols* and *Nietzsche contra Wagner*.

* * *

In *Zarathustra* Nietzsche had attained—or so he believed—the ideal of the artistic genius, as set forth in *Richard Wagner at Bayreuth*. 'The

[1] TI, p. 80.   [2] WP, 808.   [3] EH, p. 71.   [4] WP, 852.   [5] CW, p. 95.

whole of *Zarathustra*,' he writes, 'might be classified under the rubric music';[1] he habitually refers to it as a tragedy. Inevitably, in *The Genealogy of Morals* and its sequel, he himself assumes the historical role he had formerly assigned to Wagner.

Whether his interpretation of history can be upheld, is a point we shall consider later; whether, even if it could be upheld, his estimate of *Zarathustra* was just, one may well question here and now.

In one sense, it obviously was not. *Zarathustra*, with all its merits, fails to realize the classical perfection he was aiming at. It resembles less a Doric temple than a Gothic church—one of those twelfth-century churches built onto time and again. The work as a whole lacks proportion. In fact, there is no work as a whole. Though the first three Parts do constitute some sort of unity, the fourth was a baroque extension; and, we may be fairly sure, had Nietzsche fulfilled his intention of writing yet further instalments, though it might have approximated more nearly to a tragedy in the accepted sense, it would have been even less of a unity than it is. It would have come to resemble *Faust*.

This much admitted, however, the truth remains that *Zarathustra* does fulfil, to an almost uncanny extent, the spirit of his earlier aspirations. Curiously enough, moreover, its very incompleteness lends weight to his claim: since, not withstanding his classical *desideratum*, it was precisely the overmastering urge to growth that prevented him from realizing it. If none of his great projects was ever carried out to the end, that was simply because he grew out of them. 'It is too bad! Always the old story! When a man has finished building his house, he finds that he has thereby learned unawares something which he absolutely *ought* to have known—before he *began* to build.'[2]

Probably it was the same with Goethe, who, towards the end of his life, warned Eckerman against attempting a large work; and probably, as Nietzsche opined, it was a necessity of the age they lived in. Unlike the envied Greeks, unlike the men of the Renaissance, they were not in a position to take anything for granted—neither a credible picture of the whole of life, nor its counterpart, an integrated culture. They were not free to concentrate whole-heartedly on artistic creation; the very force of their creative instinct drove them out of the pale of art. As he insisted in *David Strauss*, the moderns were first and foremost *seekers*—seekers of that which would enable them, or their successors, to be the artists they wished.

'To have attained an ideal,' Nietzsche observes in *Beyond Good and Evil*, 'is precisely thereby to have surpassed it.'[3] In the first three Parts

---

[1] EH, p. 97.   [2] BGE, 277.   [3] BGE, 73.

of *Zarathustra* he had attained his ideal of the artistic genius, so far as was possible to a man of the nineteenth century. Precisely thereby he did surpass it. As we saw at the beginning of this chapter, he found himself immediately confronted with a new task—that of working out the implications of his mission—and in consequence, with a new ideal. We are now in a position to see just what this new ideal was. It was nothing more nor less than that of the philosophical genius, as set forth in *Schopenhauer as Educator*.

The Greeks, it will be recalled, had never, in his opinion, been fully conscious of what their achievement implied. They had never evolved a philosophy adequate to their experience. With the possible exception of Heraclitus (and even he imposed a semi-moral order upon existence), they had 'misunderstood the tragic'.[1] And, like Schlegel (another adherent of the Romantic Myth), who cited 'the majesty of antiquity' as 'a remarkable example of the perishable nature of merely instinctive greatness', Nietzsche thought it was due to this that their culture had succumbed so quickly to rationalism. The new-born Hellenism of Germany, he had declared in *The Birth of Tragedy*, was more auspiciously situated, since side by side with Wagner stood Schopenhauer, 'whose philosophy we may unhesitatingly designate as Dionysian wisdom comprised in concepts'.

Even then it had been sufficiently evident whom he had really in mind—and it had become still more so in *Schopenhauer as Educator*. He himself it was, and no other, who was to provide that picture of the whole of life, whence future generations might learn the meaning of their own. Now, in 1884, he at last felt ready for the undertaking. He, the Aeschylus of the new dispensation, would be likewise its Heraclitus—'the first tragic philosopher'![2]

Beyond Good and Evil bears the subtitle 'Prelude to a Philosophy of the Future'. This philosophy, this 'translation of the Dionysian into the philosophic pathos',[3] was to be the substance of *The Transvaluation of all Values*: and, notwithstanding all past experience, notwithstanding his own admission, 'I am not sufficiently *limited* to construct a "system"—even my own',[4] Nietzsche had conceived it once more in the grand style. To this, accordingly, we must now direct our attention.

[1] WP, 1029.   [2] EH, p. 72.   [3] *Ibid.*   [4] N, XIV, 354.

X

THE COSMOLOGIST

The most important thing to remember about *The Will to Power, an Attempted Transvaluation of all Values*, is that it was never written. All that survives of Nietzsche's most ambitious project is a vast assortment of notes accumulated over the years 1884–8; a dozen plans of the contents; and a single completed section, 'The Antichrist'. Of that 'enormous host of problems',[1] which, he told Brandes, he could see lying spread out at his feet in relief, we can gain a fairly clear idea; the 'conception as a whole', in which they were to find their solution, must always be a matter of inference and more or less dubious conjecture.

The book was conceived, as we might expect, shortly after the completion of Part III of *Zarathustra*. In the early summer of 1884 Nietzsche informed Overbeck and his sister of his intention to devote the next five or six years to 'the elaboration of my philosophy';[2] thenceforward his letters were seldom free from references to this *magnum opus*. But progress was arduous and intermittent. Whereas, in August 1884, he could speak of 'hours when this task was clearly present to me, when an unbelievable philosophical (and I would say more than philosophical) whole was spread out before my eyes',[3] a year later, 'my philosophy', he confessed, 'if I am justified in calling by that name what torments me to the very roots of my being, cannot be communicated any more, at all events in print'.[4] He had already turned aside to compile the fourth part of *Zarathustra* and *Beyond Good and Evil*. The following year saw the publication of *The Genealogy of Morals*.

With this, he declared later, his 'preparatory activities'[5] had reached their term. An epoch in his life had come to an end. Henceforward he would have to keep to himself more than ever, publishing nothing for a number of years, if he was to gather strength sufficient to pluck the last fruit of his tree. In fact, a few months of silence did elapse between *The Genealogy of Morals* and *The Case of Wagner*: months during which the necessity of 'building an intellectual edifice'[6] alternately weighed on him 'like a load of five tons' and uplifted him with abounding enthus-

---

[1] L, 4, 5, 88.   [2] L, 7, 4, 84.   [3] L, 28, 8, 84.
[4] L, 3, 7, 85.   [5] L, 17, 9, 87.   [6] L, 24, 3, 87.

iasm. Not until the beginning of 1888 was he able to tell Overbeck once more, 'the outlines of what is without doubt an incredible task, the task now laid upon me, emerge ever more clearly from the clouds'. By that time, however, his conception of both the nature and the magnitude of the task was undergoing a change; and if we are to form any just idea of what had been taking shape in his mind, there is no option but to consult the multitudinous notes.

That his failure—for such we must account it—even to begin *The Will to Power*, represents a major tragedy in the history of philosophy, can hardly be denied. Great and fertile as his completed works are, they constituted, in Nietzsche's own eyes, no more than a prolegomenon to something that would have overshadowed them all; and however sceptical we may remain towards his more extravagant claims, there is no reason for disputing this. A careful perusal of the notes leaves the impression of a gigantic quarry, strewn with blocks of chiselled marble. Almost every stroke reveals the hand of a master: the edifice for which they were intended could hardly have been unworthy.

At the same time, those critics are right who insist that the failure had its compensations. Had these fragments not survived in their existing form, something precious would have been lost: namely, the glimpse they afford into the workings of Nietzsche's mind. Their very ambiguities and contradictions are eloquent. *The Antichrist* is a straitened production compared with the 'Criticism of Religion' on which it is based—and that not only because it was cast as a polemic. Nietzsche's very greatness resides in the absolute freedom he allowed himself to follow any argument to its ultimate conclusion, no matter how seemingly absurd; to let no premise go unchallenged, least of all a premise he himself was disposed to favour. There are moments when every other philosopher does seem wanting in 'intellectual probity'[1] beside him. And it is just in those writings of his that were never intended for publication that this *terribile demonstrazione* appears most conspicuously.

Furthermore, while it would be foolish to acclaim the raw material an adequate substitute for the finished product, or to pretend that we can see in these notes what was still partially concealed from himself—that unbelievable philosophical (and more than philosophical) whole—neither inference nor conjecture need be quite so dubious as they often have been. It is possible to discern the broad outline, at least, of the world-view towards which he was feeling his way. Not only are we informed of his aim—'under a title which carries some risk, "The Will to Power", it is a new philosophy, or, more exactly, an *attempt at a new*

[1] WP, 460.

interpretation of occurrence which seeks provisional expression'[1]—but we already possess, in *Beyond Good and Evil*, a number of his cardinal thoughts in definitive form. He has placed in our hands the end of a golden string; with its aid we can penetrate far into the labyrinth.

The Will to Power is the title; the Will to Power is the theme: and what Nietzsche understood by the Will to Power we have already partially elucidated. It is his name for the 'deepest self' in man: for that primary impulse or tendency out of which all our instincts have originated, and which they are appointed to serve. In Chapter VIII, I likened it in passing to Freud's Eros: and though this likeness will have to be qualified before we have done, there will be no danger of doing violence to Nietzsche's thought if, for the time being, we consider it simply, in Freud's words, as the urge 'to establish ever greater unities, and to preserve them thus'.

Early in *Beyond Good and Evil*, he gives unequivocal expression to this thesis, at the same time issuing a warning against the moral prejudice which immediately makes itself felt, when we are confronted with a postulate so repugnant to idealistic presuppositions—a warning we do well to lay to heart:

'All psychology hitherto has run aground on moral prejudices and timidities, it has not dared to launch out into the depths. In so far as it is allowable to recognize in that which has hitherto been written, evidence of that which has hitherto been kept silent, it seems as if nobody had yet harboured the notion of psychology as the morphology and *Development-theory of the Will to Power*, as I conceive of it. The power of moral prejudices has penetrated deeply into the most intellectual world, the world apparently most indifferent and unprejudiced, and has obviously operated in an injurious, obstructive, blinding, and distorting manner. A proper physio-psychology has to contend with unconscious antagonism in the heart of the investigator, it has "the heart" against it: even a theory of the reciprocal conditioning of the "good" and the "bad" impulses, causes (as refined immorality) distress and aversion in a still strong and manly conscience—still more so, a theory of the derivation of all good impulses from bad ones. If, however, a person should regard even the emotions of hatred, envy, covetousness, and imperiousness as life-conditioning emotions, as factors which must be present, fundamentally and essentially, in the general economy of life (which must, therefore, be further developed if life is to be further

[1] N, XIV, 418.

developed), he will suffer from such a view of things as from sea-sickness.'[1]

As usual, Nietzsche was speaking from experience; his cynicism began at home. To nobody, as we know, had this notion been more repugnant at first than to him. He had had more than his fair share of idealism to mortify, before he could take the malicious joy he sometimes did take in mortifying other people's. His hostility to those 'beautiful, glistening, jingling, festive words—honesty, love of truth, love of wisdom, sacrifice for knowledge, heroism of the truthful'[2]—was proportionate to the enchantment they had exercised over his own youth. To see such heroism reduced to a species of egoism had not given him the same satisfaction as it gives our current intellectuals—he possessed it himself. In fact, he had displayed it in the reduction; and it was precisely because his honesty, his love of truth, had involved him in suffering, that he diagnosed it as a species of cruelty, and pronounced cruelty necessary to life:

'In effect, to translate man back again into nature; to master the many vain and visionary interpretations and subordinate meanings which have hitherto been scratched and daubed over the eternal original text, *homo natura*; to bring it about that man shall henceforth stand before man as he now, hardened by the discipline of science, stands before the *other* forms of nature, with fearless Oedipus-eyes, and stopped Ulysses-ears, deaf to the enticements of old metaphysical bird-catchers, who have piped to him far too long: "Thou art more! thou art higher! thou hast a different origin!"—this may be a strange and foolish task, but that it is a *task*, who can deny! Why did we choose it, this foolish task? Or, to put the question differently: "Why knowledge at all?" Everyone will ask us about this. And thus pressed, we, who have asked ourselves the question a hundred times, have not found, and cannot find any better answer. . . .'[3]

It was the Will to Power, striving to establish ever greater unities, that had thus inexorably driven him to seek a formula that fitted the facts; and it was because it fitted the facts, and only because it did so, that he had eventually adopted the formula, 'Will to Power'.

This theory of the primary impulse or tendency in man, then, in itself constitutes the first great step in Nietzsche's synthesis: 'our intellect, our will, also our sentiments, depend on our *valuations*; these correspond to our instincts and their conditions of existence; our instincts are reducible to *Will to Power*. The Will to Power is the ultimate fact we are able to

[1] BGE, 23.   [2] BGE, 230.   [3] *Ibid.*

descend to.'[1] And the second great step, which likewise has its analogue in Freud, might have been predicted of a *quondam* Schopenhauerian. It is the straightforward identification of this Will with the 'intelligible character' of the whole animate and inanimate world: the thesis, in other words, that action, wherever manifest, is of essentially the same kind as human action.

Supposing, Nietzsche writes—again in *Beyond Good and Evil*—'supposing that nothing else is "given" as real but our world of desires and passions, that we cannot sink or rise to any other "reality" but just that of our impulses—for thinking is only a relation of these impulses to one another'—may we not, *must* we not, pose the question, 'whether this "given" does not *suffice* for understanding, in terms of something similar, the so-called mechanical (or "material") world also?'[2]

'Granted, finally, that we succeeded in explaining our entire instinctive life as the development and ramification of one fundamental form of will—namely, the Will to Power, as *my* thesis puts it; granted that all organic functions could be traced back to this Will to Power, and that the solution of the problem of generation and nutrition—it is one problem—could also be found therein: one would thus have acquired the right to define *all* active force unequivocally as *Will to Power*. The world seen from within, the world defined and designated according to its "intelligible character"—it would simply be "Will to Power", and nothing else.'[3]

This, of course, is the sort of conjecture that sends a chill down the spine of many scientists, even today. But that is of no importance. In the first place, as Schopenhauer argued with the utmost cogency, science can never dispense with at least one *qualitas occulta*—the most it can do is systematically to investigate and record its manifestations: 'it is an illusion to suppose that something is *known*, when all we have is a mathematical formula for the occurrence; it is only *designated, described* —nothing more!'[4] In the second place, science insists, with ever-increasing emphasis, on the continuity between the inorganic, organic and human worlds. If, therefore, the postulate of a basic tendency towards the acquisition of power fits the facts of human nature, and enables us to predict new ones, there is reason to suspect that it may fulfil the same role with regard to the rest of nature; and, if this does prove the case, to conclude in addition that the occult quality whose manifestations we observe is of the same kind as that whose manifesta-

[1] N, XIV, 327.   [2] BGE, 36.   [3] *Ibid.*   [4] WP, 628.

tions we not only observe but experience: in other words, that it may legitimately be designated 'will'.

Science, Nietzsche has said already, set out with the intention of tracing the unknown back to the known; it has ended by tracing the known back to the unknown. But 'a force of which we cannot form any idea is an empty word'.[1] It follows that 'the triumphant concept "*energy*", with which our physicists created God and the world, needs yet to be completed: it must be given an inner will which I designate as the "*Will to Power*". . . . There is no help for it, all movements, all "appearances", all "laws" must be understood as *symptoms* of an *inner* occurrence, and the analogy of man must be used for this purpose.'[2]

He advances this conjecture, be it noted, expressly as an 'hypothesis'; as an hypothesis it must be considered; as an hypothesis he himself considers it. It can neither be dismissed nor adopted until the attempt has been made to see whether or not it fits the facts, all the facts, and nothing but the facts. 'The *will* is to be *deduced*—is not an immediate fact such as Schopenhauer required. It remains to be seen whether it is a *legitimate* deduction.'[3] His own procedure is to assume tentatively that the Will to Power does constitute the single reality, and, on the basis of this assumption, to attempt his own re-creation of God and the world. In the ensuing pages I propose to retrace this attempt.

* * *

One thing is immediately obvious: Nietzsche's theory marks a complete break with both Idealism and Materialism. On the one hand, he is careful to distinguish between his own standpoint and Schopenhauer's. The 'so-called mechanical (or material) world' is not to be regarded as an illusion: other Wills are just as real as our own, and the multiplicity of phenomena is by no means a product of the mind. 'There is no such thing as will: there are only punctuations of will, which are constantly increasing or decreasing their power.'[4] On the other hand, he retains Schopenhauer's contention, that the true being of everything consists in its action: 'a quantum of power is characterized by the effect it exerts and which it resists';[5] to think these away, is to think away the quantum itself. The ultimate constituents of the world are 'dynamic quanta in a relation of tension to all other dynamic quanta: the essence of which resides in their relation to all other quanta, in their "effect" upon the latter'.[6]

In the beginning was the event. Nietzsche's theory excludes from the outset the Cartesian 'substance' in both its forms, mind and body—and

---

[1] WP, 621.   [2] WP, 619.   [3] N, XIII, 261.
[4] WP, 715.   [5] WP, 634.   [6] WP, 635.

therewith the Cartesian dualism. 'The concept "substance"', he writes, 'is an outcome of the concept "subject"':[1] and the concept 'subject' reflects a mistaken psychology. 'We distinguish ourselves, the agents, from the action, and everywhere we make use of this scheme—we try to discover an agent for every occurrence. What have we done? We have *mistaken* a feeling of power, tension, resistance, a muscular feeling, which is already the beginning of the action, for a cause; or we have understood the will to do this or that as a cause, because the action follows it.'[2] In reality, we ourselves have no existence apart from the sum-total of our activities, conscious and unconscious; no more has anything else.

The distinction is perpetuated in language. For example, 'when I say the "lightning flashes", I have set down the flash once as activity and a second time as subject; thus a being is accredited to the occurrence, which is not one with it, which rather remains, *is*, and does not "become"'.[3] This 'being' is a fiction nonetheless—there is no such thing as a thing. 'A "thing" is the sum of its effects, synthetically united by means of a concept, an image.'[4] The whole distinction of subject and verb is a relic of animism. When, therefore, Descartes conceived the soul on the analogy of the body, he was merely reversing the aboriginal act whereby the body was conceived on the analogy of the soul. ' "Something is thought, therefore there is something that thinks": this is what Descartes' argument amounts to. But this is to postulate our belief in the substance-concept as already true *a priori*: that there must be something "that thinks" when there is thinking is merely a formulation of our grammatical usage, which postulates an agent for every action.'[5]

As a practised philologist, Nietzsche was keenly aware that language embodies at every turn the prepossessions of 'our most remote and foolish, as well as most intelligent forefathers.'[6] This is a theme to which he constantly recurs. In *Beyond Good and Evil*, for example, he suggests that the family-likeness of all Indian, Greek and German philosophizing may be attributed to 'the unconscious domination and guidance of similar grammatical functions':[7] their respective syntaxes exercised an invisible spell over the philosophers, so that their systems in the end might amount to little more than the recovery of forgotten myths embodied in speech. In regions where the subject-verb distinction was less marked, quite different results would be reached. As Anatole France once put it: '*un métaphysicien n'a, pour constituer le système du monde,*

---

[1] WP, 485.   [2] WP, 551.   [3] WP, 531.   [4] WP, 551.
[5] WP, 484.   [6] WP, 409.   [7] BGE, 20.

que le cri perfectionné des singes et des chiens': only most metaphysicians have been sublimely oblivious to the fact. They have tended rather to treat their terms as 'a wonderful *dowry* from some kind of wonderland'.[1] What we need before all today, Nietzsche infers, is 'absolute scepticism towards all traditional concepts (like that which a certain philosopher may already have possessed—and he was Plato, of course: for he taught the *reverse*).'[2] Most of what is serviceable in linguistic analysis might be described as a footnote to this aphorism.

Along with Descartes' ego goes, of course, Democritus's and Dalton's atom—since 'the hypothesis of the existence of atoms is simply a consequence of the subject and substance concept'[3]—and with that, the whole basis of the mechanistic science of Nietzsche's day. The quantum of power usurps the place of that discrete particle whose movements were supposed to determine the configuration of the world. The atom, he asserts, is no more necessary or plausible than the soul: both terms may indeed be retained, but their content must be drastically revised. And here—need it be said?—his originality shows up to the best advantage.

Mechanistic materialism and the Cartesian ego, Whitehead remarks in one of his lectures, after a reign of two-and-a-half centuries, were challenged simultaneously, the one by science, the other by philosophy. The credit for the philosophical challenge he assigns to James, whose essay, *Does Consciousness Exist?* appeared in 1904. But Nietzsche challenged both together: and the year in which the bulk of *The Will to Power* was written, 1887, happens also to have been the year of the Michelson-Morley experiment, now generally taken to mark the beginning of the end of classical physics. It was Michelson and Morley who relegated the physicists' ether to the status of 'nominative of the verb "to undulate"'.

'When it is understood that the "subject" is nothing that *acts*, but only a thing of fancy, there is much that follows.'[4] There is indeed. Not only does 'the world of *acting atoms*' disappear, but 'the belief in cause and effect between phenomena which we call things also falls to pieces.'[5] Nietzsche, as we have seen, was not slow in drawing this conclusion.

If the primary constituent of matter is nothing that acts, but rather activity itself, Will to Power, then we must banish from our minds the concept of anything that is merely the passive recipient of external impacts and compulsions. Wherever there is action, there is interaction; and it is 'a matter of indifference whether cause and effect be put on this side or that'.[6] In any given situation, 'it is a question of a struggle between two elements unequal in power: a new adjustment is arrived at,

[1] WP, 409. [2] *Ibid.* [3] N, XIII, 61. [4] WP, 552. [5] *Ibid.* [6] WP, 551.

according to the measure of power each possesses'.[1] No one element is at liberty to act independently of the other—indeed, of all the others—but it is not, on that account, to be regarded as a victim of circumstances; on the contrary, its own activity, the activity which it *is*, is an indispensable factor in the entire fluid situation.

Nietzsche was inclined to associate the opposite supposition, inherent in conventional determinism, with a pusillanimous wish to excuse weakness and disown responsibility. For this reason, he speaks of the concept 'cause and effect' as 'dangerous'.[2] If we choose to speak of one total state as the 'effect' of a preceding one, he says, we are at liberty to do so; but let us never forget that we are thinking at one remove from reality, substituting abstractions for dynamic events. 'One should not wrongly *materialize* "cause" and "effect", as the natural philosophers do (and whoever like them naturalizes in thinking at present), according to the prevailing mechanistic doltishness which makes the cause press and push until it "effects" its end; one should use "cause" and "effect" only as pure *conceptions*, that is to say, as conventional fictions for the purpose of designation and mutual understanding—*not* for explanation.'[3]

Statements like this must not be allowed to mislead us. Nietzsche's challenge to mechanistic determinism implied no belief in free will, whether applied to human beings or electrons. He is emphatic on this point. 'At present we no longer have any sympathy with the concept "free-will": we know only too well what it is—the most egregious trick devised by theologians for the purpose of making mankind "responsible" in their sense,—that is to say, for making mankind dependent upon theologians.'[4] Wherever this trick has been played, he reiterates, the appetite for judgement and punishment has been at work. In truth, 'no-one is responsible for the fact that he exists at all, that he is constituted as he is, and that he happens to be in certain circumstances and in a particular environment. The fatality of his being cannot be divorced from the fatality of all that has been and will be.'[5] To require anything to be other than it is, is to require everything to have been otherwise that it was—a preposterous arrogance.

If the activity of a quantum of power is not caused by the push and pressure of external forces, neither is it caused by the quantum itself—because there is no quantum apart from its activity: 'the *causa sui* is the best self-contradiction that has ever yet been conceived, it is a sort of logical violation and unnaturalness'.[6] Because there is no quantum apart from its activity, it is not free to 'manifest itself otherwise than in con-

---

[1] WP, 633.   [2] WP, 552.   [3] BGE, 21.
[4] TI, p. 41.   [5] TI, p. 43.   [6] BGE, 21.

formity with its degree of strength'[1]—hence the predictability of phenomena. 'To speak of events as being necessary is tautological.'[2]

Nevertheless, Nietzsche contends, our customary conception of 'natural laws', bound up as that too is with the mechanistic world-view, and charged with misleading associations, ought to be discarded outright. For, if the spontaneous clash of like (but never identical) forces is the ultimate fact we are able to descend to, then chance, 'divine chance', is the master of the ceremonies of existence; and not only are all the regularities we discern and formulate in nature results of chance, but they may well be only temporary results: it is unlikely, at all events, that a 'law' would be found even approximately valid at every stage of evolution:

'We find a formula, in order to express an ever-recurring kind of succession: we have *not* thereby *discovered a "law"*, still less a force which is the cause of the recurring succession. The fact that something always happens thus and thus is interpreted here as if a being always acted thus and thus in obedience to a law or a law-giver: whereas apart from the "law" it would be free to act otherwise. But precisely that inability to act otherwise might spring from the being itself, which did *not* behave in such and such a way in response to a law, but because it was constituted in such and such a way. It means only: something cannot also be something else, cannot do now this and now something else, is neither free nor unfree, but merely thus and thus. *The fault lies in the fanciful projection of a subject*'.[3]

There is no law which ordains that an atom should behave as it does; on the contrary, it is the behaviour of the atom that ordains the law. The world we know 'has a "necessary and calculable course"', *not*, however, because laws obtain in it, but because laws are absolutely *lacking*, and every power effects its ultimate consequences every moment.'[4]

It all appears obvious enough, once we have grasped it: and now that science itself has routed mechanistic determinism, it is not so difficult to grasp. Yet how topsy-turvy do many of the commonest scientific expressions now sound! 'Even these indeterminate events are governed by statistical laws'; 'whether we are thinking about electrons or not, and whether we are experimenting with them or not, their motion is determined by the equations of the Heisenberg dynamics': I take these examples at random from the work of a distinguished scientist[5] who

[1] WP, 639.   [2] *Ibid.*   [3] WP, 632.   [4] BGE, 22.
[5] *Philosophy and Physics*, by Sir J. Jeans, Cambridge, 1943, pp. 151, 171.

happens also to have charged philosophers with the use of ambiguous, ill-defined terms.

Behind this clinging to an outworn legalistic terminology, Nietzsche thought he could once more detect an ideological bias: ' "Everywhere equality before the law—Nature is not different in that respect, nor better than we": a fine instance of a secret motive, in which the vulgar antagonism to everything privileged and autocratic . . . is once more disguised'.[1] Quite possibly he was right: and if so, it may throw some light on the vexed question of 'class-science', hitherto the subject of so much dogmatism and derision, and so little serious scrutiny. Class-prepossessions, petrified in linguistic usage, may well govern the interpretation of observations, and by so doing retard discovery. It is certain, at all events, that had Nietzsche's theory been examined on its merits, physicists would have been better prepared than they were for that wholesale revision of traditional concepts which their own experiments eventually forced on them, at the beginning of the twentieth century.

* * *

Nietzsche's breach with both Idealism and Materialism is no less apparent in his biology than in his physics. On the one hand, he ridicules Schopenhauer's notion that every individual member of a plant or animal species is merely the single facet of an eternal, immutable Idea. On the other, he holds fast to Schopenhauer's contention that the living creature represents a distinct and original grade in the objectification of Will. That is to say he is at one with him in substituting for 'the presupposition that the organism is merely an aggregate of physical, chemical and mechanical forces', the conception of the organism as a synthesis, ordaining laws of its own.

'According to the view I have expressed,' Schopenhauer concludes in a remarkable section of *The World as Will and Idea*, 'the traces of chemical and physical modes of operation will indeed be found in the organism, but it can never be explained from them; because it is by no means a phenomenon even accidentally brought about through the united action of such forces, but a higher Idea which has overcome the lower ideas by *subduing assimilation*.' This, apart from the metaphysical formulation, was completely in accord with Nietzsche's theory. He had conceived the Will to Power in the first place as an urge to establish ever greater unities, and the unities of his psychological and artistic experience were of this kind. If the Will to Power was, as he was assuming, the essence of every phenomenon—if there was, *ex hypothesi*, 'no other

[1] BGE, 22.

force, either physical, dynamic or psychic'[1]—then the living organism
could not be other than a 'third reality'. Even the simplest protozoan
would be more than the sum of its constituent molecules; even the
simplest multicellular plant or animal, more than the sum of its cells. So
far from its being possible to predict the properties of the whole from
an acquaintance with those of the parts, the properties of the parts themselves could only be fully understood in terms of their relationship to
the whole:

'One sees in chemistry that every body extends its power as far as it
is able; thus a third reality is born.

'One cannot *deduce* the properties of a child from even the most
exact knowledge of its father and mother. For these properties are the
effects produced on us by a third: but the effects of the first, and
those of the second, i.e. *their* characteristics, will not add up to the
"effects of the third".'[2]

Elsewhere he defines man in particular, as 'an assemblage of atoms absolutely dependent, in his movements, on all the forces of the universe,
their distribution and their modifications—and at the same time un-
predictable like every atom, a being in himself'.[3] And here again, of
course, his originality shows up. It was not until several years afterwards
that the experiments of Driesch and others resulted in the expulsion of
the mechanistic presupposition from biology; and to Bergson is generally given the credit of having (in Whitehead's words) 'introduced into
philosophy the organic conceptions of physiological science'. But Bergson was only building on the foundations Kant and Goethe had laid,
as every German Idealist had done.

The higher Idea, Schopenhauer continues in the passage quoted, is
always born out of a conflict between the lower ideas. Once it has
emerged, it subdues them to its purpose. But, 'since the higher Idea or
objectification of will can only appear through the conquest of the lower,
it endures the opposition of these lower Ideas, which, although brought
into subjection, still constantly strive to obtain an independent and complete expression of their being'. The more completely the wills of the
parts are dominated by the will of the whole, the greater the health, and
incidentally the beauty, of the organism. Here also Nietzsche follows
him. The organism is 'an intricate complexity of systems struggling for
the increase of the feeling of power.'[4] The greater part of its energy is
taken up with preserving its own hierarchical structure; only with what

---

[1] WP, 688.   [2] N, XIII, 277.   [3] N, XII, 303.   [4] WP, 703.

is left over can it go on to encompass its aim.

But what *is* its aim?—Simply, of course, to manifest its power still further. 'Physiologists,' he writes, 'should bethink themselves before putting down the instinct of self-preservation as the cardinal instinct of an organic being. A living thing seeks above all to *discharge* its strength: "self-preservation" is only one of the results thereof.'[1] Only upon this assumption, he argues, can we account for the most elementary facts of life. If self-preservation were an end in itself, it would be hard to account for the fact, for example, which Schopenhauer himself remarked, that every living creature appropriates more than it needs to repair its own wastage. Again, if happiness were the end, whence that everlasting quest for obstacles exhibited by even the protozoan? The Will to Power, on the other hand, can only manifest itself against obstacles, and therefore courts pain as the condition of its pleasure; gratified by 'subduing assimilation', it goes on appropriating until its capacity is actually exceeded:

'The will to power can manifest itself only against *obstacles*; it therefore goes in search of what resists it—this is the original tendency of the protoplasm, when it extends its pseudopodia and feels about it. Appropriation and incorporation is above all a desire to overpower, a forming, a building-onto and rebuilding, until the vanquished is completely absorbed into the aggressor's sphere of power, and has increased the latter. If this incorporation does not succeed, then no doubt the whole structure falls to pieces, and the duality appears as result of the will to power: in order not to let slip what has been conquered, the will to power divides into two wills (on occasion without completely abandoning its relation to the two).[2]

In the same way, Nietzsche explains that very war of all against all, which Schopenhauer described with such horrified fascination.

Finally, he contends, the process of evolution itself can only be made intelligible by virtue of some such assumption: first, because apart from reproduction there would be nothing for Natural Selection to operate on; and secondly, because, were it not for that sovereign urge towards 'subduing assimilation', every mutation would be disastrous to the individual exhibiting it.

The second point is particularly noteworthy, demonstrating yet again Nietzsche's instinctive grasp of biological problems: for no physiologist today would belittle the part played by the plastic power of the

---

[1] WP, 650.   [2] WP, 656.

whole in internal adaptation. A new organ, if it is to be of any value, has to be co-ordinated with every other, both structurally and functionally, to a nicety almost unimaginable. In other words, 'the formation of an organ is a matter of interpretation . . . the organic process continually presupposes interpretation':[1] 'greater complexity, sharp differentiation, the contiguity of the developed organs and functions, with the disappearance of intermediate members—if *that* is *perfection*, then there is a Will to Power apparent in the organic process by virtue of which, *dominating*, *shaping*, and *commanding* forces are continually increasing the sphere of their power, and persistently simplifying things within that sphere.'[2]

Nietzsche, it should be understood, although no Darwinist—although, indeed, inclined to be less than just to Darwin—never disputed either the truth or the importance of Darwin's theory so far as it went. Only, he affirmed, 'the influence of environment is nonsensically *over-rated* in Darwin: the essential factor in the process of life is precisely the tremendous inner power to shape and to create forms, which merely *uses*, *exploits* "environment"':[3] and there can be little doubt that he was right. As Whitehead put it, there are 'two sides to the machinery involved in the development of nature. On the one side, there is a given environment with organisms adapting themselves to it. . . . The other side of the evolutionary machinery, the neglected side, is expressed by the word *creativeness*. The organisms can create their environment.'[4] It was the neglect of this creativeness that Nietzsche wished to rectify.

Darwin himself, of course, like many great innovators, was more conscious of the limitations of his theory than some of his *soi-disant* disciples. He knew that Natural Selection accounted for nothing apart from 'heredity' and 'adaptability', and that neither of these words was more, in his day, than the 'designation, the identification of a problem'.[5] He was keenly alive to the difficulty (it was insoluble before Mendel's experiments became known) presented by the promiscuous crossing of individuals which did and did not exemplify a new variation; he confessed himself baffled by the apparition of the eye, presupposing as it seemed a long and intricate succession of modifications individually devoid of survival-value. Yet even Darwin tended to minimize the reciprocity between organism and environment; even he was disposed to assign the former a predominantly passive role—and what was merely a tendency with him became an article of faith with his followers:

[1] WP, 643.　　　[2] WP, 644.　　　[3] WP, 647.
[4] Whitehead, *Science and the Modern World*, Cambridge, 1927.
[5] WP, 645.

'A fool this honest Britisher
Was not. . . . But a philosopher!
As *that* you really rate him?
Set Darwin up by Goethe's side?
But majesty you thus deride—
    Genii majestatem!'[1]

Nietzsche's squib misfired insofar as it was aimed at Darwin, who never dreamed of setting up as a philosopher—but it was merited by the Darwinians.

This bias was yet another expression of mechanistic materialism; and once again Nietzsche thought he could trace the workings of an ideological factor: 'these biologists *continue* the moral valuations ("the intrinsically higher worth of altruism", the antagonism towards the lust of dominion, towards war, towards all the non-utilitarian, and towards the order of rank and of class)'.[2] The reduction of the role played by the organism to some questionable 'instinct of self-preservation' was connected, in his view, with the social conditions prevailing in the Workshop of the World: 'over the whole of English Darwinism there hovers something of the suffocating air of over-crowded England'[3]— an *aperçu* remarkably shrewd, seeing that, whether he knew it or not, both Darwin and Wallace were decisively influenced by Malthus's *Essay on Population*.

Had *The Will to Power* been published as intended, evolutionary theory might have owed much to Nietzsche. As it was, another half-century had to elapse before what is known as the organismic, or holistic, interpretation won widespread acceptance from biologists. Yet Smuts's 'holistic principle' is hardly to be distinguished from Nietzsche's Will; and the first creative evolutionist ought to be accorded the honour he deserves—even though, like the vast majority of mankind, great and small, at all times and places, he was unfavourably disposed towards democracy.

* * *

Nietzsche made use of his psychological theory to throw light on physics and biology. In turn, he now made use of his physics and biology to throw fresh light on psychology. If we wish to form a picture of the mind, he writes more than once in his notes, 'the essential thing is to start out from the body and to use it as a general clue. It is by far the richer phenomenon, and allows of much more accurate observation.'[4] Belief in the body, he adds, is much more soundly established than

[1] EH, p. 186.   [2] WP, 681.   [3] JW, 349.   [4] WP, 532.

belief in the spirit—'it has never occurred to anyone to regard his sto-mach as a strange or a divine stomach!'[1]

What we should look to find, therefore, is not the 'mind', as an en-tity, a monad, but rather an organization or collective action. The ana-logy of the body enables us to conceive the subject 'as a number of regents at the head of a community (not as "souls" or as "life-forces"), as also of the dependence of these regents upon their subjects, and upon the conditions of a hierarchy, and of the division of labour, which made possible both the part and the whole.'[2]

Of the mind thus conceived, he infers, such operations as enter con-sciousness constitute only the smallest fraction. For instance, 'the care and cautiousness which is concerned with the inter-relation of the bodily functions, does *not* enter into consciousness, any more than does the *storing activity* of the intellect'.[3] The conscious intellect, it is all-import-ant to remember, has been developed for and by our relationship with the outer world:

'As a rule *consciousness* itself is understood to be the general sensorium and supreme court of appeal; but it is only a *means of communication*: it was developed by intercourse, and with a view to the interests of inter-course. . . . "Intercourse" is understood, here, as "relation", and is intended to cover the action of the outer world upon us and our neces-sary response to it, as also our actual influence *upon* the outer world. It is *not* the conducting force, but an *organ of the latter*.'[4]

Elsewhere he affirms that consciousness and speech have developed *pari passu*, both as means whereby the earliest human communities achieved control of their environment: a conclusion which, as I write, is being advanced as something of a novelty by Professor J. Z. Young.

The actual operations of the mind may also, he suggests, be con-strued by analogy with those of the body, or even of the crystal, its very first activity being 'the *making like* of the new';[5] that is to say, 'the harmonization of the new material with the old schemes'—another contention of Professor Young's. 'The process of making equal is the same as the assimilation by the amoeba of the nutritive matter it appro-priates'[6]—it is a process of abstraction and rejection, of building and rebuilding, essentially of transformation and falsification, effected by the Will to Power. And here, of course, he takes up the thread of an argu-ment already alighted upon in the essay *On Truth and Falsity*, and un-ravelled further in *Human, All-too-Human*.

In the continuous flux of becoming, no two sensations are ever

[1] WP, 659. [2] WP, 492. [3] WP, 524. [4] WP, 524. [5] WP, 499. [6] WP, 501

identical; yet we identify them, and out of this identification has arisen our faith in the 'subject'—'the fiction that many like states of ours are the effect of a single substratum'.[1] No two 'things' are ever identical, yet we bestow the same name upon them, and out of this verbal equation (Adam's first recorded activity) has arisen our belief in identical things. Since the subject is the presupposition of the thing, and the thing the presupposition of our ideas of time, space and motion (considered as relations between things), we have here the origin of all those *a prioris* which, as Kant discovered, govern our perceptions, conceptions and thoughts.

That verbal equation was indispensable to speech; speech indispensable to the ascendancy of the human species. 'The inventive force which devised the categories worked in the service of our needs of security, quick intelligibility, in the form of signs, sounds, and abbreviations. . . . It was the powerful who made the names of things into law, and, among the powerful, it was the greatest artists in abstraction who created the categories'.[2] Only those, therefore, who were capable of perceiving, judging and thinking according to these categories survived the struggle for existence: and today they have become, in consequence, part and parcel of our mental apparatus, to abandon which would mean 'to cease from being able to think'.[3] To this context belongs Nietzsche's famous definition of truth: '*Truth is that kind of error* without which a certain species of living being cannot exist.'[4]

From his point of view, then, the emergence of consciousness, *pari passu* with speech, is to be looked upon in precisely the same light as the emergence of any other organ, whereby one animal species is distinguished from another. Accidental in origin, it has been preserved and developed, like the eye or the hand, because of its usefulness to the body —that is to say, the whole of which it is a part, 'that prodigious synthesis of living beings and intellects which we call "man" ':[5]

'What is astonishing is much rather the body: one never ceases to marvel at how the human *body* has become possible; that this prodigious collectivity of living beings, all dependent and subordinate, and yet, in a certain sense, again commanding and endowed with voluntary activity, is able to live, grow and subsist for a certain space of time as a whole; and, manifestly, this is *not* due to consciousness. Of this "miracle of miracles" consciousness is only an instrument, nothing more—in the same sense as the stomach is an instrument.'[6]

The intellect also is strictly 'utilitarian': not, however, in the sense

[1] WP. 485.   [2] WP, 513.   [3] WP, 487.   [4] WP, 493.   [5] N, XIII, 248.   [6] *Ibid.*

understood by the English utilitarians, not as a means to self-preservation or happiness—'man does not aspire to happiness; only the Englishman does that'[1]—but as a means to the increase of power. 'Knowledge works as an *instrument* of power'.[2]

Consciousness is a means, not an end—and as yet, in Nietzsche's view, a very imperfect means. As 'a new-comer among the organs, an organ still infantile',[3] it is neither accurate within its own province, nor properly co-ordinated with the rest. It still requires 'interpretation'. Indeed, where that interpretation is lacking, it may actually work as much harm as good: 'that which has brought about man's victory in his struggle with the animals is at the same time the cause of his peculiarly painful, dangerous and morbid development'.[4] As we know it today, at any rate, it must be regarded as a transitional phenomenon: and so, therefore, must man as we know him—'*he is the animal whose species is not yet fixed*':[5]

'Put briefly: perhaps the whole of mental development is a matter of the *body*: it is the *history*, growing perceptible, of the fact that a *higher body is in process of formation*. The organic is still ascending to higher levels. Our craving for knowledge of nature is a means whereby the body would perfect itself. Or better still: hundreds of thousands of experiments are being made to alter the nourishment, the modes of life and lodging of the *body*: the consciousness and valuations within it, all kinds of desire and aversion, are *symptoms of these alterations and experiments. In the last resort, it is not a matter of man: he is to be surpassed.*'[6]

In the words of Zarathustra, man is 'a bridge, and not a goal'.[7]

Let it be insisted, even at the risk of repetition (for Nietzsche himself insists on it), that this is not materialism, as generally understood. The 'body' referred to here is not the 'flesh' as distinct from the 'spirit'. That the 'spirit' is a part of the body is precisely the point he is trying to make: and the 'higher body' appertains to the 'higher man'.

Every organ, according to his theory, is striving to obtain an independent and complete expression of its being; whether it succeeds or fails being dependent upon the power of the Will. In a healthy organism the various 'underwills' in the hierarchy, from the molecule up to the spirit, are overpowered and subdued to 'the service of a higher instinct which rules the whole'.[8] Conversely, the successful self-assertion of a part against the whole constitutes a definition of ill-health, whether

---

[1] TI, p. 2.   [2] WP, 480.   [3] N, XIII, 164.   [4] N, XIII, 276.
[5] *Ibid.*   [6] WP, 676.   [7] Z, Prologue, 4.   [8] WP, 651.

physical or mental; since it betokens a danger of the entire synthesis breaking down—a weakening and dissolution of the Will.

From Nietzsche's standpoint, therefore, if 'spiritualism', postulating the absolute supremacy of the intellect, must be treated as a symptom of ill-health, so, and no less, must materialism, subordinating the intellect to carnal needs. Both these valuations represent a successful self-assertion of the part, or—it comes to the same—a relative deficiency of Will. In fact, he classes the étatist, the hedonist and the ultilitarian along with the priest, as a type of morbidity. To judge from *The Twilight of the Idols*—into which he flung pell-mell many of the best (and worst) ideas of *The Will to Power*—there was scarcely a trend of contemporary thought that did not strike him as decadent in one or other of these ways: and probably he was not far wrong.

Nevertheless, it was the hypertrophy of consciousness that chiefly alarmed him; 'whoever lives among the most conscious Europeans knows even that it is a disease'.[1] Contemporary materialism, he held, was little more than a violent reaction against contemporary spiritualism. For this reason he almost invariably chose to present his doctrine in physiological terms. So few people were aware of the very existence of the Self that misunderstanding was inevitable in any case: he would rather be taken for a belly-god than a god.

It was, most probably, for the same reason that, when he began to 'philosophize with the hammer', he opened *The Twilight of the Idols* with his ringing challenge to Socrates. For Socrates—he was now more than ever convinced—marked 'a moment of the most *profound perversity* in the history of values'.[2] He it was who had set mankind on the road to this hypertrophy of consciousness.

* * *

Socrates, we are given to understand, was a monstrosity, whose grotesque physiognomy reflected the anarchy of his passions; a decadent, who, as a foreign observer declared to his face, harboured all the worst passions and vices. The key to his nature is the answer he returned to this charge, 'but I overcame them all'—that being a true admission at once of his strength and his weakness. It was his strength that he did succeed in overcoming his passions; his weakness, that he was reduced to overcoming them by reason: for 'when a man finds it necessary, as Socrates did, to create a tyrant out of *reason*, there is no small danger that something else is playing the tyrant.'[3]

Socrates, of course, was a plebeian, and at war not only with his own instinctive life, but also with that of the nobility: 'the dialectician's irony

[1] JW, 354.   [2] WP, 430.   [3] TI, p. 14.

is a form of mob-revenge: the ferocity of the oppressed lies in the cold
knife-cuts of the syllogism!'[1] Hence the fate meted out to him. By the
time he appeared on the scene, however, the Athenian nobility was
nearly as decadent as himself: 'his case was at bottom only the extreme
and most apparent example of a state of distress which was beginning to
be general: that state in which no one was able to master himself and in
which the instincts turned one against another'.[2] Hence his posthumous
triumph. The nobility needed Socrates; or rather, they needed his
method—and not least of them his foremost disciple, Plato.

Plato, Nietzsche confessed, 'with me becomes a caricature';[3] and that
is true. His attitude towards Plato was ambivalent. For some things
he admired him above all philosophers; for others he detested him: and
since it was the latter that mainly concerned him in his polemical writings, his admiration is not often apparent. Yet even a caricaturist only
exaggerates, he does not invent, the salient features of his victim; and
what Nietzsche singles out for attack is just what the majority of Europeans have clung to with reverence and awe: for 'mankind has always
repeated the same error':

'It has always turned a means to life into a measure of life: instead of
finding the measure in the highest ascent of life itself—in the problem of
growth and creation—it has employed the *means* to a very definite kind
of life for the exclusion of all other kinds, in short, for the criticism and
selection of life. i.e. man gets to love the means for its own sake and
forgets that it is a means: so that now it emerges into his consciousness
as an end, as the measure of ends. i.e. *a certain species of man* treats its
conditions of existence as legally binding conditions, as "truth",
"good", "perfection": it *tyrannises*.'[4]

In Plato, Nietzsche saw, not merely the tyranny, but the apotheosis
of reason, and the categories of reason; the perfect, final, fascinating—
and deadly, systematization of the tendency he deplored. Here those
linguistic formulae, which had developed *pari passu* with consciousness
as a handy instrument in the service of life, were suddenly hypostatized.
Not merely such mechanical concepts as 'cause' and 'effect' were
accorded ideal validity: 'goodness', 'truth' and 'beauty'—these too
were torn from the contexts they belonged to, in which alone they had
meaning, and turned into 'eternal values'. These abstractions from
reality were actually held responsible for reality! Finally, the abstraction
of all abstractions, the most refined, the most rarified concept of the lot,

[1] WP, 431.   [2] TI, p. 14.   [3] WP, 374.   [4] WP, 354.

'the One', was postulated as the First Cause. 'I fear we shall never be rid of God', said Nietzsche, 'as long as we believe in grammar'.[1]

This hypostatization, this deification of mere verbal generalizations, invented for the purpose of intercourse and to promote man's power over nature—this was, in his view, 'the greatest error which has ever been committed, the really fatal error of the world':[2] and this was Plato's doing. He it was who had devised the 'ideal world', and who, not content with according it higher *reality* than the world we know, had had the colossal, the almost megalomaniac, presumption to accord it higher *worth*! In Plato the dialectician, the deductions of the intellect were pitted against the evidence of the senses; the 'real world' was used to condemn the 'world of appearances'. And why?—Simply, in the last resort, because Plato's intellect was pitted against Plato's senses; because he had not the Will to overcome himself, and in so doing to overcome the world; because he could not endure, let alone redeem, this life of flux and becoming, of change, suffering and death.

Plato thought he was arresting the decadence of Athens by reinstating the noble virtues. In reality he was doing the reverse. It was of the essence of the noble virtues that they had sprung directly out of the life of a people still healthy, spontaneous and complete. There had been no law which ordained that a noble should behave as he did, justly, truthfully, or beautifully; on the contrary, it was the behaviour of the noble which had ordained the law. The only necessity he had obeyed was the necessity of his inmost nature. 'One cannot stress the fact hard enough, that the great Greek philosophers stood for *the decadence of all the Greek faculties*, and made it contagious. This "virtue" rendered abstract was the greatest temptation to self-abstraction'.[3] Plato's actual achievement was to carry his own inward division to its limit, to petrify it—and project it into the very nature of the universe. Thereby he, the great decadent, played into the hands of the slaves and priests. 'When Socrates and Plato adopted the cause of virtue and justice, they were *Jews* or I know not what.'[4]

To understand Nietzsche's indictment of Plato is to understand Nietzsche. He returns to it again and again; it belongs to the heart of his teaching. Platonism, he says elsewhere, 'was the *greatest of all re-christenings*, and because Christianity adopted it, we are blind to the astounding fact'.[5] All that Christianity had done, he thought, was to add a new set of virtues to those already hypostatized; Love, Forgiveness and Humility had been awarded a place in the pantheon alongside Justice and Truth: but equally as commandments to be obeyed, as ideals imposed

[1] TI, p. 22.   [2] WP, 584.   [3] WP, 428.   [4] WP, 429.   [5] WP, 572.

from above—and 'virtues are as dangerous as vices, insofar as they are allowed to rule over one as authorities and laws coming from outside, and are not first engendered out of ourselves'.[1] To this very day, in consequence, we can scarcely conceive an ideal as anything but an idea. So deeply is this habit of mind ingrained in us, that even now, when once in a generation or two the rare man does arise who attempts to turn right way up what Plato turned upside down, it is he, the rare man (the Nietzsche or the Lawrence) whom we label presumptuous and perverse.

'Moral fanaticism (in short: Plato) destroyed paganism by trans-valuing its values and poisoning its innocence':[2] and what has the history of western philosophy been but "a succession of footnotes to Plato"?

'It is a *woeful* history: man looks for a principle, from the standpoint of which he will be able to contemn man—he invents a world in order to be able to slander and throw mud at this world: as a matter of fact, he snatches every time at nothing, and construes this nothing as "God", as "Truth", and, in any case, as judge and condemner of *this* existence. . . .

'The history of philosophy is a *secret raging against* the prerequisites of life, against the feeling of the value of life, against the championship of life. The philosophers have never hesitated to affirm a world, provided it contradicted this world and supplied them with a handle with which to calumniate this world. Up to the present it has been the great *school of slander.*'[3]

Schopenhauer's system, in this perspective, represents merely the *reductio ad absurdum* of a tendency running through all philosophy. In Schopenhauer, the secret hatred comes out into the open—that is all.

In a brilliant chapter of *The Twilight of the Idols*, entitled, 'How the "True World" ultimately became a Fable', Nietzsche recounts the rise and fall of this dualism in a series of apophthegms. Whereas Plato had presented the True World as accessible to the sage—'it was a para-phrase of the proposition, "I, Plato, am the truth" '—Christianity only promised it to the repentant sinner after death. Kant, going a stage further, declared that it could not be proved at all, let alone promised, though it was still a consoling possibility, bearing with it a moral obligation—'the idea has become sublime, pale, northern, Königs-bergian'. With that the ascent was completed. Even to Comte, however, an idea so diluted begins to be questionable—'grey of dawn . . . the cock-crow of positivism'; whilst to the Nietzsche of *Human, All-too-Human*

[1] WP, 326.　　　[2] WP, 438.　　　[3] WP, 461.

it is frankly unacceptable—'bright daylight; breakfast, the return of common sense and cheerfulness; Plato blushes for shame and all free-spirits kick up a shindy'. Finally, scepticism towards the True World is found to involve scepticism towards the world of positivism as well. There are no facts, only interpretations: nothing is true, and everything allowed:

'We have abolished the True World: what world survives? the apparent world perhaps? ... Certainly not! *In abolishing the True World we have also abolished the world of appearance!*

(Noon; the moment of the shortest shadows; the end of the longest error; mankind's zenith; *Incipit Zarathustra*.)'

It is Nietzsche's briefest and brightest epitome of the Romantic Myth.

Objectively, the act he defines here as the abolition of the True World, is nothing other than the realization that there are no eternal, let alone transcendental, standards of right and wrong; that man is a valu-ing animal, but nonetheless an animal, whose virtues and ideals represent a language of signs, indicating physiological prosperity or the reverse; that 'when we speak of values, we speak under the inspiration and through the optics of life: life itself urges us to determine values: life itself values through us when we determine values';[1] in other words, that 'morality is just as immoral as anything else on earth; morality itself is a form of immorality'.[2] In *The Will to Power* Nietzsche refers to 'the great liberation which this insight brings: the homogeneity of all occur-rence is *saved*'.[3] It is the occasion of man's reintegration into nature.

Subjectively, the act is nothing other than the 'interpretation' of consciousness; the restoration of health or wholeness to the human organism, so long imperilled by the successful self-assertion of a part. It is the overtaking of reason by the Will, which, henceforth, can employ it once again as an instrument—an instrument all the more valuable for the mastery and subtlety it has acquired in the course of its long domina-tion.

That interpretation was what Nietzsche had accomplished in 1881. Or rather, it was what life had accomplished through him—for, naturally, he neither could nor did take any credit for being the creature he was: if he felt free to blazon his achievement abroad, it may well have been because, in the depths of his nature, he knew that 'he' was not respon-sible at all. Then it was that he had learned to envisage himself as a developing organism, whose very will to truth became the means to its self-surpassing. Then it was, too, that he had realized the presumption

[1] TI, p. 31.   [2] WP, 308.   [3] *Ibid.*

of condemning the world—since there was no standpoint outside the
world from which it could be condemned—and become what he was in
Zarathustra, a Yea-sayer.

* * *

'The highest state to which a philosopher can attain', Nietzsche writes
'is to maintain a Dionysian attitude towards life—my formula for this is
amor fati.'[1] He applied to philosophers and philosophies the same
criterion as to artists and works of art. Just as he approached an opera
with the question, 'Has hunger or superfluity been creative here?'—so
he approached a world-view asking, 'How much truth can a spirit
endure? for how much truth is it *daring* enough?'[2]—and, of course, the
classification he arrived at by this 'measure of value' cut clean across any
based on dialectical ability.

He contended that any point of view could be 'established' by subtle
reasoning; but that 'behind all logic and its seeming sovereignty of
movement, there are valuations, or to speak more plainly, physiological
demands for the maintenance of a particular mode of life.'[3] The kernel
of every philosophical system was the moral, and the moral was the man.
This applied as much to Buddha as to Bentham, to Spencer as to
Aquinas.

It was for this reason that he never hesitated to pass judgement on the
early Greek philosophers, although so little of their argumentation has
survived. To his question, 'How much truth can a spirit *endure?*' it was
answer enough that Parmenides, for example, had repudiated the world
of flux, whereas Heraclitus had pronounced it divine. The belief in
Being was fundamentally reactive; it arose from the fear of Becoming:
'*pain inspires* these conclusions: at bottom they are *wishes* that such a
world might exist; the hatred of a world which leads to suffering is likewise revealed in the fact that another and *more valuable* world is imagined:
the metaphysician's *resentment* of the actual is creative here'.[4]

It was for this reason also that he seldom bothered to 'prove' his own
aperçus. He thought it both more honest and more instructive to present
them just as they came. 'A man should neither conceal nor misrepresent
the *facts* concerning the way in which he conceived his thoughts: the
deepest and least exhausted books may well always have something of
the aphoristic and impetuous character of Pascal's *Pensées*'.[5] To one
of his disciples, who has demanded his reasons for an opinion, Zarathustra
retorts impatiently that it is as much as he can do to retain his opinions
alone, without having to muster the evidence in addition.

Such an attitude undoubtedly has drawbacks. But it has advantages

[1] WP, 1041.   [2] *Ibid.*   [3] BGE, 3.   [4] WP, 579.   [5] WP, 424.

too. Has anybody ever really been influenced by the imposing Euclidean panoply in which Spinoza encased his vision? If Nietzsche partially exempted Spinoza, as he did, from his wholesale censure of modern philosophers, it was because, *nothwithstanding* this panoply, the *Ethics* had expressed, and thereby transmitted, an affirmative outlook on life. His standpoint was very like Keats', who confessed that he had never been able to perceive how anything could be known for truth by consecutive reasoning, declaring that what Imagination seizes as Beauty must be Truth. To both, a view was acceptable insofar as it satisfied the whole man, in other words, effected a reintegration. Only, what Keats called Imagination, Nietzsche called Will to Power: 'the criterion of truth lies in the enhancement of the feeling of power'.[1]

Let us hope it is unnecessary to insist that Nietzsche was not, in this celebrated dictum, promulgating a philosophy for propagandists and advertisers. The time-honoured charge of anti-intellectualism can always be taken to denote ignorance of his works. Far from implying an attack on the scientific method, his dictum was actually a defence of it: since it is precisely in natural science that this criterion is most clearly adopted.

The truth of a scientific hypothesis is invariably assessed by the multiplicity of phenomena it succeeds in reducing to unity. What Nietzsche contended was that this realization of ever more comprehensive syntheses was motivated, consciously or unconsciously, by the urge to dominate nature, in theory and practice: 'natural science seeks, by means of its formulae, to teach the *subjugation* of the forces of nature'.[2] The greater the synthesis, the greater the feeling of power. His dictum could therefore, without distortion, be put the other way round: the criterion of power is the enhancement of the feeling of truth. In fact, he sometimes did put it that way round.

At the same time, he wished to emphasize that this domination of nature has a subjective correlate. For man does not stand over against nature; he is not a detached, dispassionate observer of phenomena unconnected with himself. His most scrupulous observation bears the character of an action and interaction: 'knowing means: "to place oneself in relation with something", to feel oneself conditioned by something and oneself conditioning it ... not a process of *sounding* beings, things or objects "in-themselves".'[3] It follows that, in systematizing phenomena, we are systematizing our own relations with phenomena; in other words, reducing to unity the multiplicity of our own valuations. The ordering of the objective world is simultaneously an ordering of the subjective. Every extension of power over nature involves the emer-

[1] WP, 534.   [2] N, XIII, 79.   [3] WP, 555.

gence of a new complex of power within the human organism itself; in order to achieve power over nature, one must achieve 'a certain power over one's self'.[1]

It was a fault on the part of the physicists, he pointed out, that they overlooked this: 'in the end, without knowing it, they left something out of the constellation: precisely the necessary *perspectivity*, by virtue of which every centre of force—and not man alone—constructs the rest of the world *from its point of view*—that is to say, measures it, feels it, and moulds it by its own standard of force. . . . They forgot to reckon with this perspective-*fixing* power . . . but even the chemical investigator needs it: it is indeed *specific being*, which determines action and reaction according to circumstances'.[2] He believed that physics itself would have ultimately to take account of this factor—and his belief has been vindicated. Both relativity and quantum theory are distinguished by its elucidation. As Jeans puts it well: 'complete objectivity can only be regained by treating observer and observed as parts of a single system; these must now be supposed to constitute an indivisible whole, which we must now identify with nature, the object of our studies. It now appears that this does not consist of something we perceive, but of our perceptions; it is not the object of the subject-object relation, but the relation itself.'[3]

Nietzsche applied to aesthetic and ethical theory the same criterion as we apply to scientific. He admitted, in fact, no essential differences between them. Our data are always valuations; our valuations reflect the conditions of our existence: 'for a very small part, the conditions necessary to the existence of the individual, for a much greater part those necessary to the human species, for the greatest part of all those that make possible life itself.'[4] The data of aesthetics and ethics belong to the first two classes respectively, those of science to the third. If our artistic valuations still vary from man to man, that is because they have rarely, contributed to the survival of the species. If every aesthetic theory bears the stamp of its author on its face, that is because it is manifestly a systematization of his own relations with phenomena—because, in other words, the 'subjective correlate' is more in evidence. But the instinct that impels a man to seek a common denominator in the works he admires, to establish an order of rank among them, to account for their significance to himself, is the same that impels the natural scientist: and to acknowledge the presence of the subjective correlate is by no means to favour 'subjectivity'.

Whether it be a person, a people or an historical movement that

<hr />

[1] WP, 403. [2] WP, 636. [3] Jeans, *op. cit.*, p. 143. [4] N, XIII, 257.

engages us, we are—Nietzsche agreed with Leibniz—like artists seated about a model: each sees her from his own particular angle, none can see her entire. 'There is only a seeing from a perspective, only a "knowing" from a perspective.'[1] It follows that 'the *more* emotions we express over a thing, the *more* eyes, different eyes, we train on the same thing, the more complete will be our "idea" of that thing, our "objectivity" ':[2] and the justest man will be the most pre-eminently endowed with the capacity for making his own a host of different viewpoints, without allowing any of them to absorb him exclusively: 'in effect, wherever the plant man flourished vigorously, one does find powerful instincts *competing* with one another (for instance, in Shakespeare) and yet held under control.'[3]

This capacity, we have already seen, Nietzsche regarded as his own *forte*. A man of innumerable masks, he himself was for ever adopting new perspectives; turning the same thing round and round in his mind to see it from every possible angle. 'To look upon healthier concepts and values from the standpoint of the sick, and conversely, to look down upon the secret work of the instincts of decadence from the standpoint of him who is laden and self-reliant with the richness of life—this has been my longest exercise, my principal experience'.[4] It was in this way that he would study a Socrates—now with the eyes of an Alcibiades, now with those of a Thrasymachus, a Pyrrho, a Meletus, a Timaeus— his reason incessantly active to accommodate the diverging viewpoints. This activity was reason itself; this accommodation, this order of rank, the substance of his ethical theory.

If Nietzsche derided 'objectivity', therefore, considered as 'contemplation without interest', this was not because he favoured 'subjectivity', but simply because he knew—too well—the origin of his own comprehensiveness. It was that very state of distress he had diagnosed in Plato—the state in which all the instincts turn against one another, the chaos without which there is no dancing star. He virtually *was* Thrasymachus and the rest, by turn. To be enormously multifarious was his fatality, to be yet the reverse of chaos, a seldom-attained ideal, which, like all genuine ideals, sprang straight from personal necessity. 'Detached', 'dispassionate', 'disinterested'—'oh, how very much are we the reverse of this!'[5] To reduce to unity the multiplicity of his valuations; to overcome, not one bias, but many—why, the survival of his personality depended upon it! And that was just why he put such faith in his theory. Its justice was proportionate to the variety of bias it transcended:

[1] GM, III, 12.   [2] *Ibid.*   [3] WP, 966.   [4] EH, p. 11.   [5] WP, 426.

'Insight: all valuation implies a definite perspective: the *preservation* of the individual, of a community, a race, a State, a Church, a belief, a culture. Thanks to our having *forgotten* that there is only a perspective valuing, one man may swarm with a host of contradictory valuations, and *therefore with a host of contradictory impulses*. This is the *expression of sickness in man*, as opposed to the animal, in which all the existing instincts serve a quite definite purpose.

'This creature full of contradictions, however, has in his being a great method of acquiring *knowledge*: he feels many pro's and con's, he elevates himself to *justice*—to comprehension *beyond the values good and evil*.

'The wisest man would thus be *the richest in contradictions*—he who has, so to speak, antennae for all kinds of men: and betweenwhiles his great moments of sublime harmony—the rarest of *chances* even in us! A sort of planetary movement.'[1]

Such a moment Nietzsche had experienced in *Zarathustra*: the synthesis preached in the poem was the source of the poem itself. Hence the belief he entertained, that—his own state of distress being general, as it had been in Plato's time—*Zarathustra* would do for Europe what Plato's *Republic* had done: re-establish its values for centuries.

In natural science, aesthetics and ethics alike, the criterion of truth was integration; of integration, the feeling of power. Nietzsche's application of his dictum to philosophy was a natural sequel or conclusion. For what was the philosopher, as he conceived him, but precisely the most multifarious man of all—the man who, to be equal to his vocation, must have been scientist, artist *and* teacher, and whose world-view, accordingly, if it was to satisfy the whole man, must represent a synthesis of science, aesthetics and ethics? The philosopher, he had written at the time of *Philosophy during the Tragic Age of the Greeks*, 'is contemplative like the plastic artist, responsive to the feelings of others like the religious, logical like the man of science: he tries to let all the tones of the universe re-echo within himself and then to project this whole chord into concepts outside himself.'[2]

Such a world-view as this, he had then believed, was to be found in *The World as Will and Idea*. Schopenhauer had brought into harmony his own competing talents, converting him, as he said, into a little 'solar system'.[3] Now, at long last, a new one was taking shape, in *The Will to Power*: one which would—this time he was confident—prove capable of raising mankind from the heights of sceptical disillusionment to the height of tragic contemplation, of providing it with a picture of the whole of life whence it could learn the meaning of its own.

[1] WP, 259.   [2] N, X, 131.   [3] TS, III, 2.

Thus, towards the end of his work, Nietzsche brings himself and his own activity completely within the compass of his vision. The same drive that constitutes the atom, the amoeba and the amphibian, constitutes the author of *The Will to Power*. Not merely the observer as mathematician, but the observer as philosopher—that is to say, the whole man—is incorporated completely in the observed. And, just as the formulae of Einstein and Dirac involve a transcendence of time as we know it, so does Nietzsche's own. He stands once again where he stood in 1881, and once again the universe presents itself *sub specie aeternitatis*. The title of the concluding section was to have been 'Eternal Recurrence':

'And do you know what "the world" is to me? Shall I show you it in my mirror? This world: a monster of energy, without beginning, without end, a fixed and brazen mass of energy, which grows neither bigger nor smaller, which does not consume, but only transforms itself; an unalterably great whole, a household without expenditure and losses, but likewise without increase and income, surrounded by nonentity as by a frontier; nothing vague, running to waste, nothing extended to infinity, but definite energy occupying a definite space, and not a space which would anywhere be "empty", rather energy everywhere, play of energy and waves of energy, at the same time one and many, aggregating here and simultaneously diminishing there; a sea of forces storming and streaming in itself, forever wandering, forever rolling back, with vast years of recurrence; with an ebb and flow of its formations, driving out from the simplest into the most complex, from the stillest, firmest, coldest, into the hottest, wildest, most self-contradictory, and then turning home again from abundance to simplicity, from the play of contradictions back to the joy of unison; affirming itself even in the likeness of its courses and years, blessing itself as that which must eternally return, as a becoming that knows no satiety, no disgust, no weariness: this my *Dionysian* world of eternal self-creation, of eternal self-destruction, this mystery-world of the twofold lust, this my "beyond good and evil", without goal, unless there be a goal in the happiness of the circle, without will, unless a ring bear good will towards itself—do you want a *name* for this world? A *solution* to all its riddles? A light also for you, most hidden, strongest, most undaunted men of the blackest midnight? —*This world is the will to power—and nothing besides*! And even you yourselves are this will to power—and nothing besides!'[1]

* * *

This, then, is Nietzsche's translation of the Dionysian into the philo-

[1] WP, 1067.

sophical pathos, his new interpretation of occurrence. What are we to
say of it?

One thing is immediately apparent—the resemblance, namely,
between his later philosophy and his earlier. Again and again, in the
notes that make up his last work, we are reminded of the first of all. His
own remarks on 'Art in *The Birth of Tragedy*' could be applied as well
to *The Will to Power*; *The Will to Power*, more completely than *The
Birth of Tragedy*, fulfils the promise he had held out to Rohde in his
early twenties, that one day, thanks to the intergrowth of science and art
in his mind, he would give birth to a centaur. It is, of course, the
resemblance inevitable between philosophies designed to elucidate, in
one case a surmise, in the other an experience, of 'the Dionysian'.

At the same time, there are striking contrasts. The condition of his
surmise becoming an experience had, after all, been his wholehearted
submission in the interim to the scientific imperative, 'I will not deceive,
not even myself':[1] and this was bound to leave its imprint on everything he subsequently wrote. In fact, two features in particular set
The Will to Power in a class apart from *The Birth of Tragedy*.

In the first place, Nietzsche's earlier world-view was essentially pre-
scientific. Derived as it was from Schopenhauer, it represented no more
than an original variant of the first attempt ever made by an Aryan-
speaking people to solve the mystery of existence. His metaphysical
unity of the Will was a traditional religious postulate; he himself called
it a God:

'Once on a time, Zarathustra also cast his fancy beyond man, like all
backworldsmen. The work of a suffering and tortured God did the
world then seem to me. . . .

'Ah, ye brethren, that God whom I created was human work and
human madness, like all the Gods!'[2]

In all his writings from 1876 onwards, this postulate is renounced.
Science knows nothing of a unity subsisting beyond the multiplicity of
phenomena: as far as it is concerned, the flux of becoming is final; and
Nietzsche is at one with it. 'Philosophy, in the only shape in which I still
subscribe to it, is the most general form of history: an attempt in some
way to describe the heraclitean becoming'.[3]

His mere retention of the word 'Will', therefore, should not mislead
us. In this respect, the resemblance between his earlier world-view and
his later amounts to no more than that which Koestler has remarked,

[1] JW, 344.   [2] Z, 3.   [3] N, XIII, 23.

between the age-old belief of the Vedanta and 'the modern physical conception of the universe as a multidimensional continuum in which all phenomena may be described in terms of a unitary space-time geometry, and in which apparently substantial events dissolve into patterns of ripples, moving as it were across the veil of Maya—that is, the phenomenal world.'[1] *The Birth of Tragedy* is pre-scientific; *The Will to Power* might almost be called post-scientific.

It is, at all events, scientific from beginning to end; and Nietzsche's nearest-of-kin, as he himself acknowledged, were not the authors of the Vedanta, but the early Greek cosmologists. Thales has been acclaimed the father of both western philosophy and science; Russell has pointed out the impossibility of drawing any sharp distinction between the mystical and the physical in Heraclitus; and it was precisely Heraclitus, as we have seen, whom Nietzsche saluted as his predecessor. In *Ecce Homo* he recalls that Heraclitus may even have conceived the Eternal Recurrence—in which case, a cynic might add, the Great Noon struck about 550 B.C., and his watch was two-and-a-half millennia slow. It would be truer to say that *The Will to Power* marks the recovery of philosophy and science from an estrangement that dates back to Plato, and has been a source of impoverishment to both.

'We are again approaching today,' he wrote in 1885, 'all those fundamental types of world-interpretation which the Greek spirit invented through Anaximander, Heraclitus, Parmenides, Empedocles, Democritus and Anaxagoras'.[2] He himself certainly was; and in this, once more, he may well prove to have been prophetic. For, whether we like it or not, there is little doubt that any picture of the whole of life which secures the allegiance of Europe now will be scientific in form.

What is more, while every attempt to elaborate such a picture at present must be premature, and therefore dangerous (the data by no means warrant such generalizations as Dialectical Materialism), it is reasonably certain that the holistic principle, already widely acknowledged as a common denominator of physics, biology and psychology, will occupy a central place. If we wish to locate Nietzsche's nearest-of-kin among the moderns, it is to those who have approached philosophy from the standpoint of science, rather than their opposite numbers, that we have to turn. Among our own countrymen, Whitehead—who, like him, owed much to Spinoza and Leibniz—stands out as indubitably the first.

The second feature which sets *The Will to Power* in a class apart from *The Birth of Tragedy*, however, also sets Nietzsche apart from every

---

[1] A. Koestler, *Insight and Outlook*, Macmillan, 1948.   [2] WP, 419.

scientific philosopher: for this is that 'fundamental nihilism',[1] which, he believed, he shared only with Burckhardt and Taine.

In *Philosophy during the Tragic Age of the Greeks*, it may be recalled, he had defined the starting-point of Thales' cosmology as 'a metaphysical dogma, which had its origin in a mystic intuition, and which, together with the ever-renewed endeavour to express it better, we find in all philosophies—the proposition: "*Everything is one*".' In all philosophies, and equally in all sciences, philosophy and science being 'two forms of a single thought'.[2] This mystical intuition, he had then believed was the voice of the All-one-Will; his own philosophy, therefore, which proclaimed that Will as the One, was in effect the best and the truest.

Now, on the contrary, whilst the Will—that is, the urge to establish ever greater unities—is once again posited as the intelligible character of existence, it is, simultaneously, defined as a fundamentally *falsifying* force. The starting-point of his whole system is the inquiry, 'whether this creating, rationalizing, adjusting and falsifying be not the best-guaranteed *reality* itself: in short, whether that which "fixes the meaning of things" is not the only reality: and whether the "effect of the outer world on us" be not only the result of such will-exercising subjects.'[3] His whole argument derives from the premise that a quantum of power, at whatever level it is envisaged, is concerned exclusively with its own domination and ascendancy: 'even in the inorganic world all that concerns an atom of energy is its immediate neighbourhood: distant forces balance each other. Here is the root of *perspectivity*, and it explains why a living being is "egoistic" to the core'.[4] Every organism, man included, 'interprets' the world from its own point of view.

It is the old argument of *Human, All-too-Human*—and, of course, the old conclusion follows. Since, although we can neither perceive now nor even conceive the 'amorphous and unadjustable world consisting of the chaos of sensations',[5] which would be the real and true as opposed to the false and apparent, we can, by lifting ourselves above and beyond the whole process, realize that such must be its nature, and that the 'real and true', accordingly, is 'neither one nor even reducible to one',[6] every philosophy also must be pronounced a falsification. In every philosophy, Nietzsche had concluded in 1879, he could find only one thing irrefutable—the fact that somewhere, at some time, somebody had viewed the world in that way: it is to this conclusion that he returns in *Beyond Good and Evil*. 'As soon as ever a philosophy begins to believe in itself', he writes, 'it always creates the world in its own image; it

[1] L, 23, 5, 87. [2] N, X, 133. [3] WP, 569.
[4] WP, 637. [5] WP, 569. [6] WP, 536.

cannot do otherwise; philosophy is this tyrannical impulse itself, the most spiritual Will to Power, the will to "creation of the world".'[1]

Inevitably, therefore, we are brought face to face with the question, whether his own philosophy, inspired as it manifestly is by the self-same mystical intuition, the self-same tyrannical impulse, can be assigned to any different category? Must not this world-view, likewise, be pronounced, at least a human, at most a super-human, interpretation of phenomena? The answer is self-evident: if Nietzsche is right, he is wrong. And this, of course, is precisely the answer he has all along intended us to reach!—'Granted that this also is only interpretation—and you will be eager enough to make this objection?—well, so much the better.'[2]

In the last resort, Nietzsche holds as firmly as ever to his absolute scepticism. 'So far as the word "knowledge" has any sense at all,' he maintains, 'the world is knowable: but it may be interpreted *differently*, it has not one sense behind it, but hundreds of senses—"perspectivity" '.[3] To the extent to which truth can be willed, it behoves us to will it: but we must never forget what the will to truth itself proclaims, that absolute truth is unattainable. There are no antitheses in nature; even the antithesis, 'true and false' is merely an instance of 'the excluded middle', 'according to my way of thinking, "truth" does not necessarily mean the opposite of error, but, in the most fundamental cases, merely the relation of different errors to each other: thus one error might be older, deeper than another, perhaps altogether ineradicable, one without which organic creatures like ourselves could not exist'—such would be Kant's synthetic propositions *a priori*—'whereas other errors might not tyrannize over us to that extent as conditions of existence, but when measured by the standard of those other "tyrants" could be laid aside and "refuted".'[4]

In the last resort, Nietzsche will not allow that even that 'complete objectivity' attained through the incorporation of the observer in the observed is really objectivity. If his own interpretation of the universe is superior to others, it is superior, not because more absolutely true, but only because the creation of a superior man—and, to the extent to which he succeeds in transmitting it, capable of creating other superior men: 'the question is, how far a judgement is life-furthering, life-preserving, species-preserving, perhaps species-rearing.'[5] This is his answer to the question, 'What is the value of truth?'

As the expression of a reintegrated man, it is the world-view appropriate to a new species; but though this species is the latest, it does not

[1] BGE, 9.   [2] BGE, 22.   [3] WP, 481.   [4] WP, 535.   [5] BGE, 4.

follow that it is the last, to emerge. In time, it may be superseded; in space, it may already have been:

'That the *worth of the world* lies in our interpretations (that somewhere perhaps yet other interpretations than the merely human are possible); that the interpretations made hitherto are perspective valuations, by virtue of which we maintain ourselves in life, i.e. in the will to power, for the growth of power; that every *elevation of man* carries with it the overcoming of narrower interpretations; that every further reinforcement and extension of power opens up new perspectives and means belief in new horizons—this runs through all my writings. *The world that concerns us at all* is false, i.e. is no set of facts, but a poetical rounding-off of a meagre sum of observations; it is "in flux", something evolving, a falsehood continually superseding itself, that never draws near the truth—for there is no "truth".'[1]

It is only when we finally apprehend this, Nietzsche gives us to understand, that we can be said to have touched the heart of his philosophy. Follow his thought to the limit, and we shall find that he is not to be identified even with his own system. The last fruit may fall from his tree; the tree will go on growing as before.

Thus, while his later world-view can justly be described as mystical, it cannot be described as religious. His unique combination of mysticism with scepticism precludes us from describing it even as pantheistic. 'The concept, "the All" '[2] is banished from the outset; his universe is explicitly a 'universe of discourse':

'I think that we are today at least far from the ludicrous immodesty of decreeing from our nook that there *can* only be legitimate perspectives from that nook. The world, on the contrary, has once more become "infinite" to us: insofar as we cannot dismiss the possibility that it *contains infinite interpretations*. Once more the great horror seizes us—but who would desire forthwith to deify once more *this* monster of an unknown world in the old fashion? And perhaps worship the unknown thing as the "unknown person" in future? Ah! there are too many *ungodly* possibilities of interpretation comprised in this unknown, too much devilry, stupidity and folly of interpretation,—also our own human, all-too-human interpretation itself, which we know.'[3]

Whereas in *The Birth of Tragedy* Nietzsche had believed in the actual existence of his Dionysus (nothwithstanding a certain doubt 'right in the background of the book'),[4] in *The Will to Power* he does not. Doubt

[1] WP, 616.   [2] WP, 331.   [3] JW, 374.   [4] WP, 853.

has darkened into disbelief. Whereas in *The Birth of Tragedy*, he had unconsciously created a God in his own image, in *The Will to Power* he creates a world in his own image consciously—and probably he was the first to do so.

That is why he characterized his philosophy as *tragic* optimism. For, though he had overcome that 'great horror', in the third Part of *Zarathustra*, and learned, as he put it, to 'dance on the verge of abysses',[1] it was continually seizing him anew. Like Stavrogin, he believed, but he could not believe in his belief. In Nietzsche, as in Goethe, there was a Mephistopheles as well as a Faust; but in Nietzsche it was Mephistopheles who had the last word.

[1] JW, 347.

XI

THE REVOLUTIONIST

When Nietzsche composed the first Part of *Zarathustra*, he was confident of a hearing at last. He assured his publisher, Schmeitzner, that he would find it a lucrative proposition; and was surprised, as well as disgusted, when the latter gave precedence first to an edition of five hundred thousand hymn-books and then to a cargo of anti-semitic pamphlets: 'these are truly experiences for the founder of a religion!'[1] During the five months' delay caused by this obstruction, he actually planned to locate a building—perhaps 'some castle formerly fitted up by the Benedictines'[2]—to house himself and the many new friends who were bound to seek him out. His old dream of a monastic community was once again in full flower.

The reception the poem actually had must have been completely dumbfounding. Not that the opinions of reviewers were other than he had expected, but the absolute indifference of all his more intelligent countrymen was something he was quite unprepared for. It was not until, in desperation, he began sending presentation copies of his books to distinguished personalities abroad that he met with any response whatever. In the meanwhile, he was compelled to resign himself to publication at his own expense. The third and fourth Parts of *Zarathustra* found seven readers.

In his autobiography, and in many of his letters and notes, Nietzsche makes light of this disappointment. He even boasts of it: 'my triumph is just the opposite of Schopenhauer's—I say "*Non* legor, *non* legar".'[3] That the Germans, who had stultified the Renaissance and resented Goethe and Napoleon, should likewise have turned against him, was only to be expected: had they done anything else, then indeed he would have had cause for misgivings! From time to time, he would startle his fellow-guests at the *pension* by declaring that in fifty years' time his name would be famous throughout Europe: it was precisely because he was so far in advance that he could not hope to find readers any sooner. 'I should regard it as a complete contradiction of myself, if I expected ears and hands ready for my truths today: the fact that no one hears me, that no one knows how to take from me today, is not only comprehen-

[1] L, 1, 7, 83.   [2] L, 5, 83.   [3] EH, p. 56.

sible, it seems to me right.'[1] There was justice in this estimate too.

Nevertheless, not even the author most confident of posthumous recognition can cheerfully forego all influence on his own contemporaries—'he must communicate, provided he is an artist, a genius of communication';[2] and still less can he do so if, like Nietzsche, he is persuaded that it depends on himself whether or not there is to be a posterity capable of appreciating him. Underlying this attitude of his, there was actually a manifest contradiction. He could have vindicated it only as a believer in the inevitable progress of history; it was just because he did not believe progress historically inevitable that he attached such urgent importance to his message.

In the concluding aphorism of 'The Natural History of Morals', he gives memorable expression to the hopes and fears that beset him continually at this time:

'There are few pains so grievous as to have seen, divined, or experienced how an exceptional man has missed his way and deteriorated; but he who has the rare eye for the universal danger of "man" himself *deteriorating*, he who like us has recognized the extraordinary fortuitousness which has hitherto played its game in respect to the future of mankind—a game in which neither the hand nor even a "finger of God" has participated!—he who divines the fate that is hidden under the idiotic unwariness and blind confidence of "modern ideas", and still more under the whole of Christo-European morality—suffers from an anguish with which no other is to be compared: he sees at a glance all that could still *be made out of man* through a favourable accumulation and augmentation of human powers and endeavours; he knows with all the knowledge of his conscience how unexhausted man still is for the greatest possibilities, and how often in the past the type man has stood in presence of mysterious decisions and new paths: he knows still better from his painfulest recollections on what wretched obstacles promising developments of the highest rank have hitherto usually gone to pieces, broken down, sunk, and become contemptible. The *universal degeneration of mankind* to the level of the "man of the future"—as idealized by the socialistic fools and shallow-pates—this degeneracy and dwarfing of man to an absolutely gregarious animal (or as they call it, to a man of "free society"), this brutalizing of man into a pigmy with equal rights and claims, is undoubtedly *possible*! He who has thought out this possibility to its ultimate conclusion knows *another* loathing unknown to the rest of mankind—and perhaps also a new *mission*!'[3]

[1] EH, p. 55.   [2] TI, p. 80.   [3] BGE, 203.

This passage is of crucial importance for an understanding of the later Nietzsche. It behoves us to lay it to heart. Perhaps it is easier for us to do so today than it was for his readers fifty or sixty years ago.

'I am forty,' he had reminded Gast soon after the completion of *Zarathustra*, 'and I find myself at the very point I proposed, when twenty, to reach at this age.'[1] How true that was, we have seen in the foregoing chapters. But, as he knew only too well, it was true in more senses than one. If he had attained the ideal of the artistic genius, as set forth in *Thoughts out of Season*, he had also exposed himself to the formidable consequences, as set forth in *The Future of our Educational Institutions*: that smug indifference or hostility which had been the common lot of the foremost representatives of German letters. He it was now who was at war with the spirit of his time; who had to endure the complacent patronage of professor and journalist, and to hear his message dismissed as 'morbid' and 'pathological'. 'Every time a "success" is registered, the mass of the vulgar appears on the scene; to have to listen to the opinions of the petty and poor in spirit is a veritable martyrdom for him who has learned, with a shudder, *that the destiny of mankind depends on its success in realizing a higher type.*'[2] The anguish he had long since discerned in Hölderlin, Kleist and Wagner was now his own; and his own, in turn, made him all the more sensitive to theirs.

Continually, in his later writings, Nietzsche dwells on the fate of such men: 'the isolated, those who feel the want of education, who do not know how to explain themselves, degenerate, and their degeneration serves as an argument against their existence ("genius"="neurosis"!)'[3] At times their fate seems even to have obsessed him, as though he could see in it a grim forewarning of his own—and then the very pity he felt became a danger: 'the manifold torment of the psychologist who has discovered this ruination, who discovers once, and then discovers *almost* repeatedly, throughout all history, this universal inner "desperateness" of higher men, this eternal "too late" in every sense—may perhaps one day be the cause of his turning with bitterness against his own lot, and of his making an attempt at self-destruction—of his "going to ruin" himself.'[4] He felt a need to steel himself against his compassion: in one of his letters he cites the 'excessive hardness' of his books as a 'sort of revenge'[5] he took on his vulnerability; and the whole fourth Part of *Zarathustra* was devoted to the prophet's passing of this, his 'final test'.[6]

Simultaneously with this revival of his obsessive concern for the genius, went, of course, a revival of his old, never finally conquered

---

[1] L, 5, 3, 84.   [2] WP, 987.   [3] N, XIV, 296.
[4] BGE, 269.   [5] L, 1, 2, 88.   [6] EH, p. 18.

detestation of the petty and poor in spirit, 'the newspaper-reading *demi-monde* of intellect, the cultured class.'[1] If pity for the higher man was his final test, this loathing was, he confessed, his greatest danger: and slowly, steadily, notwithstanding his efforts to combat it, it began to get the upper hand—loathing for his countrymen first of all, who had spurned the gift he had offered them, loathing that gradually extended until it embraced the greater part of mankind.

Like Leonardo at a similar turn in his affairs, he began to day-dream of titanic convulsions which would put an end to this thankless species. 'I utterly hate all men, myself included,'[2] he burst out in one of his letters, and there was nothing rhetorical about it. Lanzky, who was with him at the time, recalls with what exultation Nietzsche heard of the eruption of Krakatoa, by which two thousand Javans and some thirty-six thousand neighbouring islanders were destroyed overnight. He would get his friend to read him the communiqués, ejaculating, 'two thousand human beings annihilated at a stroke! It's magnificent! This is how humanity should come to its end—how one day it will end!'—and he hoped that the tidal wave might reach as far as the Mediterranean, engulfing the populace of Nice, himself and Lanzky included. Had he lived sixty years later, it is clear, he would have greeted the obliteration of Hiroshima and Nagasaki with all the enthusiasm of a B.B.C. news commentator.

There is no escaping it: hardly had Nietzsche completed the third Part of *Zarathustra* before his love began to turn into hatred, his hope into utter despair. A prophet is never without honour save in his own country and among his own kin: it is the monotonous refrain of one after another of his letters. Although, in his notes, he tried to console himself with the thought that present-day man ought not to be judged by the present-day German, and compiled an exhaustive inventory of 'the strong points of the nineteenth century', he had really ceased to believe that this pitiful creature would ever respond to the summons, Become what thou art!—'It cannot be helped: we must go forward,—that is to say, *step by step further into decadence* (this is my definition of modern "progress"). We can hinder this development, and by so doing dam up and accumulate degeneration itself and render it more convulsive, more *volcanic*: we cannot do more.'[3] He had ceased to look for that new nobility which, by virtue of its own conquest of nihilism, would be capable of leading Europe towards a new Renaissance.

Behind all the vauntings of his autobiography, there lurks a profound and bitter disillusionment: and inevitably this disillusionment affected

[1] BGE, 263.   [2] L, I, 85.   [3] TI, p. 101.

his whole vision of the future. For if there were not enough men capable, like himself, of overcoming nihilism within their own souls—*since* there were not enough—nihilism, he believed, must ultimately overcome them. The dissolution of the traditional values of Europe would proceed to its logical conclusion—in that world-shaking convulsion he had predicted in *Schopenhauer as Educator*. Just as the scepticism of the eighteenth century, unconquered and unreconciled, had erupted finally in the French Revolution and twenty years of European war, so would the new and more radical scepticism, which he himself had perfected, blow what remained of European civilization to perdition. 'What I am now going to relate,' he writes in the Preface to an unfinished treatise on nihilism, 'is the history of the next two centuries. I shall describe what will happen, what must necessarily happen: *the triumph of Nihilism.* This history can already be written; for necessity itself is at work here.'[1]

* * *

Nietzsche was like an uncommonly sensitive seismograph. He felt and recorded the tremors of the distant earthquake long before news of it had reached his contemporaries. It is dangerous to be so sensitive. As he told Gast, 'my machine is one of those which may *fly in pieces.*'[2] Yet how amazingly accurate it was while it lasted! He knew that Christianity in all its forms had lost its hold upon Europe; he derided what he called the peculiarly English superstition that Christian morality could long outlast the religion that gave it birth; and the words in which he voiced his forebodings speak now into our very ears:

'My friends, we had a hard time as youths; we even suffered from youth itself as though it were a serious disease. This is owing to the age in which we were born—an age of enormous internal decay and disintegration which, with all its weakness and even with the best of its strength, is opposed to the spirit of youth. Disintegration—therefore uncertainty—is peculiar to this age: nothing stands on solid ground or on a sound faith. People live for the morrow, because the day-after-tomorrow is doubtful. All our road is slippery and dangerous, while the ice which still bears us has grown unconscionably thin: we all feel the mild and gruesome breath of the thaw-wind—soon, where we are walking, no one will any longer *be able* to walk!'[3]

It might have been written of the generation that grew up in the 1920's and 1930's.

Of this dissolution of traditional values, he detected the preliminary symptoms in that philosophical pessimism which, by the time he was

[1] WP, Preface, 2.   [2] L, 14, 8, 81.   [3] WP, 57.

writing, had become the fashion of intellectual Europe. He himself, having long ago been through all that, knew that it would not stop there. Belief in the Christian God being dead, belief in the various substitutes designed to slake the metaphysical thirst would not be long in following it to the grave. Sooner or later, men would be faced, as he had been, with the question, What is the value of existence?—and the answer, It has no value!—And then, unless they were strong enough to assume the terrible responsibility of consciously *creating values*, despair would master them finally. 'The logic of Pessimism leads finally to nihilism.'[1]

Nietzsche believed, indeed, that this stage had been reached once before, three thousand years earlier, in India. Buddhism, the religion *par excellence* of world-weariness, resignation and denial of the Will, had been its outstanding expression. He foretold, accordingly, the rise of a European Buddhism. But, his own experience had taught him, besides the nihilism of weakness there was possible a nihilism of strength—a nihilism which, not content with meditating over the 'in vain', takes a hand and drives to destruction: a vast upsurge of this, he also foretold, would distinguish the twentieth century.

The scepticism of weakness, he says in *Beyond Good and Evil*, springs from 'nervous debility and sickness'.[2] 'Where do we not find this cripple sitting nowadays!'[3] he exclaims; and goes on to contrast the paralysis of Europe with the native vigour of Russia. One day, Russia may *compel* Europe to find a will of its own, and the sense of a common purpose, if only in self-defence—'so that the long comedy of its petty-stateism, and dynastic as well as its democratic many-willedness, may finally be brought to a close. The time for petty politics is past; the next century will bring the struggle for the dominion of the world—and the *compulsion* to great politics.'[4]

The scepticism of strength, on the other hand, is 'the scepticism of daring manliness, which is closely related to the genius for war and conquest, and made its first entrance into Germany, in the person of the great Frederick:

'This scepticism despises and nevertheless grasps; it undermines and takes possession; it does not believe, but it does not thereby lose itself; it gives the spirit a dangerous liberty, but it keeps strict guard over the heart; it is the *German* form of scepticism, which, as a continued Fredericianism, risen to the highest spirituality, has kept Europe for a considerable time under the dominion of the German spirit and its critical and historical distrust. Owing to the insuperably strong and tough

---

[1] WP, 11.   [2] BGE, 208.   [3] *Ibid.*   [4] *Ibid.*

masculine character of the great German philologists and historical critics (who, rightly estimated, were also all of them artists of destruction and dissolution), a *new* conception of the German spirit gradually established itself—in spite of all Romanticism in music and philosophy—in which the leaning towards masculine scepticism was decidedly prominent: whether, for instance, as fearlessness of gaze, as courage and sternness of the dissecting hand, or as resolute will to dangerous voyages of discovery, to spiritualized North Pole expeditions under barren and dangerous skies.'[1]

This was Nietzsche's own kind of scepticism—the scepticism of *Human, All-too-Human*—and the inference is unmistakable. Germany, he believed, or the German spirit, would take the lead in that upsurge of destruction, whereby the remains of European civilization would be blown to perdition. In Germany, at all events, would be manifest first and foremost the despair of meaninglessness eternal.

Well, too well, could Nietzsche describe himself as 'an instinctive philosopher and anchorite, who found his advantage in isolation—in remaining outside, in patience, procrastination and lagging behind; like a weighing and testing spirit who has already lost his way in every labyrinth of the future; like a prophetic bird-spirit that *looks backwards* when it would announce what is to come; like the first perfect European Nihilist who, however, has already lived through Nihilism to the end—has it behind, beneath and outside himself'.[2]

* * *

'Nihilism is at our door: whence comes this most gruesome of all guests to us?' The opening sentence of the treatise on nihilism bears a startling resemblance to that of *The Communist Manifesto*. In truth, Nietzsche and Marx had more in common than appears at first sight, and it may be instructive to compare them.

To begin with, both these men saw the successive phases of an historical dialectic embodied, not in Hegel's national empires, but in social classes. Both were critically alive to the way in which 'the feelings peculiar to certain social ranks are projected into the universe',[3] colouring not only their philosophical, but equally their scientific, concepts. Both aspired to the formation of an *élite* which, espousing 'the elucidation of action, and not merely an airy permutation of concepts',[4] should point the way to a new synthesis. Marx's celebrated dictum, 'the philosophers have only given various interpretations of the world, the real task is to change it', could be paralleled many times over in Nietzsche's works.

[1] BGE, 209.   [2] WP, Preface, 3.   [3] WP, 677.   [4] WP, 605.

Marx's initial vision, again, was almost certainly 'beyond good and evil'; his *élite* of philosopher-kings, recruited from all classes, intended to be animated by it. The 'classless society' he anticipated was a society whose every member, simply by obeying his own self, would the better enable others to obey theirs; and clearly there is no incompatibility between 'classlessness' envisaged in this way and that natural hierarchy among men which Nietzsche very properly emphasized. They complement one another. It would be precisely in such a society that the wisest would be accorded the respect and responsibility they deserved. Only among equals is inequality truly understood.

Lastly Marx, like Nietzsche, foresaw the imminent catastrophe of bourgeois-Christian civilization. Although he read history in terms of economics, rather than philosophy, his prescience was none the less sure: and, like Nietzsche, he believed it impossible, for his own countrymen at all events, to forestall the catastrophe. 'One day,' he predicted, 'Germany will find herself on the level of European collapse, before she has ever stood on the level of European emancipation.'

Only at this point do the two apparently part company: for, of course, Marx's hatred of this civilization was such that he positively exulted in its doom. Far from wishing to do anything to forestall it, he flung himself body and soul into the task of precipitating it. Seeing in the proletariat the appointed agent of its destruction, he allied himself with the proletariat. He even went so far as to oppose whatever reforms might mitigate the proletarian's frustration, lest they should mitigate his revolutionary ardour, and to greet with sombre enthusiasm the restriction of economic power to fewer and fewer hands, since the fewer the capitalists left, the easier would be their expropriation. Thus, he became the advocate of 'slave-morality', the modern representative *par excellence* of the 'Judaic spirit'.

Marx, in other words, fell into the selfsame error that Nietzsche exposed in his rival Dühring—the error of supposing that a 'positive state' like justice can spring from the 'reactive feelings';[1] that the bourgeois order had only to be overthrown for a nobler one to rise in its stead. He relapsed into sheer negation, and rationalized his relapse by an appeal to Hegelian Idealism: re-christening the Human Essence 'the ensemble of social relations', and endowing the 'means of production' with the supernatural power of the Idea—the power, that is, of bearing the Chosen People inexorably out of the House of Bondage into the Promised Land.

It was by virtue of this Idealistic presupposition that Marx was able to

[1] GM, II, 11.

accord 'proletarian' concepts an absolute validity denied to all others. Progress once posited as independent of the motives and morality of men, it followed that any action which might assist the 'means of production' to achieve their end (seemingly collectivization), being virtually the Will of God, was justified; the class appointed to be the instrument of this consummation, being virtually Messiah, could do no wrong. His theory affords a striking illustration of Nietzsche's dictum, 'though the religious instinct is in vigorous growth, it rejects the theistic satisfaction with profound distrust.'[1]

The working man's vision of a revolutionary utopia, in Nietzsche's view, was a compensatory dream, equivalent to the early Christian vision of the Last Judgement. The reality, he maintained, would be vastly different; and he wished it could be demonstrated somewhere for the edification of the dreamers. 'The earth is big enough,' he wrote, 'and man is still unexhausted enough for a practical lesson of this sort and *demonstratio ad absurdum*—even if it were accomplished only by a vast expenditure of lives'.[2] It is greatly to be regretted that he never encountered Marx. He was always pining for a foeman worthy of his steel; in the author of *Capital* he would have found him. One thinks regretfully of the polemics that might have thundered to and fro between Sils Maria and Hampstead!

The strange thing is, however—and this is the point of our comparison—that once Nietzsche had finally despaired of present-day man, his own thought pursued an almost identical trajectory. He too began positively to exult in the thought of the imminent catastrophe; he too began to work for it! Once more the feasibility of a complete overthrow of all things presented itself to him, and he no longer shrank from the thought. Possibly, beyond this upheaval and desolation there might be a chance of a new hope; and even if there was not, would not complete annihilation be better than the wretched existing state of affairs? Was not a volcanic convulsion, indeed, precisely his heart's desire? If present-day man would not repent and flee from the wrath to come, *since* he would not repent, let it come, and the sooner the better! *Après moi le déluge!*

Nietzsche, needless to say, did not ally himself with the proletariat. By the time he was writing, the social legislation of Bismarck and Lassalle had already robbed the workers of their revolutionary ardour. They had adopted the religion of smug ease; in no essential respect did their ideals differ from those of the bourgeoisie. The socialism they still professed would at most carry one stage further the levelling spirit of

[1] BGE, 53.   [2] WP, 125.

democracy, itself a derivative of Christianity: 'modern socialism would fain create a profane counterpart of Jesuitism: everybody a perfect instrument'.[1] But, as we have seen, he detected another force, already largely emancipated from Christianity, and far more closely related to the scepticism of the strong—the force of militarism. And he threw in his lot with that.

There is no room for doubt on this score. More and more frequently now the old paean in honour of warfare began to make itself heard in Nietzsche's writings. Whereas, in 'We Fearless Ones', he had contemplated with 'silent rage' the nationalism and race-hatred 'on account of which the nations of Europe are at present bounded off and secluded from one another as if by quarantine',[2] now, on the contrary, 'I am delighted at the military development of Europe', he cries, 'also at the inner anarchical conditions.'[3] Whereas he had predicted with contemptuous disgust that Germany, in order to preserve its artificial *Reich*, would have to 'plant itself between two mortal hatreds',[4] now this very development excites his sombre enthusiasm: 'the *maintenance of the military state* is the last means of either upholding or securing the great *tradition* of the supreme type of man, the strong type. And every idea which perpetuates the enmity and distance in rank of states may to that end seem justified (e.g. nationalism, protective tariffs)'.[5]

Far from seeking to avert the disintegration of Europe, Nietzsche now flung himself body and soul into the task of precipitating it. He even went so far as to oppose all attempts to arrest the advance of democracy and socialism—'the *levelling* of the mankind of Europe is the great process which should not be arrested; it should even be accelerated'[6]—since a mass-man would thereby be created who, when the hour struck, would fall like ripe fruit into the hands of the military. All that was needful, he confided, was to make sure that the military themselves remained untouched by the contagion, and to cleave, wherever possible, a yet deeper gulf between them and their destined subjects.

Modern Europe, as he saw it, was arriving at a condition of decadence analogous to that of the ancient world, when it was overrun, defeated and subdued by the hardier races of the north. The military were summoned to perform the role of those hardier races. 'Problem: where are the *barbarians* of the twentieth century? Obviously they will only show themselves and consolidate themselves after enormous socialistic crises. They will consist of those elements which are capable of the *greatest hardness towards themselves*, and which can guarantee the *most enduring*

[1] WP, 757.   [2] JW, 377.   [3] WP, 127.
[4] JW, 377.   [5] WP, 729.   [6] WP, 898.

will-power'.[1] Thus Nietzsche emerges as the advocate of active nihilism, the modern representative *par excellence* of the anti-Judaic spirit.

* * *

No more than Marx, of course, did he believe, or profess to believe, that this upsurge of destruction would prove final. 'Nihilism,' he wrote, 'represents an intermediate, pathological condition (the vast generalization, the conclusion that there is *no purpose* in anything, is pathological).'[2] He himself had already outlived nihilism; Europe would eventually do likewise. He, the new Goethe, who had overcome the twentieth century, would have his counterpart in a new Napoleon, who would succeed, where the first had failed, in uniting Europe and ultimately the world—and that would be sufficient atonement for all that had gone before. 'The Revolution made Napoleon possible: that is its justification. We ought to desire the anarchical collapse of the whole of our civilization, if such a reward were to be its result.'[3]

The new Napoleon—he can be envisaged either as an individual or as a type—would lay the foundations of a super-State. Then, at long last, the decisive questions would be posed: 'How shall the earth as a whole be ruled? And to what end shall man as a whole—no longer as a people or as a race—be reared and trained?'[4] And then, at long last, Nietzsche too would come into his own—*Voilà un homme!* For was it not precisely for 'such colossally creative men, such really great men as I understand them',[5] that he had prepared his evangel of the future? He had given them their gospel in *Zarathustra*; he would shortly be giving them their theology—and, as if to point the moral more clearly, he contemplated writing *The Will to Power* in Corsica:

'For the reader must not misunderstand the meaning of the title which has been given to this Evangel of the Future. "*The Will to Power: An Attempted Transvaluation of all Values*"—with this formula a *counter-movement* finds expression, in regard to both a principle and a mission; a movement which in some remote future will supersede this perfect Nihilism; but which *presupposes* it, both logically and psychologically, and which positively cannot come, except *on top of* and *out of* it.'[6]

It is a grandiose dream, and by no means an ignoble one. But we—who live in the midst of the nihilistic interregnum—find ourselves driven to ask, Is it anything more than a dream? That the world will be united,

[1] WP, 868.   [2] WP, 13.   [3] WP, 877.
[4] WP, 951.   [5] *Ibid.*   [6] WP, Preface, 4.

and soon, admits of little doubt. The consummation Nietzsche foresaw is visibly preparing itself. The one thing more likely than the establishment of a super-State is the total collapse of the more advanced technological societies, and a reversal of human life to the primitive subsistence-level. (As he himself reminded the optimistic Darwinians, evolution not infrequently proceeds through the elimination of specialized types and the survival of the simpler and more adaptable.) But, even supposing the world united, what guarantee is there that it will be at the hands of such colossally creative men, and not of their very opposites?— that the super-State will be governed by a Julius Cæsar and not by a Cesar Borgia?

Nietzsche tried to meet these objections. 'Danger, severity, violence, peril in the street and in the heart, inequality of rights, secrecy, stoicism, seductive art and devilry of every kind,' he writes, 'are necessary to the elevation of man.'[1] The conditions prevailing in the interregnum, in other words, will be of a kind ideally calculated to promote a form of natural selection, as the result of which, though incalculable numbers of higher men may perish, those that survive will be 'as strong as the devil'.[2] These were the conditions, he argues, that prevailed in the Italy of the Renaissance. He does not add that they prevailed throughout the Dark Ages.

The argument, however, is so manifestly untenable that it is hard to believe that he himself could ever have been convinced by it. Granted that a society torn and terrorized by the hired gangs of rival lords is no *more* stultifying than one duped and debauched by the hired liars of rival press-lords, is there any evidence that it is *less* so? What sort of a selection would that have been, which a cannon-ball might have effected at Metz, had it struck Nietzsche instead of his neighbour? Not merely does he leave out of account the difference between medieval and modern warfare (which, if anything, 'selects' the most contemptible types), but it begs the fundamental question, whether the artists of dissolution and destruction are always, or even often, artists of reconciliation and creation.

That was what he wanted to prove; and he failed completely to do so. The early stage of every Cæsar, he asserts, is a Catiline—as though we could infer from that that the later stage of every Catiline is a Cæsar, and Voltaire, had he lived long enough, would have been a Goethe, and Robespierre a Napoleon. At bottom, Nietzsche's forecast was based on nothing more substantial than an analogy: he, the author of *Human, All-too-Human*, had, in the fullness of time, created *Thus Spake Zara-*

---

[1] WP, 957.   [2] WP, 131.

thustra. It presents yet another example of the old Hegelian optimism, only this time without the Hegelian rationalization.

It is possible, of course, just possible, that the world will be united at the hands of some such philosopher-king as he pictured. We have no right to rule out the possibility, however unfavourable the omens. And yet, the longer one considers it, the less psychologically probable it appears. He would have, indeed, to have 'a heart transformed into brass'[1] who could employ the means necessary, not simply to gain the victory, but to eradicate the after-effects (to sterilize or exterminate the million monstrosities resulting from radio-activity, the 'physiologically bungled and botched', as Nietzsche would call them). It is barely conceivable that even a potential creator could assume that responsibility without going to ruin himself. He forgot how intimately his own hardness was bound up with his sensitiveness—he, who by his own confession, could no more murder than break his word. 'The Roman Cæsar with the soul of Christ!'[2] It is either a solecism or a definition of the Grand Inquisitor.

'Napoleon was corrupted in the struggle for power, like Bismarck. For the coming century I foresee an eruption of petty despots.'[3] Nietzsche was on firmer ground here. We have lived long enough to see for ourselves what type of man comes to the top in time of modern war. A super-state founded and consolidated by heroes such as these would legislate, not for the Superman, but for the Last Man. It would be a totalitarian world-tyranny.

Did Nietzsche ever envisage that alternative? Or was he completely deluded by a compensatory dream, as naive and as self-contradictory as Marx's own? It seems that he did. On one occasion, at least, he did admit to himself that something more than militarism would be required to create the order he wished for Europe. He actually specified it:

'A peace party, without sentimentality, which forbids itself and its children to wage war; which forbids recourse to justice; which brings on itself fighting, contradiction, persecution: a party of the oppressed, at least for a time; very soon the great party. Hostile to feelings of revenge and resentment. . . .'[4]

A party of *satyagrahis*, destined to re-enact, in the conditions of a new world *imperium*, the role of the Christian Church under the Roman Cæsars!

But Nietzsche pursued this thought no further: and the reason is not far to seek. Had he not despaired of present-day man, he would never have looked for a Napoleon in the first place; he would have looked for

[1] BGE, 203.   [2] WP, 983.   [3] N, XIV, 65.   [4] WP, 748.

a Mirabeau instead—for one who would go on striving, even at the eleventh hour, to forestall the catastrophe. As it was, his despair was at once the cause and effect of a relapse into sheer negation on his own part: a relapse so violent that, in the name of Cæsar, he really did proclaim Cesar Borgia, and in the name of Napoleon—Hitler.

* * *

The tendency towards sheer negation, and its corollary of militarism, is not, of course, new in Nietzsche's writings. It appears in *The Greek State*, and from time to time in *The Joyful Wisdom*; it can be traced in a number of his notes of the period of *Zarathustra* itself—it is, indeed, part and parcel of that loathing and hatred of the small man which the prophet overcomes in Part III. From *Beyond Good and Evil* onwards, however, what has hitherto been no more than a bass accompaniment comes near to drowning the air of *amor fati*. Nietzsche frankly admitted this. 'Now that the yea-saying part of my life-task was accomplished,' he wrote in *Ecce Homo*, 'there came the turn of the nay-saying, nay-doing half; the transvaluation of all values accepted hitherto, the great war . . .'[1] The great *war*! His books, from being 'victories', had turned suddenly into campaigns.

Brandes, the earliest and one of the most discerning of his critics, was quick to remark Nietzsche's renewed taste for the polemical style, hinting plainly that this was something he ought to have outgrown. Brandes was puzzled by it too, as well he might be in view of Zarathustra's affirmations. But in truth the style was the man; had he looked more closely, he would have found the solution to the puzzle in *The Genealogy of Morals* itself:

'Let us come to the conclusion. The two *opposing values*, "good and bad", "good and evil", have fought a dreadful, thousand-year fight in the world, and though, indubitably, the second value has been long preponderant, places are not wanting where the fortune of the fight is still undecided. It could even be said that, in the meanwhile, the fight has been raised to an ever higher plane, and has on that account become ever more intense, ever more spiritual: so that nowadays there is perhaps no more decisive mark of the "*higher nature*", of the more spiritual nature, than to be in that sense divided, and actually to be still a battle-field for these two opposites. The symbol of this fight, written in characters still legible throughout all human history, is "Rome against Judaea, Judaea against Rome".'[2]

The mark of the higher nature is to be still a battle-field: not a syn-

[1] EH, p. 114.   [2] GM, I, 16.

thesis, be it noted, but a self-contradiction! Nietzsche, by the time he wrote this, was once more at war with the Judaic spirit in himself—that terrible, nagging conscience which harked back and bound him to Naumburg—and therefore he was at war with it outside himself as well. He was fighting Tolstoy's battle in reverse.

For a moment, in Zarathustra, he had overcome, by accepting, this spirit, which, as he supposed, he had inherited from his priestly forebears; consequently, 'see how Zarathustra goes down and speaks the kindest words to everyone! See with what delicate fingers he touches his very adversaries, the priests, and how he suffers with them from themselves!'[1] Now he is no longer capable of such forbearance. Even when he continues to affirm in theory 'that economy in the law of life which draws its own advantage even out of the repulsive race of bigots, the priests and the virtuous',[2] the bitterness of his language betrays him; and soon, 'the priest', we find him exclaiming, 'the shepherd of souls, should be looked upon as a form of life which must be suppressed'[3]— suppressed, not surpassed. In the words of The Dawn of Day, having ceased to love himself through grace, he has ceased to love anyone.

'Only the wholest people can love'.[4] The keynote of Zarathustra is struck in the prophet's counsel to the Fool, 'where one can no longer love, there should one pass by'. In some of Nietzsche's later notes, he sounds like the Fool in person. Only listen to this:

'The annihilation of declining races. The decay of Europe. The annihilation of slave-tainted valuations. The dominion of the world as a means to the rearing of a higher type. The annihilation of the humbug which is called morality (Christianity as a hysterical kind of honesty in this regard: Augustine, Bunyan). The annihilation of universal suffrage —that is to say, that system by means of which the lowest natures prescribe themselves as a law of the higher natures. . . .'[5]

Nietzsche himself is now a nay-sayer; he, of all men, now reacts— against the reactive.

Inevitably, the very features he has pointed out as characteristic of the nay-sayer begin to appear in his own works. Out of the Christian 'good and evil', he has virtually made a new 'evil'; and, like the anarchist and anti-semite, he allows this to prescribe his 'good'. His whole conception of master-morality undergoes a subtle distortion; it becomes merely the negation of slave-morality.

'Ye highest men who have come within my ken,' Zarathustra mocks at one point, 'this is my doubt of you and my secret laughter: I suspect

[1] EH, p. 108.　　[2] TI, p. 32.　　[3] WP, 51.　　[4] WP, 296.　　[5] WP, 862.

ye would call my Superman—a devil!'[1] His mockery is abundantly justified: the good and the just hold up their hands in horror at the thought of a spontaneous virtue. It does not follow that everything that they call 'evil' must, on that account, be good. Yet this, in effect, is what Nietzsche now maintains. Like Blake in his *Bible of Hell*, he virtually equates his 'beyond good and evil' with the Christian's 'evil'.

It is in *Ecce Homo* that he tells us how once he 'whispered to a man that he would do better to seek for the Superman even in a Cesar Borgia than in a Parsifal':[2] and had he left the point there, no one could well have objected. We have only to read *Zarathustra* to see that the Super-man veritably is about as like Parsifal as Goethe is like Till Eulenspiegel. But Nietzsche could not leave it there. Such was his animosity towards the Church, that the thought of a murderous atheist enthroned in the Holy See filled him with exultation—'*déniaiser la vertu*—a secret joy!'[3]—It would have been the crowning symbol for the negation of slave morality in the very nerve-centre of Christendom. Accordingly, in *Beyond Good and Evil*, this 'man of prey', this 'healthiest of all tropical monsters and growths',[4] actually is presented as a desideratum!

'He who fights with monsters should be careful lest he thereby become a monster. And if thou gaze long into an abyss, the abyss will also gaze into thee.'[5]

Nietzsche being once more a battle-field, the history of Europe in his eyes must perforce remain a battle-field also. It is no accident that in *The Genealogy of Morals*, Rome, and not Athens, should be pitted against Judaea. The Romans, 'primeval forest creatures',[6] stand in the same relation to the Greeks as Borgia to Leonardo: they stand for unity and domination for its own sake. In Nietzsche's soul at this moment 'the Greek idea as against the Roman . . . the idea of culture as a new and finer nature, without distinction of inner and outer, without convention or disguise, as a unison of living, thinking, appearing and willing', has practically ceased to count; all that matters is the reassertion of aristo-cratic prerogative. His own synthesis being disrupted, he can no longer even anticipate an historical synthesis: the thousand-year duel must end, not in a reconciliation of Rome and Judaea, but in outright victory for Rome.

* * *

Zarathustra, to be sure, contains no positive indications as to the organization of the society over which the prophet is destined to preside; nor as to the means by which it is to be brought into being. Nietzsche's

[1] Z, 43. [2] EH, p. 58. [3] WP, 425. [4] BGE, 197. [5] BGE, 146. [6] WP, 959.

purpose in the poem was simply to proclaim a goal—the creation of Superman. To discover the conditions of its realization, to do whatever the changing situation allowed to promote such conditions—these were the tasks to which his warriors were called; and how far and how fast they could proceed would depend, in the first instance, on how many of them there were. 'Zarathustra's mood is not one of mad impatience for Superman! It is peaceful, it can wait: but all action has derived some purpose from being the road and the means thither—and must be done well and perfectly.'[1] It took the Greeks generations to rear a type as perfect as Thucydides; it would not take fewer to embody his own ideal.

The one thing that emerges clearly from the poem itself is that the new nobility he looked for, the nobility of men who had become what they were, would constitute a kind of Jesuit Order. As early as *Human, All-too-Human*, Nietzsche had pictured the 'enlightened' banding themselves into a body 'equally admirable through self-conquest, indefatigableness and dedication';[2] in his later notes this conception reappears —although, of course, he stresses the difference of their aim from that of the sixteenth-century Jesuits (or their modern counterparts, the Communists):

'The overriding consideration of jesuitism, equally of socialist jesuitism: government of mankind with a view to their *happiness*, happiness of mankind through the keeping up of illusion, of faith. *To this I oppose my contrary movement: government of mankind with a view to their surpassing. Surpassing by means of doctrines that will make them perish, except for those who endure them.*'[3]

He looked for the emergence of a new Church, which, while neither claiming infallibility nor practising persecution (he consistently regarded the tendency to preserve, rather than repress, opposition as one of Europe's major advances), would emphatically discountenance the protestant-plebeian assumption that any man, whatever his qualifications or lack of them, is entitled to pontificate on morals—an assumption unthinkable in medicine. It would be a Church hierarchically organized, like the Catholic; and, like the Catholic, would treat the State as a means to its end, the production of a higher man: 'a Church is above all an authoritative organization, which secures to the *more spiritual* men the highest rank, and so far *believes* in the power of spirituality as to forbid itself all grosser appliances of authority.'[4]

On the evidence of *Zarathustra* alone, therefore, one might reason-

[1] NZ, 76.   [2] H, I, 55.   [3] N, XIV, 73.   [4] JW, 358.

ably deduce that the new ecumenical society he looked for would be analogous to medieval Christendom. The act of self-transcendence taking the place of that resurrection, which, by the earliest Christians, was supposed to commence at baptism, the *élite* would look on all men as potential recruits, even were their talents only of the second or third order. In principle, it would be a 'classless society': and the conclusion of Nietzsche's Romantic Myth would thus, like all the rest, correspond exactly to Wagner's.

Whatever may or may not have been in his mind when he actually composed the poem, however, such was emphatically not the deduction that Nietzsche himself drew. On the contrary, in *Beyond Good and Evil* and its successors he reverts to the standpoint, not of *Thoughts out of Season*, but of *The Future of our Educational Institutions*.

In those addresses, it will be recalled, his impatience with all who were incapable of benefiting from a classical education—with all, that is, whom a classical education could only turn into Philistines of Culture—had led him to the savage verdict that creativeness in every form was the prerogative of a tiny minority. It is the same argument (and the same tag) that finds expression in *The Twilight of the Idols*: ' "Higher education" and a vast crowd—these terms contradict each other from the start. A higher education can only concern the exception: a man must be privileged in order to have a right to such a great privilege. All great and beautiful things cannot be a common possession: *pulchrum est paucorum hominum.*'[1]

Nietzsche had subsequently abandoned this verdict. Even in *Philosophy during the Tragic Age of the Greeks* there had been a manifest contradiction between his portrayal of the Greek philosophers 'undisturbed by a wanton, noisy race of dwarfs, creeping about beneath them',[2] and of the Greek nation as one in which 'we should ever find reflected only that picture which in her highest geniuses shines forth in more resplendent colours'; and by the time of *Richard Wagner at Bayreuth*, he had come to the conclusion that 'the masses are neither better nor worse than the educated. . . . One uplifts or debases them accordingly as one uplifts or debases oneself.'[3] Yet, in the fierce indignation of his final works, all this is once more forgotten. It is not only the old paean in honour of war that sounds forth anew in *Beyond Good and Evil*, but also the old paean in honour of slavery.

The new ecumenical society he envisaged was actually constituted, not on the medieval Christian, but on the ancient Indian, model. It was to be a society of rigid castes. Early in 1888, he procured a copy of *The*

[1] TI, p. 56.   [2] GP, 1.   [3] N, XI, 142.

Laws of Manu, and was instantly captivated by it. It rounded off his ideas on religion, he told Gast, in the most remarkable manner: and no wonder!—

'I confess that the impression it has given me is that everything else we possess in the nature of great moral codes is simply an imitation or even a caricature of this work: above all Egypticism. Even Plato strikes me as being, in all important points, merely the well-schooled *chela* of a Brahmana. While from the standpoint of Manu's Law-Book, the Jews seem to be a Chandala race, that has learned from its masters the principles according to which a *priesthood* can prevail and organize a people. ... The organization of the Middle Ages seems like a monstrous groping after the recovery of all the ideas on which the primeval Indo-Aryan community rested—but in this case we have to reckon with the additional bias of *pessimistic* values that found their forcing dung in the general decadence of races. Here, again, the *Jews* appear to have been only "intermediaries" (middle-men)—they invent nothing.'[1]

No words of Nietzsche's could throw a more searching light than these on what may be called the original sin of his political philosophy.

Christianity is grounded on the dogma that every man, whatever his race or class, is potentially a son of God. This dogma, a Jewish invention, was formulated by the Church in direct and conscious opposition to the teaching of Plato: and the organization of the Middle Ages, insofar as it is distinctive at all, derives from it. It was thanks to this that social classes were conceived as functional, and that the ranks of the priesthood, even to the papacy itself, were open to the sons of knights, burgesses and serfs alike. As Carlyle exclaimed, 'How, like an immense mineshaft through the dim oppressed classes of society, this Institution of the Priesthood ran, opening, from the lowest depths, and towards all heights and towards Heaven itself, a free road of egress and emergence towards virtuous nobleness, heroism and well-doing for every born man!' It was thanks to this that the priesthood saw it as its mission to promote the spiritual welfare of every member of society—to transform every man, if possible, into a higher man.

The religion of Manu is grounded on precisely the opposite dogma: that spirituality of the highest order is the prerogative of a single, distinguishable, hereditary caste. It was for this reason and no other that Nietzsche found it so congenial: 'what a wretched thing the New Testament is beside Manu, what an evil odour hangs around it!'[2] Once that premise is granted, everything else follows logically.

[1] L, 31, 5, 88.   [2] TI, p. 46.

The vast majority of mankind either cannot, or need not, or ought not, to respond to the summons, Become what thou art! They belong to a different species from the *élite*—different not merely in degree, but in kind. Grant this and it follows, first of all, that the *élite*, from whose ranks alone the Superman may eventually emerge, will be as little concerned for the spiritual welfare of the majority as they will for that of their cats and dogs. To speak of 'spiritual welfare' at all, in such a connection, would be absurd! They may even prefer not to soil their own hands with 'the *unavoidable* filth of all political agitation. The Brahmins, for instance, understood this fact. With the help of a religious organization, they secured to themselves the power of nominating kings for the people, while their sentiments prompted them to keep apart and outside, as men with a higher and super-regal mission.'[1]

It follows again, that the value of the majority of mankind will be determined, simply and exclusively, by their material usefulness to the *élite*. They have no end in themselves: 'ordinary men . . . exist for service and general utility, and are only so far entitled to exist.'[2] They may therefore be sorted out and trained as agriculturalists, merchants, doctors, soldiers, etc.—or, if the fancy should happen to take a ruler, crossed with one another, like pigs or poultry, to see what new varieties may be bred. In the *Laws of Manu*, Nietzsche observes approvingly, 'the task is set of rearing no less than four races at once: a priestly race, a merchant and agricultural race, and finally a race of servants—the Sudras.'[3]

It is noticeable that, in order to justify this conception, he has recourse to the time-honoured simile of the 'social organism'—a simile first employed by the Roman patricians to explain their position to the plebs. But—the point is significant—Nietzsche's idea of an organism has undergone a sea-change. He no longer regards it as a synthesis, endowed with a will of its own, over and above the wills of its component parts. A society conceived on that model could only resemble Rousseau's: it would be a society animated and regulated by a 'General Will', proceeding from the tendency of each to seek his final perfection. Now, on the contrary, Nietzsche conceives the organism as a multiplicity of parts dominated by the strongest, the instincts—which, in their turn, are all contending with each other for sovereignty. It is by virtue of this that he is able to pronounce as the essential of a good and healthy aristocracy 'that it should *not* regard itself as a function of either the kingship or the commonwealth, but as the *significance* and highest justification thereof—that it should therefore accept with a good conscience the

[1] BGE, 61.   [2] *Ibid.*   [3] TI, p. 46.

sacrifice of a legion of individuals who, *for its sake*, must be suppressed and reduced to imperfect men, to slaves and instruments.'[1]

Finally, it follows from his premise that those who cannot be employed in any useful capacity, the 'physiologically bungled and botched', will have to be exterminated outright. Manu's name for these outcasts was Chandala; and his code prescribes for them a mode of living calculated to ensure their ultimate extinction. Nietzsche cites the relevant clauses at some length in *The Twilight of the Idols*; and, in his private notes, accepts the conclusion without flinching. Indeed, he accepts it with something very like exultation: 'we', after all, 'are the *noble*! It is much more important to maintain *us* than *that* cattle!'[2]

'Humanity as a mass sacrificed to the prosperity of the one *stronger* species of Man,' he cries in *The Genealogy of Morals*, 'that *would be* a progress'![3]—and so indeed it would, did it mean the self-surpassing of humanity, man's self-overcoming for the benefit of Superman. But that is no longer his meaning. Under the pressure of loathing and despair, the whole ethic of *Zarathustra* has been distorted out of recognition. The 'new love' he had proclaimed in the poem, which is hard because it seeks the emancipation of others, has become 'hard, full of self-conquest, because it needs human sacrifices'[4]—and needs them almost literally. Against the sickly and morbid sympathy of the pitiful he has nothing better to pit than a brutal callousness, sanctioned in the name of nature:

'It is not nature that is immoral if she is without pity for the degenerate: on the contrary, the growth of physiological and moral evil in the human race is the *result of a morbid and unnatural morality*. The sensibility of the majority of men is morbid and unnatural.

'How comes it that humanity is *corrupted*, morally and physiologically?—The body goes to pieces if an organ is *interfered with*. One cannot derive the *right of altruism* from physiology, any more than the right to succour, to equality of lots: these are all premiums on the degenerate and handicapped.

'There is no *solidarity* in a society which harbours sterile, unproductive and destructive elements—elements, moreover, that will have a progeny still more degenerate than themselves.'[5]

The decadent must be suppressd—without malice or resentment, certainly, but equally without compunction.

But who are the decadent? Obviously, Nietzsche's whole edifice rests on the assumption, not only that certain elements are incurable (both

[1] BGE, 258.   [2] WP, 873.   [3] GM, II, 12.   [4] WP, 246.   [5] WP, 52.

they and their progeny), but that 'we, the noble', are in a position to tell which they are. It is a sizeable assumption, and he himself was alive to the difficulties. 'Men have always *confused* the weariest with the strongest', he observes, 'and the strongest with the most harmful';[1] again, the symptoms being so markedly similar, how are we to know whether an individual is 'afflicted with sickness or excess of health?'[2] In the end he discovered a solution—the racial theory.

It was not the racial theory of Gobineau. Although, like Wagner, Nietzsche admired the author of *The Inequality of Human Races*, there is no evidence that he subscribed to the dogma of the innate superiority of yellow people over black, or white over yellow. Rather, he seems to have assumed the inheritability of acquired characteristics, and deduced from this that slaves, for example, transmitted their revengefulness to their offspring, aristocrats their nobler impulses. Since, however, certain races like the Iberians or Dravidians had long been relegated to the lowest stratum of society, the implications were practically identical. The conclusion could be hazarded that wherever Iberian or Dravidian features manifested themselves, the instincts of decadence might be looked for; conversely, that the instincts of health were associated with the 'Aryan' type (a type which, like Gobineau, Nietzsche believed to be rarer in Germany than in France). It was in accordance with this theory that he derived the evils of democracy from an intermingling of races, consequent upon the levelling of classes; and could not socialism itself be regarded as a monstrous recrudescence of the primitive communism of the Celts? It was likewise in accordance with this that he took pains to establish his own descent from one of the aristocratic houses of Poland.

In fact, the theory was altogether invaluable. Not only did it provide a complete and conclusive justification of the caste-system—since the more generations practised a particular craft, the more expertise they would acquire; but it shifted the emphasis everywhere from education to breeding. If the emergence of Superman could be secured by the mating of complementary types, neither the motives nor the morality of individuals was of more than secondary consequence. Thus Nietzsche, who had once maintained that it was in the voluntary choice of his wife that a man gave expression to his truest individuality, pronounces in favour of marriages arranged by authority—and even of a system of stud-breeding: 'some exceptional men ought to be given the opportunity to father children on numerous women, and some women, exhibiting particularly favourable traits, ought not to be bound by the

[1] WP, 48.   [2] WP, 1009.

accident which has attached them to a single man.'[1] We might begin forthwith, he suggests on another occasion, to encourage an intermarriage of Prussians and Jews, whereby the latter would acquire some dignity, and the former some intelligence.

This, of course, is the part of Nietzsche's philosophy that was afterwards so exquisitely handled by Shaw in *Man and Superman*: and we are in no position to deny that there was any truth in it. The study of heredity has not advanced nearly far enough for that. Moreover, because it invariably carries, as in this case, political implications, even such advances as have been made may not really be advances at all. When the *furor politicus* seizes a scientist, he becomes as arbitrary, evasive and unreliable as any journalist. Almost everything that has been written on the subject may well be suspected of *parti pris*, and never more so than, when it is presented as 'objective'. At present, we simply do not know what psychological characteristics, if any, are innate in the different races; we do not know whether acquired characteristics are inherited; we do not even know what characteristics are acquired: and we shall not know any of these things until it becomes possible for a British geneticist, for example, to acknowledge that the late Herr Rosenberg was right—should the evidence happen to point that way.

But—and this is what matters—neither did Nietzsche know. He knew even less about the subject than we do: and that is why we may legitimately call his racial theory a rationalization. His dogmatic addiction to it, equally with his evident relish for the prospects it opened up, can only be accounted for by his determination to prove certain classes of men irredeemable. And the prospects were pretty grim. There is no need to list them all. They are, unhappily, all too familiar today. A few more quotations will suffice:

'*On the future of marriage*:—a *super-tax* (on inherited property), also a longer term of military conscription for bachelors of a certain minimum age (within the community). *Privileges of all sorts for fathers* who lavish boys upon the world: in some circumstances plural votes. A *medical certificate* as a condition of any marriage, endorsed by the local authorities, in which a series of precise questions, addressed to the betrothed and to the medical officers, must be answered ("family histories"). As a counter-agent to prostitution (or as its ennoblement), leasehold marriages, legalised (for years, for months), with provision for the children . . .'[2]

'A criminal should not be deprived of the possibility of making his

[1] N, XII, 188.   [2] WP, 733.

peace with society: provided he does not belong to the *race of criminals*. In the latter case, war should be waged on him, even before he has done anything malicious (first operation, as soon as he is in our power: castrate him).'[1]

'To utilise the degenerate. A new *penal* right: the guilty can be *utilised* as a subject of experiment (for a new dietetic regime). Punishment is sanctified when one man is *expended* to the greatest advantage of the men of the future.'[2]

Considering that the Jews have suffered longer repression than any other people in Europe, one might expect Nietzsche to go on from this to class them among the bungled and botched; and in point of fact, the writings of his final period do betray some falling-off in his partiality for them. In *Human, All-too-Human*, he had hailed them as continuators of the Greek scientific spirit; in *The Dawn of Day*, as 'a people which, like the Greeks, and even in greater degree than the Greeks, clung and still clings to life.'[3] He had dismissed the 'Jewish problem' as one that would solve itself, as soon as Europe was united and they ceased to extend across otherwise watertight frontiers; he had even predicted that they might emerge as the ruling *élite*—and broken out into hosannas at the thought: 'when Israel shall have changed its eternal vengeance into an eternal benediction for Europe, that seventh day will once more be when the old Jewish god may rejoice in Himself, in His creation, in His chosen people—and all, all of us, will rejoice with Him!'[4] Now, notwithstanding his emphatic maxim, 'to associate with no man who takes any part in the mendacious race swindle',[5] he occasionally lays himself open to the charge of anti-semitism.

At this point, however, Nietzsche did find the facts too strong for him. Not only could he scarcely forget Spinoza and Heine, Mendelssohn and Offenbach; but, as it turned out, whatever he himself wrote, the Jews were the first to understand. Rée, Brandes, Helen Zimmern —'it is amazing to see the extent to which this race now has the spirituality of Europe in its hands!'[6] Consequently, while failing to acknowledge that the logical conclusion of his theory was likewise its refutation, he did go so far as to indite one sentence which Adolf Hitler, otherwise so faithful to these precepts, most unfortunately overlooked: 'anti-semites—another name for "bungled and botched".'[7]

* * *

Most of the notes just cited belong to the few months immediately succeeding Nietzsche's study of *The Laws of Manu*. It is clear that he was

[1] WP, 740.   [2] N, XIII, 368.   [3] D, 72.   [4] D, 205.
[5] GM, p. 226.   [6] L, 20, 7, 86.   [7] WP, 864.

tempted at that time to follow Plato's example, and actually legislate for the society of the future. In the end he forebore. 'The superior reason of such a procedure lies in the intention to draw consciousness off step by step from that mode of life which has been recognized as correct (i.e. *proved* after enormous and carefully examined experience), so that perfect automatism of the instincts may be attained—this being the only possible basis of all mastery of every kind of perfection in the art of life.'[1] He realized that in the absence of any such experience, it would be premature to attempt such a feat. His own principles prevented him from capping his *Republic* with a *Laws*: and perhaps it is just as well.

Not that we have the least right to blame Nietzsche for the despair and loathing that are at the root of his political philosophy. These were only the defects of his virtues. 'The duel between Nietzsche and civilization is long since over,'[2] wrote an English politician in 1911, going on to assert of *Zarathustra* that 'the greatest difficulty that one experiences before such a doctrine as his is the difficulty of taking it seriously.' In spite of all that has occurred since, the attitude of parliament, pulpit and press is still Mr. R. M. Kettle, M.P.'s. Because it still is, and because one need no longer be a prophet to 'divine the fate that is hidden under the idiotic unwariness and blind confidence of "modern ideas"' (it is no longer even hidden), only a saint could presume to condemn such despair and loathing.

Nevertheless, one must blame Nietzsche for representing his despair as a victory, and his loathing, not as a defect, but as a virtue. For it is never the things a man stands for that determine his influence in the short run; it is the things he stands against; and by allowing his aversions to sprout and harden into a monstrous system, he did more than generations of commentators to stultify his own deepest insight and make the message of *Zarathustra* of none effect. Although his political philosophy is in reality little more than a parasite, flourishing at the expense of his philosophy as a whole, it has gone far towards killing its host—and some of its spores have already germinated grotesquely.

In the happy heyday of liberalism, when everybody was dominated by the idea that ideas could not dominate anybody, this would have seemed of small account. To whom did it matter then that the dons read his books backwards, that they mistook the fungus for the oak, and that all that appears in the majority of philosophical text-books under the heading 'Nietzsche' is still only a more or less inaccurate description of the fungus? Today, on the other hand, when philosophy has once more stepped out of the cloister, exchanging cap and gown for the trappings

[1] A, 57.　　[2] Introduction to Halévy's *Life of Nietzsche*.

and accoutrements of war, we can begin to see that it does matter—that it matters more than anything else. The only fit speech for despair is silence.

Nietzsche dealt his doctrine a blow from which it may never recover. The despair that drove him to proclaim catastrophe inevitable, made him an agent of catastrophe. He went to ruin as he feared, and became the prophet of ruin:

'I know my destiny. There will come a day when my name will recall the memory of something formidable—a crisis the like of which has never been known on earth, the memory of the most profound clash of consciences, and the passing of a sentence upon all that which theretofore had been believed, exacted, and hallowed. I am not a man, I am dynamite. . . .'[1]

Nietzsche went insane in 1889—just fifty years before the Second World War. He was ahead of his time to the last.

[1] EH, p. 131.

XII

THE ANTICHRIST

(1)

In his popular *History of Western Philosophy*, Bertrand Russell has been pleased to epitomize Nietzsche's message in the words of the mad King Lear:

> 'I will do such things,—
> What they are, yet I know not; but they shall be
> The terrors of the earth. . . .'

A more imaginative historian than Russell, faced with those last tense weeks in Turin, would rather have recourse to Kent's

> 'He hates him
> That would upon the rack of this tough world
> Stretch him out longer. . . .'

Not that Nietzsche was particularly unhappy at that time: he was particularly cheerful. Notwithstanding occasional forebodings, his spirits throughout the autumn and winter of 1888 never ceased to soar. Rarely had he enjoyed such prolonged freedom from pain, rarely felt so confident of his powers. His letters to Strindberg and others show him possessed once again by the feeling that everything happening to him is meaningful—'there no longer remains any such thing as an accident in my life.'[1] At first glance it would seem as though the mood of *Zarathustra* had returned.

Yet we have only to look a little closer to realize how far otherwise it was. For one thing, the strained and hectic references to his 'mission' that feature more and more frequently in his correspondence suggest a man whistling to keep up his courage rather than one wholly self-reliant. Although he had always been accustomed to 'cast his words ahead of his deeds'—to indenture himself, so to speak, to the task in hand—the element of self-dramatization in these forecasts is new. At times one is uncomfortably reminded of his own description of the philosopher's decline, 'forcing into the light whatever of the agitator and actor lurks in him.'[2] Signs are not wanting even here that 'the long real tragedy is *at an end*, supposing that every philosophy has been a long tragedy in its origin.'[3]

[1] L, 7, 12, 88.   [2] BGE, 25.   [3] *Ibid.*

315

Again, his first sip of fame after so long obscurity seems to have gone straight to his head. No longer content to let the last fruit of his tree ripen in silence, he becomes suddenly impatient for immediate, tangible success. 'Thoughts that come softly like doves guide the world',[1] Zarathustra sang; now Nietzsche wants his progress heralded by trumpets: and, his friends being equipped only with panpipes, has no option but to blow his own. *Ecce Homo* was intended to alert every mind for 'the destructive thunderbolt of the *Transvaluation*, which will send the whole of civilization into convulsions'.[2] A far greater celebrity than Brandes had given him could hardly have wrought such an effect, had his self-command not already been sapped. 'Often struggling with protracted disgust, with an ever-reappearing phantom of disbelief, which makes them cold, and obliges them to languish for *gloria* and devour "faith in themselves" out of the hands of intoxicated adulators: what a *torment* these great artists are and the so-called higher men in general, to him who has once fathomed them!'[3]

Finally, the works of 1888 bear their own witness. For all their ease and brilliance, they lack the warmth, richness and humour of *Zarathustra*. Halévy puts it well: 'his lucidity is extreme, but disastrous, since it exercises itself only to destroy. As one studies the last months of this life, one feels as though one were watching the work of some engine of war which is no longer governed by the hand of man.' A great war the *Transvaluation* had in fact become.

Unable to contain himself any longer, in the late summer Nietzsche actually began this *magnum opus*. But how harsh and crude his berries still were, is shown by the fact that he could only recast it in the form of a polemic, or rather of a series of polemics, in the style of *The Genealogy of Morals*. His final design read as follows:

TRANSVALUATION OF ALL VALUES

BOOK I
The Antichrist: An attempted criticism of Christianity.

BOOK II
The Free Spirit: A criticism of philosophy as a nihilistic movement.

BOOK III
The Immoralist: A criticism of the most pernicious species of ignorance: morality.

BOOK IV
Dionysus: The philosophy of the Eternal Recurrence.

[1] Z, 44.   [2] EH, p. 130.   [3] BGE, 269.

In view of this, it is almost laughable to find him, in *The Twilight of the Idols*, describing his nature as one 'which is affirmative and which concerns itself with contradiction only indirectly and with reluctance'.[1] Much truer rings the statement (only a few pages further on), 'my taste, which is perhaps the reverse of tolerant . . . on the whole it is not over-eager to say *yea*, it would prefer to say *nay*'.[2] The mere juxtaposition of these quotations tells a tale.

Far from marking the end of his inward division, Nietzsche's last works reflect it *in extremis*: so helplessly, indeed, that the ultimate shattering of his personality follows like a logical *finale*. One is tempted to apply to himself his own further words concerning Rousseau: 'in Rousseau there was undoubtedly some brain trouble. . . . His periods of insanity are also those of his misanthropy and mistrust. . . .'[3]

At this point, however, I can hear the reader (supposing a reader to have reached this point) charging me with the very procedure I have censured in other critics: that is, with judging Nietzsche by a standard of my own, which I have as yet done nothing to vindicate. And the charge is perfectly just. He himself was far from admitting that his 'relapse into nihilism' was a relapse; he contended that the negations of *Beyond Good and Evil* were as healthy as the affirmations of *Zarathustra*: and so far I have ignored these contentions. There can be no valid appraisal of *The Antichrist*, much less of his work as a whole, until they have been faced and refuted. I think they can be refuted.

* * *

In the foregoing chapters I have made frequent mention of Freud. He had much in common with Nietzsche—more even than those other two great moulders of the modern mind, Marx and Einstein. In particular, he agreed with Nietzsche that all our instincts can be derived from two fundamental *Triebe*, 'Eros' and 'Thanatos'—the one aiming 'to estab-lish ever greater unities and to preserve them', the other aiming to 'undo connections and so to destroy things'. He agreed, further, in identifying these *Triebe* with 'the pair of opposing forces, attraction and repulsion, which rule in the inorganic world',[4] and therefore in hailing Empedocles as his forerunner. It is, on the face of it, likely that something of value will emerge from a closer comparison of their theories; and it is by way of such a comparison that we can best approach the problem in hand.

What I have just said may appear to contradict the equation drawn earlier between 'the Will to Power' and 'Eros'. But this contradiction is more apparent than real. In all healthy biological functions, according

---

[1] TI, p. 57.   [2] TI, p. 112.   [3] WP, 100.
[4] S. Freud, *An Outline of Psycho-analysis*, Hogarth Press, 1949.

to Freud, Thanatos is subservient to Eros: 'thus, the act of eating is a destruction of the object with the final aim of incorporating it, and the sexual act is an act of aggression having as its purpose the most intimate union.' One might, therefore (and many psychologists do), deny the separate existence of Thanatos altogether, treating it simply as the obverse of Eros. In which case the latter becomes indistinguishable from the Will to Power: for while Nietzsche's Will, like Schopenhauer's, does actually include the two—'the instinct to cleave to something, and the instinct to repel something, are in the inorganic as in the organic world the uniting bond'[1]—he also gives precedence to Eros:

'And he who hath to be a creator in good and evil—verily, he hath first to be a destroyer, and break values into pieces.

'Thus doth the greatest evil belong to the greatest good: that, however, is the creating good.'[2]

Throughout life, Nietzsche maintains in *Zarathustra*, creation involves destruction. There cannot be the one without the other. Just as a chick has to break its egg in order to grow (the analogy preceding these lines provides a fine illustration of Aristotle's dictum, 'a good metaphor implies the intuitive perception of the similarity in dissimilars'), so must even a philosopher be continually demolishing earlier systems, his own included. He must be capable of 'cruelty', towards others and towards himself:

'The thinker who has learned that in us, side by side with all growth, reigns the law of decay, and that such ruthless annihilation and dissolution are necessary for the sake of creation and birth, must furthermore learn to take a kind of delight in this spectacle in order to endure it; otherwise he will lose his aptitude for knowledge. He must, then, have the capacity for a refined cruelty, prepare for that with a firm heart.'[3]

It was on the strength of this conviction that Nietzsche claimed that 'almost everything that we call "higher culture" is based on the spiritualizing and intensifying of *cruelty*'[4]—a tenet which Freud could hardly dispute. They were both, like Dostoievsky, 'cruel geniuses'.

At the same time (in a note of 1883), Nietzsche distinguished sharply between this and the cruelty 'which follows from physical degeneracy (sadism, etc.)'[5]—and the distinction is obviously important: for sadism is a delight in destruction for its own sake. Both Nietzsche, who invariably equates degeneracy with incapacity for creation, and Freud, who sees in it a slight excess of Thanatos, attribute this delight to frustration:

[1] WP, 655.   [2] Z, 34.   [3] N ,XIII, 43.   [4] BGE, 229.   [5] N, XIV, 82.

'Superior spirits run no small danger of learning, one day or another, to look out for the terrible joy which is to be found in destruction, in demolition stone by stone, in the event of creative activity being absolutely denied them, for want of tools or by some other cruel misfortune. For such spirits, there then remains no other alternative; they may feel themselves constrained to destroy, gradually, insidiously, and with diabolical delight, just what they have loved most. Whether a great soul manifests itself beneficently and creatively, or destructively, is a matter of chance. One day a poet might well venture to show us how a God, *through disgust of man, became the tempter and destroyer of man.*'[1]

The resemblance of Nietzsche's theory to Freud's is at this stage really impressive, and of itself provides confirmation of its truth. There was assuredly nothing extravagant in his claim to be 'a peerless psychologist'.[2] Moreover, where they begin to diverge, it is Nietzsche who exhibits the greater insight: on two counts.

In the first place, he states unequivocally that 'it is only if one postulates an *ideal* to be attained, that the words "healthy" and "morbid" make sense':[3] whereas Freud always tended to assume that the 'healthy' was something self-evident, 'given'—indeed, that it was synonymous with the normal. It was thanks to this that he opened the way to the vicious practice of treating as 'maladjusted' all who fail to conform to the ephemeral standards of a particular social order (the psychiatric social worker is blood-brother to the totalitarian inquisitor).

In the second place, while readily admitting that his own ideal too is ultimately a matter of 'taste', Nietzsche both can and does point out that it is at least in line with the general tendency of evolution towards the achievement of ever more complex syntheses—and that we have no standpoint for which to condemn this tendency. Freud, on the other hand, was inclined to regard the syntheses attained by the artist and philosopher, through the sublimation of their instincts, as in some way inferior to those attained at the biological level—and even organic syntheses as mere substitutes for inorganic. He retained, in short, the Schopenhauerian assumption that the whole process of evolution is in reality a gigantic blunder. Had he been more consistent, he would have treated the ascendancy of Eros over Thanatos (but for which this process could never have taken place) as morbid, not as healthy; and, like Schopenhauer, have done all in his power to further the extinction of the species.

I find myself in agreement with Nietzsche on this matter. His argu-

[1] N, XIII, 44.   [2] EH, p. 64.   [3] N, XII, 78.

ments seem to me unanswerable. It is, however, precisely because I agree with him that I pronounce his later nihilism diseased: for, by his own confession, the lust for destruction which begins to triumph in *Beyond Good and Evil* was of the very nature defined in the passage just quoted. It is in the section of *Ecce Homo* devoted to *Beyond Good and Evil* that the following sentences appear:

'Who can guess *what* kind of relaxation is made necessary by such an expenditure of goodness as *Zarathustra* is? Speaking theologically— now pay heed, for it is but seldom that I speak as a theologian—it was God himself who, at the end of his day's work, lay down under the Tree of Knowledge as a serpent. It was thus that he recovered from being God. . . . He had made everything so beautiful. . . . The Devil is simply God's idleness on that seventh day.'[1]

The cruelty of Nietzsche's final period is sublimated sadism—and not always sublimated. The Dionysus of *The Twilight of the Idols* is the deity of the Babylonian Sacaea.

Moreover, the arguments Nietzsche adduces in support of destruction for its own sake only weaken his case: for he continues to appeal to the example of nature in general, and nature, as we have seen, fails to endorse his appeal. We search the organic world in vain for an instance of such destructiveness. He points to the primeval forest creeper (*Salvo matador*); but, as Koestler happens to observe, 'ivy may strangle a tree in its climb towards the light, but it will grow just as well upon a wall, and the destruction of the tree is accidental. Animals kill to devour, in competition for food or mating partners, but their aggressive-defensive behaviour can always be shown to be causally related to the self-assertive tendency, and the assumption of an instinct of cruelty or destruction *per se* is entirely gratuitous.'[2]

Whichever way we approach the matter, this lust for destruction has to be pronounced a perversion; and, when Nietzsche invokes *Zarathustra* in defence of it, a perversion of his own doctrine. Create, and destruction will take care of itself: that is the gospel of *Zarathustra*. Destroy, and creation will take care of itself: that is the gospel of *The Twilight of the Idols*. By the use of the always-equivocal term 'Will to Power', Nietzsche concealed the difference between them, yet it is the difference of life from death, of heaven from hell. And if Dionysus is rightly interpreted as 'the joy of procreative and destructive force, as *unremitting creation*',[3] and the Dionysian as one who has realized 'a temporary identification with the principle of life',[4] then he must be said,

[1] EH, p. 116.   [2] A. Koestler, *Insight and Outlook*.   [3] WP, 1049.   [4] WP, 417.

in addition, to have betrayed both himself and his God.

The tendency to sheer destruction is very deep-rooted in Nietzsche. Though disappointment and disease exacerbated, they did not originate it. It finds vent not only in his attitude towards man, but equally in his attitude towards God.

Every theory of knowledge, he contended, betrays an *arrière-pensée*, and is symptomatic of health or sickness. The predetermined object of Kant's critique was the reinstatement of God; that of his own, God's dethronement. His atheism was not the outcome of a 'disinterested' epistemology; his epistemology was the outcome of his atheism. That is why, in the fourth Part of *Zarathustra*, it is the Murderer of God who first alights on the Eternal Recurrence.

His scepticism, we might say, was symptomatic of a kind of cosmic claustrophobia: and it is not difficult (it may be too simple) to divine the original cause. 'The ingenuity with which a prisoner seeks the means of freedom, the most cold-blooded and patient employment of every smallest advantage, can teach us what tools Nature sometimes makes use of in order to produce Genius. . . . She, Nature, begins it in a dungeon and excites to the utmost its desire to free itself.'[1] Nietzsche began life in a dungeon. He saw the Christian God first as Frau Nietzsche had seen Him—that is to say, as a magnified Frau Nietzsche; and his loathing for this petty, pitiful, protective and retributive deity was precisely equivalent to his loathing for the people who had invented Him. How often must Naumburg have echoed to the protest of *The Dawn of Day*: 'Are we never to have the right of remaining alone with ourselves? are we always to be watched, guarded, surrounded by leading-strings and gifts? If there is always someone round about us, the best part of courage and kindness will ever remain impossible of attainment in this world. Are we not tempted to fly to hell before this continual obtrusiveness of heaven, this inevitable supernatural neighbour?'[2] I have often thought that the nursery at Naumburg must have been adorned with one of those 'all-seeing Eyes' so beloved of pious Victorians.

The Murderer of God speaks in a similar strain. How could he, the Ugliest Man (whose grotesque physiognomy, no doubt, reflected the anarchy of his instincts), endure this universal sensorium? It was the pity of God, he declares, that had made Him insufferable:

'But he—*had* to die: he looked with eyes which beheld *everything*,— he beheld man's depths and dregs, all his hidden ignominy and ugliness.

'His pity knew no modesty: he crept into my dirtiest corners. This most prying, over-intrusive, over-pitiful God had to die.

[1] H,I, 231.   [2] D, 464.

'He ever beheld *me*: on such a witness I would have revenge—or not live myself.'[1]

Nietzsche's loathing of God was equivalent to his loathing of the small man: he was the small man's God. His 'theoretical' and 'practical' nihilism were intimately related. If we have pronounced the one morbid, therefore, must we not pronounce the other so too? The answer is inescapable.

As he himself insisted, however, to explain is not to explain away; and whether or not his atheism was the cause or result of neurosis, it is not refuted thereby. If, as he did, we make health the criterion of good, then indeed we are entitled to call the morality of *The Antichrist* bad. But it is only if we go on to make health the criterion of truth that we are entitled to call his atheism false—and for that there is no warrant whatever. 'There is no pre-established harmony between the promotion of truth and the welfare of mankind.' It may take a madman to live without illusions.

Zarathustra conquers his nihilism. In him, creation prevails over destruction, Eros over Thanatos: he personifies health for this reason. In his teaching, the denial of the intrinsic value of existence is merely the obverse of a triumphant proclamation of values; the craving for independence gives way to a feeling of absolute sovereignty; the murder of God is commemorated by the apotheosis of man: 'but that I may reveal my heart entirely unto you, my friends: *if* there were Gods, how could I endure it to be no God!—*Therefore* there are no Gods!'[2] But Zarathustra never denies the findings of nihilism. How could he?—They are implicit in all his claims.

Zarathustra converts even the nightmare of the Eternal Recurrence into a glorious dream. But he could not accomplish this feat did he not still believe in the Recurrence: and his belief may be justified. For if health is no criterion of truth, still less is a sense of humour; and if a theist may dub the Recurrence the *reductio ad absurdum* of a world without meaning or purpose, so may Nietzsche dub God the *reductio ad absurdum* of a world having both. The conclusion in either case is the same: *credo quia absurdum est*. That his epistemology is a symptom of sickness is no argument against that epistemology. It has to be judged on its merits.

There may have been madness in his method; there was certainly method in his madness—and the method is all-important. The time has come, therefore, to pose the problem directly: how much, if anything,

---

[1] Z, 67.   [2] Z, 24.

of Christianity survives his threefold critique? Can he be said to have demonstrated, first, that the Christian interpretation of the world is incompatible with the modern scientific; secondly, that if science is right, it is wròng; and thirdly, that the only absolute truth is that absolute truth is unattainable?

* * *

Many of the Fathers of Christianity, Greeks that they were and steeped in Hellenistic science, were entranced by the spectacle of an ordered universe. Contemplating the seemingly immutable laws of nature—still, in their day, a relatively novel discovery—they experienced an awe like Kant's in the presence of the starry heavens. So intense was their aesthetic satisfaction that according to St. Athanasius, 'as they tell of Phidias the Sculptor that his works of art by their symmetry and by the proportion of their parts betray Phidias to those who see them, although he is not there, so by the Order of the Universe one ought to perceive God its maker and artificer, even though He be not seen with bodily eyes'. To them, this Order was nothing short of divine. It was only because so many men were impervious to it, Athanasius goes on to contend, that God, the infinitely patient, found it necessary to manifest Himself in a human form as well, that they 'might be able at any rate from what resembled themselves to reason to Him and contemplate Him.' Jesus personified 'the Framing Wisdom which is in the creation'—the Logos.

Now Nietzsche, as we have seen, was no less opposed to this identification of the real with the rational than he was to that of the rational with the real. Whatever goodness, beauty or rationality we find in things, he claimed, we ourselves have laid in them. 'The general character of the world, on the other hand, is to all eternity chaos; not by the absence of necessity, but in the sense of the absence of order, structure, form, beauty wisdom, and whatever else our aesthetic humanities are called.'[1] It was this contention that he wished to uphold by his constantly iterated assertion that 'things' and 'identical things' are our inventions, that logic and mathematics, accordingly, apply only to a fictitious world. He attempted, in short, by dispelling the 'shadows of God', to invalidate the whole conception of the Logos: and the question we have to decide is whether this attempt was successful.

There can be little doubt that in one sense it was. Nietzsche's critique of abstraction must, on any account, be reckoned the first of his two major contributions to the theory of knowledge. Not, of course, because it was wholly original—it is implicit in all great poetry, and many great

[1] JW, 109.

poets have tried to explicate it—but because it took a poet who was also a great philosopher to formulate it systematically, and a philosopher who was also a great poet to translate his formulae back into act.

That the real is the unique, the inimitable, the *nonpareil*; that we depart from the real in proportion as we substitute the word, the concept, the species, the law; that the constraint we are under to create these forms is a 'constraint to adjust a world by means of which *our existence will be assured*';[1] that abstractions are tools in the service of life, which, however fine—and the finer the better, for who wants inaccurate tools? —ought never to tyrannise over life; that life surpasses itself anew as often as, acknowledging this, we ourselves become what we are, the unique, the inimitable, the *nonpareils*: these doctrines of Nietzsche's are immortal; and with them he sounded the death-knell of idealisation.

At the same time, it has to be remembered that the very compulsion he experienced to dissolve the orthodox interpretation resulted in a new interpretation. He could only show that it was, to use his own philological metaphor, 'interpretation and not text',[2] by making the activity of interpretation itself the 'intelligible character' of the world; and although from an orthodox standpoint this activity may be pronounced evil, ugly and irrational, from his own it was nothing of the sort. On the contrary, as *vis creativa*, the Will to Power was actually his criterion of 'the good'. A world of perpetual creation, therefore, could only appear to him as divine as an ordered world did to the Greeks. As long as he believed in it, he was virtually a pantheist; and in one of his most illuminating notes he himself acknowledges, with something like a start of surprise, how closely his *amor fati* resembled the *amor intellectualis* of Spinoza:[3]

'At bottom only the moral God has been overcome. Is there any sense in imagining a God "beyond good and evil"? Would pantheism in *this* sense be possible? Do we withdraw the idea of purpose from the process, and affirm the process notwithstanding? This were so if, within that process, something were *attained* every moment—and always the same thing. Spinoza won an affirmative position of this sort, so far as every moment has a *logical* necessity: and he triumphed by means of his fundamentally logical instinct over such a conformation of the world. ... If every *fundamental trait of character*, which lies beneath every act, and which finds expression in every act, were recognized by the individual as *his* fundamental trait of character, this individual would be

---

[1] WP, 521.   [2] BGE, 22.
[3] The resemblance at one point in *The Twilight of the Idols* is so obvious that his English editor points it out in a footnote.

driven to regard every moment of existence in general, triumphantly as good. It would simply be necessary for that fundamental trait of character to be felt in oneself as something good, valuable, and pleasurable.'[1]

Nietzsche was right: he had overcome only the 'moral God'—the Logos as universal Reason. The Logos as perpetual creation, he had not only failed to dislodge, but gone far towards re-establishing. And this Logos has also had its champions within Christianity—Nicolas Berd-yaev for one. If Christians in general have neglected creativity, leaving it to others to re-affirm, they have only themselves to blame. They have only themselves to blame that certain thinkers today, knowing nothing of the 'procession of the Logos', have begun discussing the 'task of Eros'.

* * *

This brings us to the second question, however: whether, just because it is also an interpretation, Nietzsche's world-view must be set down as a lie?—For that, as we have seen, was his own deduction. His standpoint in this respect was the exact reverse of Spinoza's. 'I know not whether my philosophy is the best,' Spinoza said once, 'but I do know that it is true': 'I know not whether my philosophy is true,' Nietzsche might have said, 'but I do know that it is the best.' It appeared to him literally too good to be true. The more pleasure he derived from his vision, the more he distrusted it: 'people seek a picture of the world in *that* philosophy which gives them the greatest sense of freedom, i.e. in that which gives free play to *their strongest instinct*. This is probably the case with me.'[2] The more he distrusted it, the more strongly he grew persuaded that the activity of interpretation was essentially a falsifying activity (and his critics, of course, have been quick to seize on this deducation, blandly unaware that it if applies to his picture of life, it applies no less to their own). Was this persuasion justified?

Here, once more, the answer seems to be: yes, and no. It was justified in one sense and not in another: for the word 'falsification', as Nietzsche uses it, is itself ambiguous. Ironically enough, in view of his keen eye for linguistic deceptions, he uses it indifferently to denote 'invention' and 'simplification'; and these two activities are scarcely identical. A portrait-painter who simplifies his subject cannot be said to invent it: if he does invent it, he will soon learn the difference when he tries to dispose of his portrait.

In all cognition, Nietzsche gives us to understand, the equalization of

[1] WP, 55.   [2] WP, 418.

unequals is the essential factor. Not merely concepts, but even the data from which concepts are derived, percepts, are really abstractions which, through force of habit, have acquired the status of realities. 'The senses function in the same manner as the "spirit"; they appropriate things, just as science subjugates nature by means of concepts and numbers.'[1] An organism forms its image of the object by the selection of relevant from irrelevant impressions, and the re-combination of the former according to a pattern prescribed by itself. That is, it assimilates the new to the old, old impressions having determined this pattern; it matches whatever comes its way to its already existing stock of experience.

If, therefore, we pronounce abstraction tantamount to invention, the conclusion is inescapable, that all our 'knowledge' is literally fictitious, corresponding to nothing whatever in the world outside ourselves. And this, on occasion, is what Nietzsche actually maintains. 'What would truth then be, all our truth? . . . An unprincipled falsification of the false? A higher degree of falseness?'[2] It is, in fact, by virtue of this pronouncement that he arrives at his conclusion that even relative truth is a chimera —a conclusion which, though he seems not to have realized it, borders on solipsism.

But can this pronouncement be sustained? Surely not—at all events by the arguments he himself adduces. For while it is conceivable, as he suggests in the essay 'On Truth and Falsity', that a human community might impose on its members some entirely arbitrary equation, going on to eliminate all who failed to adopt it, it is quite inconceivable that an exactly similar process of elimination should have prevailed throughout the course of evolution. In making this inference, Nietzsche overlooks the plain fact, that 'natural', no less than 'artificial' (i.e. human) selection presupposes a selector—and that the natural selector can be nothing other than nature itself. To the proposition, 'truths are errors necessary to survival', it is only necessary to rejoin that errors *necessary to survival* are truths—at any rate part-truths.

Again, while it is simple enough, by insisting that 'thought consists in falsifying by transforming, sensation consists in falsifying by transforming, willing consists in falsifying by transforming',[3] to build up a picture of cumulative falsification, which, if it does not actually make nonsense of knowledge, considerably depreciates its sense, we ought not to overlook the fact that every successive 'falsification' corresponds to a fresh range of data. The sum of observations from which we construe the object is by no means so meagre as this would suggest. Indeed, when he calls 'the harmonization of the new material in the old schemes—(Pro-

[1] N, XIV, 50.   [2] WP, 542.   [3] N, XIV, 34.

crustes' bed)',[1] the *essential factor* in cognition, Nietzsche contradicts his own premise, that the Will to Power, far from always taking the line of least resistance, 'goes in search of what resists it'. While we, for example, are undoubtedly aware of a reluctance to modify or abandon old schemes of thought—'the power of the spirit to appropriate foreign elements reveals itself in a strong tendency to assimilate the new to the old, to simplify the manifold, to overlook or repudiate the absolutely contradictory'[2]—we are also, as he avows, aware of a counter-tendency, to acknowledge and master the contradictory, even at the expense of those old schemes and the sense of security conferred by them. *Simplex sigillum veri* tells only half the story.

He himself draws attention to this factor in another connection:

'Little by little, thanks to the sharpening of the senses and the attention, entailed in the conflicts and development of exceedingly complex forms of life, cases of identity or likeness are admitted ever more rarely: whereas to the lower organisms everything seemed "eternally the same", "one", "constant", "absolute", "neutral". Little by little the external world is thus differentiated; but for incalculable periods of time on earth a thing was thought of as identical and consubstantial with a single one of its properties, its colour for example. Only very gradually have the many distinct qualities pertaining to a single thing been granted; even the history of human language betrays a resistance to the multiplication of epithets. . . . The more refined the senses, the stricter the attention, the more numerous the demands of life, the harder also it became to admit that our "knowledge" of a thing, a fact, amounts to a definitive knowledge, to a "truth". Finally, when our methodical caution brings us to the point we have reached at the present day, we no longer claim the right to speak of truths at all, in an absolute sense—we have abjured our faith in the knowability of things, likewise our faith in knowledge. The "thing" is no more than a fiction (the "thing-in-itself", a contradictory fiction—forbidden!). But equally knowledge itself—absolute, and consequently relative knowledge—is likewise only a fiction.'[3]

This line of thought could perhaps be made to yield the opposite conclusion: namely, that if reality is 'to all eternity chaos', knowledge, as a process of differentiation, approximates ever more closely to reality, and closest of all in this very realization.

[1] WP, 499.
[2] BGE, 230.
[3] N, XIII, 21.

Be that as it may, Nietzsche's equation of abstraction with invention can hardly be justified by the reasons he himself adduces. One is forced to pronounce it arbitrary—an extreme reaction against the doctrine of Ideas. Plato and Schopenhauer having turned similarity into identity, he himself turned it into nonentity. Not content with affirming that an idea is something 'to which nothing corresponds exactly, although many things correspond to it a little',[1] he proceeded to deny that it corresponded to anything whatever. Whereas, according to Plato, the pair of robins that follow me round my garden are merely imperfect reflections of a single, immutable, presumably hermaphroditic Robin, according to Nietzsche, I am probably mistaken in thinking them robins at all: they may resemble each other no more than they resemble me. This, at all events, is what the essay *On Truth and Falsity* suggests: and if I understand it aright, it may not unreasonably be dismissed as one of the extravagancies and vices of the philosopher. It is only when he denotes by 'falsification', 'simplification', that Nietzsche is completely justified.

His repeated contention that knowledge spells falsification in this sense, on the other hand, is incontrovertible—and invaluable. We do not have to deny that the robins I see are robins, in order to admit that they are not the robins they see; we do not have to subscribe to the syllogism, 'there are many kinds of eyes—even the sphinx has eyes—therefore there must be many kinds of "truth", and consequently there can be no truth',[2] in order to admit that nothing would be properly characterized before 'every being had addressed it the question, What is that? and returned an answer'.[3] If 'creating is an act of selecting and of finishing the thing selected',[4] then every body of knowledge veritably is an artistic creation, and to that extent false, subjective, illusory. Since what is relevant to one, moreover, is irrelevant, or differently relevant, to another, every being does veritably live in a world of its own contrivance; and even though these worlds be not mutually exclusive, none can be called definitive or final. His insistence on the specific relativity of truth represents his second major contribution to the theory of knowledge.

Here, indeed, he is supreme: no other philosopher, not even Leibniz, having made the conception of 'perspectivity' so completely his own. Nietzsche was, as we have seen, himself endowed, to his joy and sorrow, with the great dramatist's capacity for adopting numberless viewpoints: hence his seeming inconsistency. He might have exclaimed with Whitman, 'do I contradict myself?—Very well, then, I contradict myself: I

[1] N, XIV, 46.   [2] WP, 540.   [3] WP, 556.   [4] WP, 662.

am large, I contain thousands': what he actually did say was, 'I have many beneath me.' He might have employed, with Kierkegaard and Dostoievsky, the method of 'indirect communication', christening his masks by different names—in which case he would never have been blamed, but only praised, for his inconsistency: he preferred to incur the blame, by christening all but one by the same name—and he was wise to do so; since this blame only goes to show how ingrained the habit still is of looking to a philosopher for final truth—the very habit he wished to contest. His lifelong refusal to imprison himself in a definitive system—even his own—was the seal of his superiority. In future, it will always be the sign of a second-rate mind to claim (as even Schopenhauer still could) to have discovered and presented *the* truth. 'The world, on the contrary, has once more become infinite to us.'

Understood in this way, Nietzsche's absolute scepticism is a prophyllactic against dogmatism, and all that Berdyaev denotes by the term 'objectification'; the fact that he remained to the last 'master of his convictions', the quintessence of his theory and practice. 'We must ourselves', he once wrote, 'be like God: just towards all things, kind, "solar"; and as we have created them, incessantly create anew'[1]—and that is precisely what he did. He painted his portrait, only to wash it out before the colours had time to fade: 'it is in the annihilation of even the most beautiful appearance that Dionysian joy attains its summit.'[2] He wove his interpretation, only, the moment the pattern was complete, to toss it aside as one 'falsification' among innumerable others: and as often as he did so, the observer was reincorporated in the observed. 'We thus realize to ourselves ... the tragic artist himself when he proceeds like a luxuriantly fertile divinity of individuation to create his figures (in which sense his work can hardly be understood as an "imitation of nature")—and when, on the other hand, his vast Dionysian impulse then engulfs the entire world of phenomena in order to anticipate beyond it, and through its annihilation, the highest artistic primal joy, in the bosom of the Primordial Unity.'[3]

Does all this, however, invalidate his world-view? Not in the least: it confirms it. For, though symbol and reality can never be the same—though Nietzsche will not allow even the formula, Eternal Recurrence, to be more than 'the very nearest approach of a world of Being to a world of Becoming'[4]—it was precisely this Dionysian rapture that his world-view was designed to body forth. 'Dionysus speaks the language of Apollo. Apollo, however, finally speaks the language of Dionysus;

[1] N, XII, 170.   [1] N, XIV, 366.   [3] BT, 22.   [4] WP, 101.

and so the highest good of tragedy'—and of tragic philosophy—'is attained.'[1]

* * *

Nietzsche did not succeed in demonstrating either the incompatibility of a Christian interpretation of the world with the modern scientific, or its absolute subjectivity. What he did demonstrate (so far as such a thing is possible) was rather its relative truth. But we have still to ask the final question: whether, that is, in the very realization of the relativity of truth—when we are lifted, at least for a moment, above and beyond the whole process—knowledge itself is not transformed, and absolute truth made accessible after all?

Nietzsche, of course, denied this too:

'Nowadays I am not much impressed when somebody remarks, with the modesty of philosophical scepticism or a religious resignation, "the essence of things is unknown to me", or somebody else, who, though braver, has yet to learn sufficiently what is meant by criticism and distrust, "the essence of things is for the most part unknown to me". I object to both that they still presume and claim to know far too much: as though the distinction they both draw at the outset, the distinction between "the essence of things" and the phenomenal world were legitimate! In order to make good such a distinction, it would be necessary to represent our intellect as possessed of a contradictory character: on the one hand, designed to see from a perspective (after the manner required of creatures of our species, if they are to maintain themselves in existence), and on the other hand, endowed simultaneously with a faculty for conceiving this seeing *as* a seeing from a perspective, the phenomenon *as* a phenomenon; as capable, in other words, both of believing in "reality" as though that alone existed, and also of judging this belief a perspective-limitation with respect to a true reality. But a belief judged in this way is no longer a belief: as a belief, it is dissolved. In fine, we must not conceive our intellect in such a contradictory way, as at one and the same time a belief and a knowledge that this belief is only a belief. Let us get rid of the thing-in-itself, and along with it, of one of the vaguest concepts there are, the "phenomenon". This whole antinomy, equally with the older one of "matter" and "spirit", has shown itself useless.'[2]

Nietzsche will not allow that even at 'the height of contemplation' when the Self is not only reincorporated into nature, but knows itself reincorporated, the activity of valuation is suspended, or objectivity

[1] BT, 21.   [2] N, XIII, 48.

attained. The eternity of Becoming is itself apprehended in time, and can, for this reason, only be conceived as an eternal recurrence of Becoming. He will not exempt anything whatever from the flux. Perspectivity is ultimate and inescapable, phenomenality all-inclusive. Hence his horror of 'the abyss', for him synonymous with 'the void'; his incessant and terrifying oscillation between 'cosmic claustrophobia' and a kind of cosmic agoraphobia.

'Error reached its zenith', he wrote, 'when Schopenhauer taught: *in the release from passion and will* alone lay the road to "truth", to knowledge; the intellect freed from will *could not help* seeing the true and actual essence of things.'[1] He clung to this assertion to the end: and nobody, who has appropriated his critique of Idealism, can wholly regret that he did. *If* there is such a thing as 'disinterestedness', it can only be attained through the reduction to interest of virtually all that has gone by the name—including not merely that possessive 'love', which he identified with the Christian, but even the 'new love' he sought to substitute. *If* there is such a thing as Being, it can only be apprehended through the annihilation of every concept of Being. This book is for those who have either submitted or are prepared to submit to the full impact of Nietzsche's critique.

Nevertheless, it is clear that his theory, in the passage just quoted, flies in the face of his practice. What he here declares impossible to do was what he himself was continually doing. He himself was continually incorporating the observer in the observed; and that this incorporation was no theoretical exercise, the whole of *Zarathustra* bears witness. 'Under the charm of the Dionysian, not only is the covenant between man and man again established, but also estranged, hostile or subjugated nature again celebrates her reconciliation with her lost son, man.' Only one conclusion is feasible. If this conscious reconciliation is an intellectual impossibility, then, under the charm of the Dionysian, the intellect is either transformed or transcended.

Nietzsche refused to accept that conclusion. He had delivered his verdict on transcendentalism in *Human, All-too-Human*, and nothing could make him go back on it—not even the experience that converted the physician of *The Dawn of Day* into the visionary of *The Joyful Wisdom*. To have admitted two kinds of knowledge would have been like admitting a new dualism; to have admitted a new dualism would have been to open the back door to God. Rather than that, he preferred to plunge into a *circulosus vitiosus*.

Yet the result of his refusal is chaos. Reducing the knowledge he

[1] WP, 612.

actually possesses of the interpretative function of the intellect to the level of an interpretation, he virtually denies that knowledge: just as, reducing his 'beyond good and evil' to the level of his own 'good', he virtually denies 'beyond good and evil'—with what fatal repercussions we have seen. In fact, these two reductions are one and the same. His moral confusion is found, after all, to be bound up with an intellectual confusion, and that, in its turn, with an extreme reaction against Idealism. To put it another way: his inveterate atheism issued in hopeless contradictions, and these contradictions are its refutation.

The more persistently, determinedly, heroically, Nietzsche struggles to annihilate Being, the more inexorably he vindicates Being. Surely he must himself have realized this on occasion?—There is evidence that he did. Not even he was able consistently to abjure the reward of his renunciation. To Rohde he might write (and by 1887 it was probably true), 'I have not yet abandoned all hope of finding a way out of the abyss, by means of which we can arrive at "something" ';[1] but to himself he had already confided: 'You say that this is the spontaneous decomposition of God?—It is nothing more than the casting of a skin: he divests himself of his moral integument, and soon you will find him again—beyond good and evil.'[2]

Nietzsche never published such *pensées* as this: he was not sufficiently sure of himself. They were found among his posthumous papers. Had it not been for the piety of his friends and relatives, we might never have known how close he came to acknowledging the reality of the Logos. But that he did come close—and that, not in his moments of weakness, but at the period of his maximum strength—is barely contestable. The abyss was not always empty.

'Modern man has generally applied to a God his faculties of idealization, *moralizing him* more and more. What does that signify? Nothing good, the diminution of human strength.

'The reverse would be possible in itself; and there are indications of it. God conceived as emancipation from morality, concentrating in himself the antinomies of life in all their plenitude, *redeeming* them, *justifying* them through divine martyrdom; God as what is beyond and above this miserable, beggarly morality of good and evil.'[3]

Dieu est mort: vive Dieu!

* * *

In the magnificent parable of 'The Madman' (*The Joyful Wisdom*, Aph. 125), Nietzsche epitomized his message once and for all. He him-

[1] L, 23, 5. 87.   [2] N, XII, 329.   [3] WP, 1035.

self had no doubt where his chief significance lay: in his being the first atheist. The revolt against God is the mainspring of all his thought, as it is of the twentieth century's. If the twentieth century has not yet caught up with him, that is because it has not dared face the ultimate consequences of this revolt. It is still a timid century.

Nobody will blame it for that. It is a fearful thing to fall out of the hands of the living God—just how fearful, Nietzsche's destiny reveals: for he did face them. As Karl Jaspers has said, along this road there is no possibility of going beyond him: the last word has been spoken. But what was the last word?—as we have seen, it was inconclusive. He did not succeed in invalidating the Christian conception of the Logos; it could be held that he vindicated it—as a principle of perpetual creation, Eros.

Nevertheless, we must beware of aligning ourselves with those facile debaters known to G. K. Chesterton, who, 'by a typical transition, passed from the gratifying thought that Nietzsche attacked Christianity, to the natural inference that he was a True Christian.' Not only was Nietzsche neither a True Christian nor a false, but his significance, both negative and positive, is bound up with the fact that he was neither.

No one can be called Christian, in even the most unorthodox sense, who does not acknowledge in Jesus Christ the 'divine martyr' who reveals the nature of God: and Nietzsche was as far from acknowledging that in his period of maximum strength as he was in his moments of weakness—indeed farther. We have still to take up his final challenge, thrown out in what were almost the last coherent words he uttered, the last words of *Ecce Homo*:

'You have understood me? *Dionysus* versus *the Crucified.*'

(2)

From the time of *Zarathustra* onwards, Nietzsche was more or less continually measuring himself against Jesus of Nazareth. His interpretation of history compelled him to do so. His mission being, as he saw it, to turn right way up what Plato had turned upside down, he had no option but to look on the *Transvaluation* as a new *Republic*. Jesus, 'God on the Cross', being the symbol under which the first great transvaluation of values had triumphed in the ancient world, he had no option but to look on Zarathustra as a counter-symbol, himself as a counter-Jesus. The title he eventually chose for the first book of the *Transvaluation*,

The Antichrist, was a challenging assertion of this role. So was the title, *Ecce Homo*.

On the strength of this, it is now *de rigeur* among theologians to claim that Nietzsche really revered Jesus more than any other figure in history; and those last mad notes of his, signed alternately 'Dionysus' and 'The Crucified', are invoked in evidence. For this claim there is little warrant. Indeed, it is positively misleading. If the notes can be taken to prove anything at all, it is that he identified Jesus with the decadent half of himself, the Judaic, just as he came to identify Dionysus with the anti-Judaic, the Roman. Like all the pathetic memorials of his breakdown, they reflect the final disruption of a personality. He is identified in turn with every one of his contending instincts ('I am Prado, I am father Prado also. I venture to say that I am Lesseps as well'),[1] because he no longer possesses any identity of his own.

Nietzsche pitied Jesus, certainly; he thought his own suffering had allowed him 'to have intercourse with the anchorites and the misunderstood of every age'.[2] He might even have written of Jesus what he wrote of Socrates, 'I confess that he is so close to me that I am nearly always struggling against him.'[3] But he did not revere Jesus, let alone regard him as his superior. On the contrary, he pronounced him unintelligent compared with Socrates, and fanatical compared with Plato —since Plato, he suspected, had never really believed in his belief.

He saw in Jesus always the embodiment of his own earliest ideal—an ideal he had long since discarded. The greatness of the Hebrew lay in his potentialities, not his actual achievement. This is stated unequivocally through the lips of Zarathustra:

'Verily, too early died that Hebrew whom the preachers of slow death honour: and to many hath it proved a fatality that he died too early.

'As yet he had known only tears, and the melancholy of the Hebrew, together with the hatred of the good and the just—the Hebrew Jesus! then was he seized with the longing for death.

'Had he but remained in the wilderness, and far from the good and the just! Then, perhaps, he would have learned to live, and love the earth—and laughter also!

'Believe it, my brethren! He died too early; he himself would have disavowed his doctrine had he attained to my age! Noble enough was he to disavow!'[4]

Whether accepting Schopenhauer or rejecting him, Nietzsche never

[1] L, 5, 1, 89.   [2] NZ, 75.   [3] N, X, 217.   [4] Z, 21.

ceased to see Jesus through Schopenhauer's eyes, as the 'personification of the denial of the will to live'.

It is perfectly true, all the same, that *though* he did not revere Jesus—perhaps *because* he did not—his interpretation of history, and therefore of his own role in history, stands or falls with his representation of Jesus. If he was mistaken in this, he was mistaken in much else as well: and I, for one, believe he was radically mistaken.

* * *

In saying this, I do not mean to dispute Schopenhauer's elucidation of the highest common factor in all the great world religions. In the religion of Jesus, as in Buddhism and Hinduism, there undoubtedly is an element of world-negation, which it was one of Schopenhauer's outstanding merits to have brought to the fore again, at a time when prevalent optimism was in danger of eclipsing it altogether. Jesus preaches the end of this world, and its supersession by the Kingdom of God. His preaching originates in an act of self-transcendance, which is at the same time a transcendence of life.

Nietzsche, moreover, who had studied the Eastern religions on his own account, showed himself even better-informed than his master on this matter, since he realized that, along with life, morality itself was transcended. Quoting the disciple of the Vedanta, 'the good and the evil he shakes from off him, sage that he is; his kingdom suffers no more from any act; good and evil, he goes beyond them both', and the Buddhist's 'good and evil, both are fetters: the perfect man is master of them both', he declares in *The Genealogy of Morals*, 'the fact that they remained *true* on this point is perhaps to be regarded as the best piece of realism in the three greatest religions, otherwise so completely steeped in morality.'[1]

He realized that in Buddhism at least 'a subtle transcendence of morality is thought out.'[2] It was for this reason that he rated it the highest of the three, and thought Europe only just ripe for it:

'Buddhism is the only really *positive* religion to be found in history, even in its epistomology (which is strict phenomenalism)—it no longer speaks of the "struggle with *sin*", but fully recognizing the true nature of reality it speaks of the "struggle with *pain*". It already has—and this distinguishes it profoundly from Christianity,—the self-deception of moral concepts beneath it,—to use my own phraseology, it stands *beyond* good and evil.'[3]

If he censured Buddhism, therefore, it was because, *notwithstanding* its

[1] GM, III, 17.　　[2] WP, 155.　　[3] A ,20.

transcendence of morality, it continued to preach a denial of life; because even its amoral Beyond was pitted against the phenomenal. And here he was probably correct: for rich as the Indian tradition is in varieties of holiness, it can hardly be disputed that the saint who has virtually ceased to live, even while his body still breathes, occupies a pre-eminent position. His is the ideal that recurs most persistently, and, as often as it does recur, commands the deepest veneration. In Hinduism, too, even when action is not wholly discountenanced as incompatible with sanctity, it is rarely allowed that sanctity should determine the action. The warrior of the *Bhagavadgita* is enjoined to discharge the duties of his caste in a spirit of total detachment: the duties remain what they were.

Whether or not this ideal is true to the Eastern religions, however, it is completely untrue to the religion of Jesus of Nazareth. In representing the Hebrew as a 'Buddha on a soil only very slightly Hindu',[1] Nietzsche, like Schopenhauer, flew in the face of facts. Nowhere in the Gospels is there the slightest suggestion of 'an instinctive hatred of all reality, a flight into the "intangible", into the "incomprehensible" ';[2] let alone of 'a feeling at one's ease in a world in which no sort of reality is any longer visible, a merely "inner" world, a "true" world, an "eternal" world.'[3] If these are symptoms of morbidity, morbidity is conspicuous by its absence.

'Ye may be the children of your Father which is in heaven, for he maketh his sun to rise on the evil and on the good, and sendeth rain on the just and on the unjust.' In those words, the transcendence of good and evil is explicit; and Nietzsche was right, doubly right, when he insisted that this blessedness, according to Jesus, was something to be experienced, not only after physical death, but here and now; and that every man capable of experiencing it was potentially a 'son of God'. 'With the word "Son", *entrance* into the feeling of the general trans-figuration of all things (beatitude) is expressed, with the word "Father", *this feeling itself*, the feeling of eternity and perfection.'[4] But—the very words make it unmistakable—this beatitude, so far from implying a denunciation of reality, is an 'eternal affirmation of all things, "a tre-mendous saying of Yea and Amen" '; and, so far from issuing in a renunciation of life, spells the beginning of a new life, the keynote of which is spontaneity.

Jesus's own example bears this out. 'I am opposed,' Nietzsche says, 'to the importation of the fanatic into the type of the Saviour: the word "*impérieux*" which Renan uses in itself annuls the type.'[5] There is, in-

---

[1] A, 31.   [2] A, 29.   [3] *Ibid.*   [4] A, 34.   [5] A, 32.

deed, no place for the hero-will in either Jesus's character or his teaching; any more than there is for asceticism *per se* (the man whom his contemporaries could describe as a wine-bibber and a glutton was assuredly no St. Anthony). His bearing is characterized throughout by an effortless beauty and grace; he summons men to live and grow as naturally as the lilies of the field: 'consider the lilies of the field, how they grow; they toil not, neither do they spin: and yet I say unto you, That even Solomon, in all his glory, was not arrayed like one of these.' It was only by dismissing this saying with a Voltairean jibe, that Nietzsche could sustain his thesis of a Saviour who had still to learn how to live and love the earth. It sounds, like most of the parables, the authentic accent of all great poetry.

It was only, again, by dismissing the narrative of the Temptation and the simile of the house swept and garnished—not to speak of 'whosoever shall lose his life, shall preserve it'—that he could bring himself to declare, 'the faith which raises its voice here is not a faith that has been won by a struggle, —it is to hand, it was there from the beginning, it is a sort of spiritual return to childishness.'[1] Jesus had reconquered his innocence; if he spoke of becoming as a little child, what did he more than Zarathustra?

Jesus does not so much command as communicate. He does not lay down a new moral law, which has only to be obeyed; he quickens the impulse that may carry a man beyond morality: 'Jesus said to his Jews: "The law was for servants;—love God as I love him, as his Son! What have we Sons of God to do with morals!"'[2] He never prescribes the actions of the reborn man; insofar as he enunciates an ideal, it is an ideal that follows inevitably upon rebirth. 'A man as he *ought* to be,' said Nietzsche, 'sounds to me in just as bad taste as: "A tree as it ought to be".'[3] But, on the lips of a forester, 'a tree as it ought to be' has a very definite meaning: it means a tree not stunted by adverse winds nor trimmed to an alien mould, a tree which has succeeded in realizing the full potentialities of its species: and men might expand like oaks and hawthorns—'a grand democracy of forest trees'.

Jesus, to be sure, did not believe that all men would respond to his summons: he frankly declared that it was not for us to decide who would or who would not—the wheat and the tares must be allowed to grow up together. But even among those who did, he looked for no uniformity. Their performance would vary, both in degree and in kind, according to their natural 'talents'. If he proclaimed the essential equality of the 'sons

---

[1] A, 32.   [2] BGE, 164.   [3] WP, 332.

of God', therefore, it was not an equality that conflicted with hierarchy: the two principles were at one in his doctrine.

Again, though his name for the vital centre in man, the plastic power, was 'love', and this name has lent itself to every manner of abuse, to equate that love with an irresistible horror of suffering is to do violence to both his preaching and his practice. The teaching of Jesus was a hard one—and he himself was hard enough for it. Gentle Jesus, meek and mild, exists nowhere but in stained-glass windows. Not only did he face persecution and promise it to his disciples, but he never shrank from inflicting pain and urged them to follow his example. 'If any man come to me, and hate not his father, and mother, and wife, and children, and brethren, and sisters . . .'—it is one of the hardest sayings on record. He came not to bring peace, but a sword—and his polemics against the good and the just betray a master of spiritual warfare. If the Jesus of *The Antichrist* is a eunuch, it was Nietzsche who emasculated him.

All the same—and this is essential—destruction for its own sake derives no authority from the Gospels. Even the Law, Jesus affirmed, he came not to destroy but fulfil. There is no trace of reactiveness here. His life, in fact, was one long summons to creative action: and so was his death. For it was such action, and such alone, that could determine the advent of the Kingdom. 'The Kingdom of heaven suffereth violence, and the violent take it by force.'

That sentence, as Schweitzer has shown, is crucial: and marks the fundamental distinction between the religion of Jesus, on the one hand, and Hinduism or Buddhism on the other. In the religion of Jesus, world-negation passes over immediately into world-affirmation: or rather, the two elements are combined. The world is admitted to be doomed, to be transitory, to be void of intrinsic value, to be destined for no temporal millennium; at the same time, its supersession by the Kingdom of God is posited as dependent upon the creative action of men: the harvest presupposes the sowing; the sowing, the sower. 'The essence of Christianity,' says Schweitzer, 'is world-affirmation which has gone through an experience of world-negation. In the eschatological world-view of world-negation, Jesus proclaims the ethic of active love.'

It was this unique combination of elements that Schopenhauer overlooked; and Nietzsche followed in his steps. Perhaps he could not have done otherwise. Perhaps, before Schweitzer elucidated the late-Jewish eschatology, a convincing representation of Jesus was impossible, and he had no option but to do what Tolstoy and others had done, namely, imagine a type which fitted some of the facts, and dismiss the others as interpolations. At Bonn, he had studied the work of 'the incomparable

Strauss',[1] on the sources of the synoptic Gospels, only to conclude that texts so disputable could never yield what he wanted—a world-view to rely on and live by; later on he belittled the whole attempt to arrive at an authentic portrait. The fact remains that he was wrong. If his representation of Jesus is a little more plausible than the Orthodox, that is its only merit.

* * *

Nietzsche was mistaken about Jesus: that is why he could not revere him, but only pity and patronise. He was also, as it happens, mistaken about St. Paul, whom, as the founder of the Church, he could only abuse and anathematize. The Church representing, in his view, a travesty and a betrayal of everything Jesus had stood for, his hatred for the apostle was proportionate to his affection for the master: he would admit no redeeming feature in this 'pernicious blockhead',[2] 'this appalling impostor'.[3] Yet in this case the mistake is less easily explained or excused: first, because we possess reliable documents on which to base a representation; and secondly, because, in all antiquity, it would be hard to find a figure more resembling Nietzsche himself.

To begin with, Paul, like Nietzsche, was brought up a Pharisee of the Pharisees. The victim of a rigorous orthodoxy, imposed from earliest childhood, he knew all there was to know of the bitter results of repression. His letters are crowded with reminiscences of the savage, unsuccessful war he had waged on his instinctive nature; his incurable thorn in the flesh may well have been a legacy from it. In the name of the Law, he had striven to subdue his desires, and the sole outcome had been to exacerbate them. 'He knew from experience that he—violent, sensual, melancholy and malicious in his hatred as he was—*could* not fulfil the Law; and furthermore, what seemed strangest of all to him, he saw that his boundless craving for power was continually provoked to break it, and that he *could not* bear up against this thorn.'[4] Paul—or rather, Saul—must, as Nietzsche infers, have been heartily sick of the Law long before he dared to admit it, and partially identified with its breakers, even while persecuting them.

Such a conflict as this, we know, cannot persist indefinitely: and in Paul it came to a head on the road to Damascus. What happened there? According to Nietzsche, Paul suddenly realized that he had only to acknowledge Jesus the Christ to be exempt from obedience to the Law —more than that, to wreak his revenge on the Law: 'his mind was suddenly enlightened, and he said to himself: 'It is *unreasonable* to persecute this Jesus Christ! Here is my means of escape, here is my complete

[1] A, 28.   [2] WP, 169.   [3] A, 45.   [4] D, 68.

vengeance, here and nowhere else have I the *annihilator of the Law* in my hands!" "[1] He thereupon experienced an immense emotional release, accompanied by visionary symptoms.

This interpretation, however, is transparently superficial—as superficial as Freud's. It locates the Damascus road on the first stage of the journey from the Underworld. What actually took place was infinitely more revolutionary. Far from reacting against the Law, Paul surpassed it. In other words, he passed beyond good and evil; and it was precisely on this account that he was able to salute in Jesus 'the first to be reaped of those who sleep in death'.

That this was the case, his whole teaching makes clear beyond cavil. Paul perceives, indeed, that his very adherence to the Law has been the cause of his division and 'death'. Once, as a child, he had lived 'without the law'; subsequently, 'the command came home to me, sin sprang to life and I died'. The passions, he reiterates, become evil and malignant when regarded with evil and malignant eyes: 'why, had it not been for the Law, I would never have known what sin meant! . . . The command gave an impulse to sin, and sin resulted for me in all manner of covetous desire—for sin, apart from the Law, is lifeless.' For this reason he will not allow that the Law proceeded directly from God.

At the same time (and it is here that he differs from Marcion), neither will he allow that it was a purely devilish imposition: 'what follows from this? That "the Law is equivalent to sin?" Never!' On the contrary, it is something to be blessed in retrospect, 'for through the Law I died to the Law, that I might live for God'.—No Law, no 'death'; no 'death', no resurrection. All things work together for good!

Nietzsche held Paul responsible for 'the doctrine of *Resurrection*, by means of which the whole concept "blessedness", the entire and only reality of the Gospel, is conjured away—in favour of a state *after* death!'[2] From this, in his view, followed the poisoning of the world by the theory of vicarious sacrifice and the practice of self-laceration. Yet the slenderest acquaintance with the Epistles should have sufficed to convince him that the resurrection referred to by Paul is an experience undergone here and now. Nietzsche was actually echoing Paul, when he spoke of himself as having died many times over.

The 'risen' are those who, having been beyond good and evil, have already entered upon a new life; the distinctive feature of which is the *supersession* of the deadly conflict of mind and body. They are those who are guided no longer either by the Law, or by the passions provoked by the Law, but by that which is deeper and stronger than either—what

[1] D, 68.   [2] A, 41.

Paul called 'love' or the spirit of Christ. It is by virtue of this that they constitute together the Mystical Body of Christ, and experience day by day the glorious liberty of the sons of God.

'Wherever the Spirit of the Lord is, there is open freedom.' Paul's doctrine is first and foremost one of emancipation, from both sin and the sense of sin. To the risen, he affirms, all things are lawful, even though not all are expedient; and that is why, like Jesus, he discourages asceticism for its own sake. Thanks to the Incarnation, body and mind alike are sanctified—the body is made a temple of God. To say of Paul, as Nietzsche says, that even he 'could not help admitting the awkward fact that the body still remained',[1] is like saying of Sigmund Freud that even he could not help admitting that men had a sexual instinct.

Paul's teaching on marriage illustrates this. Like Nietzsche (and incidentally, like nearly every other philosopher), he 'shudders mortally at *marriage*, together with all that persuades him to it—marriage as a fatal hindrance on the way to the optimum';[2] he treats it, in general, as a thing not expedient, inasmuch as family ties may distract a man from his task, especially in times of persecution; he counsels his converts to avoid it: 'not that I want to restrict your freedom; it is only to secure decorum and concentration upon a life of devotion to the Lord'. On the other hand, Paul is emphatic that what is good for one may not be good for another, and that it is for each to discover for himself the conditions of his own best performance: 'thus both are right, alike in marrying and refraining from marriage.'

Paul's attitude here is not at all unlike Nietzsche's; nor is his attitude towards the past: for, of course, he was liberally endowed with the historical sense; his experience was turned immediately to the illumination of history as he knew it. He sees mankind in the likeness of one man, struggling from the innocence enjoyed by the patriarchs, who lived without consciousness of sin, through the conflict engendered by the Law, in whose name the offspring of the promise was crucified, towards that reintegration of which Christ is at once the prototype and symbol. This interpretation of history is the source of his apocalyptic enthusiasm:

'The destiny of the Jews, yea, of all mankind, seemed to him to be intertwined with this instantaneous flash of enlightenment: he held the thought of thoughts, the key of keys, the light of lights; history would henceforth revolve around him! From that time onward he would be the apostle of the *annihilation of the Law*!'[3]

That is Nietzsche's description of Paul at the date of his conversion.

[1] WP, 659.   [2] GM, III, 7.   [3] D, 68.

It might equally well be a description of himself in the summer of 1881:
and the likeness is not accidental. Christianity inherited its belief in a
meaning of history from the Prophets—it was one of those 'Jewish
accretions' which Schopenhauer wished to see expunged—and, though
he did not know it, Nietzsche inherited it from Christianity. Of all the
astonishing statements contained in his notes on religion, none is more
flatly at variance with the facts than that which reads: 'Christianity ... is
from top to bottom unhistorical, since it denies that the millennia to
come can show anything that is not now, and has not been for the last
eighteen hundred years, within reach of anybody. If, despite that, the
spirit of the present epoch is historical through and through, this only
goes to show that mankind is no longer submissive to the Christian
yoke, that it is becoming pagan once more, as it was thousands of
years ago.'[1] The Romantic Myth, in all its forms, is secularized apocalyp-
ticism.

Paul to be sure, formulated his vision in the terms of late-Jewish
eschatology. To this belongs his belief in an imminent end of the world,
a resurrection of the dead with the dying, a judgement of men and angels.
His mysticism can never be wholly divorced from the world-view it re-
informed, and it is mistaken to try and divorce it. Even so, to speak of
Paul as importing Jewish conceptions into the primitive Buddhism of
Jesus is preposterous—and not only because there never was such a
primitive Buddhism. Insofar as his world-view was Judaic, he shared it
with Jesus himself; insofar as his mysticism was original, it combined,
like Jesus's own, the two elements of world-negation and world-
affirmation.

This eschatology, it scarcely needs saying, lent itself to abuse.
Whether or not it had originated in the compensatory dreams of the
oppressed, it certainly helped to reinforce them. It may even be true, as
Nietzsche thought, that Jesus and Paul paid dearly for addressing themselves to the Chandala. The herd-solidarity, the resentment, the escap-
ism, of the slave were bound to adapt the Gospel 'according to a scheme
embodying *profoundly different needs*'.[2] It is by no means unlikely, as he
followed Bauer in presuming, that the portrait of the Saviour was 'enriched retrospectively, with features which can be interpreted only as
serving the purposes of war and propaganda.'[3] At all events, much that
Jesus opposed found its way into Christian doctrine, and much that
he affirmed was distorted out of all recognition.

Nevertheless, to hold Paul responsible for this corruption is to do
violence to the documentary evidence: his own teaching was abused as

[1] N, X, 273.   [2] WP, 195.   [3] A, 31.

much as Jesus's. Furthermore, when all is said and done, the corruption was never so complete as Nietzsche supposed. To say that 'the whole of the Christian *creed*—all Christian "truth" is idle falsehood and deception, and is precisely the reverse of that which was at the bottom of the first Christian movement,'[1] is to be guilty of more than over-simplification. Even Schopenhauer had to admit, with a sigh, that the pessimism, asceticism and life-denial of the Church were for ever being qualified, not to say overwhelmed, by precisely the opposite valuations.

* * *

In one of his notes for *The Antichrist* (those notes that are often more suggestive than the book itself), Nietzsche distinguishes two 'powers that have mastered Christianity'—meaning by Christianity in this case the religion of Jesus: 'Judaism (Paul); Platonism (Augustine).'[2] Paul, we are given to understand, completed a process begun by the first apostles, at a time when belief in the End was still strong; Augustine, a process begun by John at a time when it was already receding. Between them they laid the foundations of Christian Orthodoxy.

So far as Paul is concerned, there is no warrant for this supposition. In him, it was the religion of Jesus that mastered Judaism. But can as much be said of Augustine? Was it, in this case, the religion of Jesus that mastered platonism? The point, obviously, is of very considerable importance, since Nietzsche's case against Christianity was fundamentally his case against Plato, and *The City of God* was the charter of medieval Christendom.

He charged Plato, as we have seen, with dividing the universe, because he was powerless to heal his own division; with inventing an ideal world, because he could not stomach (i.e. digest and assimilate) the real. He saw in his dualism, in short, a symptom of decadence: and there is much to be said for the diagnosis. It is, in fact, powerfully corroborated by Augustine himself, who, as a neo-platonist, was confessedly a man thus divided.

In Augustine, as in Saul, instinct and reason were violently at odds. His sensuality was in continual revolt against his intellectual ideal. He was melancholy and malicious in his hatred of the flesh; and, in his autobiography, he shows how intimately related his world-view was to this state of distress. Incapable of conceiving the body except as evil and in perpetual warfare with the spirit, he could only picture the world and God as two mutually exclusive 'substances', and was tormented by the problem of evil: 'I sought "whence is evil", and found no way . . .'

The essence of Augustine's conversion to Christianity, however—

[1] WP, 158.   [2] WP, 214.

the central fact, to which he returns again and again—was precisely his surmounting of this cleavage: in himself first of all, and by consequence in his world-view. This is what constitutes the climax of the *Confessions*: the realization, which seems to have reached him in a flash, that to condemn the nature of the universe, in the name of some purely human, relative 'good', was little less than megalomaniac; and that, in the Light of Eternity as he puts it, 'whatsoever is, is good':

'And I saw that all things did harmonize, not with their places only, but with their seasons. And that Thou, who only art Eternal, didst not begin to work after innumerable spaces of time spent; for that all spaces of times, both which have passed, and which shall pass, neither go nor come, but through Thee, working, and abiding. And I perceived and found it nothing strange, that bread which is pleasant to a healthy palate, is loathsome to one distempered; and to sore eyes light is offensive, which to the sound is delightful.'

It is this realization that prompts Augustine to invoke the Psalms of David—those Psalms which Nietzsche acclaimed for their triumphant affirmation of life.

It is this also that accounts for the peculiar affinity he felt with Paul: 'for he who extols the nature of the soul as the chief good, and condemns the nature of the flesh as if it were evil, assuredly is fleshly both in his love of the soul and hatred of the flesh.' He is at one with Paul in his conviction that 'if the Law be present with its command, and the Spirit be absent with His help, the presence of the prohibition serves only to increase the desire to sin'; at the same time, he is at one with him in his gratitude for 'those silent contritions of my soul' which have proved the preconditions of his knowledge. It is no accident that both men are labelled predestinarians and fatalists: they were, for they loved their fate.

Nietzsche was as mistaken about Augustine as he was about Paul. If their religion was Christianity, therefore—and this can hardly be contested—he was mistaken about Christianity itself. 'Platonism for the people'[1] is exactly what this religion was *not*. The example of Augustine, moreover, artist in words that he was, and profoundly versed in ancient philosophy, refutes not only the allegation that '*Christianity* is a nay-saying to the natural',[2] but, even more emphatically, the allegation that 'it is opposed to every *intellectual* movement, to all philosophy: it takes up the cudgels for idiots, and utters a curse upon the intellect.'[3]

The charge of 'anti-intellectualism', indeed, is just as foolish when

[1] BGE, Preface.   [2] WP, 147.   [3] WP, 154.

applied to the Fathers of the Church as it is when applied to Nietzsche. The 'wisdom of this world', which they attacked, was the same that he attacked, namely, the wisdom of Plato; and if their gospel was 'foolishness to the Greeks', would not his own have been? Tertullian, to be sure, denounced both science and art as redundant since the coming of Christ—but Tertullian was condemned as a heretic; Clement of Alexandria averred that there were two Old Testaments, the Bible and Greek philosophy—and Clement was canonized. Far from destroying what was left of classical culture, after the blond beasts had done their work, Christianity did much to preserve it; and it was just because it did so, that it was able, in the fullness of time, not merely to endure, but to inspire, the culture of the late Middle Ages.

Nietzsche was blind to that culture—that unity of artistic style in every aspect of the people's life. The very vividness with which he perceived and portrayed the hellenic world may have been responsible for his blindness: to the eye trained on Minerva, the moon itself is a blur. Yet the culture of the Renaissance too was rooted in it. The Renaissance was not all a revolt; nor were its foremost representatives aware of a wide discrepancy between their practice and Catholic precept. 'Raphael said Yea, Raphael *did* Yea,—consequently Raphael was no Christian':[1] thus spake Friedrich Nietzsche. But Raphael Sanzio, in his 'Transfiguration', spake otherwise—and his opinion is not to be discounted.

* * *

With all his magnificent faculties for the task of *transvaluing values*— 'more faculties perhaps than have ever yet dwelt side by side in one individual'—Nietzsche was still lacking in one. He never made up for his premature abandonment of theology at Bonn. His lack of a rigorous grounding in philosophy and natural science he acknowledged and often deplored: he also took steps to remedy it; his ignorance of theology, he was not even conscious of: and it was the most serious ignorance of all.

In a note of 1885–6, we find the following illuminating sentences:

'The two noblest types of man I have ever encountered personally were the perfect Christian—I hold it an honour to be descended from a family which has always taken its Christianity seriously, in every sense— and the perfect Romantic artist, whom I have found to stand on a much lower level than the Christian. It is evident that when one turns one's back on *these* two types, because they no longer satisfy one, one will not easily be content with any other contemporary species of man. Thus I am condemned to solitude, for all that I can well imagine a human type in whom I should take pleasure.'[2]

[1] TI, p. 67.   [2] N, XIV, 358.

It is clear from this confession that the only type of Christianity known to Nietzsche was 'Naumburg Christianity': that is to say, the melancholy, repressive, puritanical type, of which Pascal's may be called the apotheosis. 'Christianity', he once said, 'should never be forgiven for having ruined such men as Pascal.'[1]

Of specifically Christian mysticism, he had no knowledge whatever. He read only those pietists (if he read them at all) of whom Schopenhauer happened to approve: and Schopenhauer—need it be said?—was not a Christian at all, but a Gnostic. Elsewhere I have entitled him 'the perfect nineteenth-century representative of Gnosticism'.[2] Not only was his whole attempt to construct a theodicy from Oriental and Platonic sources alone (excluding everything Judaic) a repetition of the attempts made by Valentinian, Basilides and Marcion; but, in *The World as Will and Idea*, he explicitly favours the Docetists and Manichees. They were, he says, the most thoroughly consistent Idealists—which is true. It is precisely because they were, that their doctrine was condemned by the Church.

Nietzsche saw Christianity, as he saw Christ, through Schopenhauer's dark glasses; and, of course, he was confirmed in his habit by his long discipleship to Wagner. For Wagner, truth to tell, was no more a perfect Romantic than Aunt Rosalie was a perfect Christian. He was a very imperfect Romantic. Had he been anything else, he would never have fallen for Schopenhauer. The fact that he did so fall constitutes the final refutation of his claim, in *The Art-Work of the Future*, to have transcended the old division of flesh and spirit. The perfect Romantic says Yea, the perfect Romantic *does* Yea—consequently he is no Schopenhauerian.

Romantic art at its highest—Beethoven's for example—is 'a yea-saying to the point of justifying, to the point of redeeming even, all that is past';[3] and possibly the same applies to Romantic philosophy. Hegel himself, after all, was not 'dipped in the bath of Spinoza' for nothing. True, he hypostatized Reason, and thereby repeated the error (if it was an error) of Plato: but was this Reason of his, distinct from the Understanding, really so remote from the Will to Power? True, he spoke of the real as the rational, the rational as the real, and had he meant by the rational the moral, Nietzsche's objection would have been justified—there is nothing moral about the death of a Raphael: but was Hegel's

---

[1] WP, 252.
[2] For a fuller discussion of this subject, cf. the author's *The Seed of the Church*, Sheppard Press, 1947.
[3] EH, p. 113.

'rationalism' anything other than 'the great pantheistic sympathy with pleasure and pain, which declares even the most terrible and questionable qualities of existence good, and sanctifies them'?[1] Was Hegel an Hegelian?

Had Nietzsche really encountered a perfect Romantic, his eyes might well have been opened to specifically Christian mysticism. The example of Blake shows how easily the morality of *Zarathustra* can be comprised in Christian concepts. As it was, his attack on Christianity must be pronounced, first and foremost, an attack on Gnosticism. His very symbolism goes to prove this:

'Then he looked enquiringly aloft—for he heard above him the sharp call of a bird. And behold! An eagle swept through the air in wide circles, and on it hung a serpent, not like a prey, but like a friend: for it kept itself coiled round the eagle's neck.

"They are mine animals," said Zarathustra, and rejoiced in his heart.

"The proudest animal under the sun, and the wisest animal under the sun,—they have come out to reconnoitre".'[2]

The eagle and the serpent are Persian symbols, which the Gnostics (like Shelley in *The Revolt of Islam*) took to represent pride of life on the one hand, and intellect or spirituality on the other. Only, whereas they were unable to conceive these two powers except as in perpetual warfare—light against darkness, Ormuzd against Ahriman—Nietzsche presents them as reconciled: intellect once again borne aloft on the wings of the Will to Power.

Still more significant, of course, is his resurrection of Zarathustra himself, the explanation of which he gives in *Ecce Homo*:

'People have never asked me, as they should have done, what precisely the name *Zarathustra* signifies on my lips—on the lips of the first immoralist: for that Persian's tremendous distinction in history is, that he was just the reverse of an immoralist. Zarathustra was the first to see in the struggle between good and evil the very fly-wheel of existence. The translation of morality into the metaphysical, as force, cause, end-in-itself, is *his* work. At bottom, however, the answer is already given in the question. Zarathustra *created* this most portentous of errors, morality: *consequently* he must also be the first to acknowledge it. . . . Do you understand me? . . . The self-surpassing of morality through truthfulness, the self-surpassing of the moralist in his opposite—in *me*—that is what the name Zarathustra signifies on my lips.'[3]

[1] WP, 1050.   [2] Z, Prologue, 10.   [3] EH, p. 132.

The conception was a beautiful one. Nietzsche resurrected Zarathustra, as Blake did Milton and Shelley Prometheus, in order that he should repent of his dualism, and proclaim the transcendence of good and evil. But it underlines only the harder his fundamental fallacy; for, had he but known it, Zarathustra had come back already, in the Manichees, and repented—in the person of Augustine.

Nietzsche, like Heine (whose disciple he was in this respect), 'consistently designated Manicheeism by the name of Christianity'. We have only to realize this, to realize that his Romantic Myth is a half-truth and his fundamental contrast an untruth:

'Dionysus *versus* the "Crucified": there you have the contrast. It is *not* a difference in regard to the martyrdom, but the martyrdom has different meanings. Life itself —life's eternal fruitfulness and recurrence —causes anguish, destruction and the will to annihilation. In the other case, suffering, the "Crucified as the Innocent", stands as an objection to life, it is a formula for life's condemnation. One divines: the problem is that of the significance of suffering: whether a Christian or a tragic significance. In the former case, it appears as the path leading to a holy state; in the latter, *existence* is regarded *as holy enough* to justify immensely greater grief. The tragic man says Yea even to the bitterest affliction: he is sufficiently strong, rich and capable of deifying; the Christian says Nay even to the happiest of earthly lots; he is so weak, poor and disinherited as to suffer from life in any form. The God on the Cross is a curse upon life, an admonition to deliverance from it; Dionysus dismembered is a *promise* of life—it will for ever be born anew and return home out of destruction.'[1]

This challenge cannot be sustained; and neither can Nietzsche's messianism. His transvaluation of values had been anticipated by two thousand years.

* * *

Nietzsche never succeeded in making his own the, distinctively Christian 'perspective'. He never saw what the mysticism of *Zarathustra* had in common with that of the Gospels and Epistles; or that in *The City of God* an attempt had already been made to turn platonism right-way-up: and for him as an individual, this failure was unmitigated disaster. As his note on the perfect Christian and perfect Romantic goes to show, it isolated him even more than was inevitable. Blake himself was not so finally excommunicated.

Standing, as he believed, clean beyond the Christian tradition, which

[1] WP, 1052,

is also the European tradition, Nietzsche was driven to look for his 'predecessors' among men as lonely as himself. Perpetually on the point of succumbing to desperation and bitterness, he had to draw what encouragement he could from those who had already succumbed. If only—one is tempted to exclaim—if only he could have realized how close he stood, not indeed to the Jesus of *The Antichrist*, but to the authentic Jesus of Nazareth!

However, it is idle, and what is more, disloyal to his genius, wholly to regret this failure. After all, whatever he may have lost by it, we have gained. His wholesale repudiation both of Christianity and of Christ was the very condition of his significance. Nothing can detract from that.

Nietzsche's negative significance lies in his ultimate scepticism. His positive significance lies in his being the first European to re-discover the standpoint of Jesus and Paul, and present it in terms of a world-view as appropriate to the twentieth century as theirs was to the first. Only a man persuaded that his discovery was both original and antagonistic to Christianity could have succeeded in that. Had he realized even for a moment how much his mysticism had in common with theirs, he would have been tempted to emphasize the affinity by adopting or adapting their idiom. As it was, he presented it without so much as a Christian overtone; and the importance of that is tremendous—for two reasons pre-eminently.

In the first place, the world-views, Judaic and Greek, in which European mysticism has expressed itself for the last two millennia, have become unintelligible. Just as only a few scholars can now decipher Paul's meaning in the original Greek, so only a few can decipher it in the original eschatology. The time was ripe, and more than ripe, for a re-presentation in terms of twentieth-century cosmology.

In the second place, along with a multitude of formulae reflecting the distinctively Christian synthesis of world-negation and world-affirmation, Christianity in all its forms has upheld a mass of others which can only be designated Gnostic. The dogma of the Virgin Birth, for instance, was far more appropriate to Plato than it is to Jesus of Nazareth. Though pessimism, asceticism and life-denial may never have conquered the Church, they have always wielded enormous power within it—and still do, even where the heroic austerities of the Desert Fathers have dwindled down to 'outspoken sermons' on bathing-costumes. Not only was Nietzsche the first man to present the Gospel in twentieth-century terms, but he was also the first to present it in terms that lent no support to Gnosticism.

Thus Spake Zarathustra is no more proof against abuse than any other classic of religion; it may be less so than most. But, more than most, it has the power to open contemporary eyes to truths they are in peril of losing sight of, truths that are all-important. For this alone we should honour Nietzsche. We should honour him only the more highly if, once they have been opened, those eyes turn back to an authentic 'higher man', who, despite every temptation to denial and despair, remained the spokesman of creation; who kept faith in humanity to the last; and whose tragedy, complete as it is, reveals more fully than any fiction the nature and workings of the Logos.

Such at all events is one man's conclusion; and he has not been un-mindful of the maxim of *The Dawn of Day*: 'those earnest, able and upright men of profound feelings, who are still Christians from the heart, owe it to themselves to make one attempt to live for a certain space of time without Christianity: they owe it *to their faith* that they should thus for once take up their abode "in the wilderness"—if only in order to acquire the right to pronounce on the question as to whether Christianity is needful.'[1] It is the conclusive tribute to Nietzsche's greatness that whoever (under what obscure compulsion?) grapples honestly with his works, does find himself, sooner or later, driven into that wilderness. Conversely, whoever in the wilderness of the twentieth century is already lost and seemingly alone, will discover in those works a trail blazed out beforehand. What Nietzsche bore, he bore on our behalf. *Requiescat in pace.*

[1] D, 61.

INDEX